Awakening the Buddhist Heart

Integrating Love,

Meaning, and

Connection into

Every Part of

Your Life

BROADWAY BOOKS

NEW YORK

AWAKENING

THE

BUDDHIST

HEART

Lama Surya Das

BROADWAY

AWAKENING THE BUDDHIST HEART. Copyright © 2000 by Lama
Surya Das. All rights reserved. Printed in the United States of America. No
part of this book may be reproduced or transmitted in any form or by any
means, electronic or mechanical, including photocopying, recording, or by
any information storage and retrieval system, without written permission
from the publisher. For information, address Broadway Books, a division of
Random House, Inc., 1540 Broadway, New York, NY 10036.

Broadway Books titles may be purchased for business or promotional use or
for special sales. For information, please write to: Special Markets
Department, Random House, Inc., 1540 Broadway, New York, NY 10036.

BROADWAY BOOKS and its logo, a letter B bisected on the diagonal, are
trademarks of Broadway Books, a division of Random House, Inc.

Visit our website at www.broadwaybooks.com

Library of Congress Cataloging-in-Publication Data
Das, Surya.
Awakening the buddhist heart: integrating love,
meaning, and connection into every part of your life /
Lama Surya Das.
p.   cm.
Includes index.
1. Compassion (Buddhism)   2. Love—Religious aspects—Buddhism.
3. Spiritual life—Buddhism.   4. Buddhism—China—Tibet—Doctrines.
BQ4399.S87 2000
294.3'444—dc21   00-036083

FIRST EDITION

Designed by Dana Leigh Treglia

ISBN 0-7679-0276-9

00   01   02   03   04   10   9   8   7   6   5   4   3   2   1

To my late Dzogchen master,

Nyoshul Khenpo Rinpoche

1932—1999

ACKNOWLEDGMENTS

I want to gratefully acknowledge the good friends whose encouragement and assistance helped make this book possible, and who all help me to open my very own heart.

Thank you to Lauren Marino, my fine editor at Broadway Books; Susan Lee Cohen, my literary agent; Julie Coopersmith, who always reminds me to go deeper and helps make it all possible; and Kathy Peterson, for her loving support and "being there."

I also want to thank my copyeditor Nancy Peske, my assistant Julie Barker, as well as all the friends and colleagues who shared their many stories and gave support and encouragement, especially Maggie Sluyter, Deb Bouvier, Ram Dass, John Halley, Lucy Duggan, Christopher Coriat, Chad Gillete, Paul Crafts, Ron Goldman, Charles Genoud, John Makransky, Roger Walsh, Michele Tempesta, Vincent Duggan, Philip Carter, and Cheryl Pelavin.

Contents

INTRODUCTION   1

CHAPTER ONE   *Spiritual Intelligence—*   3
Connecting to the Bigger Picture

CHAPTER TWO   *Awakening to a Deeper Love—*   27
A Buddha's Love

CHAPTER THREE   *Connecting to Your*   41
Life Experience

CHAPTER FOUR   *Developing Authentic Presence*   61

CHAPTER FIVE   *Letting Go, Getting Real*   81

CHAPTER SIX   *The Connection Reflex—*   107
Building Meaningful
Relationships

Contents

CHAPTER SEVEN *Finding Our Sacred Place in Nature* 135

CHAPTER EIGHT *Joyfully Crazy and Wonderful Awakenings* 157

CHAPTER NINE *Spiritual Alchemy— Embracing Life's Lessons* 175

CHAPTER TEN *Learning to Love What We Don't Like* 197

EPILOGUE *A Prayer for the New Millennium* 219

APPENDIX *The Bodhicitta Practices of an Awakened Heart* 221

INDEX 247

Nothing worth doing is completed
In one lifetime,
Therefore we must be saved by hope.
Nothing true or beautiful makes
Complete sense
In any context of history,
Therefore we must be saved by faith.
Nothing we do, no matter how virtuous,
Can be accomplished alone.
Therefore we must be saved by love.

—Reinhold Niebuhr

INTRODUCTION

The Buddhist heart is alive and well in all of us. It is just a matter of awakening to it. This luminous spiritual jewel is what the Dalai Lama calls "the good heart," representing our own inner goodness—our most tender, compassionate, and caring side. That is why the Dalai Lama always says, "My religion is loving-kindness." The loving heart is our share of the true, good, and beautiful—something genuine to cherish and venerate.

This basic goodness is our true nature, or Buddha-nature—our highest, wisest self. Our best Self. It is like the little Buddha within each of us. This radiant innate jewel represents what we aspire toward as well as who we truly *are*. These two aspects—a developmental, growth-oriented, "higher educational" side and the innate, timeless, immanent side—are like two sides of a single hand. It is a helping hand as well as a hand that is complete in itself. This is what Tibet's Dzogchen masters call "Buddhahood in the palm of your hand"; it is all right there. You may feel far from it, but it is never far from you.

As we enter a new century and a new millennium, and in the light of all the challenges, changes, and uncertainty we must face daily, it seems increasingly important to awaken our Buddha-like hearts through spiritual connections. We can make spiritual connections within ourselves, with all the various aspects and facets of ourselves and our life—physical, mental, emotional, psychological, spiritual—recognizing that everything we do and feel is part of our spiritual journey.

What better time to awaken our hearts and make meaningful connections with others as well through the avenue of friendship and relationship? We can do this with our families, our romantic partners, and our colleagues, through work, with our neighbors, our society, our country, and our world; we can do this with our pets and animals and all creatures, great and small. Moreover we can extend ourselves to include in our radiant heart's awakened embrace all things, animate and inanimate—everything that is in our natural environment. And we can connect with that which is greater than, yet within and all around, each of us.

Where better to make this spiritual connection than here and now, with our best selves and with each other, in every part of our lives? Awakening the Buddhist heart that beats within each of us will bring us directly into intimate relatedness to one and to all, unveiling our innate spiritual connectedness to the source and ground of our very being, thus informing every aspect of our daily lives with purpose, meaning, and love.

Chapter One

Spiritual Intelligence—
Connecting to the Bigger Picture

Life is about relationship—the relationship we have with ourselves, with each other, with the world, as well as the connection to that which is beyond any of us yet immanent in each of us. When our relationships are good, we feel good; when they are bad, we feel awful. Let's accept it. We need each other. We need to feel connected; we need to feel each other's presence and love.

The most ancient scriptures of India say that we are all part of a universal web of light. Each of us is a glowing, shining, mirrorlike jewel reflecting and containing the light of the whole. All in one. One in all. We are never disconnected from the whole. This intrinsic knowledge of our place in the greater picture is part of our spiritual DNA, our original software—or "heartware."

Nonetheless, at one time or another most of us feel disconnected from this knowledge of our place in the great web of being. We lose sight of where we belong, and instead, we experience intense feelings of loneliness, alienation, and confusion. Trying to find the way back to our place in the whole is what the spiritual seeker's search is all about. It represents a journey home to who we are.

How about you? Do you ever suffer from a sense that you are lost and wandering—almost as though you have been through some kind of an emotional holocaust? Most of us here in America are very fortunate. We have little idea of what it's like to live in a war-torn country. Even so, from the safety of your own secure home, do you sometimes feel as though you have an uncanny sense of what it must feel like to be a displaced person—unsafe and at the mercy of strangers? Mother Teresa said, "The biggest problem facing the world today is not people dying in the streets of Calcutta, and not inflation, but spiritual deprivation . . . this feeling of emptiness associated with feeling separate from God, and from all our sisters and brothers on planet earth." "Loneliness," she said, "is like the leprosy of the West."

Mother Teresa was talking about the pain associated with feelings of isolation and separateness. These feelings are common to mankind. They can overtake any one of us in a heartbeat, even in the very midst of happiness and joy. Loneliness implies a lack of meaningful connection. For most people, it is a familiar travelling companion. Even when we're surrounded by people we know, we can feel separate and apart. Separate from what, we might ask? Separate from others, separate from ourselves, separate from the Divine, separate from meaning, separate from love. Separate from a sense of belonging.

The promise of spiritual life is that we will be able to heal these feelings through love and an experiential understanding of the essential interconnectedness of all beings. The Dalai Lama of Tibet, for example, often says that no matter how many new faces he sees each day, he never feels as though he is meeting anyone for the first time. That's because the Dalai Lama knows that every single one of us is on an infinite journey that began aeons ago. According to Tibetan Buddhism we have each had so many births that in all probability our paths have crossed time and time again. Wondrously connected one to the other, we have been for each other brothers, sisters, cousins, aunts, children, fathers, mothers, and mates. At the heart of Tibetan Buddhism is this belief: Each person we meet has at one time been a close, caring family member and should be treated with the respect and love such a relationship deserves.

Don't we all need to feel the light and warmth that emanates from others? Don't we all want true love? Don't we all hunger for genuine communication, and deeper and more authentic connections? Don't we all recognize that the quality of our individual lives is determined by the quality of our relationships both external and internal? When our relationships are superficial, we feel as though we are leading superficial lives; when our relationships reflect our deeper commitments and aspirations, we feel as though we are walking a more meaningful and satisfying path.

Love comes through relating. That's why we must connect.

Connecting to the sacred in our relationships is a way of satisfying our spiritual hunger with love—thus nurturing ourselves, as well as nourishing the world. For just a minute, stop and think about your relationships. Think about all those with whom you interact—at home, at work, and in the community. Think about family, friends, coworkers, and even those with whom you have only a nodding acquaintance. Don't leave anybody out, not even your pets. Whenever you think about the important relationships in your life, remember that each of us also has a connection with the natural world and all the wild creatures that live on our planet—as well as with the planet itself.

Some of our relationships seem deep and meaningful; others are merely casual. But on a spiritual level, they are all important; they can all be deepened and improved. Relationships are essential for ongoing spiritual growth and development. They help us find meaning and purpose; they help us experience love—human as well as divine. Learning to love is the first lesson in Spirituality 101. The connections we make as we live our incredible lives offer us the opportunity to acknowledge and connect to the divine in ourselves as well as in others. Ask yourself: Who did you love today?

Although spiritual seekers and saints historically have often been associated with self-sacrifice and reclusive, solitary lifestyles (often monastic, and frequently cloistered), here in the modern world, other traditions and styles of spirituality are emerging. Contemporary seekers realize that we can't retreat permanently; it is not very helpful to pass negative judgments on worldly values. Instead we need to find new and better ways of walking the soulful path of awakening, by integrating the heart of love in every aspect of our lives. In this way we learn to dance gracefully with life.

It is a fundamental Buddhist tenet as well as a larger, more general fact of life that we are all interconnected and interdependent on each other. I find it very gratifying to see that so many Western seekers and students of truth and Dharma are sincerely striving to combine social activism with spiritual growth. As seekers, we want to find ways to do spiritual work within our relationships. We aspire to help improve the quality of our own lives as well as the lives of those around us. In this way we are hopeful that we will be better able to live in congruence with our most deeply held inner principles and values. We who inhabit this planet all share a common karma as well as a common ground. We already live together; we need to learn to work together. We need to learn to love others—even those we may not like. This is the greatest challenge of all.

For the sake of clarity, Tibetan teachings traditionally divide our spiritual efforts and practices into two categories:

❋ Inner—those efforts we make primarily for ourselves

❋ Outer—those efforts we make primarily for the benefit of others and the world around us

The inner-directed goal of a spiritual life is to realize the innate purity and primordial perfection in each of us. This expresses itself in how we see—and treat—ourselves. Through inner work, we realize the truth, wisdom, clarity, and peace of mind that is latent in each of us. No one else can give it to us or provide it for us. We must find it for ourselves.

The outer goal expresses itself in how we feel about others, how we perceive them, as well as how we treat them. By learning to better love and care for ourselves as well as each other, we get closer to that which is greater than any one of us. When we serve and foster one soul, we serve the whole world. This is spiritual connection. Through spiritual practice, we connect in all directions at once—a little like tuning into some vast cosmic Internet. As we refine our outer and inner efforts, becoming more and more skillful through practice, we realize that these efforts are one. The great naturalist John Muir once said, "I only went out for a walk and finally concluded to stay out till sundown, for going out, I found, was really going in."

What does this mean for us day to day as we go about our lives at home, in the office, or at the shopping mall? As seekers, we want to be able to improve our relationships at work; we want personal connections that bring us the abundance and joy they initially promise. How can we grow together spiritually with the people we care about? How can we share meditation, silence, song, and prayer with those we love? How can we spiritually enrich every relationship?

We all have special bonds with certain people, including those we may even think of as "soul mates." But what about the bonds we share with people we don't love or respect? What about people toward whom we feel anger, annoyance, distrust, and contempt? What can we learn from those we love as well as those we don't? Can we, for example, learn to love people we don't even like? Buddhist teachings tell us that all of our bonds are sacred; they remind us that sometimes our adversaries provide us with the most precious teachings. We never really do anything alone; we always have help, even though sometimes that help comes in very strange forms. We are surrounded by an array of helping, loving hands.

One of the most difficult things we all struggle with are feelings of existential despair—a sense that there is little or no meaning or purpose to our existence. Sometimes it just all seems too much, and we lose our sense of place, our feeling of fitting in, of being understood, of belonging. As much as we may be rushing here and there, we don't always know where we are going. We haven't found our bearings, the polestar of our existence. We just keep on keepin' on with no respite in sight.

Spiritual teachings universally remind us that we are integral and essential parts of a greater pattern. There is an exquisite meaning and coherence to life. I'm not talking now about a perfectly ordered theistic universe or a fixed destiny. What I'm describing are cosmic principles and universal laws that are always at work. I believe we can discover and align ourselves with these principles, perhaps even become masters of them. No matter how lost we may be, it is possible to find our place within the whole. We *can* get "there" from here—wherever here may be for you right now. "Here," after all, is within the word "there."

Life sometimes seems so chaotic, like a terrifying maelstrom that exists only to whip us about. But in truth, it's really more like a mandala or hologram. There are constellations, patterns, and even directions to be found within the vastness and mystery of it all. At the end of my freshman year of college, I came back to stay with my parents on Long Island, and I took a summer job at a law firm in Manhattan. I remember what it felt like on my commute to work each morning, popping out of a subterranean, dark, Bosch-like netherworld of subways and train tunnels, not knowing exactly where I was. During my first days at my job, I walked out onto the teeming streets during lunch hour, and all I knew was that I was someplace in midtown, whatever *that* meant. People were swirling around like floodwaters in those concrete canyons amidst skyscrapers that were so densely constructed that even at midday, the sun was completely hidden. I had no orientation, no sense of direction. Where was I? I remember walking around with no idea of where I was going, feeling somewhat nervous that I would not find my way back to the office, and then suddenly I came upon a bus stop and a blow-up map of Manhattan. I saw that if I wanted to amble, it was just a short walk to Central Park and an easy stroll to the Museum of Modern Art. Rockefeller Center was just a block or two away, and if I wanted to venture further after work, I could get on the Fifth Avenue bus and go straight down to Greenwich Village, a favorite teenage haunt of mine. The large blow-up subway map provided me with a view from above, instantly rescuing me from the bewildered feeling that I was lost in a maze. I knew where I was, and I knew what was around me, and I saw how it all fit together.

Spiritually speaking, we've all experienced feelings of being so lost in the dense thickets of our lives that we can't see the paths or figure out how large the forest really is. At those times we lack an overview, a world map, an awareness of the bigger picture. But some people seem to have a deeper and better sense of who they are, where they are standing, and where they are going. They seem to have a better sense of how to navigate the highways and byways of life without losing their way. Simply put, they seem to have a better sense of their spiritual center. This is like having an internal compass, an internal true-ing device.

FINDING A SPIRITUAL CENTER

Just as the unexamined life is a life poorly lived, no life is complete without some effort to connect with the deeper meaning of our existence. Whether we are Jewish, Christian, Buddhist, Hindu, Muslim, or non-believer, we all have spiritual DNA; that graceful, radiant inner spiral connects us above and below, leading both within and without.

When we, as seekers, begin to reconnect more deeply with our loving hearts—our spiritual centers—we begin to achieve greater realization of the profound wisdom and intuitive awareness that is a natural part of each of us. This is spiritual intelligence; it naturally recognizes the heart connection and the inseparability of self and other.

When we take standard IQ tests, what we're being tested for is our ability to see the connections between things—numbers, words, mathematical concepts, and geometric shapes. Spiritual intelligence is very similar. People whose spiritual intelligence is highly developed are able to see the connecting patterns and principles that help create meaning and order out of the seeming chaos of life. Spiritual intelligence gives us the wisdom to see the relationship between the whole and its many parts, the one and the many, the ordinary and the extraordinary, the mundane and the divine, the light and its shadow. Spiritual intelligence is existential awareness.

The more we cultivate our innate spiritual intelligence, the more we become aware of and intuitively sensitive to what those around us see and feel. Cultivating a heightened spiritual discernment and awareness helps us become better mates, parents, and friends. Ultimately it can lead us to mind reading, clairvoyance, healing powers, shape shifting, and the development of other psychic abilities as well as deepening our inner wisdom and compassion.

Over the years, a fair amount of esoteric material has been written about Tibet—some fascinating, some strange at best. Many Westerners, for example, including a number of my friends and contemporaries, initially became interested in learning more about Tibet through the eccentric writings of a man who called himself Lobsang Rampa. Rampa, who was in fact a British plumber, presented himself to readers as a Tibetan lama. Later, when it was discovered that this was an Englishman who had never even been to Tibet, Rampa announced that a Tibetan lama had taken hold of his body, and that he, Rampa, was channeling this information.

Rampa's most famous book, which was a bestseller in the U.S. and England some forty years ago, was called *The Third Eye*. In it, there is a very dramatic scene that takes place in the bowels of the Potala Palace, the centuries-old home of a succession of Dalai Lamas, all of whom were during their lifetimes the spiritual and political leaders of Tibet. In this fictional scene, the then Dalai Lama goes down to the deep basement which holds the gold-plated, lotus-positioned, mummified remains of previous Dalai Lamas. There, he subjects himself to an operation in which a wooden corkscrew is used to open his "third eye," the inner wisdom eye located in the center of the forehead.

I've been to the Potala Palace, and I've seen the gilded embalmed remains in their tomb monuments. But the corkscrew operation should not be taken literally. It's obviously a fictional technology. However, the concept of an inner wisdom eye, an eye that is so spiritually aware that it sees beyond everyday illusion, is not so farfetched. In fact, one of the first books by the present Dalai Lama is called *Opening the Wisdom Eye*.

For Tibetans, the possibility of heightened awareness is taken for granted; in fact it is often raised to the level of science and is even part of medical procedure. New York City's master Buddhist professor, Robert Thurman, describing Tibetan medical diagnosis, writes:

> "The trained Tibetan doctor develops a combination of memorization, anatomical learning, subtle visualization and contemplative heightening of sensitivity. He or she trains the six tip corners of the first three fingers of each hand to be attuned to the twelve channels of communication from the patient's body. Placing these fingers anywhere on the body . . . but preferably on the radial arteries of the two wrists, the doctor becomes a psychic CAT-scan machine. He or she lets the awareness enter into the body of the patient, travel through the blood, lymph and neural systems into various organs and vessels, and emerge with a detailed picture of the exact physical condition of the patient's body."

We all can learn to raise our spiritual intelligence and heighten the power of our incandescent awareness. If we elevate our gaze and open wide our wisdom eyes, ears, and innermost tender hearts, our spiritual intelligence will soar. We will possess higher knowledge as well as uncommon common sense. This is the sacred intelligence that can help create win/win scenarios in all our relationships.

THE COMPONENTS
OF SPIRITUAL INTELLIGENCE

What is spiritual intelligence? And how do we get it? How can we each find a higher or deeper transcendent spiritual vision and perspective? Some vegetarians say that it's spiritual to be vegetarian; people who are kosher believe that it's spiritually necessary to be kosher. In Judaism, following the Torah is spiritually intelligent. The word "Islam" means surrender or submission to God's will; in Islam, surrendering to God's will is spiritual intelligence. That's not so different from Taoism where spiritual intelligence is equated with learning to be one with the flow of things, the Tao. Some people might say we become more spiritually intelligent by meditating and sitting around trying not to think. However, Tibetan lamas say that when we practice that type of mind-wiping meditation we run the risk of being reborn as cows—dumbly chewing their cud over and over again.

But all of this seems very generalized and is missing a certain specificity. From where I sit, spiritual intelligence has three separate components. They are:

I. A SENSE OF THE BIGGER PICTURE

Have you ever tried to look at the world with a God's eye view—an overarching or divine point of view? Think about this for a minute. Even if you don't believe in God—and most Buddhists don't—imagine what an omniscient being would see. Some say that Buddha, who was perfectly enlightened, was omniscient. What do you think he perceived as he lived an enlightened life? Remember that the Buddha himself said he was able to remember at least five hundred previous lifetimes. From his unique vantage point, it would be almost impossible to become overly invested in petty day-to-day problems. I think the Buddha, who often referred to his students and followers as children, had seen so many things come and go that he was able to keep everything in perspective.

I spend a lot of time flying around the country on teaching tours, and I love looking out of the plane window while passing over places like the Rocky Mountains, the Great Lakes, the midwestern farmlands and plains, great rivers like the Mississippi, and large man-made cities too. When you fly over the

Grand Canyon, the pilot often points it out, and everyone looks out the window. I like peering down over rows of neatly laid out houses on streets that from a distance look like accessories for a miniature model train layout. From thousands of feet up in the air, even New York City appears to be a gleaming anthill. I love being high above the clouds where the sun is always shining. This reminds me of deep spiritual memories, of a sacred timeless time and spacious space. The feeling is one of *been there, known that.*

From the perspective of being high up in a plane, we get a small sense of the bigger picture, the long view, the eagle's vision. Most spiritual traditions make a special place for elders, those members of the community whose age and experience makes it easier for them to offer a larger, wiser perspective on life. As we mature spiritually and become elder-like in our attitude toward life, it becomes easier to get beyond our own petty prejudices and short-term thinking and move further away from selfishness and self-interest toward stewardship and guardianship.

When we take the long view, we are better able to be spiritually intelligent in our relationships. Margot, for example, is very upset that her son, Josh, failed a geometry test. She's worried about Josh getting into a good college, and because of this she's been coming down pretty hard on him. When she is able to step back and take a God's eye view, she can see that it's just a small test, and not the major calamity that she fears. Life will go on . . . and on. Still, it is hard to remember that sometimes.

My friend Patti says that when her son was three and a half years old, he had a table with four little chairs, and he used to lug one of the chairs with him everywhere, climbing on it and turning it upside down. He was really rough on those chairs. First one broke, then another, and finally a third. Patti got angry at the little boy. "Can't you be more careful?" she said in an angry tone of voice. Her son started crying. "Mommy," he said, his little lip trembling, "I'm your only son, and you're making me feel bad because of a chair." Patti said that even though her son is still a little kid, he exhibited a wisdom that was, at that moment, superior to her own.

If we're going to relate to others successfully, we need a firm sense of perspective and a clear idea about what's important in the long run. That means that often we have to let go of our rigid ideas and fixed positions on a wide variety of things. We need to focus on those values and virtues that we know are important in the long run and let go of some of the issues and concerns that are fundamentally superficial or even comic. Sometimes when we look at life with a long view, all we can do is laugh at our foibles. Doesn't it sometimes seem as though we are all Moe, Larry, and Curly, continuously falling all over ourselves in our clumsy silliness?

Buddhism teaches that we are usually feeling something— pleasure, displeasure, or indifference. But these feelings change, all the time. We have good years, and we have bad years; good hair days and bad hair days. We can be elated one week, sad the next. We can be calm one moment, excited the next. Nothing stays the same. The long view helps us let go of our attachment to feelings that aren't giving us real satisfaction.

2. THE ABILITY TO DISTINGUISH THE REAL FROM THE UNREAL

It is taught that when the Buddha achieved perfect enlightenment, the veil of illusion was lifted from in front of his eyes. He was able to see truth; he was able to perceive reality. Illusion and delusion are part of the human condition. In a world that is filled with deceit, manipulation, and exploitation, not to mention spin doctors, it's easy to get cynical about truth. It's easy to become confused about what we're really hearing, seeing, experiencing, or feeling; it's too easy to believe what we're told, even when, in our heart of hearts, we know it's not true.

The Buddha saw and experienced life with perfect clarity of

vision. Keep in mind that when the Buddha began his path, he was a human being, like you and me. When the Buddha became enlightened, he still retained all his humanity, but he had transcended his human limitations and attachment to mere appearances. He realized freedom and deathless bliss, "nirvana."

The Buddha became enlightened through his own efforts. If he were living today, indeed if he were one of our neighbors, we might look at him and say, "Wow, that guy really keeps working on himself." The Buddha's hard work paid off; through his efforts, he was able to realize absolute truth—ultimate reality. In Buddhism, the true nature of the world is called "sunyata," or emptiness/openness.

Most of us, of course, have to be content with relative truth or relative reality. Because we believe in the possibility of enlightenment, however, we continue to strive toward the deepest truth. The path to ultimate reality takes hard work. If we value truth and reality, we do this work by chipping away at the falsehoods, both large and subtle, in our own lives. If we continue to look at any object or situation and use our minds to peel away the layers of projections, concepts, and reactivity, we get closer and closer to reality and absolute truth—things just as they are, in all their naked, unalloyed splendor. That's part of becoming more and more enlightened. We can become a little more illumined every day that we walk the path.

Take a book off a shelf and look at it. At first glance it looks like paper and print, but get beyond mere surface appearances, and think about the ink and the trees that created the paper. If you were to try to get that book down to its most basic form, you would have to consider atomic and molecular structure. And what about the words in the book you're examining? Do they reflect truth? Does the book convey different levels of meaning? Many of us have had the experience of reading and rereading a book, finding new and deeper truths each time.

The search for truth is the seeker's search. We keep analyzing, reflecting on, and unwrapping the experiences we encounter in an attempt to find fundamental truth. Every day we can bring the search for truth to our dealings with friends, family, and coworkers. All we need to do is make truth a value, a touchstone. All things flow from that commitment.

Recently I was in a shoe store with a woman friend who was trying to buy some sandals. As I sat there waiting, somewhat impatiently, I noticed an elderly woman who was trying to find a pair of sneakers that fit. "None of them are right," she complained. "They're either too big or too small. In this one, my big toe is hitting against the end of the shoe." She was with several family members who were trying to convince her that the sneakers she had on *did* indeed fit, and that she was imagining the tightness, and she was wavering in her conviction. Finally, just as her family and the salesperson had finished convincing her that she should buy the pair she had on, another woman, a senior citizen with beautifully dyed red hair, entered the store and sat down next to her. "Tell me," the first woman said to the newcomer. "Do you think this sneaker is too tight?" "Let me see," said the redhead. She reached down and poked the sneaker with her thumb. "Absolutely," she decreed. "Your big toe is hitting the side. You're not going to be able to walk in them." I could see the first woman's entire family groan silently and roll their eyes up in unison.

This little vignette was a classic lesson in reality. If the woman had brought home the sneakers, and they pinched her big toe, she would have had to live with the consequences. This kind of thing happens to all of us. We fail to acknowledge the truth of what's happening in our own lives as it's taking place. We see what we want to see, hear what we want to hear, and ignore the messages we find distasteful. As a result we end up living our lives feeling the pinch. We ignore reality every time we spend money we don't have; we ignore reality every time we close our eyes to our own unhappiness or the suffering of those around us; and we ignore reality every time we construct fantasies that help us avoid what we don't want to see.

The Buddha saw "what is." He saw things exactly as they are. This may sound ordinary, but in fact, it's totally extraordinary. You may think that everybody sees reality, but check it out. I'm sure you'll discover that we can all walk down the same street, and yet we'll see and hear different things. One person's flower is another person's pollen season. A firm grip on reality helps us be aware of both the flower and the pollen.

3. AN UNDERSTANDING OF KARMA—CAUSE AND EFFECT

Your karma is the result of everything you do, think, say, and feel. Right now, it's a summer day, and this morning the room in which I am working is hotter than normal. Yesterday I failed to pull the blinds on the west side of the house, and the blazing afternoon sun heated my study all day long. Now I'm uncomfortable. I'm also at least partially responsible. That's karma. There is no one else to blame.

The thing about karma is that everything we do has some consequence. For every cause there is an effect. Buddhism teaches that our karma was created by past behavior—some of it in other lifetimes, some of it within the last hour. It also teaches that no matter when karma is created, it can be changed, worked with, expiated, purified, and transformed. That means our destiny is in our own hands.

Understanding karma helps us get more accurate insight into how things work. The teachings about karma explain causation and show us how things fit together. The Buddha taught that all psychological and physical phenomena are interdependent. He said that everything we do, say, or even think conditions the next act, word, or thought. This, one of the most essential Buddhist teachings, is known as the Chain of Conditioned Arising.

Let's say, for example, that when you were a child, your mother hated being in the city in the summer and took you to the country, and you enjoyed the experience. You responded to her negative feelings about the city, and you also liked the experience of being in the country. Now as an adult, when you are forced to spend your summer weekends in a city, you feel acutely deprived; you respond more positively to the smells, sights, and sounds of the country. One day, you go to visit a friend who lives in a bucolic area; strolling through town, you see some local real estate ads. Impulsively you walk into a real estate agency, and before the day ends you make an offer for a small house and sign a large check.

Now, how does this work? You have an impulse based on past experiences. Your impulse leads to a thought; the thought becomes a movement (words and deeds) that will bring you to the country each weekend. This establishes a pattern. Through repetition, a pattern becomes a habit. You may now regularly find yourself on a crowded highway driving to and from the country every weekend during rush hour. Habitual patterns help form our character, which in turn determine our destiny. This is karmic evolution. This is how we constantly shape and reshape our lives—for better or for worse.

Each impulse we have lays down an imprint; when it's repeated it becomes a groove. The groove creates a channel, and energy as well as more material things start to be pulled and channeled more and more in that direction. Once a groove is firmly established, it's hard to change. If we want to alter our behavior, we have to make strong conscious efforts to do so. Buddhist teachings about karma tell us that every time we do something, we are psychologically, physically, emotionally, and even morally imprinted and conditioned in a way that makes it more likely that we will behave the same way the next time.

When we want to change the way we are with ourselves or with the rest of the world, we need to do a little karmic intervention in order to alter old habits and behavior patterns. This is very difficult. Joanna, for example, approaches most situations passively. She has never been able to take a proactive approach, and she has suffered accordingly. Right now, she is struggling to become more direct, assertive, and outspoken in her life. For her, this is very hard work. I know other people who find Joanna's passive approach to life unfathomable. Joanna's friend Sarah treats every situation as though it is a potential battle zone; she is always trying to restrain her tendencies to jump in and take over. Both Joanna and Sarah realize that changing their behavior will change their experiences and their destiny. When we change our attitudes as well as our intentions, wishes, and aspirations, we are able to change our behavior and thus change our karma. This is the first principle of self-mastery and the Buddhist practices that bring inner freedom and autonomy.

One of the most important teachings about karma is this: It's not what happens to us that matters most; it's what we do with it. Yesterday a student who was about to go on retreat called me. She told me that one of her tires went flat while she was driving in the country during a rainstorm. She had never bothered to sign up for any road service like AAA; she had a cell phone, but the battery was dead; she was wearing shorts and a T-shirt and had no umbrella or warm clothing in the car. She used her flat tire as a learning experience. As soon as she got home, she became a member of a road service; she purchased a device so she could charge her phone from the car battery; she put an umbrella, a heavy sweatshirt, and a blanket in the trunk of her car; and she got some flares and a flashlight as well. To learn from experience makes us grow wiser with our years.

I often meet people who say to me, "Everything in my life is a mess, so I guess I must have done something wrong in my past life. . . . Haha!" I find this approach to problems somewhat distressing. The Buddha said, "If you want to know what your future life will be like, look at your life right now." We are creating the future, and we are doing it today. We always have choices. We all have to fight the impulse to become rigid caricatures of the people and personality types we have always been. It is spiritually intelligent to stay open to new possibilities and new ways of being. Just because we—or our parents or grandparents—have always acted in a certain way doesn't mean it has to continue. We are not victims of our past; we all have choices. If a behavior or way of thinking doesn't have the positive payoff of making our lives happy, it can and should be changed. We could all afford to be a little more flexible and adaptable. Understanding the law of karma helps us do that.

Seekers living today have tremendous spiritual mobility, not just to change their religions, but to change their karmic behavior patterns. Change is now a positive value in our society, and we have many more tools at our disposal than earlier generations had. We don't have to travel great distances to find the best teachers to help us. We can read their books, watch videotapes, or listen to audiotapes; we can connect with many of them on their websites or on-line. We can go into therapy in order to change patterns that no longer work. We can attend seminars and support groups. We can talk openly to friends in a way that earlier generations would not have dreamed possible. These opportunities are part of our collective karma; spiritual intelligence reminds us to take advantage of them.

CONNECTING TO THE BIGGER PICTURE—
A PRACTICE

Kalu Rinpoche, who died in 1989 at his monastery in Darjeeling, India, was one of the great Tibetan meditation masters of his time. When I first went to India, I lived there in his monastery off and on for eight years. One of the first teachings Kalu Rinpoche gave was known as the Four Mind Changers. It's an ancient practice designed to help us connect to a deeper reality.

This reflective exercise is a basic Buddhist preliminary practice. This kind of examination helps us turn our hearts and minds to Dharma—truth and reality—and away from worldliness, confusion, and ordinary habits; it sharpens our spiritual intelligence by raising our consciousness and heightening our awareness about who we are and how we all fit together in this world and this universe. Kalu Rinpoche advised that we practice it before we begin any meditation or prayer session, but this kind of reflection can be done at any time—while taking a walk, riding a subway, or waiting for a bus.

This reflection on four basic thoughts can help us sort out our values and priorities and become more conscientious about our spiritual practice. We use this exercise to keep us grounded in reality and conscious of what's truly important.

Reflect on the following:

I

I HAVE BEEN BLESSED WITH A LIFE IN WHICH I CAN DO MANY THINGS TO FURTHER MY OWN HAPPINESS AND THE HAPPINESS OF THOSE AROUND ME.

Life is an amazing opportunity filled with freedoms and choices too wondrous to describe. It would be a shame to waste this wondrous opportunity by engaging in useless and meaningless activities; it would be a pity to waste this life by not fulfilling one's spiritual potential. The chances that exist for each of us today to be more loving, kind, helpful, and compassionate shouldn't be squandered or thrown aside. We all have innate wisdom and goodness; this life provides extraordinary opportunities, great and small, to be wise and virtuous. When we keep this in mind at every moment, we turn toward truth.

Consider your own life; think about the many opportunities you have to be true to yourself and what you know is important. Think about ways you can deepen your commitment to those values you hold most dear. Each day as you reflect on this, try to reinforce and firm up your intentions and bring them into action. Take some practical steps in this direction, no matter how small. Take this contemplation into action.

II

LIFE IS SHORT; THERE IS NO TIME TO WASTE.

Recently I was visiting friends, and their children were watching a videotape of *The Wizard of Oz* with Judy Garland. I think we've probably all seen the movie. Judy Garland was an enchanting, multitalented girl, and on screen she remains breathtakingly young. Of course, she died almost twenty years ago, but in this classic film she is frozen in time. Whenever I look at this movie, I find it hard to believe that Judy Garland is no longer a fresh-faced preadolescent belting out "Somewhere over the Rainbow." But she's not. Like everyone, she had problems, grew older, and died. In my own life, it seems like yesterday that I watched the movie for the first time as a young child.

How about you? Don't you have trouble believing the speed with which things pass? One moment you're in high school worrying about which college to attend, and almost the next thing you know you're a full-fledged adult with adult concerns, belief systems, responsibilities, and travails. How does this happen? Is it really true that each of us will grow up, mature, grow old, and die? Sometimes it seems so inconceivable that we choose not to think about it, but we become wiser when we accept the tenuous, short-lived nature of life. Myself, I know I am going to die, but if I am totally honest with myself, I find it hard to believe.

The Buddha told his disciples and followers to think about death and the remembrance of mortality/impermanence. He said that death was his greatest teacher. He told people that remembering how little time we have in this lifetime would help us spend our days on earth more wisely. Reflecting upon death is not meant to be a morbid practice. In fact, it can have the opposite affect; it can help ground us in the *here and now* and make us appreciate the wonderful miracle of life each moment as it's given to us now. The Buddha said:

> *"The universe and its inhabitants are as ephemeral as the*
> *clouds in the sky;*
> *Beings being born and dying are like a spectacular dance*
> *or drama show.*
> *The duration of our lives is like a flash of lightning*
> *or a firefly's brief twinkle;*
> *Everything passes like the flowing waters of a steep waterfall."*

III

THE JOURNEY THROUGH LIFE ISN'T SUPPOSED TO BE EASY; IT'S SUPPOSED TO BE REAL.

Here's a fact of life: Nobody gets away scot-free. In every life, we are destined to find some disappointment, dissatisfaction, pain, and illness. We are bound to feel confused, insecure, and anxious. The Buddha termed our passage on this earth and the cycle of birth and death that we all experience as "samsara." The word in Sanskrit is literally translated as "journeying," or cycling and recycling.

Regularly contemplating the travails of our journey helps us to stay realistic about what life is and isn't. Don't be depressed by these thoughts. Instead recognize the joys that can be found by staying grounded and real. Every dip and rise, every twist and turn is part of the infinite journey; why turn aside from any of it?

Too many of us resist authenticity, preferring instead an air-brushed approach to the world. This is easy to do since we live in a time where our values and our vision of reality are influenced and shaped by images that are unreal and false. We watch popular television shows, and we come away thinking that everyone is supposed to be young, beautiful, thin, and rich. We have a false view of a world created by jaded Hollywood values. We create fantasies for ourselves based on what we see and read in contemporary entertainment media or what I call "airbrush reality." Too much airbrush reality on a day-to-day basis and we become airheads.

Reflect on the frustrations, joys, and sorrows of a real life. When you are sitting around with nothing to do, and your mind wanders, try to keep it from getting caught up in fantasies of perfection. Don't get caught up in the sizzle; instead, focus on substance and reality. It is right before you, this very moment; don't overlook it.

IV

OUR KARMA IS THE ONE THING WE CARRY WITH US ALWAYS.

As we become more and more conscious, heart-centered, and spiritually awake, we begin to better see how everything we do shapes and creates our destiny. Reflect on the laws of karma and the patterns that have unfolded in your own experience. Reflect on the passages and transitions—the bardos—of your life. My Tibetan teachers often told me that when we die, the only thing we can take with us is our karma. We each have our own personal karmic bank account.

Thinking about your karma helps you face the truth about your own experience; it helps you make changes when necessary. We all do and say things that don't work to make us happy. What about you? Focus on ways you can change and improve your karma. Don't think about changing anybody else's behavior—just your own. What can you do today to change the way you feel tomorrow? Keep your plans manageable and doable within the next 24 hours. Ask yourself the following questions:

Can I improve my attitude toward one person or situation in my life?

Can I let go and be less attached to a situation or thing that is causing me pain?

Can I let go of some negative feelings and cultivate a more positive, loving attitude toward the people in my life who make me angry?

Can I do something today that will help the planet?

He who understands karma understands Dharma and realizes reality.

The Buddha said:

"Wherever we go, wherever we remain,
the results of our actions follow us."

Chapter Two

Awakening to a Deeper Love—

A Buddha's Love

I went to my first meditation course in Bodh-Gaya, the village in India that has grown up around the tree under which the Buddha attained enlightenment. . . . out of curiosity someone asked me, "Why are you practicing meditation?" The first thing that came to my mind was an image of the Buddha in the main temple near the Bodhi tree, and I found myself saying, "I'm practicing so that I can have the love of a Buddha, so I can love people the way the Buddha did."

—From *A Heart as Wide as the World*
by Sharon Salzberg

We all want and need love. In fact, most of us are almost constantly seeking it—often more than anything else in life. That's because like seeks like, and we *are* love. We all have hearts of love. We are the energy of love, like the invisible God's visible body of love, or Buddha's body of love manifesting in this world. It happens through us. Love is not just something we do or experience. Love is a way of being—our most beautiful and unobstructed way of being. It is our truest and deepest calling.

The central theme of Mahayana Buddhism revolves around how we can answer that call by opening our hearts and learning to love and care for others, as well as ourselves. Buddhism teaches us how to transform ourselves so that we will be able to love as purely, unselfishly, and unconditionally as the Buddha loved. Many seekers are highly drawn to this lofty noble goal. However, finding a way to embody this kind of love amidst all the stresses and strains of our daily lives is a monumental challenge. It is far easier said than done! Yet do it we must, and I believe we shall. For love is our true purpose, our true calling. Love is calling each of us home, to the vast reservoir of love within ourselves.

THE SUBTLETIES OF LOVE

Last Sunday, as Marla drove home from a weekend spiritual retreat, she felt highly motivated to do good and be good. It had been an inspiring weekend, and she had been particularly moved by a loving-kindness practice that she found extraordinarily powerful. For her entire life, Marla has been concerned with wanting to help others. The retreat reawakened Marla's commitment to live a more compassionate, caring, and loving life; she wants to apply these feelings to every issue in her life.

Only a week has gone by since Marla returned from the retreat, yet she is already feeling discouraged and disturbed by the difficulties involved in maintaining a consistently loving, unselfish attitude. This morning, for example, Marla was trying to be more loving and caring with her significant other, but Robert was being undeniably self-centered, thinking only of himself as he rushed off early—as always—to play tennis with a client, while she was left to clean up a messy house and buy food for the rest of the weekend. Meanwhile, Marla has stuff of her own she wants to do. She wants to go to the gym; she wants to meditate; she wants to read a book; and she also has some work she brought home to read.

But first she must finish her chores, so Marla forces herself to let go of her resentment against Robert as she resolutely heads off to the store. Later, when Marla returns, staggering into the house with the bundles, the first thing that happens is that a lonely, talkative friend calls to ask for some advice. Marla wants to be available and open to help others so she stays on the phone and listens for a full forty-five minutes. Marla no sooner hangs up when a close friend, Jackie, calls to say that her car "died." Could Marla please pick her up at the gas station and drive her home? Jackie is her friend. *If I don't help her,* Marla thinks to herself, *who will I help?*

Marla is backing her car out of the driveway when her sister Pam pulls up. Pam is in tears because she and her husband Chuck have just had another major fight about money; they have scheduled an emergency counseling session. Could Marla please take the baby, and could she also loan them $200 to pay the phone bill because the phone has been turned off because Chuck didn't pay it. Marla loves her sister, and she wants to help, but Pam takes total advantage. *This happens all the time,* Marla thinks. *She just arrives with her problems and I'm supposed to fix them.* More than anything else Marla wants to do good; she wants to be a good sister and a good person. But isn't this all a bit much? As much as Marla wants to be open, caring, and accepting, all she is feeling is put upon. She hasn't even had time to get all her groceries out of the bag, but she is already as busy as a small social service agency.

We all want to be good people. Spiritual seekers particularly are very likely to aspire to be more loving and less selfish. But what does it mean to be loving? What does it mean to be kind and giving? How do we know that we are giving the right things at the right time? Where and when do we draw the line? Is Marla, for example, helping Robert or their relationship by assuming most of the household chores? Is she helping her sister, or is she encouraging dependency? Is she showing love or co-dependence?

So the question remains, what is compassion? What is love? Jesus taught his disciples to give unstintingly. Buddhists are taught that the Buddha gave all he had without holding back. There are numerous teachings about the many previous lifetimes that the Buddha told his followers he remembered. There is an ancient legend that in one of these lifetimes the Buddha was a prince. One day, while he was still a young man, the prince went out for a walk; he looked down a ravine and saw a starving tigress and her cubs. The prince was so pained by the suffering of these animals that he threw himself down into the ravine in order to provide the animals with food. This was an extraordinary act of self-sacrifice. Are any of us capable of this kind of love? Would we want to be? Is this a true story, showing the depth of love that a completely unselfish person can feel, or is it merely a romanticized legend? Of course we don't know. Still, the point is there. Myths can contain greater truths than mere fact.

Love is very simple, but it has many subtleties. The great Indian poet and mystic Kabir, born in the mid-fifteenth century, devoted his life to writing poems and songs of love for God. He sang, "Subtle is the path of love." Love has so many mysteries. Love makes us lessen our selfish and self-centered view of the world. The thing about loving someone or something else is that it absolutely teaches and challenges us to go beyond ourselves. Often this is only temporary, but knowing what this feels like if only for a moment gives us a hint of what it means to truly love. Parents the world over know firsthand what it feels like to regard another as more important than one's self. This is one of the great lessons of parenthood.

Yet for all of us, many are the errors in judgment committed in the name of love. Who would argue that many of our
sufferings are due to romantic attachments? There are times
when we believe we are being loving, while everyone else
thinks we are being self-indulgent, co-dependent, and even
delusional. Our need for romance, passion, and love often gets
corrupted by greed, jealousy, fear, and the shadows of our personal histories.

If we are not conscious and awake, an unrealistic search for
romantic love can rule our lives—often at the cost of our happiness and fulfillment. Yet romantic love serves a purpose. Not
only can it give us heartache and heartbreak, it can also be like
open heart surgery—transporting us beyond ourselves and
opening realms of giving, caring, and sharing. It allows us to experience a oneness that is far beyond any mental construct or
imagination. It is a personal way to experience oneness—a gateway that can lead us beyond ourselves. Romantic love can be a
revelation of what is possible. This is the value of interpersonal
relationships and friendships. In many ways, romantic love can
be a training and an opening to the experiencing of a greater,
more divine love.

In the practical world we inhabit, love often calls for appropriate compromises and boundaries; we need to learn give and
take, and we need to stay connected to nitty-gritty reality. My
friend and mentor, Ram Dass, used to point out that transper-
sonal love and nonattachment doesn't mean non-caring. In relationships, we need to strive and sometimes even fight to make
them work, and not pretend it doesn't matter. Ram Dass would
always say, "Hold on tight; let go light." We have to try to make
wholesome attempts to make things work, and accept it when
they don't.

Love also requires honesty and self-examination. As spiritual
seekers, travelling the path of self-discovery, we always have to
question our motivations and our reasons for loving. When

Marla, for example, goes out of her way for her sister Pam, is she being truly helpful and giving or is she trying to win points in the "sibling war" by pointing out to her parents that she is the "good" sister? This is a question Marla has to ask herself.

Questions about love, compassion, and giving are part of what we all have to explore for ourselves as we walk the path of awakening. As seekers, we have to search inward and take a long hard look at our motivations and intentions as we decide what to give, when to give it, and to whom we give it.

One of my first teachers was the late great wandering Hindu holy man, Neem Karoli Baba, whom we all called Maharaji. Maharaji was famous for wearing disguises and showing up where he was least expected. One day in Allahabad, India, dressed as a tattered beggar, he appeared at the back door of one of his longtime disciples, who was a prominent and learned professor of economics—and he asked for food. The professor's sister, who answered the door, shooed him away by banging on pots and pans.

The very next day, Maharaji returned to the household, this time dressed recognizably as the blanket-wrapped swami whom they all loved and adored. As to be expected, the family provided the very best vegetarian feast before Maharaji wandered off on his way. When next the professor came to pay homage at his guru's feet, he had his entire family with him. This time it was Maharaji who shooed *them* away by banging on pots and pans. The householder was deeply shocked and upset so he later returned, this time alone, to ask the guru what had happened and why; he begged forgiveness for anything that he had done wrong. Maharaji told him, "You never know who comes from God. When I came as a beggar, your sister drove me away, banging pots and pans like I was a mongrel dog. When I came as a guru, you fed me like a king." The message, of course, is that we should treat everyone as though he or she is a child of God and has been sent by divine will.

This story bothered me for years and made me think deeply about the distinctions I make between people; it made me reflect on my own biases, prejudices, and partiality—and my capacity to give unconditionally and indiscriminately. I am the child of parents who were products of the Great Depression. In our house a greater value was placed on saving than there was on spending. I'm just now starting to experience the joy of giving and spending without reservation, and I've had to ask myself many questions about my feelings about giving. Why, for example, is it sometimes so much easier to give in situations where there is some status connected to the cause or charity? Why do we tend to blot out and erase from our minds the truly needy and the poorest of the poor as though they don't exist, while we cheerfully send beautifully wrapped birthday, Hanukkah, birthday, and Christmas gifts to people who already have much more than they need? We all do it, don't we? Often we don't even really see the needy street people we pass by when we are going to visit someone; sometimes we are carrying expensive house gifts—wine and flowers. We bring such gifts because we want to give a nice present but also because we want people to think we have great taste, or we want to be invited back. But sometimes we need to ask ourselves how much of this is true giving and how much is self-serving. Motivation is what is most relevant.

In Thailand, where the monks go out each morning to collect alms, they pass anonymously from house to house. In Japan, the monks wear large straw basket hats to cover their faces so the giver never knows who is the recipient of their generosity. This practice emphasizes the transcendental, selfless nature of generosity. That's the thing about giving in all its forms: It extends transpersonally and anonymously throughout the universe. We smile at a stranger; the stranger feels happier about the world and extends his good feeling to someone else, who in turn may pass it on. "Passing it on" is the operative term.

Several years ago, a forest fire swept the parched mountains in northern New Mexico, destroying everything in its path. Completely razed by this wildfire was the Lama Foundation, a community established outside of Taos thirty-five years ago. The Lama Foundation, which was the first East–West spiritual community of its kind in America, is located on the western slopes of Taos Mountain. This large mountain has long been held sacred by the Native Americans of the region. I have taught and led retreats there on several occasions; the disaster was a loss to all of us.

One of my friends at the Lama Foundation was particularly known for her great collection of spiritual books, handicrafts, medicine wheels, statuettes, god's eyes, and works of art—some original, many collected. We all knew how much she loved and was attached to her collection. After the fire she told me that the only pieces of her priceless, lifelong collection that had survived were the ones she had given away. This was, she said, her lesson in nonattachment and the virtue of open-handed generosity. She was glad that she knew where some of her things still remained. All that was left of her lifelong passion was what she had given to others.

GIVING MEANING TO LIFE

In Buddhism, the most loving and glorious spiritual ideal is that of the Bodhisattva, the spiritual warrior whose purpose in life is to help others find enlightenment, liberation, and truth. The Bodhisattva Vow of Mahayana Buddhism is very simple:

Sentient beings are numberless; I vow to liberate them.
Delusions are inexhaustible; I vow to transcend them.
Dharma teachings are boundless; I vow to master them.

The Buddha's enlightened way is unsurpassable; I vow to embody it.
For the ultimate benefit of all beings without exception, throughout
this and all my lifetimes, I dedicate myself to the practice and
realization of enlightenment until all together reach that goal.

Within the last twenty or thirty years, many of the great Asian teachers of their time have welcomed Western students by sharing with them the Dharma (as the Buddhist teachings of truth are known). Some of us first learned of the Bodhisattva Vow in Asia; many more learned of it in their own countries. The Dalai Lama himself has come to this country and given this vow to thousands of men and women. In Darjeeling in the early autumn of 1973, I first took the vow with my late teacher, Kalu Rinpoche. New students would sometimes ask him if they could take the Bodhisattva Vow more than once. He would tell them to take it all the time—every morning as well as every night. The Bodhisattva Vow is a living vow that we reaffirm every day, not just once in a lifetime. Kalu Rinpoche would encourage us to take refuge in the Bodhisattva Vow, explaining that taking refuge in the Vow was taking refuge and solace in our higher aspirations. In this way we relied upon the profound power of pure intention to transform our words, thoughts, and deeds.

The Bodhisattva ideal represents ultimate love—divine compassion translated into human form. With this kind of unconditional love, we consistently consider the well-being of everyone. Anything we unselfishly do for others has implications and repercussions. By making this level of commitment, we recognize that there are consequences to our actions; everything we do and say affects others. In this way, all of our connections become more meaningful. Every encounter counts.

As the Dalai Lama points out, the words don't really matter; whether you call it compassion, love, or charity, the good heart—the heart of unconditional love and unselfish caring—is universal. Whether it is Christ or Buddha, both are brothers-in-truth, driven by the awakened and loving heart of the Bodhisattva. This cosmic principle dwells in each of us. Committing ourselves to cultivating the awakened heart of the Bodhisattva is the greatest service we can dedicate to the world. The Bodhisattva is the ultimate social activist working to alleviate universal suffering throughout all of his or her lifetimes. I call this spiritual activism.

So many people go through their days feeling as though their lives are meaningless and without purpose. However, when we commit ourselves to Bodhisattva practices and the deeper love, selfless service, and boundless compassion these practices entail, by definition we endow our lives with meaning. Caring for the spiritual welfare—the most profound well-being—of others puts our lives in context. This is a reason to get up every morning. Sometimes it may feel as though we are engaged in the exhausting task of putting small drops into large buckets, but we all know that if there are enough drops, eventually the bucket *will* become full. This is a way to give your life richness and purpose.

One of the most popular Mahayana scriptures is the Avatamsaka Sutra, affectionately known as the Flower Garland Sutra. The basic teaching of this sutra is that everything is interwoven, interconnected, and mutually interpenetrating. Reading it, we think of the world as the jeweled lattice of the Hindu God Indra's web, in which each sparkling, mirrorlike jewel reflects and thus contains all the others. Like these reflecting jewels, we are not separate, and we are not one; rather we are interrelated and interconnected. This totality approach to connectedness is what the venerable and loving Vietnamese monk Thich Nhat Hanh calls "interbeing." From the light that is reflected from this vast, sacred web of interbeing-ness, we can see that we are all perfect beings perfectly evolving to a natural perfection that is beyond the limiting dualism of perfect and imperfect. Our spiritual journey is recognized, with all its ups and downs, as a perfect unfolding—an unfolding in the light, and of the light.

Before his own fully perfect enlightenment, the Buddha was just like each of us—a seeker striving for freedom and awakening. The Garland Sutra describes the Buddha's spiritual path, telling how in earlier lifetimes as a Bodhisattva he sowed the seeds of awakening in his own heart and mind through compassionate, selfless acts. In this way he cultivated what Buddhists call "Bodhicitta," a Sanskrit word that means the awakened heart-mind or the mind of enlightenment. Bodhicitta is the Buddha's heart in each of us.

When Buddhist scholars talk about Bodhicitta, they often make a distinction between two forms, which are known as (1) relative Bodhicitta and (2) absolute Bodhicitta. Relative Bodhicitta refers to the compassionate intention to attain enlightenment and liberation for the benefit of all beings. Absolute Bodhicitta (or the absolute mind of enlightenment) refers to an understanding of the central Buddhist theme of emptiness. Thus the Bodhisattva with the awakened heart-mind of enlightenment (1) strives to attain liberation for all beings and (2) realizes that the true nature of the world is emptiness, infinite openness, or sunyata.

The actual name of the Garland Sutra is the Buddhavatamsaka Sutra. When people hear the name Garland Sutra, they often think of a garland of flowers, but what this name really represents is a Garland of Buddhas. This image addresses an underlying theme of Mahayana Buddhism: The Mahayana sutras say that when we look at anything, even into the palm of our hand, we can find these infinite Buddha Fields, teeming with enlightened ones. Whether we are staring at the infinite realms of space or at the smallest molecule, what we are seeing are infinite, luminous Buddhas. Whether we are standing in the grandest cathedral or sky gazing through the highest redwoods, we see Buddha Fields without limits, veritable galaxies of Buddha light. Everywhere we look are multitudes—millions and millions of tiny Buddhas. In short, everything is permeated by Buddha-nature—or, if you prefer, by the mind of the Divine. Buddha-nature here, Buddha-nature there, Buddha-nature everywhere.

That's why the gentle spiritual warrior, known as the Bodhisattva, has limitless patience, perseverance, and courage. The Bodhisattva recognizes that no one is totally apart or separate from sacred Buddha-nature. As we strive for enlightenment and the fully realized heart mind, we begin to see that even the smallest kind word, or gentle loving gesture, has repercussions in the infinite Buddha Field we all inhabit. Karmically speaking, everything matters, everything counts, and everything is interconnected. Nothing is ever overlooked by the lord/law of karma. Knowing this lends meaning and purpose to our lives. Each of us totally matters.

I live in the countryside, and often when I am out walking I am struck by the country practice of waving. Car after car passes me on the road; the occupants wave and smile. I wave and smile back. Whether we think about it or not, this little practice of waving on a country road is a way of building spiritual connections and spreading love. Don't we feel good about the mini-relationships we build with our little waves? *How nice and kind that family looked smiling at me. How lovely the kids in the station wagon seem with their faces pressed against the back window, waving and smiling.* Even the family dog is waving his tail. We feel seen and acknowledged by these little rituals; we feel connected to our fellow travellers.

The great Indian sage Shantideva, whose name means the "Gentle Master," lived in the 7th and 8th century. He spent his life teaching others how to see the equality of self and other, and to act from this belief. He said that if you raise even *one* hand in a gesture of reverence to anything or anyone, all the Buddhas clap, rejoice, and rain down blessings. Shantideva lived in a world where people regularly put two hands together and bowed. Yet he taught that even one hand could make a difference. In a practical sense, raising a hand in reverence means that we must put down our weapons. After all, it's difficult to harm or manipulate someone when you are bowing to them. Think of this the next time you feel anger or enmity. Soften yourself by trying to experience a feeling, a glimmer, of reverence for the person who is arousing your ire. In this way we delight the ever-present Buddhas, the great accomplished Bodhisattvas—all the immortals, saints, sages, and protectors of truth and Dharma.

CHAPTER THREE

Connecting to Your

Life Experience

It's never too late to be what you might have been.
—George Eliot

I have a sane and reliable friend who swears that she remembers coming home from the hospital right after being born; her mother wrapped her in a hand-crocheted pink blanket, and placed her in a crib. From that vantage point, she says she witnessed an argument between her two older sisters, one of whom angrily threw a toy doll at my friend, the new baby. My friend has no other childhood memories until she is a bit older, but when she talked to her parents about the pink blanket and the kind of doll that was thrown at her—a bride doll—they confirmed the specifics about the argument she remembered seeing and hearing. I'm not making this up! My friend says that she also remembers talking to "voices" at the time, saying that she wasn't sure if she was in the right place and whether she was going to be able to deal with her sisters. "I don't know about this," she remembers saying. "This situation may be a little too overwhelming. I think I made a mistake."

Do you ever look at your life and wonder, did I choose this? Am I at the right address? Am I in the right relationship, the right job? How did I get here anyway? *The Tibetan Book of the Dead* explicitly teaches that we all choose our parents and the lives we lead, even if we are not as conscious about it as someone like, for example, the Dalai Lama. Some religious traditions say that this is the life that was given to us. Buddhism teaches that this is the life we chose, although not entirely consciously. The challenges we face are the challenges we chose to face. This is how we learn; this is how we grow; this is how we become more enlightened.

If that is the case, then it stands to reason that the first lesson we all need to learn is to accept and connect to the lives we are leading. For THIS IS IT. This is the path for us, and the right one. Let's make the most of it. This is the spiritual Way.

THIS IS IT. JUST THIS, HERE NOW.

There is an old Tibetan saying: "Life runs out while we are preparing to live." Even in antiquity, when life must have been somewhat slower and simpler, the sage Tibetan masters of the past recognized how easy it is to live in fantasies about the future or a time when everything will be the way we want it to be. But this fantasy-driven approach is neither productive nor ultimately satisfying. Probably one of the first lessons on the spiritual path has to do with an understanding that *this is it*. This is our chance to be happy and do good. I have been in churches that began services with the congregation singing, "Thank you for the life we are given and the song we sing today." This reality is our life. This is our song—my song and your song. This vivid song sings through us, right now.

I remember an old story about an elderly Jewish man named

Itzhak. Itzhak had spent his life trying to be a good person who honored the commandments and did good deeds. Nonetheless shortly before his death, Itzhak begins worrying about the reception he will get from God in the afterlife. He worries that he has been a failure and that he will be compared to the prophets of old and asked questions like:

Were you as good a leader as Moses?

Were you as wise as Solomon?

Did you have the vision of Isaiah?

When Itzhak finally dies and goes to meet God, he is still worrying about whether he lived up to his Lord's expectations and comparisons that might be made. With great trepidation, he waits to see which questions he will be asked. And they astonish him.

Did you have the wisdom of Itzhak?

Did you have the vision of Itzhak?

Were you genuinely and authentically yourself?

This is *your* life. Right here. Right now. Just this. Your life is your very own path. Don't wish for someone else's; instead search for ways to be like your own true self and fulfill all your own promise and possibility. You are the spiritual treasure you are trying to discover and reveal. The love and the challenges you receive from your friends, your mates, your family, and your work are all part of the process of your awakening—all grist for the mill. You are "the jewel in the lotus," as Tibetans sing in the favorite mantra, **"Om Mani Pedmé Hung."** You are the beautiful blossoming, the inner treasure.

CONNECTING TO THE LESSONS
IN YOUR OWN LIFE

Why do so many things in life go right? Why do so many others go wrong?

Why is it that so often when we look at our lives we wonder, "Why me?" or "Why is this happening?" yet when we look at someone else, we can clearly see cause and effect at work. For example:

❋ Last October my friend Meryl began to feel so exhausted that, as she put it, she didn't have the strength to get out of bed every morning. She had been fine the previous summer, following her usual daily routine. Until she began to feel tired, this was Meryl's weekday schedule:

6:00 A.M. Wake up, dress quickly, jog to gym
6:45–7:45 Work out
7:45–9:00 Jog back home, shower, dress, go to work
9:00–12:30 Work
12:30–2:00 Business lunch
2:00–6:30 Work
6:30–11:00 Work-related or social activity
11:00–11:30 Watch nightly news
11:30–12:00 Read work-related papers and material
12:00 Prepare for bed and lights out

When Meryl first began to complain of exhaustion, she started taking more vitamins, but they didn't do any good. Then she started cutting out some of her nightly activities, and began getting to bed by 10:00 and watching sitcoms until she fell asleep. That still didn't work. She began to wonder whether she needed to increase her strength training at the gym, but when she attempted to do that, she started to feel even more weary. Finally she went to the doctor, who after many tests, diagnosed chronic fatigue syndrome. *Why,* she keeps asking herself, *did I get sick?*

❋ Robert, who owns a small printing business, wants to know why he can never find a production assistant with whom he gets along. Robert likes being around highly educated people who challenge him, so inevitably everybody he hires is argumentative, overqualified, and ill-suited for a job that requires production and organizing skills. Inevitably his employees stay with him for no more than six months. All of them seem to have a difficult time understanding what Robert wants his assistant to do. Some of them become frustrated and annoyed and quit in a huff; others are more polite, giving adequate notice before leaving. More than one has simply left the office at lunchtime and not returned. *What is going wrong here,* Robert asks. *Is it me? Is it them? Is it the work?*

❊ About a year ago, Maria went into an animal shelter and adopted Gertrude, a large black and tan dog of indeterminate lineage. A few months later she was standing on a street corner with Gertrude, waiting for a light to change. A loud noise startled the dog, who broke free and bolted in the opposite direction even though Maria had been holding the leash. Ted, a man who was standing at the same corner, instinctively used his foot to step down on the dog's leash, stopping Gertrude's escape. Today Maria and Ted are deeply in love and planning a wedding next year. They both often ask each other, "How did this happen?" "Is this a miracle, or what?" "How did we get so lucky?"

Heard at Logan Airport terminal in Boston: "Unattended baggage may be lost or confiscated." Isn't that how it goes in life itself when we fail to attend to our baggage? Recently I was in Chicago teaching a five-day retreat. When I returned home and walked through the door, I smelled something strange—something damp and mildewed, like a musty old swamp, actually. What could it be? Something made me look down in the basement, and what to my wondering eyes should appear but about two or three inches of water.

I put on my boots, and waded down into the basement to assess the damage. Ruined were several boxes of winter gear and some packing material. What didn't get ruined were my file cabinets which were all raised on cement blocks a few inches off the ground.

Why did my basement get flooded? Why were some of my things ruined and others saved? Well first of all, the basement of my old farmhouse, which has stood in a field for more than a hundred years, has no drain. Secondly, I didn't notice that the water heater was beginning to leak. Oops! Water heaters typically only last from five to ten years. I had even had some indications that mine was failing because for months it had been making funny noises that I chose to ignore.

As a Buddhist, I don't believe in accidents, and yet I don't pretend to understand how all things fit together. This is part of the mystery of life with all its crazy connections and disconnections. Recently while walking down a Manhattan street, I ran into an old friend I hadn't seen in twenty years. Why were we both standing on a corner near Bloomingdale's on the same day, waiting for a light to change? Who can explain synchronicity? Yet we know it exists.

When I was growing up, many of the mothers of my friends were home watching television in the middle of the afternoon. They were addicted to soap operas. I never really watched one from start to finish, but I remember stopping in a friend's family room and asking someone else's mom what was the plotline in the show she was watching. She told me. About a year later, I was once again in my friend's home, and once again I asked his mother what was going on. I was astonished that the main characters were embroiled in the same kinds of situations. The "good guys" were still putting themselves at emotional and physical risk and the resident "bitch" was still making the same people unhappy. *Wow,* I remember thinking, *don't these people ever learn?*

When most of us stop long enough and really take the time to reflect on what we experience—good and bad—we can't help but see patterns emerging. We see how often we are careless in thought, word, and deed; we see how we have sometimes been appropriately open and caring, and we also see the times we have been determinedly argumentative and defensive.

Our lives with all their "accidents" and synchronistic happenings provide us with dozens of opportunities to learn from our experiences. The question is, Do we garner the insights and lessons we need through these experiences? Do we learn which behaviors give us joy and which cause us pain? Do we pay attention, or do we go on unconsciously year after year wondering *Why is this happening to me?* Are we like sleepwalkers dreaming our way along on a treadmill of our own unconscious making?

Karma is a very pragmatic explanation of cause and effect. We polish a piece of silver and we see the shine; we plant some seeds, and we grow our own salad; we help a friend, and we are rewarded with friendship. Right now, we can all ask ourselves, What are the paybacks in our own lives? Is what we do and say getting us what we want and need? What changes could we make in our own attitudes and actions that might produce positive effects? Do we need to become more measured and less driven? Do we need to be more open and less guarded? Do we need to be more giving and less demanding?

Enlightenment is about seeing clearly how things work; it's about knowing and understanding what is; it's about connecting to the truth of the present moment. What better place to apply ourselves to reality as it presents itself to us than in our daily moment-by-moment lives?

PAYING ATTENTION TO WHAT'S HAPPENING, AS IT HAPPENS

In everybody's life there are subterranean parts that are not getting our full attention—parts that we are sweeping under the rug and choosing to ignore. They may be skeletons—or unattended baggage—in our psychological closets. Sometimes these parts are material, as in my basement; often they are less tangible. Often there are sounds emanating from these areas—not necessarily sirens or fire alarms, but sounds nonetheless. Most of us have had the experience of being in relationships with people who are making "noises," letting us know in dozens of small ways that they are dissatisfied or unhappy. Parents of teenagers have told me that they don't need to go to a school conference to find out whether or not their children are doing well; they can read success or failure in the way a child opens and closes the door when they come home from school.

As we become more enlightened, wiser, and more spiritually intelligent about our lives, we learn to listen more closely to the messages we are receiving about how we lead our lives. We learn to hear the noises around us warning us off or cheering us on. We learn to question our own motivations and behavior. When we practice clear seeing, it becomes apparent that we need to deal realistically with the lives we have created and the people and situations around us; when we practice wisdom, it is obvious that we need to look at the world and our individual lives without any delusions or distortions.

Walking down the street one day I saw someone wearing a T-shirt that read, *"Denial is not just the name of a river in Egypt."* This made me laugh. Denial is an operative force in all our lives. We see what we are conditioned to seeing; we see what we want to see. When something happens that doesn't mesh with our version of reality, often the first response is to deny that it's taking place.

The Buddha encouraged us to look at life neither pessimistically nor optimistically, but *realistically.* Of course this is easier said than done. Whether we are examining our relationships with family, friends, coworkers, lovers, or mates, we all tend to look at the world from our own vantage point, instead of seeing the truth of what's in front of us. Many people remember the movie *Rashomon* where the same event is viewed from several different points of view. The Rashomon effect is operative all around us, all the time. I have a friend who lives in Boston; in July he was upset because he was forced to spend a summer weekend in his airconditioned apartment instead of on a New England beach as he had planned. He felt deprived. To most of the world's population, he spent an almost idyllic weekend in perfect comfort; to him, it was as if he had been imprisoned.

We also tend to see different things even when we are in the same room. I once knew somebody who was phobic about dead birds. She lived in Manhattan. "Where," I asked her with amazement, "do you see dead birds?" "Take a walk with me," she replied, "and you'll see that there are dead birds every-where." One day I did just that. As we walked, she pointed them out: dead pigeons and sparrows, hidden under cars and in alleyways. I certainly would not have noticed them if I were alone. They did seem to be everywhere. My friend had made an obsession about spotting the dead bodies, and a phobia out of that obsession. We project our karmic perceptions, and it defines and colors our experience.

In Buddhism we learn that our experiences—what we see, what we think, and what we feel—have to do with our own attachments, perceptions, and interpretations. It's all a matter of perspective. Thus we construct our reality.

UNDERSTANDING SAMSKARAS

Not that long ago, a man attended one of my lectures with his wife and her twin sister. The two women were remarkably identical. While they were standing there, an older woman became engaged in a conversation with the three of them and couldn't resist asking the man a question that he must hear with great regularity. "How do you tell them apart?" The man's reply was interesting. "They don't look at all alike to me," he said. "In fact, when I met my wife, she was with her sister. I was so attracted to my wife that I didn't pay much attention to her sister or even notice the resemblance."

For this man, when his wife walked across the stage of his life, everything clicked, and all of his antennae shot up. Why is that? Why does one person appeal to us so much more than another? Why do we choose the friends we do? Why do we gravitate toward certain occupations? Why do we find some events appealing and others completely boring? What a mystery! And yet if we look more deeply, certain patterns emerge.

There is an ancient Sanskrit word, *"samskaras,"* which is used to explain this phenomenon. "Samskara" literally means tendencies or inclinations. In Buddhism the definition is broadened somewhat to mean "impulses," or "tendencies to make certain choices because of karmic imprinting." In modern parlance, we sometimes hear people use expressions like "whatever floats your boat." This conveys the same sense as a samskara. My friend Barry often complains about his mother, saying, "She pushes all my buttons." In short, samskaras are those tendencies we have to respond positively or negatively to certain situations or people. It is deeply ingrained psychological conditioning.

Everything we do, say, think, and feel creates an impression in the mind. Everything we see, hear, smell, and taste creates an impression or impulse. Buddhist teachings say that we are all bundles of samskaras or impulses. Somebody or something pushes these samskara-buttons, and we react.

For example:

✳ When Sarah was a child, she wore a blue dress to go to a county fair with her favorite aunt and uncle. Her uncle gave her a quarter to put on a number at one of the games, and Sarah won a small teddy bear. Since that day, whenever Sarah wears blue, she feels lucky.

✻ When Theo was growing up, he had an older sister whom he resented because she was always telling him what to do. Now that he is a married man, he finds that he often responds to simple requests from his wife in the same way that he responded to his bossy sister.

Think about the dozens of samskara-buttons that reveal themselves in your life every day. We walk past luncheonettes and smell coffee brewing or pancakes being made; we want some. We hear angry noises or spooky music; our adrenaline starts flowing. We see a comfortable-looking couch; we want to sit down. Advertisers, who are in the business of sending us subliminal messages, know all about samskaras. These are the buttons they attempt to push when they want us to buy their products. If they could, they would probably implant more samskaras in us to better manipulate and direct our consumer impulses.

For each of us individually there are hundreds and hundreds of unique samskaras. Some are generational. An eighty-year-old, for example, might respond to big band music in the same way that people of my generation respond to the Beatles or a twenty-year-old reacts to the music of Pearl Jam. Some samskaras are identified with certain countries or ethnic groups, and some are familial. There are many more, of course, that are the result of one's own individual experiences. Often the people we choose as friends and romantic partners instinctively seem to know how to push our samskara-buttons.

Our samskara-buttons help create and perpetuate our karma. In fact ancient Eastern teachings say samskaras form the basis of our many attractions and aversions and therefore are driving forces behind our thoughts and our actions. Teachings about reincarnation or rebirth say that it is the samskaras which attract and repel us and are therefore part of what bring us back time and time again to this world.

When the Buddha realized perfect enlightenment, he was free from his samskaras. Never again would he be at the mercy of his likes or dislikes; he had achieved mastery of his thoughts and feelings, and with that, of course, comes freedom and inner peace.

Understanding what drives us and how our samskara-buttons are pushed helps us understand how our karma is formed. The Tibetans say that all the samskaras that drive us fall into one of eight categories, which they call the Eight Worldly Winds or the Eight Traps. These are paired up in four sets:

❀ Pleasure and pain

❀ Loss and gain

❀ Praise and blame

❀ Fame and shame

Every single one of us has these eight buttons, each of which is inscribed with these individual names. When anything in our lives pushes one or more of these buttons, we respond:

❀ Elizabeth, for example, is a beautiful woman with a very negative husband who keeps telling her that she has gained weight and is not attractive enough. Intellectually Elizabeth knows that she is attractive, and she knows that her husband is simply being cruel. But because so many of her buttons are being pushed (pain, shame, blame, loss), she loses sight of reality.

✵ Ian, who is having trouble at work, is nearly overcome with fear at the idea that he might lose his job and the status that comes with it. When his buttons are being pushed, he becomes almost irrational.

✵ Margaret believes that she will never be perfectly happy until she can move into a larger house. Just thinking about the tiny, cramped apartment she is living in gives her pain.

All of these people, of course, are allowing their lives to be dominated by the things that push their buttons, and in so doing, they are failing to find joyous freedom and spontaneous expression in the present moment. As we become more and more purified of karma and more enlightened, our samskara reaction buttons lose their hold over us. We find greater and greater freedom from conditioning as well as from unfulfilling patterns, fixations, behaviors, and neuroses; we find ourselves becoming free of illusion and confusion as well as overweening attachment and desire. We become free to be genuinely ourselves moment to moment—free to experience the natural bliss and spontaneity of just *being*. Freedom is in our hands.

CONNECTING TO YOUR
INNER SPIRITUAL WARRIOR

Initially we may have a hard time relating to the amount of work that the Buddhist path—or any other genuine spiritual path—encourages. But anyone who has walked the path knows that the greatest battles one faces are internal. The most determined demons are the demons that live within us. I think it is important for all of us to do more than just pay lip service to this idea. People often come to me for counseling about their personal lives, and in these conversations I'm made aware of how much energy and thought we all expend trying to avoid our own problems by focusing on someone else. I've spoken to many women who tell me that their biggest problems in life are caused by a male partner's relationship with his mother, for example, while men may tell me that their biggest problems are created by their partners' workaholism or attitude toward career. When we focus on our partners' weaknesses, we can deny our own karmic patterns, forgetting that it takes two to tangle.

Some of us are consistently drawn to co-dependent relationships; others of us are so enveloped in narcissistic behaviors and judgments that we can't get past our self-referring, self-preoccupied view of the cosmos. The first task of the spiritual warrior is to get honest about his or her own life and feelings. If we are going to walk the spiritual path with the courage and bravery that it and we deserve, then we have to begin facing up to a major truth:

Inside each of us is a core of essential goodness and purity. Wrapped around this core—this Buddha within—are layers of conditioned responses, attitudes, patterns, habits, and obscuring behaviors. Some of these layers reflect the goodness of our basic Buddha-nature; others do not. To fully awaken and reveal the Buddha within, we have to honestly recognize, acknowledge, and deal with the ingrained problematic conditioning that we all have. We must have the inner strength and fortitude to honestly face these parts of ourselves. There is no way around it except through it.

When we talk about becoming awake, we mean becoming fully conscious and aware of what is actually going on with us—and within us. If we're involved in destructive relationships, for example, we need to spend time unraveling why we are repeatedly attracted to these relationships. If we consistently find ourselves in unfulfilling work situations, we need to examine why this keeps happening. If we are abusing our health, we need to recognize what we are doing, and why, as a first vital step toward positive change. This level of consciousness isn't easy to achieve, but it can be done. It requires the honesty, courage, and inspired effort of a true spiritual warrior. It takes guts to open up and soften up to the tendencies, vulnerability, and shadows that abide within us.

As a Buddhist, I strive to live fully in the present moment, the here and now—the Holy Now. When I say that, some people might automatically misunderstand. They assume that living "in the now" means "living *for* the now." Nothing could be further from teachings of Buddhism, which instruct us to "live in the now" and prepare for the future whether that future is tomorrow or in the next world. The whole teaching of karma is directed at helping seekers improve their lives by altering unsatisfying behavior. In Buddhism, we foster spiritual intelligence by understanding karma and taking the long view.

CONTEMPLATING YOUR LIFE

Self-reflection helps us heal our lives. The first step in any process of change involves facing and accepting the problem that needs changing. Try the following exercise:

Sit down someplace comfortable where you can just be alone with your thoughts. Take a breather. Relax and take a few breaths. Let go of the troubles and trials of the day. Let the tension and internal conflict and friction drain away. Drop everything.

Turn inward. Slow down. Calm down. Give yourself the gift of being with yourself for a time, like a soul admitted to its own private infinity.

Now: Consider for a moment where you are in life and how you got here. Try not to run away from your thoughts.

Now: Consider for just a moment where you would like to be in a month, a year, five years, and ten years. Think about what you would like to have done and accomplished. Think about what it would be like to be on your deathbed. What would you like to look back and see that you have accomplished? What would you like your obituary to say?

Now: Consider what you have become already. Consider who and what you think you are, and what you might like to do or be if you were given the chance and the choice.

Ask yourself—this is a serious question—if someone gave you the cosmic credit card, what would you do with the rest of your life? Please think about it without editing your thoughts. Your answer could be extremely revealing.

What would you really love to do in order to make a life, not just a living? How far from that way of living are you today?

What would you do about your relationships? How would you change the way you are with others?

What would you do with your creativity? The great statesman Benjamin Disraeli once said, "Most people die with their music still locked up inside of them." What would you do to unlock your own inner music?

What would you do with your work? Do you do your work as if it matters, or are you just killing time trying to get through the week to the weekend before beginning the whole ratrace all over again?

What would you do about your health? What habits would you change to make yourself more healthy? How would you change your exercise and eating habits to make yourself feel better and be more fit?

What would you do about your spiritual life? Would you join a group of other people who are committed to a more spiritual life? Would you devote some time and energy to private contemplation, meditation, yoga, or prayer?

What would you do with your compassion and concern for the world? Would you find a way to contribute and help others? What would that be?

Ask yourself, Am I living in tune with my own interests, principles, and beliefs? Am I connecting to the sacred in my own life? Do I walk my talk and practice what I preach?

Is my life helping me develop and contribute my special gifts and talents to the world, bringing out the very best in me, and delivering satisfaction and fulfillment?

Is there any other way—perhaps a road less travelled—I could possibly still take and explore?

Ask yourself, Who am I today and who can I be?

How can I get from here to there? What is the way to my highest happiness?

Where is the next step? What is the first step? Shall I take it? What prevents me from taking such a step today?

MINDFULNESS IS THE TOOL

The single greatest tool that we can all access to help us connect to our true lives is *paying attention,* or the cultivation of conscious awareness, which Buddhists call "mindfulness." Mindfulness is how we connect to the reality of "what is." When we are fully mindful, we are vividly aware of precisely what is happening, when it is happening. When we are mindful, we are better able to see the reality of any situation. This is called clear vision. When we are mindful, we have greater mastery over our own lives. When we are mindful, we find greater joy in the small moment-by-moment pleasures of life; we are more fully present, less absentminded. We can savor life and plumb deeper into its depths rather than merely wading in the shallows.

Right now, stop what you are doing, let go of your thoughts; let go of your activities.

Breathe in through your nostrils, counting one. . . . Breathe out, counting two.

Breathe in through your nostrils, counting one. . . . Breathe out, counting two.

Do this ten times.

Now start again. Breathe in. Breathe out.

Be silent, as the world slows down. Be aware of what is crossing your gaze right now. A butterfly flits by the window. A cat stretches in the sun. A sparrow alights on the tree limb. All this in the space of a few short breaths. Take notice!

Or do this meditation with your eyes closed, becoming totally aware of sounds, like a very sensitive listening station. Enter the present moment totally through the delicious gateway of sound. Sound is a good object of meditation since it exists only in the now.

We meditate in order to train in mindfulness. In fact, the classic, most basic Buddhist meditation is called Mindfulness of Breathing. When the Buddha gave his instructions on mindfulness, he told his students and disciples that as they go through life, they should be aware of four things:

 their bodies

 their feelings and emotions

 their thoughts

 events as they occur

When we practice basic Buddhist meditation, which is called Mindfulness of Breathing, what we are doing is training ourselves to be more mindful and attentive in life. When a disciple asked the Buddha what it meant to live with impeccable mindfulness, the Buddha told him that a disciple should act with clear comprehension—clear vision—in walking, standing, eating, drinking, sitting, falling asleep, awakening, speaking, and keeping silent. This pretty much covers it.

The great contemporary Vietnamese peace activist and meditation master Thich Nhat Hanh says, "You've got to practice meditation when you walk, stand, lie down, sit, and work, while washing your hands, washing the dishes, sweeping the floor, drinking tea, talking to friends, or whatever you are doing." In other words, all the time. Can any of us afford to sleepwalk through life? Don't we all want to be more fully awake and alive?

Mindfulness is the opposite of mindlessness. Through mindless living, we dissipate our energy, and squander our lives. Through mindful living, we inhabit fully the present moment and connect more totally with whomever we are with and with whatever we are doing. Then the smallest act becomes unimaginably blessed. Mindfulness is like the wish-fulfilling jewel, the Philosopher's Stone, a genuine elixir. Connecting to it, we connect to spiritual gold. Mindful awareness is transformative.

In the hectic world we all inhabit, it seems almost impossible to be mindful all the time. As we commute to work, our minds tend to jump forward to what we're going to do once we arrive. Often we daydream about events that have already taken place. We live in yesterday or tomorrow. This, of course, is the antithesis of mindfulness. When we lose the present moment, we lose our place in life.

CONNECTING TO THE PRESENT MOMENT THROUGH THE POWER OF NOW

Take a breath; take a break. Cultivate the power of the present moment by entering into the holy now.

To do this meditation, just make yourself comfortable. Lie, sit, stand. It doesn't matter.

Breathe in slowly through your nostrils.

As you breathe in, repeat this inner mantra to yourself: "Just this, here now."

As you breathe out, repeat again: "Just this. Here now." Use this mantra as an inner form of prayer or chant of contemplation and meditation.

Inhale . . . Just this, here now.

Exhale . . . Just this, here now.

There is nothing but this moment. This sacred moment. Just this, here now.

Let everything else subside, and just go with the natural flow of things, left just as they are. Trust it.

There is no greater miracle than this. Just this. Here now.

There is nowhere else to go, nowhere else to be than just this, here now.

This is the moment we've been waiting for. This is the great crossroads of past and future. This is the goal of our journey. Just this, here now.

There is nothing extra to get rid of and nothing missing that we need to find—just this glorious, radiant, abundant here . . . now.

Right here is how we find ourselves, just as we are. Just this.

Right here is where eternity and infinity converge in the present moment. Right here is the gateway to infinity, to the timeless. Just this. Here now.

This is the eternal moment, the mystical instant, the timeless time beyond time and space—yet totally, precisely present. Just this. Here now.

Don't miss it.

CHAPTER FOUR

Developing Authentic Presence

When you meet a person who has inner authentic presence, you find he has an overwhelming genuineness, which
might be somewhat frightening because it is so true and
honest and real. You experience a sense of command radiating from the person of inner authentic presence. . . . This is
not just charisma. The person with inner authentic presence has worked on himself and made a thorough and
proper journey. He has earned authentic presence by letting
go, and by giving up personal comfort and fixed mind.

—Chogyam Trungpa Rinpoche

"Just be yourself."

How often have we heard these simple words of
wisdom? How often have we repeated them? I recently heard a mother counseling her child who was
about to go for a preinterview at the college of her
choice, "Bettina, just be yourself." In Shakespeare's
Hamlet, Polonius, the wise elder, advises his son,
Laertes:

"This above all: to thine own self be true,

And it must follow, as the night the day,

Thou canst not then be false to any man."

Whether it's couched in Elizabethan English or the current vernacular—as in "get real"—it's good advice. What a wonderful feeling it is to be able to be authentic—to be real. To just be yourself is easier said than done, is it not? Why do most of us find it difficult to be the men and women we really are?

The hard truth is that while we were growing up the most prevalent message we probably heard was not "just be yourself." In fact, most people tell me that the favored instructions of their formative years were "Do what people expect of you," or the ever-popular "Just do what we tell you." Messages such as these reinforced our own tendencies to create armor and roles for ourselves that primarily reflected societal expectations. Perhaps we exerted more effort in trying to fulfill these expectations than we did in cultivating authentic presence—our genuine, original, unfabricated, and uncontrived beingness in the world.

As we go through life, many of us get so caught up with the roles we play that we lose all sight of or sense of connection with our own authentic nature. We forget who we are. We become who we ain't. In short, the stories we make up about ourselves and others separate us from the truth of who we are; the roles we play create barriers that keep us from genuine spiritual connectedness—either with ourselves or with others.

This is particularly true when we begin to believe our own stories, our own hype about the roles we play, creating false fronts that become hardened and impenetrable; for obvious reasons this level of inauthenticity will almost inevitably cause havoc in our personal lives. Our children and mates, for example, don't always want to relate to the "great salesman," "the big boss," or the accomplished "deal maker." They want to connect with us—the real people behind the masks and costumes. They want us, not our performances. Sometimes we get into playing exhausting domestic roles at home as well. Instead of being ourselves, we begin to act like the moms/dads/husbands/wives we've seen on TV sitcoms; instead of being genuine, we become weary characters from central casting.

If the spiritual quest is the quest for truth, *and it is,* the best place to begin this search is with ourselves. What is our own truth? Who are we? How can we become more authentic and true?

GROUNDED AND REAL

As I was writing this chapter, the airwaves were thick with the sad news of the death of John F. Kennedy, Jr. People around New York City were being interviewed, talking about a man who they had come to know as a neighbor. My friends who live in Manhattan tell me that they often ran into him—at the neighborhood dog run, at local restaurants and coffee shops. Everyone seems to be particularly impressed with one quality: his effort to be a regular guy who lived a normal life, filled with normal, everyday activities. I read an interview with a messenger who had delivered a package to JFK, Jr. The messenger said that his hand was shaking, and Kennedy asked him why. The messenger told him that he felt that Kennedy was a historical figure. Kennedy replied, "I'm just a person like you." This touched my heart.

We all love people who are able to stay grounded and real, no matter what their role in life is. This is one of the reasons why so many people love the Dalai Lama. No matter how many international peace prizes and awards he wins, no matter how many world leaders he meets, no matter how many people bow in his presence, he always bows back—in the same way to everyone. He knows that we are all equal in the light of eternity. Fully present for each person he meets, in each moment, the

Dalai Lama is an inspiring example of someone with an awakened heart.

The Dalai Lama has cultivated and maintains a sense of authentic presence, and his spiritual energy is awe-inspiring. And yet as he often reminds us, he thinks of himself as a simple monk. As much as possible, he tries to follow that path and live the life of a Buddhist monk. Of course, he's a modern man. He's a diplomat; he loves science. He's very interested in the world around him. He's a human rights activist, who extends his mission to several dozen different nations every year. But he still gets up at 4:00 A.M. every morning, and meditates for two hours before he switches on the BBC World News at 6:00 A.M. He eats breakfast, sees his advisors, and receives visitors from near and far.

One of the Dalai Lama's special qualities is his determination to try to see everyone who wants to meet him. If you went to Dharamsala, in the foothills of Northern India, where he lives, if you were patient, you'd almost certainly get to see him one on one if you tried. He is happy to see everybody. He is especially focused on meeting every single Tibetan who escapes from Tibet.

The Dalai Lama knows who he is. He's just a man. He doesn't think of himself as an exalted spiritual leader. He thinks he's a human being, a guy who has things he wants to do and who does them to the best of his ability; he also has some things that he can't do because he has a big public service job right now. But as he always says, he might prefer to study and meditate, and he will retire to do so when his people can safely live again in their own country of Tibet.

Of course, the Dalai Lama doesn't say, "I'm just a simple guy." He says, "I'm a simple monk." That's very modest, as the Buddha intended his monks to be. And the Dalai Lama is an exemplary monk. He doesn't think he's a saint, a Nobel Prize laureate, or somebody we should look up to. He just thinks of himself as a monk. He's trained his whole life to be better and better at it. I always think of the Dalai Lama as fulfilling the Jewish ideal of a perfect "mensch." It's very mensch-like to know who you are, where you fit in, and that you are like everybody else. The Dalai Lama sounds humble and modest because he is genuinely humble and modest. He's also brilliant, charming, interesting, and extraordinarily present, but when he goes back to his hotel room, he takes off his Hush Puppies and reads or meditates. When he watches TV in his hotel rooms, he channel surfs. Like the Buddha of old, he is an inspiration to all of us because he is able to be such an enlightened human being right here in the world—without being totally overcome by it.

IMAGE ISSUES—A SIGN OF THE TIMES

I spent most of the 1980s in a cloistered Tibetan monastery. But once when I was back in the United States for a short visit, I saw a videotape of "Saturday Night Live." My fellow Long Islander, actor Billy Crystal, had created a well-attired character with pomaded hair and a deep tan, who joked that he'd rather "look good than feel good." Everyone laughed. Within the last two decades in this country, "looking good" has been elevated to a virtue. And "looking good" has come to mean certain things: looking successful, looking well dressed, looking well exercised, looking organized, looking "together." Since we live in a world that puts most of its emphasis on style, fashion, and performance, it's small wonder that we spend so much time worrying about image issues. Day in and day out we are bombarded by a host of messages reminding us to wear clothing with the right labels, eat food with the right labels, drive cars with the right make, enjoy the right activities, and have the right kind of kids at the right schools. It's kind of hard to focus on cultivating authentic presence when you are debating the merits of a Toyota over a Grand Cherokee, Ralph Lauren over Calvin Klein, Pepsi over Coke, or the benefits of cosmetic surgery over an expensive vacation.

Just last night I was visiting a friend's house, and I saw a bit of a television sitcom in which one of the main characters, a successful young woman—who has to go to an office party—invites her more economically challenged boyfriend to attend with her, but then, realizing that he doesn't own an appropriate suit for such an event, tries to buy him an expensive outfit similar to the ones her colleagues will be wearing. She wants him to look like everybody else who will be there; otherwise, she worries, he will not fit in—meaning that *she* won't fit in, or look good. It goes without saying that the relationship "crashed" over this issue.

These kinds of problems aren't limited to TV land. I recently counseled a woman who said that she had met "the most wonderful man in the world." She described him as being good, kind, adoring, and smart, but he was, she said, a little too short and she didn't like the way he dressed or the jewelry he wore. I felt far worse for her than for him.

We're all occasionally guilty of choosing our romantic partners and friends based upon the image they project to the world. We make judgments, good and bad, based on what we see on the outside. If someone is driving a Mercedes, we assume she is rich. If someone is carrying a stack of books, we assume he is an intellectual. If someone is walking a dog, we assume she is an animal lover. Yet there is so much more to all of us than what we superficially appear to be.

As a Westerner and a Tibetan lama, I find that people are often confused, and sometimes even disappointed, that I am not wearing maroon and gold robes or talking and behaving in ways that they expect—whatever those might be. For years, I was a monk who wore saffron robes and had a shaved head. When I left the monastery, it was my Tibetan teachers in fact who encouraged me to be more authentic to my background in terms of dress. "If you're teaching in America," they said, "teach like you're an American." That advice was first given to me in France by an incarnate lama who said, "Surya, you could afford to be more authentic." I think we could all take a page from that lesson book. It took me a while to realize that the authenticity and essence of the Buddha's teachings had nothing to do with traditional Asian dress. I am grateful to my friend the lama who said that to me.

When people hear that I am a Buddhist lama, they also seem to expect that I should be chanting and meditating around the clock. They expect me to play a particular role. A question that I'm often asked, for example, is "Are you enlightened, Surya?" When people ask me that I sense that what they are really asking is "Are you perfect?" "Are you completely blissed out, calm, and happy all the time?" "Do you know what nirvana looks like?" What they really want to know is if nirvana is possible and achievable, as well as how to get some of it for themselves. They want to know if I have some other worldly secrets for leading a spiritual life.

It might be nice to be completely blissed out all the time; then again it might become tedious and boring. I don't know because my life, like everyone else's, has its ups and downs and twists and turns. Not only do I not have any otherworldly powers or secrets for leading a spiritual life, I am certain that the components of a spiritual life are very much grounded in reality, here and now. This emphasis on truth and reality is not solely a Buddhist thought. Jesus said, "In order to enter the Kingdom of Heaven, we have to become like little children." What he meant is that we have to strip away all the accumulated layers of persona and get closer to the open, authentic, loving child that exists in all of us. The great third-century Chinese philosopher Mencius (Mengzi) said, "The great man is he who does not lose his childlike heart."

For enlightenment we don't need fancier clothes, or more degrees, or more information. We don't need bigger living spaces, more money, fancier vacations, better jobs, or more influential friends. Enlightenment is everyone's birthright. In order to realize it for ourselves we have to become more grounded, more in touch with who and what we are—what we really are, not what we pretend to be or what society and parents told us to be.

LOOSENING OUR ATTACHMENT
TO PERSONA

Buddhism is all about letting go, and yes, one of the most difficult areas for us to loosen up revolves around image or persona. At the time of the ancient Greeks and Romans, "persona" was the term applied to the large theatrical masks that actors wore on stage. The two classic masks, of course, are those of joy and sorrow that we've all seen. Actors wore their masks or persona to help audiences tell the good guys from the bad guys and the sad guys from the happy guys.

The Swiss psychiatrist Carl Jung, who helped make the word "persona" a common psychological term, said, "The persona is a compromise between individual and society as to what a man should appear to be."

According to Jung, the persona is not an accurate reflection of our individuality. Rather it is a mask that we put on in order to fulfill certain societal roles. We wear a persona, like a costume, to help us navigate life's waters. Certainly a well-defined persona can be very helpful in creating the appropriate boundaries that we sometimes need, so using a persona should not always be seen as negative. Sometimes the persona we present is actually connected to the real costumes we wear. When police officers put on their uniforms, they automatically become authority figures. The same thing is true of judges in their robes. When we see medical professionals in hospital garb, they almost by definition take on a certain aura or presence. In fact, when we were children and wore our costumes for play, didn't we assume certain roles, the moment we put them on? Don't we do that, even now, when we put on our party clothes or our exercise gear?

The persona becomes problematic and limiting when it becomes so fixed that it causes us to become frozen in place; the persona becomes problematic when it doesn't allow for growth or authentic feelings—when it insulates us and acts like a shell of armor. Years ago, I knew a very rich woman who lived on the Upper East Side of New York City, on Fifth Avenue. She had enough money to go anywhere she wanted or do anything in the world, but she was so trapped by her role that she never did anything new. Every day she woke up, left her expensive apartment, and travelled twenty blocks by cab to her office. Every night she reversed the process. All of her meals were eaten in one of four or five of the city's best restaurants. She had never been to a coffee shop; she had never been to Chinatown; she had never been to a pizza parlor or bagel joint. She had never walked through the city in which she lived, and all of her shopping was done in one of two stores—Saks or Bloomingdale's— with her personal shopper running interference and even then it was usually her personal shopper who went to the stores. She never let anyone new into her life, and all of her acquaintances were people who were almost exactly like she was in terms of career and socioeconomic status. She was never able to venture out of her role in life. Her persona had taken over.

In a less extreme fashion, this happens to many of us. We become so concerned about projecting the right image that we become afraid to be different or to do anything unusual or "out of character." We create armor so thick that nobody can get past it. We're so uneasy around people who look or act differently that we try to avoid them. One of the few times many people are somewhat able to loosen the grip of persona is when they are on vacation. For two weeks out of the year, these men and women suddenly become adventurers. Even though they normally spend every day in constrained environments in business suits, they sign up for wilderness trips or overland bike treks that allow them to loosen the constraints of the personas that they normally project. They don't worry about looking foolish if they act silly or behave in unconventional ways. They come back from their vacations feeling as though this is the only time in the year in which they are truly "alive." Doesn't this tell us something about how to feel more alive day to day, throughout the year, and what we might do to bring that about?

There is an old saying that "travel broadens the mind," and it does. It helps us get out of the mental prisons of our own making; travel helps us relax and loosen our grip on our limited versions of ourselves. When we go to a different place we are able to revisit who we think we are; we are better able to reinvent who we are. It can be exhilarating to experience, even for a moment, a sense that we could actually be anyone. In foreign cities, for example, we are less reticent about striking up conversations with strangers of all kinds—those who seem completely unlike us in appearance, age, or education and economic background. This is one of the great boons of travel.

DROPPING OUR MASKS AS WE WALK
THE SPIRITUAL PATH

Some people don't easily comprehend how a fixed persona can create a stumbling block on the spiritual path. They don't "get" how an attachment to a role, a look, or an image can stand in the way of one's inner search. What we need to understand is that the persona we create is tightly wrapped up in the stories we tell ourselves about who we are. In short, the persona is often a veritable gauge of ego clinging. When we take off our armor and discard bits and pieces of the persona, we also let go of ego grasping and clinging. Doing this helps us loosen some of the "me," "my," and "mine" thinking that we all indulge in. Many of us, after all, use this kind of thinking as a way of putting up barriers and further solidifying our masks—as in "my car," "my job," "my space." Once again, instead of seeking authentic presence, we seek image, security, and the ego's comfort zone rather than truth and freedom.

This kind of clinging isn't limited to objects. It also extends to our opinions and attitudes; we then use these opinions and attitudes to make us feel superior to others as in:

"I only eat whole grains, tofu, and a few cooked vegetables; anyone who doesn't do the same is courting physical problems."

"I have very strong views on child rearing; do what I say or you're risking your toddler's emotional well-being."

"I'm a lifelong Republican/Democrat/Liberal/Conservative/Socialist/Independent; all other points of view are wrong."

Many people, particularly from my generation, rebelled against the idea of being seen as a "suit." They were as harsh in their judgment of people who dressed in a conformist, conservative fashion as the conservatives were of the love beads and long hair that my friends sported in the late Sixties. I know people who practiced a kind of reverse snobbism, avoiding anyone who seemed different than they were. They purposely dressed down, inhabiting the margins of society; they were often proud of how little they needed to get by. For some of them, this continues to be the case. There are people who still refuse to wear suits or ties, no matter where they have been invited. They do this to make a point. Some have even worn tee shirts at the

White House. The real point, of course, is that ego is still ego, no matter what it is wearing. Being different can be but another ego trip—an attempt to flaunt an illusion of specialness. Dressing down can be just another kind of conformist dress code. Sometimes just fitting in is the simplest, most unselfish, and humble way to be.

Often these attachments to opinions and our own way of doing things are best recognized by looking at what it is that we judge in others as well as ourselves. Do we, for example, hastily judge others because of their religious or political views? Buddhism teaches that this kind of thinking—no matter what your opinion or point of view—encourages a fixated, dualistic view of the world. When we release and drop our attachment to image, whether that image is represented by appearance, possession, status, role, or attitude, we come closer to our own authentic being—our innate Buddha-nature. We can let go, relax, and simply be ourselves. It is beautiful!

SELF-ACCEPTANCE HELPS US DROP
OUR MASKS AND BECOME MORE REAL

In many way, the personas we construct are simply knee-jerk reactions to our own fears of being judged. Whether the persona we wear is shy and introverted, or exuberant and outgoing, a mask is still a mask. It's a shell, not a meaningful, beating heart. Here's a question we always have to ask: How can we love the world when we haven't learned how to love ourselves? How can we feel loved and accepted if we don't learn to love and accept ourselves?

As we become more and more certain of who we are, we become more grounded and real. We lose our concerns about what others think and are better able to reach out with love and caring. The spiritual path, as both Chogyam Trungpa and Carlos Castaneda's Yaqui Don Juan pointed out, is a warrior's path. It takes bravery to be the shining souls we are meant to be; it takes courage, and even chutzpah, to use our hearts to see beyond the superficial. And yet the heart is like an organ of perception; it could be used to guide and lead us, much like Seeing Eye dogs guide the visually challenged.

There is a Tibetan teaching tale I've always liked. It's about a learned and wise middle-aged lama who receives a visionary visit from a powerful "dakini," which is the term Tibetans use to describe sometimes wrathful female goddess-like figures who symbolize truth revealed. In this case, the dakini is Ekajati herself, a formidable, one-eyed, single-breasted protectress of the truth. She comes to issue a prophecy and tells the lama that he should take a consort from a neighboring valley. She says that if he does this, he will be able to discover and unearth hidden teachings that will be of inestimable value to subsequent generations of seekers.

The lama listens to what he is told, and immediately sends three of his monk-disciples to seek the consort that Ekajati has described. While they are gone, the lama keeps vigil in his shrine room, praying and meditating.

After a week, the monks return. But they are alone. "Where is the prophesied consort I am waiting for?" the lama asks.

"We found no one suitable for you," the monks tell him. "The only woman we saw was a ragged woodcutter, blind in one eye, wearing tattered clothes, carrying a rusty old sickle, with some gnarled branches of firewood on her bent back. She was a truly terrifying woman. Certainly not the type who would seem to be a suitable consort for someone of your sacred stature."

"That must be her," the lama says, jumping up in delight. "That harpy is none other than the great Dharma protectress

Ekajati in human disguise. Please immediately go find her and bring her here!"

The surprised and chagrined disciples are compelled to rush right back out and hunt high and low until they eventually find the woman, who appears to be as wild and crooked as the firewood she carries on her back. When the head lama sees her, he greets her with open arms and bows with an open heart that is filled with respect and delight; unlike his students, he recognized the authentic nature of the woman before him and knows a true dakini when he sees one.

The master delights in finding this woman to be his true soul mate and consort; the awesome lady in turn regally rules his household and inspires everyone who dares to enter her intense presence. As promised, the lama finds numerous spiritual treasures, revelations, and teachings which he shares with Dharma seekers. This lineage of rediscovered ancient teaching treasures remains with us today.

The point of this story, of course, is that the lama was able to see his own spiritual muse and consort for who she is only because he was supremely confident in his own judgment and sense of his own mission and purpose in life. He didn't care what others thought. In his search for authentic truth, he had no time for the superficial. He was immune to the deception of appearances.

When we are able to let go and abandon the extraneous, we are left with bare essence—the authentic Buddha-nature within. Your inner Buddha is sublimely confident and sure; he/she is at home with everyone, everywhere. When we are in touch with our inner Buddhas, we no longer need to eat in restaurants where we can see and be seen by the "people who count," whoever those people might be. We don't need to avoid people who don't share our worldview. We don't worry about being liked or fitting in; we can follow our own path, our own dancing star. When we are in touch with our inner Buddhas, we are fearlessly able to accept others because we accept ourselves, for who and what we are. We have arrived home, at home and at one with ourselves. This is the journey's goal.

YOU CAN'T IMITATE
AUTHENTIC PRESENCE

Sometimes we meet those who have a genuine sense of authentic presence. Often these individuals are powerful spiritual leaders or charismatic teachers with awe-inspiring energy. What sometimes happens to the students of such teachers is that they attempt to mimic the master's behavior. There is a Japanese Zen story about a master of old who had a unique way of teaching. This master is very well known because he answers all questions that are put to him by simply holding up one inscrutable forefinger. A young monk in the zendo (meditation hall) is very impressed by this, so impressed that he decides to imitate the master. The next time someone asks the acolyte a question, he holds up one finger. He does this again and again. It works for the master, why shouldn't it work for him?

The venerable Zen master hears of this, and after a while he calls the boy to him. "Tell me," the master asks, "who is the true Buddha?" The young monk holds up his one imitating finger. In one swift move, the master reaches out and cuts off the monk's finger with a sword. The young monk is stunned; he screams—a high, primal scream that is authentically his own. As the monk's sounds pierce the quiet of the zendo, the master holds up his one finger, and at that moment, the young monk is instantly enlightened. The moral of this strange little story, of course, is that you can't get real through imitation. By taking away the imitation, the false pointer-finger, the boy returned to his real Buddha.

Just as we all have Buddha-nature, we all have unique authentic presence. Everything about each and every one of us is different. From our fingerprints to our voice prints, each of us is authentic in his or her own way. This authenticity is something to be nurtured, cherished, and celebrated. It is probably our greatest gift, a treasure we can rediscover within ourselves, in the midst of the gritty details of our very own life.

Some people, of course, are so authentic and real that the very air around them seems to reverberate with their presence. There is a story that's told in Asia about a celebrated martial arts master of ancient China. The master was absolutely indomitable. When he was in combat he moved like a whirlwind; no one could touch him, and he seemed impervious to fear, pain, illness, or any form of attack. When he was fighting, this master would bellow *"Yaaaarghhh!!!!!!!!!!!!!!!!!!!"*—loud enough to shake the firmament.

This forceful master taught his students to face life and death with equanimity, no matter what—whether surrounded by hundreds of brigands or by a vision of hundreds of Buddhas. One night, the master was walking up in the mountains by himself, and he was attacked by a dozen or more sword-carrying robbers. He fought intensely, and managed to ward most of them off, but he was one man, and they outnumbered him twelve to one. Finally just before dawn, one of them ran a sword through his stomach, and the master shouted *"Yaaaarghh!!!!!!!!!!!!!!!"* All who heard it, far and wide, knew it was his death cry. It was so loud that the entire slumbering countryside was awakened and enlightened by the shout. Such was this master's connection to reality.

CHOOSING TO BE AUTHENTIC—
A SPIRITUAL PRACTICE

When I was growing up, many of the families in my neighborhood covered their living room furniture in plastic to protect it. I hated sitting on those slippery plastic covers. They seemed false, as well as uncomfortable. Now I know a lot of people who work in large metal and glass buildings with windows that never open. More than a few of them complain that many things in their work environment are false, including the air, which they say is so totally unnatural and stale that it sometimes makes people sick. These days it seems as though we are all somehow affected by places and situations that lack authenticity. It's a real spiritual challenge not to take on the plastic trappings of our surroundings.

There are so many times in life when we feel as though we have to pretend to be something we're not; there are so many times when we know that the people around us are pretending too. It's wearisome, isn't it? We pretend everything is fine, even when it isn't; we pretend to be brave and strong when we are frightened and vulnerable; we pretend to be happy when we're sad; we pretend to know what we're doing when we are totally confused; we pretend to know what we're talking about when we're merely voicing words. We do it so often that pretense and inauthenticity can become habits, till we are as if lost amidst all the spin and smoke and mirrors, and have lost touch with our essential selves and the fundamental reality of our own lives.

How many hours each day do we spend feeling disconnected, alienated, or as though we are playing a role? Some people complain that they feel as though they are always playing the role of sycophant—"sucking up" to people they don't want to be with. Others say their lives seem consumed with titles, achievements, and "resumes"—theirs as well as everybody else's. Many feel oppressed by the burden of constantly trying to be what others want them to be. Still others complain that some days they feel uncomfortable in their own skin. Where does this all leave us? Doesn't it ultimately make us feel as though we are eating too much junk food?

Who do we think we are fooling in the long run? Who's watching? In the crucial moments of life and death—moments of crisis, joy, and tragedy—there is no room to pretend. We are forced to be real. Maybe that's why these are some of our most memorable moments. Why does it take tragedy or crisis to force us to be on the spot, to be authentically present, to be just who we are. James Joyce wrote about one of his characters, "Mr. Bloom lived a short distance from his body." Don't we all? But that's not a terminal condition. We can reconnect and be ourselves, the genuine article, the real McCoy.

Reconnecting to Your Own Truth

One of the ways we can begin to cultivate a more authentic presence is by giving ourselves some time in which we make a commitment to be as true, honest, and real as we can possibly be. Set aside some time—it could be an hour a day, one day a week, or even one day a month. During this time, try to keep everything you do, say, and think as centered, real, and genuinely grounded in your actual moment-to-moment daily experience as possible. Be the right person in the right place at the right time by being at one with any given moment, just as it presents itself. Here are some suggestions on how to do this:

1. BE NATURAL.

Where do you feel most comfortable and natural? Think about the places and activities that make you feel most grounded. Think about the people who make you feel as though you can be yourself. Do you feel most comfortable when you're home wearing flannel pajamas and eating comfort food? Comfort and naturalness encourage healing. Naturalness is the opposite of anxiety and stress, so let the real you emerge. Don't put on airs or try to impress anyone. Hang loose and do what comes naturally. Give rein to your innate creativity; let your wholesome natural impulses guide you. Feel free and unencumbered enough—unselfconscious enough—to just be you. I think you'll love it.

2. BE SIMPLE.

As you interrelate with the world, try to keep your language and your dealings with others as simple and straightforward as possible. Keep your dealings with yourself as simple as possible as well. Don't get involved in long convoluted conversations or interior monologues. Have a simple meal; take a simple walk; perform a simple chore without hurrying; sit on a chair and look at the trees and sky. When you speak, take care to be absolutely truthful. Try not to add anything unnecessary or extraneous to your life. Instead, in the immortal words of Thoreau, "simplify, simplify, simplify."

3. LOOSEN YOUR TENDENCY TO CONTROL.

As you do inner work and become more authentic, try to let go of some of your anxieties and tendency to control situations and others. Resist the impulse to interfere unnecessarily with outcomes. Don't struggle unduly to make things happen the way you want them to. Just rest and enjoy the moment. Let others be. Let yourself be as well. Let it be.

4. BE AUTHENTIC.

Put all your stories about yourself and others aside. Instead try to become like a child and experience everything as though it were brand-new. Ask yourself, "What do I really feel?" "What do I really want?" "What is this?" Don't be unduly influenced by external values and conditions. Be honest and straightforward with yourself and others. Live moment to moment, as an intentional exercise in consciousness raising and centeredness.

5. STAY OPEN TO THE WORLD AROUND YOU.

Be inclusive and accepting. Try not to be judgmental and critical. Lose some of your armor; invite and allow others to share your experience. Be open to the sights, smells, and sounds in your immediate environment. Enjoy and appreciate reality as it unfolds. Edit and control less; appreciate more; and savor the qualities of whatever comes your way.

6. STAY AWARE.

Pay attention and be mindful of your experience moment by moment. Just relax and let yourself be. See with your inner eye; hear with your inner ear. Don't let superficial judgments get in the way of reality. Attend to the present. This is the holy now; don't overlook it.

7. STAY WISE.

Practice nonattachment and letting go of the extraneous. Let go of old judgments and attitudes. Let go of old hurts and angers. Let go of old prejudices, biases, and preconceptions. Cultivate a fresh, penetrating, vividly wakeful and acute sense of discernment and discrimination. See if you can really think for yourself and directly apprehend things just as they are.

8. BE SPONTANEOUS AND LET YOUR ENERGY FLOW NATURALLY.

Spontaneity is natural and authentic. Don't be inhibited about expressing positive energy. Sing in the shower or chant on the street if that's what you feel like doing. Don't be afraid to dance, play, or just be silly. Let your energy expand and sweep you up. Spread your arms and whirl like a dervish. Fling your hands up to the sky and shout, *"AAAAAAAhhh! Yes!"* (Why not?)

CHAPTER FIVE

Letting Go, Getting Real

What a relief it was for me to go to my first meditation retreat and hear people speak the truth so clearly—the First Noble Truth that life is difficult and painful, just by its very nature, not because we're doing it wrong. I was so relieved to meet people who were willing to say life is difficult, often painful, and who still looked fine about admitting it. Most important, they looked *happy*. This was tremendously reassuring to me. I thought to myself, "Here are people who are just like me, who have lives just like mine, who know the truth and are willing to name it and are all right with it."

—Sylvia Boorstein

The Buddha taught that this is an imperfect world; nothing is totally the way we want it to be. That's reality. By the time we become teenagers most of us have discovered that nowhere is this reality more blatant than in our interactions with others. Let's admit it: Relationships, by their very nature, are challenging.

People don't always behave the way we want them to; they don't say what we want them to say; they don't do what we want them to do; they don't treat us the way we want to be treated. But what can we do about this painful fact? What are our options and choices? After all, few of us want to retreat from the world. We know that human connection is essential to our happiness and crucial for our personal growth and well-being.

Perhaps one of the reasons spiritual masters have an easier time dealing with others is that they realize that everything, even our closest friendships, will be at least a little bit flawed, a little bit imperfect. This is the nature of life. That certainly doesn't mean that we should give up on the possibility of true friendship or intimacy. It does mean that we can find more skillful, grounded, balanced, and mindful ways of relating to each other and the world. Spiritual intelligence consistently reminds us to view personal relationships with the wisdom that allows us to appreciate their ups and downs as being part of our spiritual path and inner growth.

Our spiritual intentions and aspirations for enlightenment are abundantly clear: We are striving to become more caring and patient, more loving and generous, more wholesome, open, and wise. We can't easily cultivate these qualities in a vacuum; this practice requires interactions with others. Our relationships, whether they be fleeting or long term, casual or intense, provide personal laboratories in which we can put our spiritual intentions into practice. In fact, finding ways to skillfully and compassionately interact with others is a large part of what the spiritual path is all about.

Incorporating our spiritual aspirations into our daily interactions with others is no easy challenge. A friend of mine, Diane, recently had her car stolen. She reacted with impressive equanimity, telling herself that in the greater scheme of things losing a car is not such a big deal. Friends helped by driving Diane places, she rediscovered the joys of walking to the store, and she no longer faced the struggle of alternate side of the street parking. She stayed patient as she spent hours on the phone; she stayed calm as she spent days collecting paperwork and filling out forms for the police and the insurance company. She even cultivated thoughts of loving-kindness toward the thief! But then it turned out that there was a glitch in her automobile title; before the insurance company could make payment on her loss she needed to go to the Department of Motor Vehicles, known affectionately as the DMV, and get duplicates of some missing paperwork.

Diane dutifully arrived at the DMV at 10:00 A.M. The line snaked out to the door. Two and a half hours later she had been back and forth, going from one line to another, more than a half dozen times. She had filled out many confusing forms, some of them in error, and she was still trying to find someone who could resolve her problem. But none of the DMV employees she spoke to seemed able to help. At first Diane was quiet, patient, and polite, but finally she lost it. Her equanimity visa expired. She went "postal" at the DMV; she didn't actually kick a wastebasket, but she thought of it. Diane was not alone in her exasperation. She was surrounded by dozens of other grim-faced motorists. People were moaning and groaning; people were arguing and complaining. *Surely,* she thought, *this would test the patience of even the most committed saint or stoic Zen practitioner.* Diane wanted to stay calm and balanced, but in the stress of the moment she found herself "separating" from her intentions.

Even the most experienced meditation practitioners sometimes forget that meditation training is intended as a practice that will help us deal with others, as well as life's ups and downs, more skillfully. We see the truth of this when we observe the great meditation masters; they can remain unperturbable—as well as aware—no matter what is going on around them. It's as though they carry their own atmosphere with them wherever they go, maintaining equanimity independent of all circumstances. This is one of the many benefits of meditation. It helps us relate to life and people in a more balanced way.

When I was growing up, everyone told me how impatient and overactive I was. I loved sports, and my whole life seemed to be about quick reaction time; I always had to set my own pace, which was fast, and do things my own way. I had little tolerance for what I perceived to be a waste of time. Somehow, thirty years later, it's come about that people tell me how calm and patient I am. I have a friend who says that she both loves and hates driving when I am in her passenger seat. She loves it because I'm so calm; she hates it because I'm so damned calm. She calls me preternaturally calm, and says that it sometimes makes her even more anxious and reactive. So occasionally if we are together in her car, I act a little jumpy and reactive. It's our little joke. It usually takes her a few minutes to figure out what I'm doing, and then she gets mad at me. Then I say, "Caught you," and we both have a good laugh, which relaxes her.

USING MEDITATIVE TECHNIQUES
AS RELATIONSHIP TOOLS

Leave the body at rest, like an unmovable mountain.
Leave the speech at rest, like an unstrung guitar.
Leave the mind at rest, like a shepherd after dusk who has brought his flock home and sits content by the warm fire.
—Tibetan Meditation instruction

TRADITIONAL MEDITATION INSTRUCTION

Stop what you are doing; stop what you are thinking.
  Get comfortable. Relax.
  Find your balance. If you are sitting cross-legged on a floor, settle

your legs so they feel as though they are where they belong. If you are using a cushion, adjust it the way you like it. If you are sitting on a chair, place your feet evenly on the floor. If you are standing, let your body settle.

Keep your spine straight and your body relaxed. Let your shoulders drop.

Settle into the present moment.

Let your energy settle naturally; let your breath settle naturally; let your thoughts settle naturally.

Collect yourself.

Come home to the present moment.

Arrive where you are meant to be.

Sit in the present moment.

Breathe in, breathe out.

As you inhale, focus on the in breath. Count one.

As you exhale, focus on the out breath. Count two.

One on the inhalation, two on the exhalation.

Ride the breath.

Surf the breath.

Rest your mind on the simple, regular, calming wave of breathing.

Become aware of what you are feeling. Notice the physical sensations that your body is experiencing. Notice the sensation in your shoulders, notice the thoughts that bubble up to the surface of your mind. Notice them and simply let them go. No need to work them out or get caught up in them. Continue breathing. Focus on the in breath. Focus on the out breath. And let go.

Settle in the present moment. Stay aware of actual perceived moment-to-moment happenings: a slight pain in your shoulder, the low roar of an airplane climbing in the sky, the sound of the wind rustling through the trees, the muted voices from a neighbor's TV coming through the wall, the hissing of a radiator. Don't suppress your perceptions, feelings, or awareness; simply notice what is happening and then let it dissolve as the new moment begins. Stay awake; remain alert; pay attention.

Breathe in. . . . Breathe out. Stay focused. Let go of each breath, don't hang on. Let go of each thought; don't hang on. Note your thoughts; notice them, and let them go. If your shoulder hurts, name it "discomfort," and let it go. If the airplane noise breaks your concentration, name it "hearing, hearing," and let it go. If the temperature in the room gets chilly, name it "cold," and let it go. Let go of your worries; don't hang on. Let go of any attempts to control your mind; don't hang on. With each exhalation, let go a little more.

This is meditation.

As meditators, we train ourselves in meditative awareness. This is called mindfulness. Let's say, for example, that while I am meditating, I feel an itch in my big toe. I am aware of the feeling in the present moment, but I let go of any tendency to react at that moment. It's enough to be aware of the itchy toe. I don't have to do anything about it. I can just let it go. . . . Be aware of it, and let it be. This is the meaning of letting go.

Lama Anagarika Govinda, author of *Foundations of Tibetan Mysticism,* was a German-born Westerner who travelled to Asia to study with Buddhist masters back in the 1920s. He defined meditation as follows: "Meditation is the way to re-connect the individual with the whole, to make us aware of our continuing connection and communion, which has never really been broken off."

Meditation trains us to return to simplicity by being aware of the essentials and letting go of the extraneous. This is an invaluable skill for our complex, busy lives, where each of us has a lot we could learn to let go of. I'm not talking only about our worldly possessions; I'm talking about attitudes, behavioral quirks, habits, resentments about the past, as well as fanciful dreams about the future. Meditation helps us let go of our knee-jerk reactions and responses to people as well as situations; it trains us to let go of our attachment to discursive thinking and ego identification, which makes us perceive everything as being connected to "me" or "mine." We can apply these lessons to everything we do.

Let's say your weary and cranky spouse greets you at the door tonight complaining that you neglected to do your share of the household chores. Your immediate reaction may be defensive; you may feel angry and misunderstood. Here's where meditation techniques pay off. The principles of meditative awareness, properly applied, give you the tools to notice and be aware of "anger" without acting on it. You can have the feeling, but that feeling doesn't mean that you are compelled to lash out. You can choose to just notice the anger without judging whether it is good or bad. It simply is. This is what is known as "choiceless awareness." It means you are able to be aware of what is happening without necessarily making judgments or having preferences. You don't have to react. This gives you the time to consider the bigger picture. It gives you the time to remember your highest intentions and purpose; it gives you the space you need to be able to intentionally decide and choose how to act. In these few seconds, you might have a completely different and more compassionate thought, such as "My poor spouse must be really tired." If you respond to your spouse with empathy, caring, and compassionate concern instead of annoyance, you will be creating better, more positive karma—and a better relationship.

In Buddhist practice we learn first to meditate silently—frequently, in a room alone; or with others who are sharing the same activity. In silent meditation, it's relatively easy to recognize and be aware of the thoughts, emotions, and conditioning that intrude and interfere with our concentration. Then when we have mastered that, we take the lessons of meditation out into the world where all of our buttons, our samskaras, are likely to be pushed regularly.

These days, we are often told that faster is better, but when it comes to emotional reaction time, slower is often the wiser way to go. Meditation helps us extend our reaction time. In this way, we are given another second or two more before we respond. For example, this morning Frank walked into his office to discover that his boss, Freya, was furious at him. It seems that the computer was acting up yet again, and Freya's frustrations made her irrationally blame Frank. A few years ago Frank might have been very upset by the unfairness of Freya's anger; all of his buttons would have been pushed, and he would have been thrown into a tailspin of strong feelings that would have made him react immediately. Now, after several years of meditating, he doesn't feel compelled to respond. Instead he has control over his responses. He can take his time and make a conscious decision about what he wants to say and how, when, and where he wants to say it. Frank is aware enough to assess the situation; he knows he doesn't *have* to react. Maybe he should let Freya rant; maybe he should quit; maybe he should just sigh, breathe, and relax. Frank has choices, and he has mastery over his reactions. He is thus able to be the master of himself.

Having said that, I think it's important that we don't put too much pressure on ourselves. Reaching this level of awareness is a process. We shouldn't be too impatient or idealistic about how "perfectly" restrained and even-minded we should be. When we get embroiled in situations in which we are heavily vested, it's difficult not to react impulsively. Therefore I think it's a good idea to approach ourselves, as well as others, with compassion, patience, sensitivity, and gentleness.

I am always trying to adopt a more meditative, conscious approach to interpersonal dealings. I have learned that I have to be careful not to think of it as a quick fix prescription. We can't approach relationships with absolute dictums such as, "I won't say anything; I'll just bite my lip." This kind of absolute doesn't work very well. It's a little like unrealistic New Year's

relate to others in ways that allow us to be more true to who we really want to be; it helps us be more authentic, which, in turn, helps us ground our relationships in present reality and current time. It is time we caught up with ourselves in this way.

Bringing this level of awareness into our dealings with others is not about pretending or manipulating or trying to be dishonest with our feelings and emotions. We are simply trying to become more mindful, compassionate, and virtuous—more Buddha-like in everything we do.

The basic essential premise of Buddhism is this: Each of us, at core, is a Buddha. We are all Buddhas. Innately, each of us has the compassion and love of a Buddha; each of us has the virtue and morality of a Buddha; each of us has the patience, acceptance, and tolerance of a Buddha; each of us has the spiritual energy and endurance of a Buddha; each of us has the concentration and meditative powers of a Buddha; each of us has within us the wisdom of a potential Buddha. It is latent within us. We only have to unfold our spiritual treasure from within ourselves.

Meditation is a technique that we use to help us return to our essential, original nature—our Buddha-nature. We are training ourselves in how to respond to everything in life from that basic core of essential goodness. We are training ourselves to relinquish the illusions, fantasies, and distractions that confuse our lives; we are learning to "let go" of the conditioned responses and habits that keep us stuck. The practice of meditation is a tool that helps us cast off the barnacles of conditioning and find the beautiful, wise, and loving Buddha buried under all the sludge. *This is the real you.*

If you want to know how to react and what to do in each situation in life, ask yourself how Buddha would react—what would Buddha do? If you want to know what to do in life, ask yourself what Wisdom and Love would do in such a situation. When we start with this base, with this intention, we begin to create a blueprint, a template for how to relate to others. Life is difficult, it's true. It's up to us to try to make it easier and happier—for others and for ourselves as well so that all may have what they need and aspire to. These are the intentions of a Buddha.

LETTING GO OF EXPECTATIONS OF "PERFECTION"

Last year I took my wonderful dog, Chandi, in for grooming just before Christmas. When the grooming was finished, she looked as fluffy as a white angora rabbit. The groomer had even tied a sweet little red and green bow on her collar. After we returned home from the groomer, I made the mistake of letting her go out unattended in the fields around my house. Within minutes she had discovered the smelliest, dirtiest clump of "something" she could find, and she rolled around—and around—in it. By the time she was finished even her red bow was wet and filthy. There went my image of my perfect, beautiful dog.

It's never easy to face the fact that nothing is perfect. Don't we rail against our significant others when they reveal flaws we would rather not see? The Buddha reminded us time and again that everything is flawed. That's reality. Reality means taking off the tinted glasses we are wearing—whether those glasses are tinted with a rosy or dark hue. Meditation helps us train ourselves in clear seeing, in looking at the world without distortion, directly and objectively. As spiritual seekers, we are committed to cultivating clear seeing, clear hearing, and clear thinking—in short, clear perception. This leads to wisdom and truth.

This is an interesting approach to apply to our interactions with others since nowhere are we more likely to be guided by fantasies and unrealistic expectations than in the arena of interpersonal relationships. Don't we all cling to our fantasies about how things and others should be? We get angry at our parents because they are not always perfect; we get angry at our children because they are not always perfect; we get angry at our mates because they are not always perfect. Who doesn't cling to the "soul mate" fantasy, in which our significant other is the one person who is always able to relate to us with perfect understanding and acceptance—a charming prince or princess who can be like a savior to us.

Seekers often have a tendency to overidealize and can therefore be particularly prone to unrealistic expectations. We can, for example, be so deeply attached to our fantasies and our Prince and Princess Charming dreams that we undermine all our relationships with demands based on expectations that cannot possibly be fulfilled. We are often so filled with fantasies about what should be that we fail to acknowledge or appreciate what is. Approaching life with expectations is an invitation to frustration. However, with no expectations, we experience no disappointment.

Marge and Patti are two women married to men with similar personality quirks. Marge's husband Dan doesn't like parties and refuses to accompany her to most social events; Patti's husband John feels the same way Dan does. That's where the similarities end. Marge believes that husbands and wives should only socialize together and says she feels strange going out without her husband; on those nights when they are invited somewhere she stays home with Dan and complains about it. Patti, on the other hand, kisses John good-bye, goes out, has a nice time with her friends, and returns home a few hours later to have a bedtime snack and chat with her husband. Marge and Patti are dealing with similar issues in such different ways that it changes the entire dynamic of their relationships. Faced with the same situation, one has made a workable, satisfying choice while one has chosen not to make it work.

Buddhist teachings consistently remind us that everything is relative. Not long ago I was at a New Year's Eve gathering in the Boston area. At midnight, it was 45 degrees outdoors, and we were all commenting on how warm it was. If it had been 45 degrees on a night in July, we would all be complaining about the cold. This exemplifies how our concepts and expectations alter our experience of everything, even the temperature.

This simply points out another way in which we become attached to our views, opinions, and ideas about everything, including "how life should be." The Vietnamese teacher Thich Nhat Hanh wrote, "Attachment to views is the greatest impediment to the spiritual path."

Some of the most common misinterpretations people make about Buddhism involve the ideal of nonattachment; they often assume that being Buddhist means giving up those they love. In *The Mind and the Way,* the Theravadin Buddhist teacher Ajahn Sumedho writes:

"If you're coming from a high-minded position in which you think you shouldn't be attached to anything, then you come up with ideas like, 'Well I can't be Buddhist because I love my wife. . . .' Those kinds of thoughts come from the view that you shouldn't be attached. The recognition of attachment doesn't mean that you get rid of your wife. It means that you free yourself from wrong views about yourself and your wife. Then you find that there's love there, but it's not attached. It's not distorting, clinging, and grasping. The empty mind is quite capable of caring about others and loving in the pure sense of love. But any attachment will always distort that. If you love someone and then start grasping, things get complicated; then what you love causes you pain. For example, you love your children, but if you become attached to them . . . you have all kinds of ideas about what they should be and what you want them to be . . . as we let go of attachment, we find that our natural way of relating is to love. We find that we are able to allow our children to be as they are, rather than having fixed ideas of what we want them to be."

The Tibetan Book of the Dead reminds us that we create our own phantasmagoria; the specters that loom large on our horizon are put there mainly by our own minds. Our attitudes, opinions, and expectations are overlaid upon reality; they shape our world and get in our way. Nothing is perfect, but then again nothing is all bad either. There is an ancient Zen poem known as "Trust in the Heart Sutra"; it was written in China by the Third Zen Patriarch. One of my favorite lines from it is:

> *"Do not seek for truth,*
> *Merely cease to cherish your own ideas and opinions."*

A Buddhist sutra says, "Things are not what they seem to be, nor are they otherwise." This reminds us not to be so invested in what we think and expect. Better to remain open to life and what it brings. Be open to the moment. When we have no expectations, there are no disappointments. If we make an appointment and the person we hope to meet doesn't show up, we wouldn't be disappointed if we didn't have a certain expectation. The Buddhist lesson is that everything that is put together eventually falls apart. That doesn't mean that reality is shattered. Reality is what it is, forever free and untouched by our projections and interpretations, as well as our hopes and anxieties about it. In short, there is a certain amount of joy to be found even in a muddy dog. It's still the same lovable dog, after all, no matter how dirty she gets! I must remember that.

KEEPING OUR CONNECTIONS
AUTHENTIC AND HONEST

The best relationships we have are genuine and real. In real relationships we don't have to pretend; we aren't afraid of knowing our partners, nor are we afraid to be known. Real relationships are strengthened by authenticity and truth telling. We know this intellectually, but nonetheless in actual day-to-day relating, it's all too easy to slip back into habitual patterns that are primarily defensive and self-serving.

A large part of any Buddhist contemplative practice revolves around mindfulness. We try to stay in the present moment, in the now, and we observe ourselves mindfully. Watching ourselves, we become aware of unnecessary and self-defeating attitudes; watching ourselves we learn to let go of inauthentic behavior that keeps us stuck in the ruts of our lives. Here's a short list of some of the most common behaviors that we all need to recognize:

✺ CONTROLLING BEHAVIOR
When we're trying to control others, what we are typically doing is "watching" somebody else instead of being mindful of our own actions. Whenever we find ourselves expending energy trying to change or control somebody else, the antidote is breathing in and out mindfully and letting go of the impulse.

✺ HIDDEN AGENDAS
We've all met people who seem to approach the world almost as though they have battle plans—deeply secret agendas which only they know. To some small degree we probably all indulge in this kind of behavior. How much better and less exhausting it is to be honest and forthcoming.

❋ SUPERFICIAL VALUES

How can we be honest with our friends if our basic responses to others are being formed by superficial values? Since we occupy a world in which many try to resolve their problems by going shopping, it's easy to understand why this kind of thinking is so prevalent. Just remember: Superficial values cloud our vision; they keep us from seeing the light in our fellow beings.

❋ GOSSIP AND TALE TELLING

Have you ever been hypocritical or "two-faced" with a friend? Have you ever gossiped about somebody until that person entered the room, and then became extremely friendly and amiable? The essence of morality and virtue is represented by the wisdom of not harming others, even with words.

❋ EXPLOITATION

We all want to be in I-thou relationships that are open, respectful, and honest; nobody wants to be seen as an object. Who wants to be manipulated or used for someone else's gain? Not me and not you! Exploitation is not the true purpose of our being here together on this good earth. If and when we can connect with others, recognizing them as not much different from ourselves in terms of needs and desires, then who can we exploit, who can we objectify, and who can we deceive?

❋ DEPENDENT CLINGING

Buddhism makes a distinction between love and clinging. I think this needs repeating time and again. We need to be mindful, no matter how much we may care about specific people, that it's wise to recognize the differences between love and clinging, compassion and demanding neediness. Buddhism reminds us to cultivate balance and equanimity. In this way, our relationships are based more on openness and a free-flowing give-and-take instead of being like Velcro or sticky fly paper.

When love becomes overly laced with clinging, it can go awry; we become needy and co-dependent. Jealousy is an example of love gone awry.

❋ LIVING IN THE PAST

We all carry our own ghosts, and too often, we find ourselves relating to the people in our lives as though they are specters from the past. If we quarreled with our parents, we continue the same patterns with our mates; if we were jealous of our siblings, we run the risk of dealing with everyone with an undercurrent of sibling rivalry. It's almost impossible to have authentic, meaningful, heart-to-heart, soul-to-soul relationships until we learn to loosen the subconscious hold that our ghosts have on us. Psychotherapy and introspection can help us be able to do so.

Mindfulness is always the perfect reminder to let go of convoluted logic and tangled, self-defeating behavior. The practice of mindfulness helps us be more present and deal with situations as they occur. It helps us be attentive and let go of the past. It helps us see reality, and it helps us be more authentically true to ourselves.

BREATHE, SMILE, LET GO

Breathe In . . . Count One.
Breathe Out . . . Count Two.
Breathe In . . . Count One.
Breathe Out . . . Count Two.
Breathe In . . . Count One.
Breathe Out . . . Count Two.

Smile.
Relax.
You are fully present. Enjoy the miracle
of the present moment.
Peace and joy.

AUTHENTIC LISTENING

We bring greater spirituality as well as authenticity to our relationships by genuinely listening to the sounds and voices of the world. Start listening, and see what happens. Few among us can truly hear what others are saying. Instead we hear what we want to hear. I once saw a very funny cartoon of a dog listening to a person speaking. The dog was blotting out all the words except those that related to food. Blah, blah, blah, dinner . . . Blah, blah, blah, steak. In some ways we all do the same thing. When I was in college, I was working on a project for which I was tape recording some interviews. I would listen to the person who was being interviewed, and I would think that I had a clear idea about what was being said. Then later I would read the actual typed transcript of the interview, and I would inevitably be surprised by how little I had truly heard. Too often I discovered that I had related primarily to the things that interested me, and just like the cartoon pooch, failed to pay attention to those words that didn't automatically capture my attention.

I noticed the same thing in monastic retreat. A group of monks and nuns would gather every afternoon after lunch for intensive two- to three-hour teachings from one of our learned Tibetan lamas. Afterward, when I compared my notes with those of the others, I would sometimes discover that it was almost as though we had been listening to different teachings. This was true even of those who, like myself, had been scribbling intently, trying to write down almost every word that our teacher said. The fact is that we had all emphasized slightly different points; our interpretations of what we had heard and what were the main points were simply not the same.

True listening accurately reflects whatever appears, just like a mirror, without error or distortion. Discriminating, mirror-like wisdom can discern subtle nuances and distinctions and can recognize deeper connections, patterns, and implications.

The oral Sufi tradition says that "Mohammed is an ear." This puts an interesting spin on the role of the prophet. Mohammed is seen not only as a speaker, but as someone who is attuned to listening to the "sacred other." We also can listen and hear the sacred other, whether that other is God, mate, colleague, or child.

One of the biggest complaints that people have about their relationships is that the other is not listening; consequently they don't feel heard. It can be an act of generosity to give people an ear, which is a spiritual practice—good for us, and good for others. It doesn't mean that we can fix them or fix others, but we are helping just by giving them a hearing, by providing a sounding board. We all need it, and we are capable of doing it. It's reciprocal, like breathing in and breathing out.

LISTENING WITH THE THIRD EAR

In Buddhist centers and retreats around the world, meditation sessions often begin with the sound of a gong. At the Japanese Zen Temple in Bodh Gaya, there is a large brass gong, the size of a truck tire. Hanging next to it is a huge tree trunk–sized log. At sunset each evening two monks come out and together swing the log, striking it against the gong. I can still recall the reverberating sound, across all the years. In Tibet, practitioners are often called to meditation by gongs of different sizes; sometimes Tibetan singing bells are used for this purpose or long horns that fill an entire valley with the resonant sound.

Whenever I meditate, I slowly strike my bronze, bowl-shaped Japanese singing gong with a wooden mallet. I do this three times, letting it reverberate as long as possible. This is how I begin and end each session. When we enjoy these beautiful sounds, we may think we are ringing these instruments for our own ears, but Tibetans say we are also offering music up to the ears of all the Buddhas—including our own inner Buddhas. If we are able to hear the sounds, the little Buddha within will begin stirring. Sometimes we use large drums that resonate in our hearts and stomachs for the same reason. When I lead meditation sessions, I also typically begin by striking a gong three times—once for the Buddha, once for the Dharma, and once for the Sangha, or spiritual community.

I think it's important for seekers to remember that we can actually become awakened—enlightened—through conscious hearing. Milarepa, the enlightened Tibetan yogi, for example, is usually drawn with his hand cupped around his right ear to emphasize that he is listening to the sounds of the natural world—reading the book of nature, as it were. He's tuning in to the infinite through the finite sounds of nature. All of Milarepa's one hundred thousand songs came from true listening.

Chinese Buddhists have long celebrated the birthday of the Bodhisattva Kuan Yin, who is often depicted resembling an ethereal Chinese woman in flowing robes, not unlike Western depictions of Mary. There is a legend that says that Kuan Yin—whose name is translated as "one who hears the cries of the world"—became enlightened because she *heard* and paid attention to the suffering of the world.

The Tibetan equivalent of Kuan Yin, of course, is Avalokitesvara, the androgynous Bodhisattva of limitless compassion. Anyone who studies Buddhism will hear a lot about Avalokitesvara. Probably the best known and loved of all Buddhist sutras is the brief, one-page Heart Sutra. The legend surrounding the Heart Sutra is that in the early days of Buddhism, the Buddha himself appeared in the guise of Avalokitesvara to teach the Heart Sutra to five hundred monks and nuns who were gathered at Vulture's Peak in Rajgir, about a half day's walk from the Bodhi Tree in Bodh Gaya. The story is that many of the monks became so upset at the uncompromising proclamation of absolute truth that they actually vomited. In short, they couldn't stomach the naked unadorned truth contained within this iconoclastic discourse on ultimate voidness; it shook them up and shattered their doctrinaire concepts. The Heart Sutra, of course, resonates all the way to the present as the essence of transcendental wisdom, reminding us that form is nothing but emptiness, and that emptiness shapes up as form.

When the Buddha taught the Heart Sutra, he appeared in the form of Avalokitesvara. Having meditated deeply on the source of all sound—in other words, the source of all arisings and appearances, all sights, sounds, feelings—Avalokitesvara realized the emptiness and ungraspability of these apparition-like appearances. This great Bodhisattva was thus released from clinging to materiality or concepts.

Avalokitesvara, who embodies compassion and love, awoke to the most profound wisdom of prajna paramita (transcendental wisdom) by awakening to the truth of pure hearing. He/she heard the true sounds of the universe and plumbed the source of all sound. When I talk about listening with the third ear, I don't mean the inner ear with those little bones and pieces. I mean the real ear of listening where we're really receiving, receptive, and sensitive. I mean really being touched by the world around us and the people we meet.

THE PRACTICE OF LISTENING BEGIN
WITH SILENCE—A REFLECTION

Kabir, the medieval Indian sage and poet, sang, "God hears even the bracelets jangling on the feet of a mosquito."

What would it be like to have hearing so acute, so sensitive, so perfectly in tune with the world that we could hear everything—spoken and unspoken? Most of us are nowhere near that divine ideal; we're still struggling to hear our friends, partners, and children. We're struggling to hear the distinctions between truth and illusion in our own lives; we're still trying to learn how to listen.

Tibetan masters say there are three kinds of wisdom. First, there is hearing wisdom. That is followed by reflecting or contemplating wisdom, and then there is experiential meditative wisdom. In short, we listen and learn; then we reflect; and then we meditate and internalize. Throughout this process there is tremendous emphasis on hearing and listening.

To help us reflect on our capacity to listen and hear, Tibetan teachers often use the symbol of a cooking pot waiting to be filled with knowledge and wisdom that is nourishment for the spirit. There is even a teaching for sincere students to apply to themselves, called the Five Defects of a Vessel. This teaching helps us reflect on conditions to avoid if we are to be suitable vessels for truth and wisdom.

The Five Defects of a Vessel

I. A POT WHICH IS TURNED OVER
When we are facing the wrong direction, we are essentially unavailable to even the most nourishing substances. This is a reminder that we get to choose which direction we face. We need

to make wholesome choices and be available to hear wisdom teachings.

2. A POT WHICH IS COVERED

Have you ever tried to talk to somebody who is wearing earphones? In the same way, how can anything be poured into a vessel which, to all intents and purposes, is shut down? This reminds us to be receptive and open.

3. A POT THAT ALREADY CONTAINS SOMETHING POISONOUS

If we were to pour the purest water into a vessel that contained a toxic substance, although the toxin would be diluted, the water would still be corrupted. This reminds us to purify ourselves so that we are ready to receive.

4. A POT WHICH IS ALREADY FILLED TO THE BRIM

This symbol tells us not to be so full of ourselves and our opinions and ideas that there is no room for anything else.

5. A POT THAT LEAKS

We all know the expression "in one ear, and out the other." It is not enough to hear and be filled with wisdom; we need to learn how to retain it.

NOBLE SILENCE

Listening takes place not just through the ears, but with all the senses. Sometimes the best way to prepare ourselves to hear in a new and better way is to be still and silent. When we quiet our motor minds—and our motor mouths—we find that we are better able to open our hearts. The ancient practice of Noble

Silence helps us begin the process of hearing in a new way; this is a timeless and wise practice that helps us be more sensitive and perceptive.

Noble Silence traditionally begins with a vow to keep silent for a specific period of time. It can be an hour, a day, a week, or a month. There are practitioners who have kept Noble Silence for years. There is even a practice of lifetime silence in India called "maun." The famous master Meher Baba was a mauni baba, a silent holy man. He used a small blackboard to spell out his succinct messages, like "Don't worry, be happy," long before the reggae song was written.

If you want to try a period of Noble Silence, remember that it is a rest for all of the senses. Turn off the radio, the phone, the television. Enjoy a fast from the news. Turn off the thoughts in your head. Stay quiet. Take refuge in the inner calm and peace of the quiet mind. Don't write, don't read, don't surf the Net. Keep still. Listen to the sounds around you. What do you hear? What do you see? Open your eyes, open your ears, open your heart. Think of the ancient Christian exercise. Be still. Listen to the inner voice, and know God. This is how we learn to cultivate higher levels of hearing, perception, and vision.

"For someone deeply trapped in a prison of thought, how good it can feel to meet a mind that hears, a heart that reassures. It's as if listening mind is, in and of itself, an invitation to another mind to listen too. How much it can mean when we accept the invitation and hear the world anew."
—From *How Can I Help* by Ram Dass
and Paul Gorman

CHAPTER SIX

The Connection Reflex—
Building Meaningful Relationships

While I was in Tibet . . . there was a certain degree of respect given to the office of the Dalai Lama and people related to me accordingly, regardless of whether they had
true affection towards me or not. But if that was the only
basis of people's relation to me, then when I lost my country, it would have been extremely difficult. But there is
another source of worth and dignity from which you can
relate to other fellow human beings. *You can relate to them
because you are still a human being, within the human community.
You share that bond. And that human bond is enough to give rise
to a sense of worth and dignity. That bond can become a source of
consolation in the event that you lose everything else.*

—His Holiness, the Dalai Lama

As the Dalai Lama points out, the human bond, the
connectedness we share with each other, is an ever reliable source of strength and comfort. This is true for
all of us. Anyone who is fortunate enough to have a
friend or relative who is consistently supportive knows

how much we depend on connections such as these. Anyone who has ever been seriously ill and had to go to the hospital remembers what it feels like to have a kind doctor, nurse, or medical technician stand by the side of the gurney. It isn't just the medical expertise that's comforting; it's the human presence that makes us feel that we are not alone. Anyone who has ever relied on a kind stranger to help at roadside with sudden car trouble knows why some people refer to these Samaritans as angels.

We all reach out automatically to connect, a little like new infants who reach out to curl their tiny hands around their mothers' fingers. I call it the *connection reflex*. Just as we need others, so too they need us. It's not a choice. "No man is an island entire of itself," as John Donne wrote. We are never disconnected from the whole. This intrinsic knowledge of our place in the greater picture is part of our spiritual DNA, our original software, or heartware. But the question that we as seekers need to ask ourselves is whether our relationships—our human connections—reflect our spiritual values and intentions. Are our interactions with others an expression of our inner goodness and nobility of heart? As we communicate, work, and play with others, are we remembering our commitment to integrate spirit into everything we do and say? Or are we just going through the motions, like automatons, or worse, using others for our own ends?

Our relationships precisely mirror our satisfaction, or lack of it, with life itself. When we are unhappy, most often it's because we don't have satisfying relationships. Not that long ago, a thirty-five-year-old man named Daniel came to talk to me. Daniel told me that he felt alienated—emotionally isolated and alone. Daniel felt that much of his dissatisfaction came from how he interacts with others. He felt as though he had never been able to make the human connections that would give his life meaning. "Even in my marriage," he said, "I feel as though I am living with a stranger. I don't know my wife, and I don't feel that she knows me. Maybe it's me," he continued, "but I don't seem to be able to share my genuine feelings. Nor do I understand what it is that she's trying to communicate. The same thing is true in most of my other relationships as well. I sometimes feel as though it wouldn't matter to anyone whether I live or die."

A large part of our spiritual work here on this planet is finding ways to heal these feelings of isolation and alienation in ourselves and in those we meet. We do this by placing a value on developing deeper connections as a way of enriching our lives and our world. A good life is not about money, real estate, careers, or the stock market; it's about how well we love and are loved. It's about living with heart.

INTEGRATING RELATIONSHIPS INTO
OUR SPIRITUAL QUEST

As we work to incorporate our relationships into our spiritual quest, we are reminded that even the most classical Buddhist teachings are about relationship. When the Buddha, for example, set down his Noble Eight-fold Path to enlightenment, he talked about issues like friendliness and loving-kindness, positive intentions, ethics, wise speech, right livelihood, and right action. This has everything to do with relationship. The spiritual path isn't just about explicit religious formalities, rites, and rituals. Nor is it exclusively about mystical experience and meditative epiphanies. Most of it is simply about learning how to live an enlightened, loving life, day to day. The day-to-day antidote to alienation and loneliness is connection. The day-to-day practice or exercise that brings this about is reaching out and making genuine contact—touching and being touched.

As we go about our lives, we typically encounter and relate to many people—friends, family, and strangers. Whether these relationships are casual or intimate, we are given countless opportunities to apply the deeper values we believe in. We can put these opportunities into a spiritual framework by thinking of them as spiritual practices or exercises to help us train and strengthen our intentions.

Relating to others in a more spiritual fashion is a fairly simple and straightforward process; throughout human history, suggestions on how to do it have been given to us by the sages and masters of all the spiritual traditions. There is little that is new in the list that I'm including, but then there is nothing new under the sun; all we have are new opportunities to apply timeless wisdom every day of our marvelous lives.

CONNECTING AND REACHING OUT—
HOW TO DO IT

Accept Others as They Are—
Warts and All

When I started to think about this idea, I searched the word "acceptance" on the Net to see what came up. I discovered large numbers of support groups formed by people who were struggling together to find acceptance. One such group, for example, was formed by people who are overweight, another by men and women who are gay. It was a sad reminder of how much intolerance there is in the world, and how much we all need to stop rejecting others for how they look, what they think, and who they are. I'm still shocked by the amount of intolerance and bigotry that still exists, even in this modern age; it seems as though every time I turn on the news, another example of it is highlighted. This is one of those "When we will ever learn?" issues that we all need to address in our own lives.

The lesson of acceptance is an integral part of the spiritual path. Unconditional acceptance, after all, is about love; it's about opening our hearts and offering an unconditional "yes" to the world. I was recently reading a book by the Benedictine monk and teacher Brother David Steindl-Rast, who writes, "The 'yes' of the human heart is our full response to the 'faithfulness at the heart of all things.' In saying this 'yes,' we become what we are. Our true self is 'Yes.' " *Yes,* I thought to myself. *Yes!* Brother David stirs my Buddhist heart.

As seekers, the question we need to ask ourselves is how can we effectively say "yes" to the people around us? How can we appropriately convey acceptance and love? To get more insight into how to do this, think about the people, places, and situations that make you feel accepted. I have certain friends who I love to visit. When I walk through the door they convey a sense of great pleasure at having me there. In their homes I feel enveloped in warmth, friendship, and acceptance. We are connected, as if we are one family—one person, almost. This is spiritual connection—authentic relationship.

When we feel accepted, we feel as though we "belong," don't we? We feel as though we are on the same team; we have a place in the world, a purpose in being here; we feel aligned with others to whom we are connected in the most basic way. Therefore, doesn't it make sense that one of the simplest ways we can convey acceptance is by being inclusive and by helping others feel as though they belong as well? In short, we do this by saying *yes* to those we meet. We do this by including others in our thoughts, our prayers, and our actions; we do this by rooting out all the various shadowy forms of prejudice and intolerance in our own hearts. We do this by cultivating thoughts and wishes of well-being, loving-kindness, and compassionate concern for all that lives, breathes, and is.

The Dharma suggests that we can train ourselves to be more open and accepting of others by focusing first on the object of our greatest affection. Think about the warm feelings you have for your children or your grandparents or even your Siamese cat, for example. We continue to love and accept those we love, even though they are not always perfect. We train in loving-kindess by extending similar feelings to others, beginning with those we love the most and then working our way outward in ever-widening circles of spiritual embrace.

Let Go of Closed and Judgmental
Points of View

If you have a problem, who do you want to talk to? Someone who listens to what you have to say with an open and loving attitude, or someone who greets you with a series of judgments and fixed opinions? Do you like to hang out with people who are critical and judgmental? I doubt it. If you're like most of us, most likely these are the people you try to avoid. Or perhaps you try to straighten such people out—which most likely implies trying to bring them around to your point of view. Good luck!

My friend Anna sometimes complains about her cousin, Rosie, who is known throughout the family as "Rosie, the critic." Anna says, "I love Rosie, but I can't stand spending time with her. From the minute she walks through my door all she does is criticize. 'Why did you sauté the vegetables instead of steaming them? Why are your children wearing torn sneakers? You need a different haircut; why don't you go to my stylist? Why don't you do something about the broken tile on the kitchen floor?'" According to Anna, Rosie can't stop herself. Nothing ever pleases her; she notes every imperfection and finds fault with everything and everyone who crosses her path. Anna says that she and Rosie once went to a restaurant; at the door, the maître d' stopped them before they sat down, saying that Rosie had sent so many meals back to the kitchen that they would prefer that she not eat there anymore.

Of course, at least a little part of each of us is like "Rosie, the critic." I call this part *the inner tyrant*. The inner tyrant always thinks it knows; it's never totally satisfied, and nothing is ever quite good enough to meet its perfectionistic standards. We all have at least a few days or periods when the inner tyrant rules. When we're being severely judgmental, of course, we're losing sight of Bodhicitta, our loving intentions to express compassion and tolerance to everyone we meet.

Usually a critical attitude reflects a lack of self-acceptance. Our inner tyrant often most harshly judges ourselves. One way we can start to work on our judgmental attitudes is by softening up, cutting ourselves some slack, and showing ourselves more love and kindness. Using spiritual intelligence we can remind ourselves that in the greater scheme of things, today's critical opinions have very little significance.

DO UNTO OTHERS AS YOU WOULD HAVE OTHERS DO UNTO YOU

Professor John Makransky, my close friend and colleague, always has wonderful stories to share about the experience of parenting his two small sons. The other evening, John was downstairs in his house working when five-year-old Jonathan came to say goodnight. "Did you brush your teeth?", John asked his son.

"Yes," Jonathan answered.

"Very good," said John. "Now, did you brush your feet?"

"No, Daddy. I didn't brush my feet." Jonathan looked confused.

"Well," John said, "you had better go upstairs and tell

Mommy that you brushed your teeth, but you haven't brushed your feet yet."

So Jonathan, who was in pajamas with bare feet, started walking up the stairs slowly. Meanwhile he was thinking . . . thinking.

When Jonathan got to the top of the stairs, he stopped. Instead of going into the room his mother was in, he turned and looked back at his father. "Daddy," he said, "what do you mean 'brush my feet?' You're teasing me, aren't you?"

"Yes, Jonathan," John replied. "I am teasing you."

Jonathan put his hands on his waist and shook his head disapprovingly. "Please don't do that any more, Daddy," he said. "Put yourself in my place. How would *you* feel?"

From the mouths of babes, wisdom flows. The lesson is crystal clear: Whatever we do, whatever we say, all we have to think is how we would want to be treated. From this concept emerges a natural sense of morality as well as caring, unselfish, ethical behavior. Jesus said, "Do to others as you would have them do to you."

The Buddha said:

> *"See yourself in others*
> *Then whom can you hurt?*
> *What harm can you do?"*

DEVELOP AN AUTHENTICALLY GENEROUS SPIRIT

"The more we have, the more we have to give."

Generosity starts in the mind, with an intention to be more sincerely giving and open-hearted. The Buddha once told a follower that generosity was so important that we shouldn't sit down to a single meal without sharing it in some way. In Tibet every monk, nun, and lama begins each meal by first taking a portion of food, often rice, wadding it into a ball and throwing it outside or placing it aside to feed the hungry spirits. In this way, we are reminded of the value of sharing as well as of the depth of pain that can be suffered by those whose lives are dominated by either hunger or greed.

Giving, of course, doesn't always come naturally. That's why the Buddha once told a wealthy, but stingy, businessman that he should train himself in the virtue of generosity. The Buddha suggested that the man think of his two hands—right and left— as being separate entities, one of them poor and the other wealthy. The Buddha told the businessman to learn how to "let go" and give by taking a coin in the "wealthy hand" and giving it to the "poor hand." The Buddha told him that he should experiment with increasingly larger sums of money and greater objects of wealth until he was able to cultivate nonattachment and give generously and freely to others too.

The act of sharing means that we are beginning to let go of our clinging and greed; we are loosening our tendency to hang onto whatever we have. There are many different kinds of things, both outer and inner, that we can give. We can learn to let go on many levels; some of our most valuable gifts, of course, are inner gifts of spirit and love, which are best enjoyed by being shared. The more we have, the more we have to give. And the more we can give, the more we receive, as everyone knows.

The first principle of Buddhism's Six Principles of Enlightened Living is the perfection of generosity, which in Sanskrit is called "Dana Paramita." Dana is the wisdom of openness—internal, external, and innate. This means open hands, open arms, open mind, and open heart. When we share our bounty, in whatever form, with others, we are following through on our intention not to be greedy or selfish; we are following through on our intention to connect with the world.

Thinking about Dana Paramita reminds us that it's wise to let go. It is simply in our own higher self-interest. Externally, generosity implies being more open, giving, service-oriented, and unselfish with our material goods, energy, and time. Internally, it's about not being miserly with our emotions and our love, but being more open-hearted. Innately, just *being* represents innate generosity. Everything is available in the natural state of pure being. There is inexhaustible abundance and glory within, so exploit your own inner natural resources.

Here are some of ways we can share our bounty:

❀ SHARING MONEY AND GIFTS

There are some common reasons why it can be difficult to give. When we give others money or material objects of any kind, for example, it presupposes that there will be less left over for us. Just this morning, a friend was visiting me and asked if I had anything to drink. "I don't know," I said. "Look in the refrigerator." "Is it okay if I finish the orange juice?" my friend asked. "Sure," I replied. As I said yes, I had a knee-jerk reaction: It crossed my mind that there would be no orange juice for breakfast the next day. And for a second, I wanted to "hang on"—not "let go" of my single serving of juice. Most of us know the feeling, don't we? I mean, the truth is that in my fortunate life, there is plenty of orange juice just up the street, not to mention the various kinds of tea in my cupboard to get me through tomorrow morning—so where is the resistance really coming from?

As seekers who are trying to be more free and generous, we know that we are working on the deepest forms of giving; we are cultivating our capacity to open up, let go, and give with a genuinely open heart. In short, while sharing the orange juice is nice and a good thing, it would be wonderful if we could also be happy and grateful for the opportunity to share. Giving often creates choices. Let's say you have $200 worth of discretionary income left in your wallet, and you really would like to buy a new jacket. Walking past a store window, you see a nice looking jacket. You think, *I'd look good in that. I'd feel good in that.* But wait, you remember that a friend is having a birthday. You'd like to be able to do something special as a celebration. And your mother's radio just broke; as much as she loves listening to the radio, you know she's so worried about money that she won't buy herself a new one. And your brother and his wife are having a hard time right now; they're saving up to send your nephew to camp for the summer, and every little bit makes a difference. And your mailbox is also filled with letters from worthwhile organizations asking you to contribute to campaigns to help others. So I guess you will have to make a decision about whether to help others or buy yourself a piece of clothing. These are choices that we make.

❋ GIVE THE GIFT OF TIME AND ENERGY

Time is often the most precious commodity. When we use our time to do something for someone else, we might have less left over for ourselves. Who has enough time and energy to do everything? I know I don't. In my life, I personally am always facing the time dilemma. The phone rings. On the answering machine, I hear a student who wants me to explain part of one of my Monday night Boston Dharma talks; on the television is a basketball game that I would love to sit down and enjoy. This is a time choice I often have to make. In my own case, I'm a Dharma teacher. When I was in Asia in my twenties and thirties, my own spiritual masters were extraordinarily generous with their teachings, their time, and their energy. I'm always aware of this. When I asked them how I could repay their kindness to me, they said, "Pass it on." I consider this my responsibility.

How are you asked to give time regularly? Do you have children who would like to spend more time with you? A wife, husband or romantic partner? Do you have a friend who wants you to help her move? Do you know someone in a nursing home or hospital who would appreciate a visit? or an elderly neighbor who needs help in shopping or getting to the doctor? Are you a member of a spiritual community that needs help with a fundraiser or a specific project? In our time-starved modern society, making a conscious commitment of time and energy is always a beautiful gift.

✳ BE KIND

Think about the people in your life who have given you the gift of kindness. What is it they did that made you appreciate them? I asked some people to give me examples of kindness that had been extended to them. Here's what they said:

✳ Martha described a childhood music teacher who was *gentle* in her criticism and *encouraging* in her praise.

✳ Ed remembered the man whose new car he had recently sideswiped; he said the man *smiled* understandingly and tried to make Ed feel better about what had happened.

✳ Barbara talked about a friend who always has a kind and *supportive* word for everyone.

✳ Doug was particularly touched by the veterinarian who wrote him a letter of *sympathy* when his dog died and made a contribution in the dog's memory to a veterinarian hospital.

Kindness is an extraordinary quality. Those who are able to embody it have learned how not to be stingy with words, encouragement, and love. Those of us who are on the receiving end of kindness are always made a little bit better by the experience. Eric Hoffer said, "We are made kind by being kind."

✺ GIVE ENERGY AND COURAGE

I'm impressed by people who choose potentially lifesaving occupations that routinely require great energy and sometimes even greater courage. Firemen, of course, are one of the most obvious examples. Medical missionaries and emergency medical and rescue workers are others.

About a year ago, I read an obituary in the *New York Times* for a man I had never met, but I wish I had. The obituary headline read, "Adrian Marks, a Navy pilot who rescued 56 sailors struggling in the shark-filled Philippine Sea after the cruiser Indianapolis was sunk by Japanese torpedoes in July 1945."

The obituary said that Mr. Marks, who was eighty-one when he died, was a lieutenant during the Second World War. In that role, Lieutenant Marks, on a routine mission on a sunny day piloting a seaplane that was meant to land only in calm water, flew over American survivors of a torpedo attack in high and dangerous seas. Ignoring orders, and with the agreement and support of his crew members, Lieutenant Marks risked both his life and his crew's by putting his plane down in the midst of twelve-foot swells.

Because he did this, the plane essentially became a life raft, no longer able to take off; in short, Marks and his crew sacrificed their freedom to help others. They put as many men in their plane as they could, and then used parachute material to tie others on the wings, which were bobbing up and down on the ocean. That's how they spent the night until help came the following day. After the war, Marks went on to open a law practice in Indiana. In 1975, there was a reunion of the survivors of that event, and Marks spoke, paying tribute to the men with whom he had shared this terrifying experience. "I met you thirty years ago," he said. "I met you on a sparkling, sun-swept afternoon of horror. I have known you through a balmy tropic night of fear. I will never forget you."

I was very moved by this story; it reminded me that courageousness in caring for others has always been viewed as a Bodhisattva activity. In ancient Indian Buddhist scriptures, Bodhisattvas are likened to snow white geese, who dive down even into the depths of hell to deliver suffering creatures from pain, torment, and fear as if they were diving down into a lake. Most of us will never be called upon to literally save a human life, but most of us do have some opportunities to be fearless when it comes to saving the lives of animals and insects. And sooner or later, most of us will have opportunities to be brave enough to put our comfort and security at risk by helping other human beings. This is a way of being generous.

There are many ways to help save another's life. Not that long ago I saw a story on the news about a delivery man in New York City who had taken it upon himself to help a street person whom he regularly saw on the streets. This was a homeless alcoholic man whose mother went to church every Sunday and prayed for word of her son. The delivery man, clearly an urban Bodhisattva, spent several years giving the homeless man small amounts of money for food, trying to gain his trust in order to find out who he was and if he had any family. Finally he was able to get him to reveal a phone number, and he helped place him in a detox program and helped reunite him with his family. The two men attended a church service together, and the former street person, who was a talented musician, played a hymn for the man who was helping him find his way off the streets.

In truth, we all need at least a little bit of saving. So look around. Whose life can you help save today? Sometimes it just takes a few kind words. God saves those who save one another.

❋ SHARE WHAT YOU KNOW

My friend Lorraine recently told me that she is incredibly grateful to the instructor who helped her learn how to ski. Her instructor was so skillful and encouraging that, despite her fears, after just a few lessons, Lorraine is now actually enjoying gliding down the mountain on her new short skis, something she thought she would never be able to do.

Don't we all feel gratitude when someone takes the time to share with us what they know? Information is wealth, and not everybody is open-hearted enough to share what they know. In fact, some people hoard their information, preferring to maintain an elitist position that restricts learning and information to the chosen few—no matter what the subject. An ancient Buddhist text says that if you know where to go to read Buddhist sutras and if because of stinginess, you don't share this information with others, you run the risk of being reborn as an earthworm. So take care! You don't want to spend a lifetime with a mouthful of dirt ascending toward the surface light.

It seems as though there is often someone who takes the "I know something you don't know" attitude. We see this in all areas of expertise; maybe that's why we appreciate those who offer us information that helps us become knowledgeable. Knowledge is like freeware; it belongs to everyone.

I'm very grateful to the various friends who helped me learn how to use a computer; I'm grateful to the high school teacher who first turned me on to the joys of poetry; I'm grateful to my mother for helping me learn how to drive a car, leaving me with a series of vivid memories I will never forget; I'm grateful to the counselor in summer camp who taught me how to swim and dive; I'm grateful to my father who taught me how to ride and balance myself on a bicycle, cajoling me into not being overly nervous. And of course, I am incredibly grateful to my kind Buddhist teachers, many of whom were Tibetan refugee monks living in extremely difficult circumstances; nonetheless, they taught me how to find spiritual sanity and a more profound balance. We all have teachers in our lives to whom we are grateful. We can repay our gratitude by "passing it on" and unstintingly sharing what we know.

❋ GIVE THE GIFT OF DHARMA

All Buddhist teachings say that the greatest gift we can give anyone is the gift of Dharma. "Dharma" is a Sanskrit word with many meanings. It can be translated as teaching, truth, doctrine, religion, spirituality, or reality. The literal meaning is "that which supports or upholds." Dharma also means "that which heals."

There is an old Japanese Buddhist story that I like about a master who begged daily to raise large sums of money in order to build a temple in which people could be edified by learning Dharma. However, when the time finally came for the temple to be built, there was a famine in the land, and people were starving. Instead of building the large temple he had imagined, the master turned all the money over to the people for food. Bodhicitta, the altruistic intention to alleviate suffering and bring about spiritual deliverance, is constant and unswerving, yet the ways and means can and must be flexible enough to adapt and change.

When we give the gift of Dharma, we are giving others what they need most, whatever that might be. Therefore, if we share what we have genuinely learned through life experience and what we know about spiritual teachings, we are giving Dharma. Moreover if we are able to give someone wise advice, we are also giving someone the gift of Dharma. Often just by listening to someone's troubles, we are giving the gift of Dharma, by lending them an ear as a sounding board or a shoulder to lean on.

People in this postmodern, cynical age are often embarrassed about admitting their spiritual interest or sharing their personal spiritual treasures. Many have told me, however, that when they open up and talk with others about what's really meaningful, they discover that they are not alone. When we share Dharma, we connect on the deepest levels.

※ BECOME A GENEROUS "RECEIVER"

When Deidra was getting ready to move, she opened a closet and packed the leather briefcase that her late employer had given her once when she had been promoted. Deidra loved the briefcase, and had been very touched by the gift when she received it. However, years later, Deidra realizes that she never really conveyed her feelings to her old boss. Now, with the wisdom of hindsight, Deidra wonders why she had been so stingy with her thanks.

It's often just as important to receive with an open heart as it is to give. By definition, relationships of all kinds have to do with reciprocity and mutuality. Relationships that fall apart often do so because they are out of balance; they experience ratio strain. In her relationship with her friend Margo, Fredda is fed up because she feels as though she always gives, gives, gives. Margo, on the other hand, thinks that Fredda never allows Margo to give those things that she can. There is always an interesting connection between giver and recipient. Some people, for example, prefer the role of caretaker; they are uncomfortable when someone tries to take care of them, and they sort of "hijack" all the giving in a relationship. The thing to remember is that giver and receiver are building good karma together, so give someone else a chance to give.

Think about how much pleasure and joy we get when we give a present to a child who is truly excited and happy about receiving it. We were probably all better receivers when we were children. Nonetheless, being a good receiver is an art that's worth relearning. Say thank you. Be appreciative. Show your joy. Feel it.

EMPATHIZE WITH OTHERS

A few years back, I was with a friend who was picking up a small child from preschool. While I waited for my friend and his son, I watched a little drama unfold. One toddler—she couldn't have been more than two or three—was crying because she didn't want to leave the fingerpainting she had been working on to go home. The teacher and the child's parents were all trying to reason with her, but the little girl was having none of it. Suddenly another little boy, her own size, who already had his coat on, broke away from his mother and ran over to the sobbing child; he put his arms around her shoulders. "Don't cry, Sarah," he said. "You can finish it tomorrow. I'll help you. Please don't cry." He sounded as though he felt her unhappiness with almost as much intensity as she did. His behavior reminded me of the stories told of Tibet's little Bodhisattvas—children called "tulkus," who are the reincarnation of previous spiritual masters; these little budding Buddhas seem naturally able to feel and respond to another's pain. Inside each of us is a tender and sensitive little Buddha who is naturally able to empathize with anyone. We can reconnect with that underlying tenderheartedness in us, no matter how old and hardened we have become.

STAY OPEN AND CHALLENGE
YOUR ASSUMPTIONS

My friend Patti is an animal lover. She says that people, therefore, assume that she is prepared to baby-sit for all kinds of creatures. That's why when a friend of hers had to be hospitalized, Patti was called upon to take care of his African gray parrot, Gwendolyn. Patti had never taken care of a bird before, and she had certainly never tried to forge a relationship with one. Gwendolyn's owner, a day trader, had always told Patti that his parrot was an amazing creature who could speak in sentences and respond appropriately to all kinds of stimuli. Nonetheless, Patti was surprised by the range of the bird's vocabulary. The first time she put together a pile of clothes to be washed and walked past the parrot's cage with a laundry bag, the bird squawked, "laundry day . . . laundry day." And when she put on MSNBC on the television for the news during the day, and the ticker tape information ran across the screen, the bird yelled out, "Nasdaq. Nasdaq." Perhaps he had some stock tips!

Maybe Gwendolyn was only parroting, but she certainly used words appropriately. Over the next few weeks Patti and Gwendolyn became friends. Patti shared her breakfast with Gwendolyn every morning because she loved feeding Gwendolyn bits of toast and egg or cereal and hearing the bird say, "hmmmm . . . very good." When the bird's owner, Michael, was finally well enough to take the bird home, he came to pick her up. When Gwendolyn saw him, she yelled "Michael" and jumped up and down. Then when he came near the cage, Gwendolyn seemed to remember that she was angry at him for leaving her, and she looked the other way whenever he tried to talk to her, giving him the cold shoulder—or feathers, as it were. Finally Michael coaxed Gwendolyn out of her cage. When she was standing on his arm, the parrot couldn't stay angry any longer. She jumped up on her owner's shoulder and buried her little face in his neck. "Hello," she cried. "Hello!"

When Gwendolyn left with Michael for her own home, Patti observed the parrot's great happiness and relief at being reunited with her owner, and yet Patti was genuinely sorry to see her leave. They had become such great friends (birds of a feather . . .).

So what's the point of this story about a highly articulate parrot? Just that we all tend to make assumptions about other beings, no matter what species those beings belong to. We assume that we couldn't possibly develop a relationship with the bird that sits outside our window. We don't even think of the bird as having "feelings," even though we know that birds do form bonds. So too, we often assume that we couldn't become friends with the hundreds of people we meet each year who are somehow "different" from us.

Whenever we stereotype a group or a gender, we are making assumptions. Men often assume that women will not fully appreciate team sports, for example, which is simply not true. Women assume other things about men, I am sure—I am just not always sure what! We decide arbitrarily that people who are older, younger, richer, or poorer are different from us and couldn't possibly fit into our lives. We assume the same things about people who have more or less education than we do. Our prejudices deprive our lives of richness and texture; these assumptions leave us with fewer possibilities for making joyous connections in our daily lives.

BE "PRESENT" FOR OTHERS

"I'm Here for You"

My friend Clara recently told me that she uttered that sentence to another friend, a man who was experiencing serious personal and health problems. When she said it, what she meant was that she was prepared to "show up" for whatever was needed. She was prepared to listen to her friend talk about the troubles he was experiencing; she was prepared to drive her friend to his doctor appointments; she was prepared to simply come and sit in his living room, simply offering her "being" for support, comfort, and warmth.

Being able to just be authentically present and accounted for in our relationships is a deeply caring spiritual act. When my grandmother was in her late eighties, she was in a nursing home in Long Beach, Long Island. She was sort of losing her marbles and couldn't remember much. But I could see that as far as she was concerned, my just being with her in the present was totally and absolutely fine. I noticed that some people in my family had trouble with the fact that she couldn't remember where I lived, my name, and other such details. When I'd visit her with my local relatives, they kept trying to remind her. "This is your oldest grandson, Jeffrey. You remember Jeffrey. He lives in France now and came all the way to see you." My grandmother didn't care about France and couldn't remember my way of life. But while I was there, for those grand hours we shared, we were totally together. She knew who I was as her beloved grandson, even without such a title or label, and there we were in those moments together—totally there. All of our lifetime interconnections together had boiled down to that, and it was more than enough. It was exquisite. I loved visiting with her, sad as it could occasionally become.

That sort of sums up all of our lives, I think. If you strip away all the stories, beliefs, and fantasies, and unveil our vital, pulsing, living core, here we are, right now. We are here for ourselves; here for each other—just here. There is a symmetry, a rightness, and justness to this elemental fact.

USING THE POWER OF WORDS
TO BUILD DEEPER CONNECTIONS

Recently I was in an airport in San Francisco, waiting for a flight to Los Angeles. I had an extra half hour, so I went to a phone booth to check my home messages and make a few calls. As I stood there, talking on the phone, the woman in the next booth hung up the phone, looked at me, and said, "I'm going to New Zealand for six months, and my husband just told me that the car broke down, and he wants to know what he should do." She separated her hands and looked up to the heavens with a do-you-believe-it expression, and after we shared a nod, she hurried away.

If only for a moment, this New Zealand–bound woman needed to connect; she needed to talk and vent her feelings, even to a stranger. She needed to share her private little joke about the absurdities of life. And she did; we had our fifteen seconds of connection together. The connections we make with others, both superficial and profound, most often begin with the spoken word. As the first sentence in the New Testament book of John states, "In the beginning was the word."

We use words to convey what we think; we use words to express how we feel. When we are trying to deepen our connections or resolve differences, we typically use the power of the spoken or written word. More often than not, what we say and how we say it determines the quality of any relationship.

The Buddha was so sensitive to the power of words that one step of the Noble Eight-fold Path is called Right Speech, or Impeccable Communication. The Buddha instructed his followers to speak the truth simply, without adornment; he exhorted them to speak honestly; he told them to use their words in gentle, peace-loving ways that reflect inner wisdom, clear vision, and their intentions to help, not harm, others.

Words come in different forms and languages, from a baby's first words to power words like mantras to nonsense words like those in Lewis Carroll's classic poem "Jabberwocky." We use so many words every day, and we use them in so many ways— helpfully, harmfully, lovingly, cruelly, consciously, and unconsciously. We use words to speak to others, and we also use words to speak to ourselves—not just walking down the street, talking to the air, but in our incessant internal monologues. Not that long ago I saw a cartoon of a large stout Buddha, modeled on the large meditating stone Buddha overlooking the sea in Kamakura, Japan. The thought bubble coming out of the Buddha's head said, "I hate my thighs." Who knows, maybe even Buddhas talk to themselves.

Conscious Speech/Conscious Relationships

What we say to ourselves shapes the relationship we have with ourselves. And what we say to others shapes our relationships with the rest of the world. If there is one thing that any one of us could do that would automatically improve the quality of our relationships, it would be to become more conscious of what we say and how we say it. All of our relationships will be changed and transformed when we change and transform ourselves in this way. I guarantee it.

Have you ever had the experience of really wanting to say something that you considered important, and then not having the courage to speak your mind? Have you ever said anything you later deeply regretted? Of course you have; we all have. Not that long ago I spoke to a woman named Nancy who was incredibly upset because of a conversation she'd had with her mother an hour before her mother suffered a serious heart attack. Nancy said that her mother had been obviously upset and kept complaining of indigestion. Nancy was trying to finish a work-related project when her mother called. Because she was feeling pressured, Nancy said, she had been abrupt and not particularly sympathetic to what her mother was saying. In this case, Nancy's mother recovered, and Nancy was fortunate to have more opportunities to be a loving daughter. However, this experience showed her how important it is to be mindful and aware in all her conversations and interactions, with everybody.

An important reason for staying conscious in our speech is to avoid later regrets. Barbara says she still cringes when she remembers the time she yelled at her daughter, saying, "You're so stupid! How could you be so stupid?" Martin says that his marriage has never quite recovered from the time he told his wife, "If you don't lose some weight, I'm going to go out and find myself a skinny gal." He says he was just teasing; to his wife, however, his words felt hurtful and threatening and lingered long in her memory. Ted says that he feels that he often hurts others with his words. He has a quick tongue and a sharp sense of humor. It's easy to take a quick poke at somebody just to get a laugh. One of his biggest challenges is learning how to restrain himself. I myself often find that words seem to just tumble off my tongue, so I try to pay attention and be careful of my mouth.

We can use words skillfully or unconsciously; we can use words to heal or to hurt. As seekers, our intention is to help, not harm. Our words can help us fulfill our highest intentions. I think it would really help all of us if, before we speak, we could stop for just a moment to make certain that what we are about to say accurately reflects our heart's intentions.

A DAY OF RIGHT SPEECH—
A HEALING PRACTICE

"May this day of right speech bring gentle blessings to those around me; may the blessings extend throughout the world."

We start this practice by designating a day that will be devoted to using our words to fulfill our highest spiritual aspirations. It might be easiest to begin with a weekend, a Saturday or Sunday when there is likely to be less work-related stress and fewer deadlines or office politics. Here are some suggestions for things you can do:

❋ Put a Post-it note beside your bed the night before to remind yourself that this will be a day of "Impeccable Speech."

❋ Start the day with a heartfelt prayer that reaffirms your intention to always speak with compassion and love.

❋ Center and collect yourself each time you speak. Be mindful of all your words. Even if you want to say something as banal as "please pass the mashed potatoes," be conscious of your tone of voice, and whether you are saying what you really want to say.

❋ Find ways to keep your words gentle, loving, accurate, and positive. Do this even if you are annoyed and upset.

❋ See if you can discover better ways to talk to others that will open up new channels of communication.

❋ Don't lie and don't use words to manipulate or control others.

❋ Don't gossip.

❋ Don't say anything about anyone that you wouldn't say if that person were present.

❋ Use your words to encourage those around you.

❄ Express your most positive thoughts and feelings. Tell others that you care about them.

❄ Don't chatter; don't use words just to fill empty spaces with noise.

❄ Don't become nervous about the absence of speech; allow yourself and others to be silent.

❄ Cultivate a way of speaking that is simple and spare.

❄ Don't interrupt others; let the people around you finish their sentences and express their thoughts.

❄ Use your words to convey patience.

❄ Use your words to help your loved ones feel nourished and supported.

❄ Use your words to express gentleness and kindness.

❄ Try to make at least one person feel better because of something you say.

❄ Use your words to convey friendship, encouragement, and support.

❄ Try to phone and connect with at least one loved one with whom you have lost touch.

❄ Write a note to someone you care about, expressing your positive feelings.

❄ Take the time to express support for someone else's work or personal project.

❋ Think about the people you know who have suffered losses. Take the time today to write notes expressing your sympathy and empathy.

A day of right speech can only help your karma. Keep up the good word.

CHAPTER SEVEN

Finding Our Sacred Place
in Nature

In relation to the earth, we have been autistic for centuries. Only now have we begun to listen with some attention and with a willingness to respond to the earth's demands that we cease our industrial assault, that we abandon our inner rage against the conditions of our earthly existence, that we renew our human participation in the grand liturgy of the universe.

—Thomas Berry

Nature provides ample evidence that we live in a cause-and-effect universe. Plant some tulip bulbs in the fall; watch as the graceful flowers make us smile come the spring. Throw chemicals into a stream or river, see the marine life die and the water and nearby soil become contaminated. As we begin to clean up a dangerously polluted waterway, fish start to return—but even so, they are often still dangerously toxic for human consumption. Everything has consequences; being aware of this, we watch as karma unfolds.

Many of us spend our lives in areas where we are very insulated from a day-to-day awareness of what we are doing to the planet we live on. A few years ago, I heard a story about an eight-year-old New York boy named Johnny who joined the Cub Scouts and went away with his troop on a weekend camping trip to the Adirondacks. When Johnny returned, his father asked him how he had enjoyed himself.

"It was great!" Johnny replied. "And we found a cow's nest in the woods."

"A cow's nest?" His father was bemused and perplexed. "But cows don't have nests."

"Well," Johnny said, "we took a walk in the woods and we went to this place where there was a big pile of old broken milk bottles."

Living, as we do, in a world filled with synthetics of all kinds, it's easy to become as misinformed about cause and effect as little Johnny. We forget that we are all dependent on the earth for food and clean water. We open our freezers to remove plastic bags, which we then pop into the microwave. Voilà, minutes later we cut open the plastic and squeeze out the helping of macaroni and ersatz cheese made with soy milk and chemicals. It looks good. It even tastes okay. The subliminal message we are receiving is that food comes from freezers, wrapped in plastic.

Because we feel removed from direct contact with our food supply, we are dependent on others to take care of us. We assume that scientists, politicians, and "people in charge" will be responsible about issues like keeping our food and water supply safe. Yet of course, we also know that large businesses hire lobbyists and public relations experts, and spend fortunes making certain that senators and congressmen place more value on financial interests than they do on certain matters that affect our health and our humanity; ethical considerations are just forgotten. We have seen time and time again how often science fails Spiritual Intelligence 101 by being unwilling to take the long view or perceive the whole picture. There is an assumption that "tomorrow" will take care of the problems we are creating today.

Recently, I read an article in the *New York Times* discussing some of the reasons why wild salmon are disappearing around the world. The possible causes are many: overfishing, changing climate and water temperatures, genetic weakening. Many believe that farm-bred salmon are creating many of the problems for various reasons. Some escape from their farm pens and get into waterways, and because they are weaker and smaller than the other salmon they may be genetically creating a weaker species. Another possible reason speaks to common sense: When the farm salmon are penned up together in close quarters, diseases and parasites can run amuck, attacking and killing the fish. These multiplying parasites can then spread to wild salmon. Another reason may be that the salmon's natural predators, such as seals, have increased. Whatever the reason, the disappearance of wild salmon provides an interesting example of cause and effect problems that scientists didn't anticipate would be exacerbated when salmon began to be farmed.

There are thousands of examples such as this. Did science accurately predict the illnesses that would be caused by radioactive fallout? Is torturing innocent animals in the name of science really necessary? Sometimes all that is being achieved is a cosmetic product? Did anyone fully anticipate the new and powerful bacterial strains that would emerge as a result of antibiotic use? Friends of mine in New York City are very concerned about the possibly toxic nature of the spray that has been used in the city to combat mosquitoes; they tell me that the spray killed not only the mosquitoes but also the monarch butterflies who were beginning their yearly migration to Mexico.

From the shrinking rain forest to radioactive waste, one

could, of course, go on all day in this vein, pointing out tragic examples of man's damaging effect on the planet. Ultimately, of course, this destruction reverberates back on us all, affecting, among other things, global weather patterns and the very air we breathe. We know that there are environmental factors implicated in diseases from asthma to cancer. We're aware of the effects pesticides and chemicals have on the health of our young children. Why aren't we behaving accordingly?

The Buddha was very conscious of ecological issues even during his lifetime. He told his monks that they should each plant at least one tree every year to replace the ones that had been lost by human use. He also issued an edict telling his monks not to urinate near rivers or streams for fear of pollution. The Buddha had a special connection to trees. He was born under a tree with his mother grasping a branch; he became enlightened under a tree; and he died under a tree. If the Buddha were to appear today in Bodh Gaya near the Bodhi Tree where he realized perfect enlightenment, he wouldn't recognize the spot. During his lifetime, it was a lush forest wilderness, teeming with life. Today that section of northern India has been deforested and much of the area is now an arid desert.

We walk on common ground. That means all of us—all the peoples of all nations and all the creatures, large and small. As the earth's tenants, we have a spiritual and sacred obligation to try to become better stewards of the planet we call home. This is part of the rent we should be paying for a safer, well-preserved world. Whenever we ignore what we are doing to the earth, we do so at our own peril. We will suffer the consequences of our disregard and disrespect; so will our children and our children's children. The earth is our home. It belongs to all of us. Native Americans chant, "The earth is our mother." Right now, Mom needs our help. Unselfish service is the rent we can pay for a better world and a better life.

In Buddhism, we talk a great deal about being awake to reality and how it works. One of the major areas in which we *all* need to be a little more conscious and awake is in how we handle our relationships with the natural world. I know that I am not always as mindful about ecological concerns as I would like to be; very few of us are. I don't always recycle as diligently as I should; I don't always take the time to buy and use environmentally safe cleaning products. I'm trying to be more assiduous about this. As we become more conscious and make more intelligent choices, we see more clearly how our careless behavior has an effect on the whole. Native Americans, who had a more intimate relationship with the land, knew that if we touch any part of this universal web we inhabit, the whole world web shakes.

LOVING THE CREATURES
OF THE EARTH

". . . how terribly arrogant we have become because of a
mistaken belief that man has dominion over the birds of the
air and the fish of the seas. The word 'dominion' was actually a translation of the Hebrew word 'stewardship.' "
—Jane Goodall

The natural world provides multitudinous opportunities for practices that reflect the compassion and caring of a Bodhisattva. There is a wonderful story that's told in Tibet about an old lama who would come every day to meditate on a large rock near a calm pond. Yet, no sooner would he cross his legs, settle down, and begin his prayers and devotions then he would spot some little insect struggling in the water. Time after time, he would lift up his thin, creaky old body, catch the insect gently in his hand, and carry it to the safety of a nearby plant. The minute he settled down again, the same thing would happen.

His fellow monks, who also went off every day to meditate alone in the rocky Tibetan countryside, noticed what he was doing. Some of them became quite concerned. How could the old lama get any meditating done when all his time was spent plucking tiny insects from the placid pool? As Tibetan Buddhists, they also recognized the wisdom in saving the life of any sentient being, no matter how tiny. But still, some of them wondered if the old monk should stop meditating by the pond and move somewhere where there were fewer distractions.

One day several of them finally approached him to give their opinions and advice. "Wouldn't it be better," one asked, "if you could meditate undisturbed during the day? That way you would find perfect enlightenment more quickly and would then be able to free all living beings from the ocean of conditioned existence."

"If you want to meditate by the pond," another suggested, "why don't you do so with your eyes closed?"

"How," one of the youngest monks asked, "can you hope to develop perfect tranquility and deep diamond-like concentration if you keep hopping up and down all day long?"

The wise old lama listened quietly. Finally he bowed and spoke. "I'm sure my meditation would be deeper and more productive if I sat unmoved all day, just as you say my friends. But how can an old worthless one like myself, who has vowed again and again to devote this lifetime, and all his lives, to serving and liberating others, just sit with closed eyes and hardened heart, praying and intoning the altruistic mantra of Great Compassion, while right before my very eyes helpless creatures are drowning?"

To that simple humble question, none of the other monks could find an answer.

When we open our eyes and look around us, we see that many of the planet's creatures are suffering, and need our attention. Some men and women, with beautifully soft hearts, are particularly sensitive to the suffering of helpless animals. I know animal rescue people who go out daily to feed homeless dogs and cats. They spend their own money to take in these animals, who they neuter and spay before trying to find them good homes. This requires enormous effort. Some dog lovers volunteer at shelters where there are always needy dogs who are living in cages, waiting to be adopted; the absence of exercise increases the suffering of these animals, so volunteer dog walkers are particularly appreciated. There are also groups that rescue farm animals such as horses and donkeys and goats that are about to be destroyed often because they are too old to work. Some people work with organizations like the Audubon Society to help birds. Others concentrate their efforts on contributing time and money to organizations that are trying to preserve natural habitats. Helping animals who can't help themselves is a time honored way to do the work of a Bodhisattva and practice loving-kindness and compassion. In Tibet, it is said that these practices reverberate back, bestowing manifold blessings. Tibetan lamas teach that saving lives helps extend your own and enhances your health and vitality.

Sharon Tracy, a Buddhist who lives in New York, says that about ten years ago, she spent a weekend in Woodstock with her spiritual teacher; after she left the teacher, she was driving in a car with a friend when she spotted some poor dead creature by the side of the road. Because she had just left her teacher's presence, she said she was wide open to the experience. Suddenly she was aware of a keen sense of empathy for the suffering of all animals everywhere. For a moment, she knew what they were feeling. Sharon said that she turned to her friend, and described what she was experiencing. Her friend said, "I'm not feeling that, and I'm glad I'm not feeling that."

That day marked a real turning point in her life. Since then Sharon has devoted much of her time to aiding helpless animals. She has rescued countless cats and dogs and found them homes. She keeps several animals with severe physical problems in her apartment, where she cares for them. Using her own financial resources, she works to get as many of the dogs and cats she encounters spayed and neutered. Each evening, she drives around Brooklyn to deserted spots where feral cats congregate; there she leaves food. Before returning home, she drives to a cemetery where several wild dogs live in order to leave them food. There is a large dog living there whom she has been unsuccessful in capturing for more than ten years. Just last week, she was able to catch another of the dogs, a young female. This dog, whom she named Sunshine, is currently living in a veterinarian's office getting healthy enough to be placed in a permanent home.

Sharon says that in some ways, although this is not what she intended, this caretaking has become her spiritual practice. Unfortunately, it also makes it impossible for her to do other things she would like to. For example, she would like to make a pilgrimage to Nepal to study, but she can't. As she says, "There are all these guys waiting to be fed here."

LEARNING FROM ALL CREATURES, GREAT AND SMALL

I have a friend who declares that his relationship with his dog gives him the most perfect win/win scenario in his life. I understand because I also have a relationship with a dog, a large white sheepdog named Chandi. What joy! What love! How good for my blood pressure! Spending time with my dog is such a simple, boyish relaxed pleasure.

When we connect with the pets who consent to share our homes, not only do we feel accepted and loved, we also feel comforted and even understood. One woman recently told me that her cat has become an important part of her piano practice. Whenever she is working and concentrating on a difficult piece of music, her cat comes and sits on the piano bench with her as if to give support. A young couple I know has been going through a difficult time lately because of a stressful financial situation. They say that when they get home in the evening, playing with their two kittens is what allows them to unwind and keep from snapping at each other. Animals seem to have a definite and healing presence. They help us connect beneath the level of our own intellectual constructs. Our dog friends help us to cool out, to play, and to just take a walk; our cat friends come and sit like cosmic queens on our lap, showing us how to just be.

I realized one day that I might have gone over the top in my feelings for Chandi. I was driving to Western Massachusetts, and the dog was with me; when I looked in the rearview mirror, I could see Chandi's big serene face staring back. I was so happy. All was right with the world. *I'm driving Chandi,* I thought, *my life has meaning.* I remembered how I used to feel when my late teacher, the Dzogchen master Nyoshul Khenpo, would come from Bhutan to visit, and I would drive him around to show him the northeastern United States. My feeling of blissful contentment was very similar. In my car, driving around, being in the presence of Nyoshul Khenpo and Chandi felt so similar; I experienced the same kind of inner delight—a joyful sense of the good fortune of serving. *Am I crazy or what?* I thought to myself. *Is there no difference between my relationship with a holy Tibetan lama and my dog?* Then I realized that what I was responding to was the sense of total presence, peaceful joy, and unconditional love that Chandi emanates, and simultaneously evokes in me—not unlike what my own spiritual master evoked.

In India, when seekers make pilgrimages to revered gurus or sacred sites, they call the experience "darshan." "Darshan" means viewing or entering the presence of the sacred. "Presence" is the operative word. Nature is all about presence. When we see a great wild animal such as a lion, a tiger, an elephant, or a giraffe, even in a zoo, we are struck by its awesome presence. When we visit the Grand Canyon or a sylvan lake, we know we're in the presence of something greater than ourselves. Anyone who has ever climbed a mountain remembers what it feels like to scramble above the tree line and feel a whole new sense of grandeur, space, and freedom.

Many people say that when they are in nature, they feel closer to the sacred; they are in God's country, so to speak. I know a woman named Naomi who is an ardent nature lover and "birder." She says that viewing little birds through binoculars brings her a moving sense of intimacy and connectedness with nature, and hence with herself. For her birdwatching is an excellent mindfulness meditation practice. Describing this, she says, "We walk through the world, and fortunately there are often little brown birds around us, but they seem meaningless; we're so busy we don't really notice them. Then when they are in their natural environment, and we stop and carefully watch how they move, live, and relate to each other, we can see the precious detail that the creative force bestows on every living thing.

"Looking at birds, and any animal in nature, brings us closer to our own essential self, our own purity. Puffins, for example, will sometimes fly as much as a hundred miles out to sea to get fish to feed their babies. When I see something like that, I'm touched by the innocence; I'm reminded that things in nature are simpler and more basic."

Nature in all its forms is impressive, but it's not always filled with cute, cuddly, furry creatures. Sometimes it's just frightening; other times it can seem violent or repulsive. For some people, the unpredictable quality of the natural world is very scary. Many of us are frightened by spiders, snakes, and other creepy crawly things; some people won't take a step, no matter how well the trail is marked, because it seems so overpowering and frightening.

There is a Tibetan term, the "drala principle," which speaks to what we feel most deeply about nature. "Drala" means "beyondness" or "beyond otherness." "Drala" is beyond dualism or conflict; it's so much bigger than we are that it speaks to a largeness that is beyond our full comprehension or understanding. The spirit of nature is a good example of drala; Mother Nature is a personification of drala. When we connect to nature, or the elements of nature—fire, water, earth, air—we connect to the drala principle. When we throw a paper airplane into the air, we connect to the drala of the air. In Tibet, people write prayers on cloth flags and hang them out to flap in the breeze. In this way, they use the unseen vibrations of the drala's voices to carry their prayerful wishes into the cosmos. I was amazed the first time I saw long lines of these colorful prayer flags strung so high up on wires and ropes above perilous mountain passes; it seemed impossible that anyone could have managed to negotiate the climb that was necessary to hang them up.

Tibetans also put prayer wheels into streams to harness the power of the water element so that even while the devout are sleeping, their prayers can be going forth to bless the water, the fish, and all the other creatures. To connect to the drala by using the element of earth, many Tibetans carve mantras on stones. These "mani stones," as they are called, are often piled up until they become long walls of mantras. Sometimes they too are put into streams so that the mantras can be carried along on water.

When we garden or arrange flowers, we are connecting to the drala; when we walk in the woods, or swim in a natural body of water, we are connecting to the drala. These connections we make with the natural world help us heal and grow spiritually.

I always love it when I go to Hawaii to teach. The weather is always great, and I love the lush beauty of the islands, beaches, and beautiful fish. It's an awesome natural drala experience— everything from a volcano park with steam hissing out of the crater as you stand there, to snorkeling and swimming, moving like a fish among the beautiful tropical and slow moving, ancient, behemoth sea turtles.

A couple of years ago my friend Barbara, founder of the Buddhist Peace Park on the Big Island, suggested that I go with her to do a little exploring of the islands. We took her grandson Blake, who was about six at the time, and we went to the southernmost tip of the Hawaiian chain. We drove as far as we could and then left the car and walked over the sharp volcanic rock at the edge of the shore—all the way out to the tippy-tip of the Big Island, the last piece of land sticking out to the south in the vast Pacific Ocean. It is a remarkable site, a real power point. There, we sat down on little foam rubber cushions.

The ground there is covered with lava rock; I remember looking down and being amazed at the way the hot lava from a nearby volcano had spilled over, flowed down, and hardened in place to form the ground at the edge of the sea. I had the feeling that we were sitting out in the middle of the infinite blue Pacific. On that point, water crashes and rushes in from both east and west. It felt windy and wild even though the temperature was still warm and balmy. I was overwhelmed by the sense of nature's power and exquisitely aware of the energy of the infinite sea, sky, wind, volcano, and the igneous rock beneath us.

Little Blake was excitedly scampering around like a mountain goat—and not without our becoming concerned and anxious, I might add. We tried to get him to simply sit with us for a bit and take in the view, but he wanted to run around.

Finally, Blake said, "Lama, can we call the local gods?"

I said, "Why not?" Who was I to know more than a local boy?

So we did some chants together, and I performed some "mudras"—hand gestures of invocation and prayerful communication. Suddenly, as though on cue, a school of dolphins appeared, powerfully arching and cresting above the waves. I was impressed to say the least. I would have to say, however, that although Blake loved the spectacle, he took it in stride.

For a moment, we all felt as though we had indeed been able to summon the local deities in the form of creatures of the sea; I think we all felt deeply connected to the free-spirited creatures, who jumped and dived for our benefit. When the wave crests turned into leaping silver schools of dolphins, it was as if Mother Nature's face miraculously appeared where before there was nothing but sky. This was like encountering the drala face to face. I have never forgotten it. Now, whenever I make prayers and mudra gestures, I still see those silver seraphs swimming before me.

The invisible infinite has to take form in some way so that we can relate to it. Perhaps this is how the invisible formless, most high, manifests in Hawaii. If we were in the Amazon, it might be the jaguar. In the Rockies, it might be the golden eagle; in the Delaware Water Gap it might be a red hawk and in the Himalayas, a snow leopard, or even a yeti.

Most of us have experienced times when we have been able to lose ourselves in the power and wonder of nature. You don't have to go to the Hawaiian Islands to feel connected to nature and feel the intense energy of the universe. There may even be such a place in your own neighborhood. I know for certain that there is a place within you.

Sometimes you have to make a little effort to connect to nature, but it's always worth it. I'm often shocked when I'm on public beaches early in the morning or after six on a summer evening. Typically the crowds are gone, and one is much more conscious of the primordially wild beauty of the sea and sand. If I'm in Martha's Vineyard in the summer, I sometimes go down to Menemsha Bay to watch the sunset. There, the beach is always filled with people, and as the sun goes down, everyone bows westward, cheers, and positively loses his or her sense of propriety; for a brief moment, even the adults become like kids again. Being with a bunch of people who are uninhibitedly cheering the sun is a great experience.

Nature is healing; its silence is comforting and soothing. Nature can also help heal our relationships. Try taking a walk in the woods with a friend or romantic partner. Bring along a little picnic lunch or at least something to drink. Notice your surroundings, pay close attention to the sounds and the movements of the birds and other little creatures. See how much simpler things appear, and how much easier it is to connect with each other. Try spending a specific portion of a day together in nature practicing Noble Silence as a way of opening to deeper forms of communications.

Today more than ever, we see that no one is able to be entirely isolated. We are all citizens of planet earth. What we do today influences the ozone layer, the rain forest, the children, and the future. We all need to develop greater vision and deeper ecological understanding. Let's save the planet for our children as well as the whales.

IMPROVE YOUR KARMA AND EARTH'S KARMA— OUTER PRACTICES

I recently saw an advertisement that Home Depot had placed in a newspaper. It announced that the chain of superstores had adopted an environmental wood purchasing practice and had committed itself to stop selling products made from the trees in old growth forests in environmentally sensitive areas. The ad said that Home Depot considered the cutting down of such trees barbaric. I thought "barbaric" was an interesting and appropriate choice of words. Obviously Home Depot has realized that it is wise to protect the trees and the forests, and that it will ultimately prove to be good business as well as good sense. The entire fragile ecosystem is our home, after all. It will be hard to replace or even just replenish it.

It's incumbent on all of us to try to find ways of approaching our home planet with greater respect and less barbaric attitudes. We have to start somewhere, no matter how small our actions may appear to be. I'm sure we all have our own list of things that we can do to help the earth and its inhabitants. Here are some suggestions (feel free to add your own):

❄ Plant a tree, a garden, or even a few plants.

❄ Conserve water.

❄ Don't use a car when it's not necessary; become accustomed to walking or riding a bicycle at least some of the time.

❄ Find less toxic ways to handle insect infestations. (I'm told that ants, for example, are repelled by bay leaves.)

❄ Don't kill any creature unnecessarily.

❄ Try to avoid buying or using products that harm any beings, either in their production or application.

❄ Recycle bottles, cans, plastics, and paper.

❄ Find alternatives to wearing fur.

❄ Eat less meat (Even if you don't want to become a vegetarian, cutting back on meat consumption can make a difference).

❄ Cut back on fish as a meat substitute. (The seas also need our help.)

❋ Become more aware of practices that are damaging animals and may ultimately harm us as well (the use of hormones in farming, and the cruel slaughter of ducks to provide feathers and down, for example).

❋ Purchase nontoxic cleaning agents. Try using vinegar and baking soda to clean, and Bon Ami to scrub.

❋ Conserve electricity.

❋ Be aware of the suffering of laboratory animals and petition universities, drug companies, and research centers to look for wiser ways.

❋ Try to buy organic fruits and vegetables to reduce the use of pesticides.

❋ Become aware of the ways that certain kinds of factory farming and genetic engineering of food can harm the environment, and incorporate that information into your purchasing.

MEDITATING THROUGH THE SEASONS— INNER PRACTICE

Almost thirty years ago, after my first trip to India, my girlfriend Tina and I spent a summer living in semi-retreat in a national forest on the slopes of Mount Shasta in northern California. We had a tent, but since it never seemed to rain, we used it mainly to store things, while we slept outside. From the high slopes where we sat, we could see both sunrise and sunset, so we meditated every morning at dawn and every evening as it gradually grew dark.

I remember one morning I was off by myself, sitting under a tree, wrapped in a maroon woolen cape that Tina had made for me. I was sitting in meditation with my eyes closed, following the breath at my nostrils instead of poking my nose into anyone else's business; I was just enjoying the glorious morning moment. But then I felt a gentle touch nibbling at my left shoulder. Like a good meditator, I kept my eyes closed, and let it be. I wondered what it was. Maybe a mosquito? My mind became even quieter. Then again I noticed that the touch at my shoulder had grown slightly more insistent, turning into a veritable tug. Very quietly and slowly, I turned my head, opened my eyes, and discovered that I was staring straight into the beautiful eyes of a large doe. What was this? Maybe it was my animal ally or totem. Maybe it was a friend from another life and another mountain. We shared a moment locked in each other's gaze. Neither of us were scared or startled. It was absolutely lovely. Then the deer slowly straightened up and trotted gracefully into the deep woods. Was this a dream? This special visitation blessed my whole day—my whole week. I felt as if I had sat with the local gods. I can still see those brown doe eyes.

The great Tibetan yogi, Milarepa, lived his entire life outdoors, meditating on the mountains and in the many caves in the Tibetan countryside. "Nature," he sang in one of his spontaneous songs, "is the only book I need to read."

Meditating in nature is a beautiful way to make us more aware of the connection between our own Buddha-ness, our Buddha-nature, and nature as a whole. The Buddha meditated in the forest and along the roadside. As we know, he realized perfect enlightenment while sitting under a tree. Here are four ideas for seasonal meditations to help you on your own path of awakening.

SPRING—FLOWER MEDITATION

Most of us have seen photographs of cherry blossom season in Japan. When I lived there, I discovered that plum blossoms arrive even earlier, usually in February, as a signal that winter does not last forever. Several times in this country, I've been in Washington, D.C., just in time to see cherry blossoms herald another spring. What good luck!

Spring is a time of rebirth. We can welcome it in by praying and meditating in a garden that is beginning to bud. In New England, I sometimes see the little purple crocuses pushing through while there is still snow on the ground. Then come the daffodils, finally the tulips. What blooms first in the gardens in your part of the world?

Spring is an appropriate time to do a mindfulness meditation centered on flower arranging. In Japan, the Zen art of flower arranging is known as "Kado"—the Way (or Path) of Flowers, or "ikebana," which translates as pond flower. Literally speaking, when we practice Kado, we should let go of the Western notion of "arranging." Rather, we should approach the flowers in a meditative state of mind so that they reveal their own nature. Then we won't have to arrange them according to any preconceived pattern, but can "feel" how they want and wish to be placed.

The flowers that you choose to arrange in the spring will, of course, depend on where you live. Here in the Northeast, we have apple blossoms, cherry blossoms, pussy willows, and mountain laurel, to name just a few. Of course if you don't have access to flowers in their natural habitat, you can choose any kind of flower or greenery from a florist. Whatever flowers you decide on, the idea is to work with them mindfully and reverently. Flower arranging is like making a sacred altar.

Stay in the immediacy of the present moment, and choose your blossoms carefully one by one. Look at the flower or piece of greenery. Get a feeling of where it was grown, and how it blossomed. Cut off the bottom of the stems individually—carefully, attentively, lovingly. Find a container, whether it be a crystal vase, a ceramic bowl, or a simple metal pot, that suits the blossoms. Put water in the vase. Arrange your flowers carefully, one by one. Remain in the moment, and don't rush. In Japan, flowers are often placed asymmetrically in order to achieve a fully three-dimensional effect. Sometimes a flower is so heartbreakingly beautiful that it seems meant to be in a vase alone.

When you are finished, place your flowers somewhere where they can be viewed. If you have an altar, you might want to place them there. See if you can find a spot where the flowers can become the focal point.

When I first stayed in a Buddhist monastery in Bodh Gaya, we were encouraged not to throw out the blossoms when they began to droop. Instead it was suggested that we let the flowers wilt and die, one by one; we would observe the petals falling and then meditate on the transient beauty and impermanence of all that lives.

SUMMER—WATER-GAZING MEDITATION

Ramakrishna was a great nineteenth-century Hindu spiritual teacher in Bengal. As a young man, he practiced different disciplines including Islam and Christianity. Because of his intense mystical and spiritual experiences, he was able to see and recognize the validity and connectedness of all spiritual traditions.

One of the things that I always remember about Ramakrishna's teachings is that he told his followers that whenever they saw water, they should meditate. What did he mean by that? Did he mean that we should sit cross-legged every time we turn on the faucet or even see falling rain? It's a funny image, but I don't think that's what he meant. I think he meant that we can use water to remind ourselves of the inner lake of peace or the flowing nature of all things. Water—whether it be a waterfall, the ocean's waves, a puddle, a swimming pool, a puddle, a raindrop, or even a teardrop—reflects back on the pure, crystalline, refreshing nature of inner spirit. Water represents the innate clarity of mind; it soothes and quenches the soul.

In the summer, I love to meditate by the side of a body of water, whether it be a lake, a stream, or the ocean. But you can do it anywhere. Even a fish tank will do. Not everyone is fortunate enough to live or work near a body of pure, clean water, but I'm always astonished at how many large cities have fountains and fishponds in unlikely places. Even midtown Manhattan has a pocket park in the East 50s with an ersatz, but very satisfying, waterfall. My brilliant copy editor tells me that her sister-in-law meditated there when she was in labor.

Sit by water.
Count your breaths as if they are waves.
In breath . . . One
Out breath . . . Two
In breath . . . Three
Let the regular wavelike motion of the breath
wash away all your cares.
Let it carry you home.
Float on the breath of the present moment.
Let the water meditate for you.
Flow with it.

FALL—AN ANALYTICAL MEDITATION

When many people think of meditation, they seem to think primarily of meditations that involve resting the mind. Yet there is another kind of meditation that involves using the intellect and discriminating faculties of the mind to analyze reality.

The season of fall represents passage and the beautiful poignancy and transitory nature of life itself. What better time to use meditation and the powers of your mind to contemplate the laws of karma—cause and effect—in your own life?

Start with today. Look at how your day progressed from beginning to end. Be very detail-oriented and specific. Consider the particular events that occurred. What went wrong? What went right? Can you see how karma unfolded? Take your time. Apply your best analytical thinking to it.

You can use this technique to analyze anything. Pick your subject and maintain it. Contemplate an important relationship in your life. What have you done to create the relationship that exists? How about the last, week, month, or year of your life? Sometimes it's very easy to see the interwoven karmic connections; other times it takes work and effort. Don't back away from this analytical meditation if you become unhappy with what you are seeing. Remember this kind of meditation is a way to gain greater awareness into the nature of reality—what is—in your life and in general. Try to directly perceive and comprehend the effects of karma.

WINTER—WALKING MEDITATION

Connect to the experience of winter with a walking meditation. All you need is some comfortable clothing and a place where you can walk undisturbed for twenty or thirty minutes—even if it's back and forth in your yard or on your block. Take the dog if you have one. I always do. The minute I reach for my hooded parka, Chandi runs to the door.

If there is snow on the ground, it can be fun to walk where it crunches under your feet. Many people, myself included, like walking on beaches and boardwalks in winter weather. If you live in warmer climates, these can be good places for walking in the cooler temperatures of winter.

The path is right beneath your feet
Make a conscious step on it.
Then another. And now another.
Count your steps.
Right footstep . . . count one.
Left foot . . . count two.
Right foot . . . three.
Left foot . . . four.
Walking along the path to enlightenment . . .
Connecting with yourself
by just doing what you are doing, one hundred percent.
One step at a time.

CHAPTER EIGHT

Joyfully Crazy and

Wonderful Awakenings

I did toy with the idea of doing a cook-book. . . . The
recipes were to be the routine ones: how to make dry
toast, instant coffee, hearts of lettuce and brownies. But as
an added attraction, at no extra charge, my idea was to
put a fried egg on the cover. I think a lot of people who
hate literature but love fried eggs would buy it if the price
was right.

—Groucho Marx

There is so much joyous wisdom in humor, isn't there?
Laughing has its own uplifting energy, which can become even more spiritual when its shared. As seekers,
can we find the wisdom buried in this silly Groucho
Marx quote? It's funny, it's ironic, and it's absurd. Just
like life!

Recently I was on a beach in Brooklyn, New York,
with a friend of mine. We were sitting on our towels like
beached Buddhas staring out at the water, over our sun-
burnt bellies. To our right was a long, impressive jetty

made of rocks stretching out into the water. Suddenly a human form appeared unexpectedly around the jetty, at first swimming horizontally across the horizon and then into shore. It was a large, older man in a skimpy red bathing suit wearing a black-and-white polka dot shower cap—not a bathing cap—on his head. When he reached shore, he carefully picked a spot and laid down on the sand. But he wasn't finished with his routine. He proceeded to roll around and around, shimmying up and down on the sand, resembling a huge, amiable brown bear scratching himself on a large oak tree. He looked like he was having a whale of a great time. I should add that as outlandish as his behavior appeared, he also seemed quite sane and composed, as well as completely unself-conscious. He was clearly doing this for some purpose. (Aren't we all usually doing things for a purpose?) When he was covered with sand, head to toe—even his shower cap—he plunged back into the water and swam back around the jetty and away.

What was he doing? Was this just one scene of some bet he was trying to win, or a self-imposed task he'd dreamed up for himself while under the influence? My friend and I decided that most likely this was some health regimen that he had worked out for himself. It seemed to be working, for he was obviously a strong, physically fit man. *What,* I asked myself, *could we all learn from watching his routine?*

For me, a lesson emerged from this man's complete lack of self-consciousness. It was positively liberating to see him doing his thing, totally immersed in his own absurd antics. Watching him was a little like being entertained by a clown—at the circus, on television, or even on a street corner. When clowns frolic, and juggle, and mime, don't they also appear completely unself-conscious? But clown-like performers are acting for the benefit of their audiences. The swimmer on the Brooklyn beach was genuinely unself-conscious. He was doing what he was doing with complete focus, for his own benefit, whatever that might be. When he plopped himself on the sand, a few feet away from our towels, he knew that people would look at him. Short of covering our eyes, we had no choice. Yet he didn't care if people found his antics incomprehensible. This guy was totally oblivious; it was as if the beach were deserted.

In Tibet there is a spiritual tradition that is seen as having a connection with such incomprehensible behavior. Known as "crazy wisdom," it is embodied by enlightened vagabonds and an entire lineage of male yogis and female yoginis who throughout the centuries have behaved in ways that people didn't always understand. Some of these masters, for example, spent their lives meditating in mountaintop aeries like eagles, descending into valley villages only occasionally for alms, as bedraggled as wild animals. There are stories of Tibetan masters who vowed never to sleep indoors; masters who rarely, if ever, slept or wore clothes, even in the frigid Himalayas; masters who answered whatever they were asked by repeating exactly what was said to them. A student might question such a master saying, "How are you today, holy teacher?" and his teacher's response would be, "How are you today, holy teacher?" Such a master would often do this no matter what the question. "How are you today, crazy wastrel?" would be answered in kind: "How are you today, crazy wastrel?" Among Tibetans, teaching tales abound, even today, about some of these most colorful and unique spiritual practitioners.

The salient point to remember here is the wisdom, not just the craziness, for spiritual teachings lead us to a higher form of sanity. The "crazy wisdom" of Tibetan masters reveals a heightened form of lucidity that is able to cut through the superficial layers of social convention and customs. It is based on brilliant insight into how things actually are, as opposed to how they appear. Crazy wisdom shows a direct, raw appreciation for life as well as a cosmic sense of humor. It is what the Sufi author Idries Shah has dubbed "the wisdom of the idiots."

Tibet's inspired upholders of crazy wisdom have typically disdained speculative metaphysics and institutionalized religious forms in favor of a style that can loosely be described as "letting it all hang out." These divine madmen prefer to celebrate the unconditional freedom of enlightenment through divinely inspired foolishness. Their frequent refusal to pay homage to external religious forms and moral systems reminds us of the inherent freedom and sacredness that can be found in authentic being. This freedom often extends beyond conventional piety and morality. An enlightened Tibetan meditation master of old, Choying Rangdrol, spent his life in meditation on a floor mat, wearing only a loose sheepskin coat. He said, "Yogis want and need nothing other than the immutable nature of authentic being." Milarepa, Tibet's enlightened poet, once sang, "My lineage is crazy: crazed by devotion, crazed by truth, crazy about Dharma."

One of my favorite crazy wisdom stories is about an Indian tantric adept named Saraha, who lived in the third century. It was often the custom in India at that time for fearlessly unorthodox yogis to form relationships with women from lower castes. In this way, they helped demonstrate the possibility of freedom from concepts, such as the rigid caste system. When Saraha, who was already considered mad, went off to the jungle with a lower caste teenage servant girl, village tongues wagged.

Saraha's consort, who genuinely admired the crazy-wise master, told him that he could persevere in his meditation and yogic practices, while she would take care of daily chores and necessities. Saraha was so intensely engaged with meditation that he rarely showed any interest in food, other than to eat what was placed in front of him. One day, however, he suddenly made a strange request. "Bring me radish curry!" he said.

The young woman took great time and care to prepare the curry exactly as she thought Saraha would wish. After busying herself in food preparation, she finally brought him a plate of woven leaves, upon which was placed a generous portion of curry and some buffalo milk yogurt. Placing it in front of him she noticed that Saraha was in deep meditation, travelling to places she could not imagine. So she left him sitting there.

Twelve years passed, and Saraha did not move. All the while, the young woman stayed with him.

Suddenly, Rip Van Winkle fashion, Saraha stood up. "Where," he asked, "is the radish curry I requested?"

Saraha's consort was astonished. "Crazy master," she said. "the radish season has come and gone many times. For twelve long years, you've sat in meditation, like a radish yourself—silently stuck in the earth. Now you still want curry? You call this meditation—holding onto a radish all these years!" Thus she awakened him.

And then the young woman, like the true dakini she really was, proved her own capacity for insightful wisdom. "Sitting cross-legged," she said, "that's not true meditation. Living isolated away from family and friends, that's not genuine solitude. Authentic solitude means parting from discursive thoughts and dualistic concepts. But you've spent twelve years sitting, mentally holding an illusory radish! What kind of yogi are you anyway?"

It is said that due to the clarity of her insight, Yogi Saraha was immediately enlightened.

The pioneering Tibetan lama, Chogyam Trungpa Rinpoche, once described crazy wisdom as an innocent state of mind that has the quality of early morning—fresh, sparkling, and completely awake. He also described the principle of crazy wisdom as the starting point for an exciting spiritual journey, not just as its fruit.

The great Chogyam Trungpa was no stranger to crazy wisdom. There is an often told story about the day back in the

1970s, when the wandering American seeker and holy man Bhagwan Das was visiting Trungpa in Boulder. Trungpa was well known for his capacity to handle liquor; he and Bhagwan sat down together for a drink one night. And Trungpa promptly began literally to drink Bhagwan Das under the table. As the evening progressed, Bhagwan Das became so blotto that he didn't know or care what happened next. Trungpa took this opportunity to free Bhagwan Das from what some thought might perhaps be his greatest attachment—his long, matted, holy man beard and longer hair. When Bhagwan woke up the next morning, shorn like a sheep, he was furious. But what could he do? The crazy wisdom master, his teaching completed, was gone, and Bhagwan Das was left to deal with his own feelings and to take what he could from the irascible Tibetan master's teaching.

HOLY FOLLY

Buddhism isn't alone in its reverence for holy fools and the pure state of mind that they represent. Throughout the centuries, across the world, the archetype of the holy fool has been identified with the spiritual quest and the search for truth and meaning. The Greek and Russian Orthodox religions, for example, both have a tradition of "holy folly." In the Byzantine traditions, pilgrims, monks, and other seekers sometimes took eccentricity to the brink of madness and beyond. Like the Tibetan holy men, many practiced extreme asceticism, travelling nearly naked in the dead of winter, frequently casting off socially acceptable behavior along with their clothing. They were giving it all to God and leaving it all up to God, as it were, in unimaginable acts of self-sacrifice and renunciation.

A well-known Anglo Saxon heroic legend concerns the search for the Holy Grail and the Arthurian knight, Percival (Parcifal), whose very name means innocent fool. As the story evolves, the young and naive Percival leaves his home and, through a series of chance happenings, encounters several knights from King Arthur's court, and finally meets King Arthur himself. At first, there is no way that Percival would have been considered "knight material." However, as much because of his innocent belief as anything else, Percival is able to shock everyone by conquering the formidable Red Knight. In so doing, Percival becomes a knight.

As a knight, Percival's primary quest is to find the Holy Grail, the chalice that Jesus Christ is said to have used when sharing the Last Supper with his disciples. Percival's search takes him to the castle of the Fisher King, a wounded leader living within a wasted land that reflects the King's depressed and crippled state. The legend within the Grail Kingdom is that the king can be healed and his kingdom restored if a completely pure and innocent fool enters the kingdom and asks the right question. Then and only then will the king be healed and the Holy Grail be found. Percival, of course, is the holy fool. But even Percival's childlike innocence and pure view of the world has been distorted for he has been socialized and taught by others not to ask questions. So even though the holy fool, Percival, frames a question in his heart and mind, he fails to ask it, and thus fails to heal the king.

Many of us today walk around with too many answers. The right question, of course, can often be the key that unlocks the universe.

CONNECTING TO YOUR OWN
HOLY FOOL

Within each of us there is a holy fool, the soul who is staring out at a spiritual quest with eyes filled with wonder and awe. This is the incorruptible, eternal inner child who symbolizes trust, innocence, and purity. We all started our lives as holy fools, but for most of us it takes spiritual effort to stay connected to the little Buddha within. Still, we can reawaken that little Buddha at any age.

Friends who know such things tell me that in the tarot deck, the card for the Fool symbolizes the beginning of a journey of adventure and discovery. No one can begin a journey of discovery without tapping into the holy fool within. We can't move forward unless we access our innate purity and see the world afresh with the innocence of a child. As adults too often our vision is obscured by our jaded preconceptions and projections, which act like veils over our eyes.

We all know the story of the emperor who needs a new wardrobe and hears about an exceptionally gifted tailor. When the emperor visits the tailor he is suitably impressed by what the tailor tells him and orders a new set of the clothing, which is to be the most expensive and magnificent in the world. On the day the clothing arrives, with great fanfare the tailor opens a box, which is totally empty, and helps the emperor try on the fantasy clothing. "Look," the tailor says, pointing to air. "Notice the fine rubies on the lapels." First the emperor, buck naked, parades around his palace while his entire court oohs and aahs. Finally the emperor walks down the street so his people can admire his finery. The people clap; they shout their approval. "Look at the emperor!" They scream, "Doesn't he look beautiful in his amazing clothing?" Finally in the back of the crowd, the small voice of a child is heard. "But mommy," the child says, "the emperor is naked."

The fool is the child who knows instinctively when the emperor is naked, no matter what he is being told by society. He's not burdened by concepts or preconceived ideas about reality. He sees what is, and he's free to take chances. The fool is free to say what's on his mind. Medieval courts frequently had a fool or jester, who was one of the only people free to speak his mind to the sovereign and still keep his head.

Most of us are quite removed from such profound freedom; we are so layered and encrusted with socialized attitudes that we can't loosen up our habitualized inhibitions and canned opinions. We have so much invested in achieving a certain status, in being part of things, in fitting into the prevailing zeitgeist and its mores and values. We worry about appearances, image, and what people will think of us. We see mostly what we have been taught to see. We like the movies, books, art, theater, and dance that critics tell us to like. We eat at restaurants that have received good reviews and word of mouth. We admire the people who we are told have celebrity or status. Sometimes, in fact, it feels as though all of life is filtered through someone else's opinions. We sample everything through someone else's eyes before we experience or feel it for ourselves. Much of this comes from having been monitored and given feedback from our parents. This is a developmental issue from early childhood. Later we struggle for acceptance from our peers, and soon after from people who hold our romantic interest. Every generation has its own ideas about what is acceptable behavior, even when rebelling and being nonconformist. Many kids today pierce their navels and various body parts. In my time it was the hair thing—beards, moustaches, sideburns, and long hair.

Crazy wisdom consistently reminds us to feel what we truly feel; it reminds us to stay in touch with our own inner values. It reminds us to be genuine and sensitive—to stay in touch with the open-eyed fool within, the childlike inner soul unencumbered by socialization and convention.

The Dharma encourages us to learn to look at things with fresh vision, as if for the first time. That's why Trungpa Rinpoche, the great crazy wisdom master, titled his collection of poetry *First Thought, Best Thought*. The little Buddhas within us all have untarnished eyes, capable of seeing truth. If we can access that perspective we will bring balance and joy to our lives instead of always taking a rational and cerebral approach. We can tap into an inexhaustible inner well of spontaneous delight.

A story: Not that long ago, Dave was having lunch with some friends in a restaurant where he often eats. He ordered a bowl of chicken soup. When it came, Dave looked down and saw that he had no spoon. He laughed and he began to tell his friends a joke he had heard about a wise and learned Eastern European rabbi of old. It seems that this rabbi believed in the wisdom we can attain through personal experience, and preferred to teach by showing rather than telling. One day the rabbi and his wife walked into his favorite restaurant and ordered his favorite meal, mushroom barley soup. The waiter put the soup down in front of the rabbi and went back to the kitchen. The rabbi was very hungry and wanted to eat, but when he looked down, he realized the waiter had failed to give him a spoon. *Ah, an opportunity for a lesson.* He waited patiently until the waiter appeared again, and when he did, he said, "My friend, would you please taste this soup?"

The waiter said, "Oh, I'm very busy right now. I don't have time to taste soup. Besides my boss would be furious if he saw me eating my customer's food."

"Please," the rabbi said, "I beg of you. I just want you to taste this soup. If anyone says anything, I will explain. Do this as a favor to me."

The waiter sighed, put down his tray, and went over to taste the soup. When he looked down, he realized what the rabbi was asking. Laughing, the waiter brought the rabbi a spoon.

Dave looked at his friends, and suggested they try it with the waitress. "Helen," he said to her, "come here and taste this soup."

"Oh Dave," Helen replied, "I don't have the time to taste your soup. I'm busy. What's wrong with the soup?"

"Nothing's wrong with the soup," Dave continued. "I just want you to taste it."

"Puh-lease . . ." Helen moaned. "Don't I look busy enough for you?"

"Come on. One little taste," Dave pleaded.

"Oh all right," Helen said. She came over and looked down at the table. "Oh," she said, "you have no spoon." Having said that, she shrugged, picked up the bowl in her hands and took a sip. "It tastes good to me," she said, as she walked away to wait on another customer.

The question, of course, is who is wise, and who is foolish?

In his seminal book on this subject, appropriately entitled *Crazy Wisdom*, Wes Nisker writes:

> "Crazy wisdom is the wisdom of the saint, the Zen master, the poet, the mad scientist, and the fool. Crazy wisdom sees that we live in a world of many illusions, that the Emperor has no clothes, and that much of human belief and behavior is ritualized nonsense. Crazy wisdom understands anti-matter and old Sufi poetry; loves paradox and puns and pie fights and laughing at politicians. Crazy wisdom flips the world upside down and backward until everything becomes perfectly clear."

FOOLISH CHOICES

Recently I talked to a woman who was going through a particularly messy divorce. "I should have known," she said. "In fact, I did know. I just didn't pay attention to what I knew." She went on to talk more about her husband, saying, "He seemed to fit the bill of the kind of man I should marry. He was successful, he was attractive, he was well educated. He had all the superficial characteristics of the kind of man I was expected to marry. But as it turns out we never really had anything in common."

Listening to this woman reminded me that sometimes when we make important decisions and choices in life, we need to consult with our own inner, and holy, fool. We need to look at our choices with a fresh eye, and ask ourselves whether we are moving in a direction that brings us closer or further away from truth, from enlightenment. We need to be certain that we are not simply trying to conform to somebody else's cookie cutter version of what life should be. Sometimes the wisest action we can take is the one that appears most bizarre and least practical to everyone around us. And yet often we feel as if all our choices are defined by what others expect.

When I went off to India right after college graduation, everyone thought I was crazy. Then, when I didn't return to America for years and years, they were quite sure of it. My dad used to say that he didn't understand how I could live for so many years "without even a pot to piss in," as he so pungently put it. The surprising sense and internal logic of my personal spiritual journey was not evident to my family and friends; I must admit that it wasn't really clear to me either at the time.

Of course it is always so much easier for all of us to apply twenty-twenty hindsight and thus discern deeper, unseen patterns and higher purposes not too obvious to the naked eye in the present moment. Looking back now, I can trace my post-college trajectory through Asia and back to the West almost as if it had been scripted, and I was only following the plotline. Then, everyone thought I was crazy; now it makes perfect sense. My mother says that it took her and my late dad "decades to get used to it." That is how outlandish and nonsensical they thought my path was. But eventually they too came to see it all differently.

Now I often remind my mother that family tradition helped shape my behavior. When I was a child, my parents, my brother, my sister, and I used to take family vacations that were essentially road trips. I fondly remember driving down to Florida along the east coast, for example—three kids in the back seat of a large 1956 DeSoto with a push-button automatic transmission and a V-8 engine. Sometimes at night, my parents would stop at a drive-in movie. My mother would fit out the back seat with pillows so that we could watch the movie until we fell asleep. One of us little kids would sleep on the back window shelf, one on the back seat, and the third on the floor.

My father had a remarkable sense of direction. Even in unfamiliar states in strange places he had never been, he seemed able to give directions to others. My mother had a slightly different approach. She would say, "Harold, let's go there," pointing to a spot on a map. My mother—whose name is Joyce—would have no idea of whether or not the place was on the way to where we were going. She never asked, "Is it on the way?" Instead she would say, "I don't know. It looks like it might be good. Let's take a chance." My father would often jokingly call her "Take-a-Chance Joyce." He would make a mock motion of sharply turning the wheel, and mimic the sound of screeching tires like in a cartoon, as if we were suddenly turning completely around and heading off in an entirely new direction. But often he followed her whims. Why not? It was a vacation. Thanks to this attitude, we saw all kinds of things that weren't on the AAA roadmap. We ate in unusual places, slept in motels that weren't on anybody's recommended list, and camped in sites that would never make any campgrounds of America guide. It was always fun.

I remember till this day a farmer we met near the Finger Lakes in upstate New York, and somewhere my mother still has some shaky 8-millimeter home movie footage of this kind man, Farmer Brown, putting me up onto his horse on the edge of his pasture. In the early fifties, it was one of Take-a-Chance Joyce's off road magical detours. What a wonderful adventure! I am wearing my first pair of shoes in that film.

My parents taught me to enjoy the freedom of approaching many experiences in life from an open point of view. They taught me that we can't always follow the tourist buses. We need to give ourselves permission to find our own way, whether it seems sensible or not. If we would genuinely find and follow what Thoreau referred to as a different drummer then we must be prepared to "step to a different beat," regardless of what society's conventions might say. There is wisdom in listening to our hearts and opening ourselves up to surprise, and the magic and mystery of life. In a world gone mad, being different enough to be regarded as crazy certainly has some virtues.

CRAZY WISDOM PRACTICE?

In a bizarre piece of synchronicity, as I was writing this, someone sent me an e-mail entitled "Elevator Antics." It smacks of crazy wisdom behavior so I'm including some of the suggestions. I wouldn't want to be mistaken for Serious Das, the serious author!

Things to Do on an Elevator

1. Crack open your briefcase or purse, and while peering inside, ask, "Got enough air in there?"

2. Meow occasionally.

3. Wear a puppet on one of your hands and use it to talk to the other passengers.

4. Listen to the elevator walls with a stethoscope.

5. Say "ding" at each floor.

6. Make noises like an explosion every time someone presses a button.

7. Stare, grinning at a friendly looking passenger, and then announce, "I have on new socks."

8. When the elevator is silent, look around and ask, "Is that your beeper?"

9. Greet everyone getting on the elevator with a warm handshake and ask each of them to call you "Admiral."

10. Hand out lollipops or sticks of gum to your fellow passengers.

Of course, I realize that none of us are going to follow these elevator instructions. But for just a few minutes, think about doing any one of them, and imagine what it would mean to be free of your inhibitions about appearing different or foolish. Visualize yourself as somebody who isn't afraid of being laughed at. What freedom it must be to be able to stop worrying about what people think!

The purpose of crazy wisdom is to help burst the bubble of our fixed opinions and expectations. As we go through the day, isn't it often the unexpected thing that happens that perks us up and gives us something different to enthuse about when we get home? We can live on the brink of the mystery of being by bringing a bit more whimsy and playfulness to our serious deliberations.

LOSING MENTAL CONSTRUCTS

When I was in Asia, several teachers told me the same story about a renowned scholar monk in ancient China. He was a teacher, and he would go from monastery to monastery carrying the weighty tomes of written sutras, Dharma teachings, and his own lectures in bags on his back along trails up and down the mountains. Needless to say, he would get very tired. One day as he was walking up a mountain path, he came upon a tiny tea shack in which an elderly woman sold tea, noodles, and rice to pilgrims and travellers.

Now over the years, the monk had received many compliments on his erudition and knowledge, and he took himself much too seriously; in fact he had become quite haughty and conceited. On this particular day, when the monk approached the tea shack, he put down all the written manuscripts that contained his lifetime of commentaries on the wisdom scriptures and asked the old woman for some tea.

"Certainly," she said, "but since you are such a learned teacher, before we have tea, we must have some Dharma."

"All of my Dharma is over there," the monk said, pointing to the many manuscripts. "Can you read, illiterate old lady?"

"What good is it if your Dharma is over there, outside of yourself?" the woman replied. "What a burden that must be."

At that moment, the monk awoke to his arrogance, realizing that carrying around all this weight was not upholding the Dharma. Instantaneously, he awoke to the fact that all the Dharma was inside himself. With tears in his eyes, he bowed to the old woman three times, saying, "I don't need my commentaries on the scriptures any more. I'm free of that heavy burden. Thank you for pointing directly to the Dharma within me. I will leave them here for you to use as firewood."

And the woman said, "Now we can have our tea."

Like the holy fool, the elderly woman along the roadside reminds us that innate truth and reality function as counterpoints to those who are still burdened with the weight of concepts and accumulated knowledge.

This is the difference between mere intellectual knowledge

and spiritual realization. That is why Lao Tzu's wise *Tao Te Ching* says, "In pursuit of the world, one gains more and more. But in pursuit of the Way one gains less and less. Loss upon loss, until at last comes rest. When nothing is undertaken, nothing remains undone."

The message is: No appointments, no disappointments.

A WISE FOOL'S MEDITATION

Let yourself go.
Totally.
Breathe in and out a few times deeply.
Drop your body, drop your persona.
Let your hair down, and let it all hang out.
Drop your mind.
Unscrew your head
and shoot it—swoosh—through the nearest hoop
(a wastebasket will do).
Take the path of least resistance,
the lazy man's way to enlightenment.
Unedit yourself.
Let the uncontrived little Buddha inside wake up
And laugh, dance, sing, and shine.

No one is watching.
It don't matter how it looks.
Go for it!
Push the envelope of sanity.
Make the leap into irrationality.
Plumb the dark side of the moon,
the far side
of the brain—

the secret side of your mysterious primordial
Being.
Become a spiritual astronaut
a Way-farer
Unfurl your heart's wings
Breathe
Dance, laugh, play
Clap your hands
Soar
Sing

CHAPTER NINE

Spiritual Alchemy—
Embracing Life's Lessons

> If you know what it means to be out in the middle of an
> ocean by yourself, in the dark, scared, then it gives you a
> feel for what every other human being is going through.
> I row an actual ocean. Other people have just as many
> obstacles to go through.
>
> —Toni Murden, First woman to row solo
> across the Atlantic Ocean

Obstacles and challenges! Life is full of them, isn't it?
Sometimes it seems as though the most difficult spiritual
challenge we have to meet is figuring out the connection between the challenges on our paths and the spiritual lessons we need to learn. Let's, for example, take a
look at what Lois, a thirty-six-year-old designer, is experiencing right now. Lois feels as though the last two
years of her life have been total hell. The first thing that
happened was that her father had two heart attacks and
open heart surgery. For a while, it looked as though he
was going to get better, but just when he seemed to be

recovering, he caught pneumonia and died. Lois, who was very close to her father, was devastated. She says that her father always made her feel protected and loved; no matter what Lois did, he was her number one supporter and cheerleader. After he died, Lois felt as though she had lost her "safety zone" and quickly fell into a serious reactive depression; all she wanted to do was withdraw from the world and remain in the safety of her own apartment.

This mood couldn't have happened at a worse time because just then there was a shake-up in Lois' company. Her immediate boss was let go, and a young woman was brought in as a replacement. Lois had no history with this woman, who seemed to have zero tolerance for Lois' fragile emotional state. In fact, Lois' new boss seemed eager to replace all of the old employees with people who were younger and had no established loyalties to the earlier regime. Lois suddenly found herself under tremendous pressure to perform at what seemed to be an almost impossible level.

Lois, who was by now totally stressed, thought her mood, which alternated between depression and anger, was about as bad as it could get. But then Lois' boyfriend announced that he wanted to end the relationship. He said that he felt as though Lois had transferred her dependence on her father onto him, and he couldn't deal with it; he also said he couldn't handle her negative attitude and that she was no longer "any fun."

"What else can go wrong?" Lois asked several of her friends. About a week later, she got her answer. Lois began to feel completely exhausted, so exhausted, in fact, that she could barely get out of bed. At first Lois blamed her fatigue on depression, but it quickly became apparent that this fatigue was different—deeper and more unyielding than anything she had ever before experienced. Something as simple as walking to the corner to buy a newspaper left her feeling depleted. When she went to a doctor, he diagnosed her malady as chronic fatigue syndrome. When she tried to take a leave of absence from work, they threatened to fire her. Lois' best friend was a lawyer so Lois was able to take legal action without it costing her a small fortune. So far, she has been able to get a two-month paid leave of absence for her illness. This has helped, but Lois knows it's just a matter of time before she will have to return to her office, and she's not sure if she will be able to do it.

Right now Lois is scared. In less than a year, she has suffered so many major losses—her father, her health, her boyfriend—one right after the other. If I were to talk to Lois and tell her that what she is going through is a valuable learning experience, she would probably have an impulse to slug me. And I would understand. Who wants to hear that the pain and suffering he or she is experiencing is part of a valuable lesson? I know I don't. Last week I stood in the rain on a busy highway with my disabled jeep waiting for AAA, late for an important appointment; I would have been infuriated if somebody had stuck his head out of the window of a passing car and yelled, "It's a lesson, Surya!" And yet I have learned that all of life's trials and tribulations bring us tremendous opportunities for spiritual learning, growth, and meaningful connection.

I know men and women who have enough spiritual intelligence and discerning wisdom to look for and find the lessons in their travails. Chuck, a forty-five-year-old salesman, says that he never took the time to figure out what he might be doing wrong in his relationships with people until his business failed, his wife left him, and his teenage children stopped speaking to him. Chuck, who had always prided himself on his practical approach to life, forced himself to look at reality—at the interconnected patterns of cause and effect. If everyone he knew was angry at him, then he couldn't escape the logical conclusion that he was doing something to alienate those around him. He was thus able to learn, change, and grow from his difficulties. In this way, he reconciled with his loved ones.

My friend Deidra, now forty-one, has recovered from the anorexia that she lived with in her teens and early twenties. She told me that the worst thing about anorexia is that it made her feel separate and alienated from those around her. During the years when she struggled the most, Deidra spent much of her psychic energy concealing her illness and trying to make it seem as though she were eating normally. She says that being a full-blown anorexic was a truly terrifying experience. Nonetheless, she is grateful for what it taught her.

Deidra says that being anorexic made her aware not only of her own vulnerability, but of the vulnerability of everyone around her. Dealing with her own emotional problems gave her greater compassion and empathy for the emotional problems of others. She says this sense of everyone's suffering has permeated her awareness, her relationships, and her experience of life itself. She would not be who she is today if she hadn't known what it was like to struggle with an illness like anorexia.

Not that long ago I read a piece on the *New York Times* op-ed page. It was by James Stockdale, a retired Navy vice admiral. Stockdale had been a prisoner of war who spent four years in solitary confinement during the Vietnam War. To help put the experience of prisoners of war in perspective, James Stockdale quoted Aleksandr Solzhenitsyn:

"And it was only when I lay there on rotting prison straw that I sensed within myself the first stirrings of good. Gradually it was disclosed to me that the line separating good and evil passes not through states, nor between classes, nor between political parties either—but right through every human heart—and through all human hearts. . . . And that is why I turn back to the years of my imprisonment and say, sometimes to the astonishment of those about me: 'Bless you prison!' "

Admiral Stockdale's piece reminded me of the stories told to me by many of the Tibetan lamas who were jailed by the

Chinese. One of them was my old friend, Lama Norlha, who now teaches in New York City as well as at Kalu Rinpoche's three-year retreat center in Wappinger Falls, New York. I first met Lama Norlha in Darjeeling in the early 1970s where we lived together in a small mountainside hermitage, and he would occasionally recount his experiences.

Back in 1959 after the Chinese invasion of Tibet, Lama Norlha was placed in a prison camp, which was really just a collection of tents on the frigid Tibetan steppes surrounded by barbed wire. Lama Norlha was there with several other Buddhist monks, tortured, hungry, cold, and unsure of whether they were going to survive. Yet he told me many times that these years as a prisoner were some of the best in his life.

Everything had been taken away from him except his spiritual brothers and his meditation practice. He realized that he had no past to return to and there was no future he could count on. All he could rely on was the present moment and the eternal truth of Dharma—as valid there as anywhere else. He realized that he could continue his spiritual practice sitting in the corner of his prison tent. I remember his saying, "I had nothing else to do or be concerned about, for all had been stripped away." This always seemed to me like a great lesson, reminding us that even in the most difficult circumstances if we summon our intentions and highest aspirations we can turn our minds to the Dharma.

Lama Norlha's time in prison ended happily when he had a dream in which his guru came to him and gave him instructions and specific directions on how to leave the prison camp without being detected. Following the dream's guidance, one night Lama Norlha and several other monks crept out under a corner of the tent, through the barbed wire enclosure, and headed for the sanctuary of India. In later life when he got quite busy as a teacher, chant leader, and temple builder, he would look back and give thanks for his years of intense meditation practice in a Chinese prison.

In his classic book *A Path with Heart,* my friend Jack Korn-field wrote:

"In difficulties, we can learn the true strength of our prac-tice. At these times, the wisdom we have cultivated and the depth of our love and forgiveness is our chief resource. To meditate, to pray, to practice, at such times can be like pouring soothing balm onto the aches of our heart. The great forces of greed, hatred, fear, and ignorance that we encounter can be met by the equally great courage of our heart.

"Such strength of heart comes from knowing that the pain that we each must bear is a part of the greater pain shared by all that lives. It is not just 'our' pain but *the* pain, and realizing this awakens our universal compassion."

THE TRUTH OF "PAIN"
AND SUFFERING

The Buddha often reminded his followers that we are all going to experience illness, unexpected difficulties, aging, and death. We are all going to experience loss. This is a reality—a true "fact of life." We are all going to have many lessons in loss and suffering; no one is exempt. All religions and spiritual traditions delve into the nature and causes of human suffering. Sitting in a restaurant this summer I heard a lovely little girl, who couldn't have been more than five, ask the woman she was with, "Mar-garet, why does God let bad things happen?" Margaret re-sponded by saying that this was a question that had also plagued her for her entire life. Why do bad things happen? Isn't that a question that plagues all of our lives?

The little girl in the restaurant appeared to be a child of

privilege, wonderfully dressed, and surrounded by a group of adults who clearly adored her and thought she was pretty special. Even so, at her young age, she was asking that age-old question. Afterward, I spoke briefly with one of the adults at the table and asked if they had any idea what specifically was disturbing the little girl. I was told that the child lived in Colorado and was very aware of the killings at Columbine High School. A question that the child often asked was why God allowed guns, bombs, and other instruments of violence.

All religious and spiritual traditions have tried to give us reasons as to why we live in an imperfect world. Many of these are buried in myths and legends that provide symbolic explanations. Here in the West, our Judeo-Christian tradition points to Adam and Eve in the Garden of Eden. When Adam and Eve followed the advice of the serpent, they lost their spot in the Garden. By giving into the snake, which represents temptation and desire, Adam and Eve taste the forbidden fruit of knowledge, which implies the knowledge of good and evil—dualism and an awareness of being separate from the Divine. They thus become *self*-conscious. The spiritual path that they (and each of us) must thus follow is one that brings them through the initial childlike state of nonindividuation and along the path that eventually brings them to independence, autonomous choice, and ultimately to reunion with the Divine principle, the true source and ground of our being.

This corresponds to our own nontheistic Buddhist cosmology in which it is generally taught that we begin in ignorance and dualism and end in enlightenment and oneness. Because of our delusions, we suffer. When we recognize enlightenment, we realize everlasting peace.

All life contains both joy and sorrow. We would like to concentrate on the joy and forget the sorrow, but how much more spiritually skillful it is to use everything we meet in life as grist for the mill of awakening. Chogyam Trungpa Rinpoche used to say that the more shit you encounter along the path, the better your spiritual flowers will grow—so long as you know how to use the shit as fertilizer. We used to joke about this, calling it the "Manure Principle." In Tibetan Buddhism, we call this having "vajra" (diamond) teeth. With vajra teeth, we can grind everything we encounter into dust and digest it as easily as pablum; thus all our experiences become the equivalent of food to nourish and nurture the spirit.

When we apply this approach to life's ups and downs, we develop tremendous fearlessness, curiosity, and a greater passion for living. This vajra approach reflects the tantric principle of transforming even the greatest poisons into wisdom. The example often given is that of the wild peacocks found in India's deserts. The peacocks thrive on poisonous snakes; in fact the more poisonous snakes they eat, the bigger, more colorful their tail plumes become. This approach is very unlike that of the individual in the spiritual ivory tower who observes the world from afar. Instead, the tantric spiritual warrior jumps into the fray by leaping into the ocean of bullshit and swimming, sometimes even becoming a lifesaver.

There is an ancient Tibetan Buddhist practice that trains us in taking all of the "shit"—the suffering, heartache, and pain—the world has to offer and using it as fertilizer for greater spiritual transformation. It is called "Turning Happiness and Suffering into the Path of Enlightenment."

TURNING HAPPINESS AND SUFFERING INTO THE PATH OF ENLIGHTENMENT

Going through my old notes from my late, great teacher His Holiness Dudjom Rinpoche on the Nyingmapa practice of accepting suffering as part of the path of enlightenment, I found scribbled in my Tibetan text's margins the following quote from Dudjom Rinpoche's son, Thinley Norbu Rinpoche:

> "Same taste is the main precept. Seek to recognize that inherent wisdom or awareness is present and unaltered in both happiness and suffering. Understand that happiness no longer benefits, and suffering no longer hurts, through the experience of the same taste of all phenomenal appearances."

Most of us spend our lives seeking pleasure and trying to avoid pain. What Lama Thinley Norbu was telling us to understand is that innate nondual awareness is present in all of us, in all circumstances. We must learn to practice it in all circumstances, whether they be favorable or unfavorable.

The Buddha's life is often used as an example of this principle: He experienced great extremes of austerity and discomfort as well as respect and adoration, yet his intention to help others remained constant, and his mind was steady no matter what the outward circumstances.

> *"In the absolute expanse of awareness*
> *All things are blended into that single taste—*
> *But, relatively, each and every phenomenon*
> *is distinctly, clearly seen.*
> *Wondrous!"*
> —Lama Shabkar,
> translated by Matthieu Ricard

In this life, we cannot expect to avoid pain, suffering, illness, or loss. We can, however, train our minds so that we are better able to let go rather than hang onto life's problems; we can lead our lives so that the difficulties we face become stepping stones rather than stumbling blocks on the path to enlightenment.

We can use lemons to make lemonade.

The Practice of Accepting Suffering as the Path to Enlightenment Offers the Following Teachings:

I. LET GO OF THE IDEA OF TELLING YOURSELF THAT YOU DON'T WANT SUFFERING; INSTEAD FOCUS ON THE FOLLOWING THOUGHT: WHATEVER DIFFICULTIES LIFE BRINGS, I WILL NOT BE ANXIOUS ABOUT THEM.

Anxiety and fear is often the worst part of any negative experience. My teachers would always say that it's a waste of time to be anxious about suffering. If you are able to heal the conditions that create difficulties, then your problems are resolved. If you are unable to change anything, it's not going to do you any good to be distressed. Anxiety about life's problems and your personal unhappiness can create even greater unhappiness, as well as stress-related illnesses. Concentrate your efforts on calming and freeing the mind. Contentment and fulfillment is right there, within yourself.

2. EMBRACE YOUR DIFFICULTIES AND APPRECIATE THEM FOR PROVIDING NEW WAYS TO GROW SPIRITUALLY. TRY TO THINK OF THE POSITIVE BENEFITS AND SPIRITUAL LESSONS THAT TROUBLES CAN ALMOST CERTAINLY PROVIDE. HERE ARE SOME OF THEM:

※ Very few people begin a spiritual journey because they are blissfully happy. In fact, men and women are typically drawn to the spiritual path because they want help in dealing with difficulties. Each challenge in our lives opens the possibility of awakening our Buddhist heart.

※ When we are going through dark times, we are better able to let go of egotism and arrogance. Difficulties can help us grow in patience, understanding, and humility; they can help us seek out meaningful connection.

✻ This is an ideal time for self-reflection and an examination of those ways in which we have contributed to our own problems—our own karma. Are any of our current difficulties, for example, caused by our own carelessness and lack of mindfulness?

✻ When our troubles seem overwhelming, often we can use this as a way of growing our compassion for others. Reflect on the millions of others who—just like you—are going through tough times right now. Empathize with these brothers and sisters with whom you share so many emotions.

THINK OF YOUR DIFFICULT TIMES
AS SPIRITUAL TRAININGS

My enlightened Dzogchen master, His Holiness Dilgo Khyentse Rinpoche, said:

> *"Difficulties are like the ornament*
> *of a good practitioner.*
> *Dharma is not practiced perfectly*
> *amidst pleasant circumstances."*

It's a fact: When we use our difficulties as a way to train our minds and transform our attitudes, we can overcome anxiety and fear; we thus cultivate virtues like forbearance, humility, and acceptance. In this way we become stronger, more balanced, and mentally stable. The Tibetan Buddhist teachers are so firmly convinced that this kind of challenging training can help one overcome emotions like fear and anxiety that they do meditation training at night in cemeteries and charnal grounds.

They encourage practitioners to step up and face inner fears and use them as a propellant to contemplative energy.

When I first encountered this practice in Asia, I didn't really understand it, but eventually I came to see the spiritual benefits. When I lived in Darjeeling with my lamas, one very snowy winter it became too cold in the mountains, and I went south to visit Benares (Varanasi) on the Indian plains. There I lived along the banks of the Ganges River. Each evening a yogi friend and I would go to the stone steps of the ghat along the riverbank at one end of the city. There Hindus from around the globe would come to die and be cremated in their sacred river, as well as to watch the burning funeral pyres that illumed each night. The meditations I did at this awesome site were among the best I have ever experienced.

It was more than twenty-five years ago, but I remember as if it were yesterday the aura of severe solemnity and sacred awe surrounding these sunset proceedings. Not that I ever had a camera with me in India in those days, but I remember noticing that there were no tourists snapping photos or filming. The taking of pictures was absolutely prohibited in order to protect the sanctity of the funereal rite and the privacy of the grieving families who were present. The cremations generally occurred at dusk. Huge ravens and crows waited atop the old stone parapets of the ancient city walls and riverbank battlements, hoping for stray morsels of human flesh to pick up and carry away. Vultures loomed in the distance on the desert sands just across the wide, muddy, slow-flowing Ganges.

At first I was fearful. I remember the sickly sweet, gluey odor of burning flesh. It was frightening. And the first time I saw the corpse's distended limbs sticking out from the white gauze as the fire burnt away the shroud and the sinews dried up, pulling the hands and feet into various directions until they were extending out from the funeral pyre, I was shocked and speechless. I felt—and I still feel it viscerally—that my own body was mere firewood on the pyre of this world, this life. But the most frightening moment of all came when the eldest son of the deceased stepped forward with a large, stout stick in his hand. Alongside him was an old Brahmin priest who was intoning mantras and sprinkling consecrated water on the pyre. Bowing down to his late father's flaming corpse, the son chanted a prayer, and then raised the stick and brought it down on the corpse's skull with a sharp crack—to liberate the soul upward into Lord Shiva's embrace, as the Brahmins explained to me later.

My immediate reaction was to worry; I felt like I would become polluted or ill by contact with this scene. I was also afraid of the leprous beggars with raw exposed wounds, who lined the streets. Yet as a spiritual seeker on the path in India, I could not help but return night after night to sit on one of the cold stone temple parapets surrounding the proceedings. There I would meditate and observe the goings on, like a spectator in some Dante-esque netherworld.

This was good for me. I was twenty-two, and here, for the first time in my young and fairly privileged life, I had come face to face with the nitty-gritty facts of life and death. I realized my kinship with all who live—with all who live and die. At first it was frightening and fearsome, as well as awe inspiring. I was simply afraid—of what I could not exactly say: of the specter of death, I suppose; of being tainted or infected with death; of facing the fact of my own mortality; of ghosts, perhaps. It was mostly an unformed, unspoken fear. But soon, it became just part of my daily evening meditation—a sacred Benares sunset rite in which I could participate. It became a part of my practice, not that different from my habit of going to morning and evening chant services at Saint Ananda Mayee's ashram-temple overlooking the river at another, more gentle part of the riverside city. My original fear turned gradually into reverence and appreciation for the mystery of life, and for the natural unfolding of the process of life and death. I found that I was able to become more contemplative and less reactive and emotional about the spectacle, which to Western eyes initially seemed macabre.

By the time I was ready to return to my teacher's monastery in Darjeeling that spring, my attitude had changed. Often I would find myself sitting with the last straggling mourners, Brahmin priests, lepers, and eager crows long after the last glow of sunset had faded and the embers of the cremation pyres had begun to subside; by then night would be well advanced with the moon high over the Ganges. I think this experience helped me understand more clearly why Buddha said, "Death is my guru; death is my greatest teacher. Death, impermanence, and mortality drove me to find that deathless peace beyond the snares of birth and death. To contemplate death and your own mortality is the ultimate meditation practice."

The purpose of this kind of practice is to become so spiritually courageous and balanced that even the most difficult circumstances will reveal themselves as an opportunity for spiritual growth and deeper life-learning—what I like to call "true higher education." We Buddhists don't consider this morbid or negative in any way. This is not about seeking death; it's about embracing the opportunities that our precious lives provide even during the darkest, most frightening hours. It deepens and broadens our spiritual intelligence. In this way we become closer to absolute fearlessness and spiritual power.

BECOMING MORE BALANCED
AND CALM

All Buddhist teachers, and I am no exception, point out that all of our happiness as well as all of our despair arise from the mind.

When we search for happiness and an end to suffering, the only place to look is within the mind itself. We each contain within ourselves all that we need for personal joy, bliss, wisdom, equanimity, and peace. There is no reason to look to externals or anywhere else. When one truly embraces this thought, there is nothing to fear. We are truly free.

Until we reach this level of spiritual peace, we are in some ways always at the mercy of external circumstances. We will continue to be affected by all events, great and small. The Tibetan text on turning unhappiness into the spiritual path says that "our hair is tangled in a tree," meaning that we are bound up in external circumstances that take over and leave us tied up. In a long prayerful poem, Dudjom Rinpoche wrote, "May I tie around my own head the lead rope that is attached to my own nose," meaning may we realize autonomy and self-mastery, and not always be at the mercy of things outside ourselves.

My teachers would often remind us that obstacles and problems could be viewed as blessings that should not be avoided. Difficulties help free us from our attachment to how we want things to be. In short, they help free us from the fantasies that keep us from awakening to the joy of enlightenment, the bliss of what is. When we take this approach, we find that we are able to see and appreciate the lessons and opportunities in each experience. This applies to both the positive and the negative. Just as we are often fearful and anxious of negative experiences, and thus fail to reap the lessons that are there for us, so too we can so easily overlook and deny the blessings and simple, everyday joys in our lives.

Many seekers today, for example, complain about the level of stress they are under from the pressures of schedules and responsibilities. Often this stress is generated by the demands we place on ourselves to be better parents, friends, partners, employees, employers, neighbors—in short, to be better people. Perhaps instead of viewing our obligations as burdens, we could incorporate them into a spiritual practice with a little prayer that further emphasizes our commitment to the awakened awareness and goodness of heart embodied in the precious Bodhicitta.

We cultivate and reinforce our compassionate intentions to do good and to help, not harm, others. Because we love and care about ourselves, we naturally learn more and more to extend ourselves to others since they are really not much different than we are. In this way, each of us can transform and recondition much of our own selfish, egotistical behavior, and be more of a peacemaker and bearer of love, shedding light wherever we go.

We all long for spiritual blessings, protection, and wholeness. Yet it is not often appreciated how many blessings we all have within us and in our lives. We remember the old spiritual admonishment "Count your blessings" as we try not to overlook all that we have been given. Moreover we could practice giving blessings to ourselves and our own hopes and ideals; we could freely offer blessings to others from the fullness of our hearts. We need to overcome any tendencies to be stingy with our blessings, mistakenly assuming that blessings come from someone else. Each of us is a blessed one—you too!

When we look at everything we are experiencing—good and bad—with sacred outlook and nonjudgmental awareness, we further enhance our personal spiritual growth.

THE PRACTICE OF PURE PERCEPTION

One of the unique practices in Tibetan Buddhism is called "dak-nang," the practice of pure perception or sacred outlook. In this practice, we focus our energy on seeing this world as a perfect Buddha Field—a paradise-like realm—with all beings as Buddhas. This is a wonderful practice to keep in mind whenever we find ourselves strongly liking or not liking an experience, an event, a feeling, or a person.

We can further put this into perspective in the bigger context of what Tibetan Buddhists refer to as the Great Perfection teachings or Dzogchen. This is the ultimate revelation through which we recognize that everything that arises both within and outside us is the stately process of what we call the "Dharmakaya," or absolute dimension—the radiance of absolute truth or naked reality, stripped of illusions and conceptual imputations.

What we mean by Dharmakaya is that Buddha-nature, or primordial luminosity, is manifested and expressed through every element of our world and existence.

In short, everything is Dharmakaya—everything, including our emotions, whether they are healthy or unhealthy, positive or negative, constructive or destructive. The things we like or don't like, including physical sensations such as pain or pleasure, are all part of the blessed, radiant Dharmakaya or Buddha-nature at work—or better yet, Buddha-nature at play.

What this means is that all beings are the Buddhas in this Buddha Field. The earth is the altar, and we are the deities sitting, standing, and walking on the altar. Everything is sacred; all are holy; everything is perfectly radiant and stainless in the Buddhavision-like light of the natural Great Perfection. This is the perspective of "dak-nang," the practice of pure perception.

My late friend John Blofeld was a Buddhist author, scholar, and translator; he lived for many years in China and Tibet during the 1950s and '60s. Eventually, during the 1970s, he settled into married life in Bangkok with his Thai wife. Once when I visited him there, John told me how difficult it was for him to get acclimated to living in such a bustling, noisy city after living for decades in Himalayan monasteries and Chinese Taoist hermitages. He said that what he found particularly challenging was practicing his Tantric Green Tara Meditation for two hours in his Bangkok apartment each morning before leaving for his office.

In his apartment, John had created and decorated a lovely Tara shrine and meditation room. The room was filled with exquisite sacred art that he had accumulated over the years— beautiful statues of Buddha; small, delicate paintings; altar pieces; Chinese brocade; sacred texts; and rare books and manuscripts, along with antique offering bowls and lamps. But despite the beauty of his surroundings, John couldn't keep the discordant sounds of Bangkok morning traffic from coming through his window and interrupting his meditation.

John said the heavy traffic, especially the sounds of mufflerless truck engines and gear shifting combined with horns honking in the distance, really bugged him. After years of meditation practice and experience, he knew he could, and even should, be able to concentrate. Nonetheless, he found that he was unable either to block the intruding sounds from his mind or to integrate them into his awareness practice without being distracted or disturbed. The fact remained—he told me with a sheepish laugh—that the cacophony of the daily rush hour often made him long for his Himalayan retreats and the years of silence and solitude he had spent with his spiritual masters.

Then one day something "clicked" into place. It must have been a blessing from the "traffic gods" combined with that of his own lineage of guides and gurus, augmented of course by the good karma he'd accumulated by faithfully persevering despite the distracting noise. Whatever the reason, one morning while he was in his shrine room, meditating on Tara, he suddenly realized that all those honking horns, droning engines, and clunking gears didn't sound that much different from the blaring of Tibetan long horns and the clash of huge brass monastery cymbals wafting through his old hermitage window in Darjeeling, where John had studied Dzogchen with my own late master, Dudjom Rinpoche. In his master's monastery, John had found the sounds of the horns an enhancement to his morning meditation. Why should it be different now?

John told me that he suddenly realized—like awakening from a dream—that it was simply a matter of how he was perceiving those sounds—as distracting traffic noise, or as a celestial Tibetan ritual choir—that made all the difference. Until that moment, for no real reason other than his own interpretation superimposed upon things, he had found one set of sounds uplifting, and the other brought him down.

John then fully realized for the first time the secret of the Tibetan practice of pure perception—seeing all forms as rainbow energy, hearing all sounds as deities chanting mantras, and recognizing the Buddha light in everyone and everything. From that day on, John's morning prayers and Tara practice were totally transformed and absolutely blessed. The sacred sounds coming through his window may have been different from the sounds he had heard in his guru's distant Himalayan monastery, but—in his transformed vision—they were sacred nonetheless. Thus he found himself peacefully at home with his guru in Tara's Buddha Field, even amidst bustling Bangkok—a city that never sleeps.

THE PRACTICE OF PURE PERCEPTION /
SACRED OUTLOOK—A MEDITATION

Let's put into practice our ideal of seeing, recognizing, and appreciating the light in everyone and everything, so that all that we experience becomes an integral part of our spiritual awareness—part and parcel of our awakened/enlightened heart.

Look around the room.

See it all in a fresh new light.

Experience what you are feeling in a new way.

Open up to the luminous energy by regarding the transparent,
luminous insubstantiality of all forms and perceptions.

Breathe in light along with air,

and breathe out light again.

Visualize light pouring in like a river, along with your in breath,
and gushing out along with your out breath.

Breathe the light in and out,

filling you up

Emptying, cleansing, purifying . . .

Envision the place you are standing suffused with and surrounded
by light, haloed as in a piece of sacred art.

Envision the people around you filled with light, surrounded by
light, emanating bliss and de-light, like the sages or saints in a religious
painting.

(This may seem fabricated, but I assure you it is simply a reflection
of the actuality that is momentarily too subtle for most of us to perceive.)

Keep breathing the clear light in and out, like a continuous circle or
wheel of luminosity that turns inside and out, day and night.

Recognize others as being living Buddhas, gods or goddesses—
all splendid and divine in their own right, in their own way, their own
light.

Why be deterred by the mere appearance of their particular form or
manifestation?

Why be deterred by the illusory interaction their forms and personal-
ities have with our own?

Deep down we are all Buddhas by nature,

perfectly pure and complete luminous beings

of pure light and energy.

Honor their enlightened Buddha-nature, their innate divinity.
See them in a new light,
beyond personal distinctions, preferences and discriminations.
Breathing light, out and in, within and without,
filling and emptying our noble heart
which is pure light, illumining oneself, illumining others,
illumining the whole world:
Rest in that glorious inner sphere
of spiritual splendor,
seeing everything in an utterly new light.

Now take this sacred vision out to others who are not present.
Envision your parents, mates, colleagues, children, and neighbors in
this new light.
Embrace them with light.
Let's take this outside into the world.
Keep breathing the light in and out, back and forth,
circulating the cosmic energy throughout your own system.
As you leave the premises, gaze benevolently upon
whoever first crosses your path—human, animal, or winged insect.
Breathe in the light, then breathe it out to them,
embracing them in the radiant light of pure perception, of clear
seeing.
Notice whatever may come up and intrude
upon seeing these Buddha-like spiritual beings.
See through that momentary obscuration veiling their inner splendor
to appreciate their deeper truth and blessed being.

Carry this new way of seeing home with you, and bring it
into your family, your workplace, your daily commute.

Keep breathing light. Breathe it in and renew yourself.
Breathe it out and embrace others.

Hold your employees or boss in this light, and see how it feels. See how it changes your relationships with others, even though they don't know you are doing this.

How different this is from how we usually see things and people!

This is how we cultivate pure perceptions and achieve a sacred outlook that embraces everything and everyone—from the sublime to the mundane, from the glad to the sad—in the vast mandala of the awakened heart-mind. Amazing! Wonderfull!

Chapter Ten

Learning to Love What

We Don't Like

A Disciple asked Rabbi Shmelke: "We are commanded to love our neighbor as ourself. How can I do this, if my neighbor has wronged me?"

The Rabbi answered: "You must understand these words right. Love your neighbor like something which you yourself are. For all souls are one. Each is a spark from the original soul, and this soul is wholly inherent in all souls, just as your soul is in all the members of your body. If your hand makes a mistake and strikes you, would you then hit your hand with a stick and thus increase your pain? It is the same with your neighbor. If you punish him, you only hurt yourself."

The Disciple went on asking: "But if I see a man who is wicked before God, how can I love him?"

"Don't you know," said Rabbi Shmelke, "that the original soul came out of the essence of God, and that every human soul is a part of God? And will you have no mercy on him when you see that one of his holy sparks has been lost in a maze, and is almost stifled?"

—Martin Buber, *Tales of the Hassidim*

Why should we learn to love and connect with people and other beings we don't particularly like? Why should we love those who hurt us and cause us pain? Why should anyone want to love people like Hitler, Pol Pot, Stalin, or Idi Amin? How can we learn to love terrorists and people who cause war or genocide? How can we love drivers who are angry, careless, or drunk? How can we love men and women who are intolerant, petty, and unkind to fellow beings? How can we learn to love people who grate on our nerves? How can we learn to love mosquitoes, snakes, and slimy creatures we don't want anywhere near us? Why? Why? Why? How? How? How? When it comes to love, there are a lot of whys and hows.

There is at least one basic, simple, universal, and ultimately self-serving reason to love: The act of loving is naturally healing in and of itself. Negative feelings like anger and hate make us contract and close up; they can even make us feel and be sick. On the other hand, the more we love, the better we feel. In short, loving others is a way of loving—and healing—ourselves. When we send out pure loving-kindness, it reverberates back; sending love and receiving love go hand in hand. We love in order to feel love. That's why we love.

Being open and loving is a great feeling, isn't it? It's certainly a better feeling than hatred! What do we think about when we first hear the word "love"? Do we think of our child, our mate, our pets? Do we think of parents, siblings, or friends? Do we think of nature, a tree in the backyard perhaps, or a favorite vacation spot that brings us joy? When we talk about Dharma, spirituality, or truth and love, it really all comes down to the same thing—an exquisite appreciation of something, someone, or a certain moment in life, an appreciation of something that is beautiful and meaningful to us. That's really what we love, isn't it? How we feel in that moment. We might say we love a person or a place, but if we really look into it, what we are probably loving is how we feel when this person is with us.

Buddhism teaches that love is the antidote to anger, aversion, hatred, and fear. Buddhism also has something to say about *how* to love; it teaches us that mindfulness—authentic being—is the path to love. This answers the question of how to love. Being mindful in the present moment brings us to an understanding of "what is." Mindfulness allows us to touch our own innate Buddha-nature; it allows us to see and touch the Buddha-nature in everyone we meet. In his extraordinary book *Living Buddha, Living Christ,* Thich Nhat Hanh writes:

"When we are mindful, touching deeply the present moment, we can see and listen deeply, and the fruits are always understanding, acceptance, love, and the desire to relieve suffering and bring joy. . . . To me, mindfulness is very much like the Holy Spirit. Both are agents of healing. When you have mindfulness, you have love and understanding, you see more deeply, and you can heal the wounds in your own mind. The Buddha was called the King of Healers. In the Bible, when someone touches Christ, he or she is healed. It is not just touching a cloth that brings about a miracle. When you touch deep understanding and love, you are healed."

"LOVE" IS DIFFERENT FROM "LIKE"

When I was a young man, I thought love was always supposed to come easily and naturally. Then I discovered that in life, we are sometimes called upon to love people and situations that we don't really like. That's when love becomes more demanding and challenging.

During the 1980s I spent eight years in extended retreat, in a secluded Tibetan monastery in France. People often ask me what was the most important thing I got out of those years in a

Dzogchen retreat center, so I've thought about this question a lot. There were twenty-three of us cloistered together in a forest retreat. Some of us didn't know each other that well to start out with so it was a little like entering into an arranged marriage. There were many issues on which we didn't always agree. But I eventually learned that I could love and care about people whose opinions and habits I didn't always like or agree with. For me this was an important lesson that reinforced, in a very personal way, the Buddha's teachings on the nature of love and compassion. It was extraordinarily peace-making in my own mind and has stood me in good stead years later as I am more actively engaged in modern life and religious politics with all its trials and vicissitudes.

Spiritual teachings of all the great traditions reiterate time and time again that loving opens our hearts to acceptance and forgiveness. For me, this bespeaks an inner equanimity that is capable of appreciating all things, even as they fluctuate and morph into one kind of experience after another. Love is where we live and come from, not just what we are heading toward. It's like how we were when we were children—filled with wonder and appreciation, and open to everything. We come to perceive things with fresh eyes and ears. Everything is new and therefore miraculous and marvelous. We love it. We can embrace life fully all along the entire length of her body.

Walking the spiritual path means that we are trying to learn to love universally—not just our mates, friends, or children, but everyone. We are trying to learn to love things just as they are, for this is "truth" according to Buddha's definition. We are trying to learn to love through whatever experience we have— good, bad, or indifferent. This is a wisdom love, not just based on momentary passion, feeling, and self-reference, but rooted far more deeply in genuine caring, empathy, and unselfishness.

LEARNING DEEPER ACCEPTANCE
AND FORGIVENESS

When we talk about love, we are talking about something that is quite soulful, not abstract—not just "ah, emptiness!" or a philosophical "The Infinite." When some of us try to incorporate more loving-kindness and compassionate practices into our lives, I think we are often doing it because we want to fix something that's going wrong in our own lives. Instead, I think we should focus on appreciating everything and opening up to life's experiences with greater tolerance, forbearance, and acceptance. In order to get to that place, of course, we have to begin to work on forgiving everyone their shortcomings, even ourselves.

When I was in elementary school, I was a real hellion and often in trouble. I always seemed to get a red F in conduct, and although my other grades were much better, I was so overactive that finally they demoted me. I was sent out of the advanced class to another class to be with a group of kids who, like me, were all incipient truants and hell raisers. Still I was among the worst. The teacher of that spirited class seemed to have a real talent for dealing with troublemakers. At every opportunity, he would take us outside so we could let off energy; it was sort of like we were majoring in playground. I started to like it!

What I remember most about this teacher, Mr. LaRocca, was that he was a tough, strong guy, who wasn't intimidated by a couple of dozen rowdy kids. Once I created such a disturbance in class that he put me outside in the hallway; of course I simply ran away and played outside on the ball field. Then he put me under his desk. That's where I lived for a while. Crunched under the desk and in the dark, I couldn't do anything; I was stuffed down between his shins and a wooden hard place. I don't remember how long I stayed there, but certainly until I gave in at least a little bit. Finally he put my desk right next to his, facing the blackboard where he kept a big eye on me. This was definitely the truant's seat.

At first I saw Mr. LaRocca as being a real pain. He was my enemy, and I was out to get him with as much zeal as any hyperactive kid could muster; I also thought he was out to get me. But gradually my attitude began to change. He found out that I was interested in sports, so he took me to the library and showed me how to find and borrow the sports magazines and biographies; he encouraged me to find a way to combine the learning process with things I was naturally interested in. Most important, he didn't give up on me. Eventually I came to appreciate and even love him. Today, of course, I realize that he was a blessing in disguise. My enemy was really my best friend. That man may have saved my life. James LaRocca is the only elementary school teacher I ever visited again, years later. I still remember him with love.

Of course my grade school teacher wasn't a very threatening enemy. As we mature and become adults, we often find ourselves facing enemies who have the potential to be far more lethal and damaging. We come face to face with people whose motivations seem to be destructive, deceitful, and hurtful; we are forced to confront enemies in the form of illnesses and tragedies, such as serious accidents, cancer, heart disease, and AIDS. Some of us have chronic pain from arthritis; others have chronic fatigue. Our enemies may appear in the form of bad relationships, or addictive or self-destructive lifestyles. These are also our enemies, and this is tough stuff.

Shantideva, known as the Gentle Angel Master, said that our enemies are our greatest teachers. Our enemies teach us patience, equanimity, and love. In this way, our enemies also teach us forgiveness and acceptance.

Forgiveness and acceptance also play major roles in many Buddhist teaching tales. I've always liked a Zen story about forgiveness and acceptance in Paul Reps' classic book *Zen Flesh, Zen Bones*. It's about a Zen master named Shichiri, who, one evening while he is reciting sutras, is interrupted by a thief with a sharp sword. Shichiri, who is very involved with what he is doing, tells the thief, "Do not disturb me. You can find the money in that drawer." Shichiri goes back to the sutras for a minute, but then he calls out again, "Don't take it all. I need some to pay taxes with tomorrow."

The thief takes most of the money, and as he leaves, Shichiri says. "Thank a person when you receive a gift." The surprised intruder thanks him and leaves.

Within a week, the man is caught and confesses what he has done. When he is brought to trial, Shichiri, who has been called as a witness, says: "This man is no thief, at least as far as I am concerned. I gave him the money, and he thanked me for it."

The Zen master Shichiri's ability to accept and forgive so impressed the thief that it caused him to undergo an inner transformation. Once he was released from prison, he went straight to Shichiri and became his disciple.

It is possible to recognize that we can detest someone's actions without detesting the person; we can hate the sin without hating the sinner, as is often said. I once saw a mother chastising her small child saying, "You're a *good* child, but you just did a *bad* thing." I think this is a distinction most of us need to recognize. It's possible to judge and condemn the action, not the person doing it. We can disagree with what someone says while we continue to respect this person's right to say it. In this way, we can drop some of the burdens of anger, bitterness, and resentment that we carry around with us. We can love more broadly and still maintain our integrity and common sense.

Forgiveness is a major part of love and acceptance. When we

carry around the heavy weights of anger and unforgiveness, we hurt ourselves. Rabbi Harold Kushner said that if after two days you still haven't forgiven someone for something, it becomes your responsibility. And he was talking about the most grievous things, not just about somebody cutting you off on a traffic circle. I think Rabbi Kushner's suggestion of two days is a good one to follow, difficult as that may seem. As Buddhists we recognize that whatever someone else does is their karma to be dealt with. But if we hang on to the anger past that two-day limit, it becomes our karma too, and we are victimizing ourselves.

Whom Do You Need to Forgive?

Do you have a personal list of people whom you need to forgive? Don't we all? My friend Greta made a list of some of the people she had trouble forgiving. Here it is:

❋ Mother—for filling her daughter's head full of fantasies about the possibility of Prince Charming; for fault finding and nagging; for generally childish behavior.

❋ Father—for being "distant"; for abandoning his family emotionally, and for not protecting Greta from her mother.

❋ Brother—for being unkind and picking on her when she was still very little.

❋ First husband—for having an affair that ended their marriage.

❋ Former sister-in-law—for knowing what her brother (Greta's ex-husband) was doing and looking the other way, making Greta feel even more betrayed.

✳ Employer—for his bad temper and for taking advantage of her willingness to work hard.

✳ Friends—for being self-centered and failing to give adequate support.

✳ Self—for gaining weight and not being able to lose it.

If you were to examine your heart and your psyche, would you find a list of people and things you have difficulty forgiving? What would it look like? What grudges or vendettas are you harboring? What old prejudices are you carrying? Do you have memories of past events that fill you with hurt or rage every time you think about them? There is no need to feel guilty that these exist; simply examine these old memories and bring them into awareness. In the clear light of incandescent awareness, the old-fashioned bogeyman goes away and disappears; on the other hand, what stays unconscious continues to afflict us.

Often our deepest pockets of unforgiveness and loathing are directed at ourselves. We remember something we did or something we said, and we flinch at our behavior. We ask ourselves how we could have been so stupid, hurtful, or just plain unconscious.

In order to start the process of forgiveness, we let our minds soften up and we try to become more resilient and less rigid. We try to let go of our attachment to ideas about the past; we try to look at the world with more open and forgiving minds. When Greta, for example, allows herself to look at her mother with greater forgiveness, she sees that her mother was simply doing the best she could; from this point of view Greta is able to remember all the kind things her mother did, including the times that her mother drove her and her friends to their various after school activities. She is able to develop a more realistic and balanced view of her relationship with her mother. In this way she begins to let go of her attachment to her resentments, and focus instead on observing her life and what is happening moment to moment. As she begins to get psychologically up to date with herself, a lot of old baggage and burdens fall away, and she feels greater freedom.

Some of us have a personal history filled with people and events that loom so large in our heads that it seems as though forgiveness is barely possible. When I was teaching in Israel a few years ago, people often told me that they could never forgive Hitler and the Nazis. After I spoke about karmic responsibility and the law of cause and effect, some started shouting from the audience, "The Bible says, 'an eye for an eye, a tooth for a tooth.'" One angry audience member would egg on another, and then become even more furious. What can you say in the face of that kind of energy? It's difficult to discuss the universal law of reaping what we sow in the face of such virulent, unprocessed passions. When someone has harmed or killed a loved one, forgiveness can seem like a mighty challenge, and yet I think it's a challenge that needs to be met if we are to find any level of peace or happiness. We are up to the challenge.

What we try to do is make a spiritually intelligent distinction between forgiveness and forgetfulness. We should forgive even as we remember and learn from history. The past informs and conditions the present in ways great and small. If you, for example, know you are allergic to peanuts, mindfulness reminds you to avoid the food that can make you ill. In the same way, although the Dalai Lama forgives the Chinese Communists in his heart, he is also very realistic about their intentions when it comes to Tibet and forgets nothing about their history together in his country.

On television we sometimes see interviews with parents who have lost their children at the hand of a drunk driver or some other tragedy, and who have gone on to try to make the world better for other children by forming or being active in organizations that help protect life. They haven't allowed themselves to become paralyzed and embittered with their anger and despair; instead they have transformed their terrible pain and grief into spiritual intentions which help them to live better with their loss. Even some close relatives of murdered loved ones have found it in their hearts to forgive convicted and condemned murderers and work for clemency for them. This is a truly spiritual statement on their part.

I love the story of the elderly Mississippi laundress named Osceola McCarty, who for years secretly saved the money she earned from scrubbing other people's clothes and then gave it to a scholarship fund to help young people go to college. She had a minimal education herself, and yet instead of being bitter at her own lost opportunities, she vowed to help others—and she did. In so doing, she helped transform the lives of others as well as her own.

The past is part of the present; the only way that we can heal the past is by transforming the present. Thich Nhat Hanh says, "The ghosts of the past which follow us into the present also belong to the present moment. To observe them deeply, recognize their nature, and transform them, is to transform the past."

Staying in the present moment is, of course, a central theme of the Buddhist path; remembering this helps us deal with haunting memories and those things that we have difficulty forgiving. Teaching his followers, the Buddha said:

> *"Do not pursue the past.*
> *Do not lose yourself in the future.*
> *The past no longer is.*
> *The future has not yet come.*
> *Looking deeply at life as it is*
> *in the very here and now,*
> *the practitioner dwells*
> *in stability and freedom."*

THE ANCIENT PRACTICE OF GIVING
AND RECEIVING

Approximately a thousand years ago, an Indian Buddhist abbot named Atisha was invited to Tibet to help teach the Dharma. Legend has it that at that time Atisha had a dream in which the exalted female Buddha Tara appeared to him, telling him that if he went to Tibet, the Dharma would be greatly enhanced but his own life would be shortened by a dozen years. Atisha decided that the longevity of the Dharma was more important to the world than his own mortal existence. Although he was already sixty years of age, Atisha then travelled by foot through the treacherous mountain passes of Northern India and Nepal until he arrived in Tibet, where he spent the remaining years of his life orally transmitting teachings and founding the Kadampa school of Tibetan Buddhism. Atisha's teachings form the basis of Tibet's renowned Mahayana Mind Training, also known in Tibet as Lo-jong. These Attitude Transformation Trainings revolve around the indispensable concept of Bodhicitta and the Bodhisattva ideal.

Some hundred years after Atisha's death, a monk named Geshe Chékawa was in his lama's room one day. There, on a table near the head of his teacher's bed, he noticed a single sentence that was written on parchment. It said, "Give all the profit and gain to others, and unselfishly accept all the blame and loss." Geshe Chékawa's hair stood on end; he was so inspired by the unselfish message of these lines that he set out to try to find who had authored them. In his travels, Geshe Chékawa finally met a leper who told him that the enlightened Master Atisha was dead, but that he knew of someone who was a direct lineage disciple. In this way, Geshe Chékawa came to meet the learned layman named Drom, lineage holder of the Kadampa school.

When Geshe Chékawa questioned Lama Drom about the importance of the teaching contained in the sentence he had found in his teacher's room, Lama Drom replied that the practice of this teaching was absolutely essential to enlightenment. "Give all the profit and gain to others, and unselfishly accept all the blame and loss" formed the heart-essence of his own spiritual practice.

Geshe Chékawa apprenticed himself to Lama Drom for a dozen years, learning all he could. As time went on Geshe Chékawa began to share these teachings, first with a community of lepers because he felt a debt of gratitude to the leper who had helped him find Atisha's disciple. Tibetan oral tradition tells us that as these lepers practiced with Geshe Chékawa, they began to be healed.

In the meantime, Geshe Chékawa had a very skeptical and cynical brother who had never shown any interest in learning about the Dharma. Nonetheless, Chékawa's brother couldn't help noticing the transformation occurring with the lepers. The brother thus began to hide outside an open window to hear Chékawa's teachings. Eventually he too began to practice what was being taught. When Geshe Chékawa noticed the change in his brother's attitude, he was truly impressed. If the teachings could work even for his hard-hearted brother, they could work for anyone, he thought. And his faith and conviction in the Lojong practice was further strengthened.

Thus inspired, Geshe Chékawa began to write down Atisha's teachings, based on what Lama Drom remembered. These teachings are known in Tibet as Atisha's Seven Points of Mind Training. Out of these teachings has emerged the unique Tibetan practice called "tonglen" or giving and receiving.

Tonglen evolves from the sentence "Give all profit and gain

to others and unselfishly accept all blame and loss." This concept of giving away "the good, the desirable" and accepting "the bad, the undesirable" is quite foreign to Western ears. Most of us genuinely want the opposite; we want to breathe in only light and breathe out darkness.

In fact, this idea of breathing in "the good" and breathing out "the bad" is at the center of many New Age practices. Yet tonglen teaches us to do exactly the opposite. How can this be? This is the question many people ask when they first hear about tonglen.

Tonglen is one of the most misunderstood Tibetan Buddhist practices. In no way is it designed to make the practitioner ill or more afflicted. Its purpose is very simple: It is a mind training/attitude transformation practice meant to help us root out egotism, clinging, and dualism. It is a way to help us transform our attitudes toward those people and situations we naturally dislike, or even fear. In tonglen practice, we exchange ourselves with another; we use our mental powers to help us feel and identify with the afflictions of others. In this way, we learn to walk in someone else's shoes and better understand where others are coming from.

A belief, fundamental to the Christian faith, is that by his death, Jesus Christ took on the sins and burdens of the world. Tonglen is a Buddhist training that in many ways follows Jesus' noble ideal. Last year when I returned from a teaching trip, I received an e-mail from a woman that said in part:

"My dear lama,

I have a friend who is going through chemotherapy right now, which is causing her a lot of pain. Her suffering makes me feel helpless, and I want to find a way to comfort her. Could you please tell me how to pray and do the deeper tonglen practice so I can better take on some of her suffering? I would do anything to take on the pain if I could relieve her even half as much . . ."

The e-mail made me feel humble in the light of the writer's sincerity and natural goodness. It was apparent that she has a tender, compassionate, and loving heart. Most of us are doing tonglen because we want to be able to be as spontaneously caring as she is. Throughout the years, people have reported that tonglen practice has had a healing effect on themselves, on others, and on difficult situations and relationships. Nonetheless, although the letter writer is attracted to tonglen because she believes it might help her friend, tonglen's primary intent is to help heal the practitioner. It does this by helping us open our own inner loving hearts; it helps us be more accepting and forgiving toward both the desirable and undesirable aspects of life. In this way it gives us greater equanimity and peace, regardless of what is happening. For this reason, this is one of the best practices to deal with the most difficult situations in life, whether it's illness, a difficult mate, or an impossible job situation. It has helped me a great deal, especially when facing my greatest hardships.

In life, what we typically do is try to grasp what we want while we push away the undesirable. In Buddhist terminology this is known as attachment and aversion. By reversing these tendencies, tonglen helps us shake up our world and loosen the stranglehold of concepts such as "like" and "dislike," or "I want and I don't want."

Beginning Tonglen Practice

"Whoever wishes quickly to become
A place of refuge for self and others,
Should undertake this sacred mystery;
To take the place of others, giving them his or her own."
—From *The Way of the Bodhisattva*

Shantideva wrote *The Way of the Bodhisattva* over a thousand years ago. He said that the only way to make ourselves happy is to practice love and compassion, or Bodhicitta. Tonglen—the Practice of Giving and Receiving—is one of the principal Bodhicitta practices. It begins with an intention to open our hearts to others and also to ourselves, with the intention to learn to feel what others feel, to empathize and practice compassion. We want to allow the entire world into our hearts; we want to share what we have, what we are given. We willingly share ourselves.

We start by settling down as we would for any sitting meditation.

Get comfortable, get settled.

Loving-kindness meditations are aided by feelings of comfort and ease, so try to relax.

Use your breath to help you get settled in the present moment. Slowly, mindfully breathe in, and then breathe out through the nostrils. Breathe in gently and out gently.

Inhale . . .

Exhale . . . Relax.

TONGLEN PRACTICE—PART ONE

The traditional tonglen instructions tell us to open up to the practice by reflecting on the basic teachings of the Buddha:

✵ Be aware of the preciousness and opportunities provided by our human birth.

✵ Be aware of the fragile and impermanent nature of life—all life including our own.

✵ Be mindful of the implications of karma and our own intention to purify our actions.

TONGLEN PRACTICE—PART TWO

✿ MEDITATE ON THE OPEN NATURE OF REALITY

Things are not what they seem, nor are they otherwise. Everything changes; nothing remains the same. About this teaching, some simply say that we should "regard everything as a dream." We are trying to cultivate the mind of enlightenment—direct insight, or clear vision, into the transparent nature of self and all phenomena. This is the fundamental teaching of absolute Bodhicitta. About this, the modern-day teacher Pema Chodron writes, "The way to reunite with Bodhicitta is to lighten up in your practice and in your whole life . . . That's the essential meaning of the absolute Bodhicitta slogans—to connect with the open, spacious quality of your mind, so that you can see that there's no need to shut down and make such a big deal about everything."

At the beginning of any tonglen practice, rest in the empty, dreamlike, infinite nature of mind.

Then, the instructions tell us to:

✿ RIDE THE MOVING BREATH

Doing the meditation of "sending and receiving," we place our attention on the breath and inhale. Doing this, we visualize drawing in—taking upon ourselves—a black cloud of negativity. As we exhale, we visualize that we are giving out our goodness, our light—in short, the best part of ourselves. As we ride the moving breath, we visualize taking in the bad and exhaling the good—taking the burdens of others upon ourselves and giving away our good fortune and strength.

When they first hear about this practice, many people are confounded. They ask, "Why would anyone want to breathe in

213

the dark and breathe out the light?" But this practice, which goes against all our conditioning, provides an amazing tantric twist. It helps us face all those undesirable things we fear and try to avoid, instead of being deceived by mere appearances. Most of us have been conditioned to have a dualistic—this is good, this is bad—view of the world. After all, is darkness really bad, in any ultimate sense? Is light really good? By practicing tonglen, we begin to even out all our dualistic, judgmental views of the world. We begin to gain more inner detachment and balance. We naturally become more gentle and kind.

Many modern teachers advise that as we begin the tonglen practice—Riding the Breath, in and out—we start by focusing first on ourselves. It is easier to begin wishing well to ourselves before we begin the arduous task of evening out the differences we feel between ourselves and others. In this way, we begin approaching the spiritual ideal of treating others like ourselves by first allowing ourselves to be the recipients of our own compassionate intentions.

To do this, think about the various ways that you may feel that you need healing. Let's say, for example, that you feel confused, angry, or pained about an issue in your life.

Take this confusion, negativity, or pain and place it in front of you. Now, take a minute and allow yourself to become aware of the difficulty that your problem is causing you. Think about how healing it would be if you could be free of this negative energy. Continue breathing, and as you ride the breath, in and out, visualize that you are "Hoovering" or vacuuming up all the negativity and anger you feel as if it were a cloud of black smoke. Now, on the out breath, send out your positive energy and blessings as a ray of light. Let your positive energy and blessings gently surround your problems, whatever they might be. Breathe in the dark, the smoke, anxiety, agitation, fog, pollution, and static. Breathe out the light, the clean air, the sound of silence, the joy, the blessings, and peace and love.

TONGLEN PRACTICE—PART THREE

✻ EXCHANGE SELF-AWARENESS FOR AWARENESS OF OTHERS

Tibet's first Dalai Lama, who lived from 1391–1475, said, "Self-cherishing is said to be the source of all conflicts in this world. The cherishing of others is said to be the source of all happiness." The traditional mind-training and tonglen instructions use the phrase "Drive All Blames into One." What this means is that egotistical self-cherishing is at the root of all our troubles. We are in constant conflict, incessantly trying to get what we want and avoid what we don't want. This attitude hasn't served us well. In fact, often we find that we simply get more and more caught up in vicious and unsatisfying cycles.

As we try to reverse this tendency, we breathe in and breathe out. We keep breathing and relaxing, gentling our energies, our bodies, our minds, and our spirits. We begin first with a person we care about. We place this person in front of us in the light of awareness, and we allow ourselves to become conscious of any pain or difficulty he or she may be experiencing. Think how wonderful it would be if this person were happy and completely free of difficulty.

On the in breath, visualize yourself drawing in this person's pain. Inhale it all like a cloud of gray or dark smoke. Freely and willingly vacuum up all that pain, as if our infinitely open heart and spacious mind is a karmic Hoover—a karma cleaner.

On the out breath, visualize yourself sending out light, radiating out to this person all your blessings, all the gifts you have: strength, positive energy, health, and well-being. Give away as much as you can. Breathe out your talent, your resources, your material possessions. Don't hold back. Send it out on a ray of light that expresses all your blessings and well-being. This will enrich one and all.

Now visualize one or two other people you know and like, joining the first person. Let yourself both acknowledge and feel the troubles these new people experience. Become aware of your sincere intention to help these people. Now, on the in breath, inhale all the pain and trouble in these people's lives. Then, on the out breath, send them your light—your blessing, all that you have.

Expand your care and concern to encompass everyone you know. On the in breath, visualize yourself removing their suffering; draw it in on a cloud of black smoke. Breathe out to them all your love, caring concern, and compassion; send it out on a ray of light. Let an awareness that the karma of the world is being purified permeate your consciousness.

Be aware of your most tender, loving heart. Let the warm feelings of open-hearted compassion expand. Visualize one or more people who have given you a difficult time—people whom you need to forgive. Think about how wonderful it would be for them if they too could be free of pain and suffering. Breathe in their hardships; send them love and care on a ray of pure light that comes from the goodness of your heart.

Let your heart expand to include the entire planet and all the people and creatures on it. Give living form to your essential intention to help others. Take upon yourself the pain and suffering of the world; fearlessly breathe it in. Breathe in the darkness and let it all dissolve into the luminous, empty, openness of your infinite heart-mind, your Buddha-nature. Breathe out your light—your healing light. Let your love help heal the world. Take on the burden. It will make you stronger. Your heart will become as wide as the world.

TONGLEN PRACTICE—PART FOUR

Now visualize all those beings radiating around you filled with the light of love that you have sent out. Visualize all that light, all that love, coming back to you. Allow the healing love to fill your heart, your entire being. Feel the joy that comes from deeply connecting with and helping others.

Rest in that image. Meditate in that light. If you like, allow yourself to make a gradual transition to a natural sky-gazing meditation, water-gazing, or simple, effortless, just-being style meditation.

When we feel the pain and suffering of the world—when we can empathize with others—we naturally develop our capacity to respond with caring and compassion. When we recognize others as not much different from ourselves, we naturally feel kinship and oneness with them. This is the awakened spiritual heart in action. It cannot help responding wherever there is need.

When we realize our interconnectedness and kinship with all, we naturally respond to them as if they were our own loved ones. Thus we actualize the Golden Rule of "Do Unto Others . . ." naturally, almost effortlessly. This is the radiant heart, the awakened Buddhist heart of Bodhicitta—the luminous heart of Dharma.

Self and others are inseparable. If we let ourselves connect and link up in community with ever-widening circles—reaching out to link hands and hearts with those near and far—we can experience a oneness and healing that surpasses understanding; we can become more fully alive, integrated, and at peace. This is the secret of spiritual connection. Making a meaningful spiritual connection in each and every part of our lives is a real possibility. It is up to each and every one of us to actually do so.

EPILOGUE

A Prayer for the New Millennium

My prayer and New Millennium Resolution is this: to dedicate this life and all my lifetimes to the selfless service of spiritual enlightenment through working for the peace, harmony, and liberation of all beings. This is our heartfelt prayer and aspiration: That we may be the greatest we that we all, together as well as individually, can possibly be.

> *May all beings everywhere*
> *be awakened, healed, peaceful, and free;*
> *May there be peace in this world,*
> *and an end to war, poverty,*
> *violence, and oppression;*
> *and may we all together*
> *complete the spiritual journey.*
> —Lama Surya Das
> Concord, Massachusetts
> January 20, 2000

APPENDIX

The Bodhicitta Practices of an Awakened Heart

Following the Mahayana tradition founded by Atisha, over the centuries other mind-training practices became an important part of Tibetan Buddhism. One ancient and timeless mind-training practice that we studied extensively when I was in retreat with my teachers was The Thirty-seven Practices of a Bodhisattva. This is the work of Thogmé Zangpo, a Tibetan who lived in the late thirteenth and early fourteenth century. Thogmé Zangpo lived in a cave, meditating day and night on loving-kindness. Legend has it that all of the wild animals living nearby so benefited from his prayers and practice that they were able to live together in peace; even the wolf and the lamb would lovingly play together.

I personally found Thogmé's Thirty-seven Practices of a Bodhisattva indispensable when I was living with twenty-three others in a three-year cloistered retreat. These practices, which were taught to me by Dilgo Khyentse Rinpoche and Tulku Pema Wangyal, sum up the essence of Buddhist morality. Reading them, we are reminded time and time again of what is important in life. The Bodhisattva represents divine love and compassion translated into human form. These thirty-seven practices represent values and indicate the virtues that Bodhisattvas, the spiritual sons and daughters of the Buddha, all cherish.

When I look back over my copies of the text and translations that we used, I find countless little notes and quotes interspersed between each of the verses. The pages were turned so many times that the paper is yellowed and worn thin around the edges. When we studied these thirty-seven practices, we read Tibetan texts and translated them word by word. Here in this version, I've tried to translate the essence of them. Following each of these short practices, I've provided a commentary based on the notes and oral teachings. To help us use these practices today, I've also added a little spur for self-reflection or self-examination.

Think of each of these thirty-seven ancient and invaluable practices as a meditation to be reflected upon. As we read them, we think about our own lives; we think about the lessons of love and compassion we need to learn; we think about the ways that we can help others, and ourselves.

THE THIRTY-SEVEN PRACTICES
OF BODHISATTVAS

1. Since we are fortunate enough to be alive and to be blessed with human bodies and intelligence, let's take advantage of this opportunity to free ourselves and others from suffering. Listen to the teachings. Reflect on what you have heard. Meditate, meditate, meditate.

The Sons and Daughters of the Buddhas all follow this practice.

COMMENTARY: A basic theme in Buddhism is the preciousness of life—all life. As human beings, we are blessed with the opportunity to walk the path of awakening, for ourselves and others as well. The time honored way of doing this is to hear the Dharma—the spiritual teachings of truth; pay attention to what you have learned; then meditate with fervor and devotion, integrating these lessons into your daily life.

SELF-EXAMINATION: On this day, am I doing the best I can to take full advantage of the wondrous opportunities for growth and meaning that life provides?

2. In life, the strongest feelings are often generated by those we love and those who make us angry. We can become so preoccupied with these reactive feelings and our emotional concerns that we lose sight of what's right and wrong. We could instead cultivate an attitude of nonattachment to our feelings and be prepared to lessen the grip of our worldly preoccupations.

The Sons and Daughters of the Buddhas all follow this practice.

COMMENTARY: Renunciation is a part of most religious traditions. We give something up in order to gain something greater. In this instance, it is suggested that we stop letting our lives be solely guided by strong feelings and worldly preoccupations; instead, choose balance and a life based on deeper principles including an understanding of what is right and what is wrong.

SELF-EXAMINATION: Am I living according to my deepest heartfelt values and principles or am I just reacting semiconsciously to the vagaries and vacillations of the moment?

3. When we withdraw from excessive worldly stimulation and learn to put a priority on simplicity and solitude, our concentration, clarity, and wisdom increases as does our confidence in the Dharma and truth we've learned.

The Sons and Daughters of the Buddhas all follow this
practice.

COMMENTARY: Our lives are often so completely filled
with distracting situations that we can't focus on what's important. When we find solitude and "simplify, simplify, simplify," as
Thoreau said, our priorities become apparent. This is one of the
values of retreats. Buddhist masters would often go into solitary
retreat for years. In this new century, of course, we feel blessed
if we can find a weekend, a day, or even an hour to meditate and
reflect on ways to simplify our lives. It's wise to make certain
that we find some solitary time.

SELF-EXAMINATION: Am I consistently prioritizing
what really matters?

4. This life is transient and impermanent. All the goods
we've accumulated and relationships we've enjoyed will
change or come to an end. The mind is like a temporary
guest in our bodily house; it will someday pass beyond.
Learn to think of the larger picture beyond this one lifetime.

The Sons and Daughters of the Buddhas all follow this
practice.

COMMENTARY: The Buddha said that an awareness of
death can be our greatest teacher. Tibet's great yogi, Milarepa,
sang:

"*Fearing death, I went to the mountains.*
Over and over again I meditated on death's unpredictable coming,
And took the stronghold of the deathless unchanging nature.
Now I am completely beyond all fear of dying."

Asia is not alone in expounding this precious universal wisdom. Here in the West, the Native American Crowfoot sang in
1890:

"What is life?
 It is the flash of a firefly in the night.
 It is the breath of a buffalo in wintertime.
 It is the little shadow which runs across the grass and loses itself
 In the sunset."
                                        —Crowfoot, 1890

SELF-EXAMINATION: Am I living with a consciousness of my mortality, as if each day, hour, or minute could be my last?

5. If we spend our time with those who don't understand, encourage, and value our spiritual concerns, we will lose interest in truth and Dharma. As a result, we will meditate and pray less; we will lose sight of our vow to practice love and compassion for all others. Don't surround yourself with people who don't support your spiritual aspirations.

The Sons and Daughters of the Buddhas all follow this practice.

COMMENTARY: When walking the spiritual path, it's wise to avoid people whose conduct and influence pulls us in other directions away from our goals. Someone once said that if you want to know what a person values, look at his or her friends. Khyentse Rinpoche said, "A clear, pure crystal takes on the color of the cloth upon which it is placed, whether white, yellow, red, or black. Likewise the people you spend your time with, whether their influence is good or bad, will make a huge difference to the direction your life and internal practice take."

SELF-EXAMINATION: Do I seek out meaningful, fulfilling relationships and connections or do I gravitate toward people who pull me away from my spiritual path?

6. Good teachers and spiritual friends help us solve our problems and maintain our loving intentions. Cherish these kindred spirits, friends, and mentors.

The Sons and Daughters of the Buddhas all follow this practice.

COMMENTARY: As seekers, we need to cultivate a community of spiritual friends who will understand and value our goals. Reach out and strengthen these connections. Appreciate and value the healing gifts that these friends provide. Seek a wise teacher.

SELF-EXAMINATION: Do I fully appreciate, respect, and attend to my spiritual mentors, friends, and teachers while they are here to help guide me?

7. **How can you expect the successful wheelers and dealers of this world to help you when they themselves are mired in worldly woes? Instead, look for refuge and support in what's real and reliable.**

The Sons and Daughters of the Buddhas all follow this practice.

COMMENTARY: In life, when we find ourselves in crisis, we sometimes look for support, love, or guidance in all the wrong places. In Buddhism it is taught that we can consistently turn for help and solace to what is tried and true—the Three Jewels: the enlightened teacher; the liberating teachings; and spiritual friends/community.

SELF-EXAMINATION: Am I looking for what I need in places where it can be found?

8. **The Buddha said that our suffering and confusion is the result of our negative actions. Understand this and turn away from all behaviors that are harmful to self and others. Use all your strength to resist any tendency to cause harm to anyone.**

The Sons and Daughters of the Buddhas all follow this practice.

COMMENTARY: When we hurt others, we run the risk that our actions will boomerang back on ourselves. In some cases, we feel the repercussions immediately—often with our own immediate guilt, if not worse forms of instant karma. Other times, it may take years or lifetimes. But the laws of cause and effect are very clear. An essential spiritual rule: *Do no harm.* Cultivate the good. Be as good as you intrinsically are.

SELF-EXAMINATION: Am I scrutinizing all my thoughts and actions for any trace of nonbeneficial or unwholesome motivation?

9. **The worldly pleasures we pursue in the course of our lives can vanish in an instant, like dew on the tip of a blade of grass. There is greater satisfaction and lasting bliss to be found in walking the spiritual path and awakening the Buddha within.**

The Sons and Daughters of the Buddhas all follow this practice.

COMMENTARY: It's foolish to turn away from the path of awakening merely to fulfill our quest for pleasure. No matter how good something looks, feels, sounds, or tastes, this pleasure will last for little more than a heartbeat. Enlightenment, on the other hand, brings us freedom and bliss.

SELF-EXAMINATION: Am I too easily distracted by "cheap thrills" or am I able to keep my eye on the bigger picture?

10. **How can we think only of ourselves when others are suffering? Recognize this suffering and generate the awakened heart-mind of Bodhicitta for the benefit of all.**

The Sons and Daughters of the Buddhas all follow this practice.

COMMENTARY: Ancient Buddhist texts point out that we have all been reborn so many times that every single living creature has at one time been a loving relative, perhaps even our mother or father. These old friends and loved ones may be suffering; they may need our help. The greatest service we can provide is to cultivate and radiate Bodhicitta—the awakened heart-mind—throughout the universe.

SELF-EXAMINATION: Am I sensitive to what others are experiencing?

11. Selfish thoughts and desires will ultimately fail us. Replace these concerns with compassion for all others and the greater good. This will lead us to freedom and awakening.

The Sons and Daughters of the Buddhas all follow this practice.

COMMENTARY: Self-interest is our spiritual foe. When we think only of ourselves, we cause problems for ourselves. Cultivating love and a greater awareness of others bring us closer to spiritual maturity and great awakening. Shantideva said:

> *All the joy the world contains*
> *Has come through wishing happiness for others.*
> *All the misery the world contains*
> *Has come through wanting pleasure for oneself.*

SELF-EXAMINATION: According to Buddhist wisdom, egotism and selfishness is the root of all evil. How can this teaching help me release my own self-absorption and egotism?

12. Cultivate a nonattachment for worldly goods that is so strong that even if someone takes away everything you own, you will still feel compassion and pray for his prosperity and well-being.

The Sons and Daughters of the Buddhas all follow this practice.

COMMENTARY: We can use our monetary and worldly losses to accelerate our spiritual growth. I have a little story about this. Recently I was walking down a street on a country road in Vermont, and came upon a yard sale. I stopped to look at the various dishes, bric a brac, and clothing that had been collected. The woman who was running the sale was laughing ruefully. It seems that moments before, a car had pulled up, and while her back was turned, the driver had taken several men's shirts, jackets, and slacks that were hanging on a tree. The car then sped away. "Well," she said, "I hope somebody enjoys the clothes, and I hope everything fits." That was my lesson for the day! Of course, these were just small items. But this is the kind of attitude we need to extend to everyone, even those who cause us large financial loss, if we wish to truly transcend attachment to worldly possessions and experience content and abundance.

SELF-EXAMINATION: Can I share whatever I have, recognizing that nothing is really mine for very long anyway?

13. If we should know someone who threatens us or tries to cause us serious bodily harm, we should feel compassion for this person and show mercy by genuinely wishing that he suffers no further because of his or her deluded and misguided state.

The Sons and Daughters of the Buddhas all follow this practice.

COMMENTARY: The last two practices are very similar to the words of Jesus found in the New Testament book of Matthew:

"But I say to you, Do not resist an evildoer. But if anyone strikes you on the right cheek, turn the other also; and if anyone wants to sue you and take your coat, give your cloak as well; and if anyone forces you to go one mile, go also the second mile. Give to anyone who begs from you, and do not refuse anyone who wants to borrow from you. You have heard that it was said, 'You shall love your neighbor and hate your enemy.' But I say to you, Love your enemies and pray for those who persecute you."

SELF-EXAMINATION: Can I feel compassion even for those who wish me ill? Can I remember that they are actually harming themselves?

14. Even if someone slanders and criticizes us, spreading cruel rumors that some people may even believe, speak of that person with kindness. When you speak of him to others, praise his virtues.

The Sons and Daughters of the Buddhas all follow this practice.

COMMENTARY: When someone says unkind things about us that aren't true, it feels very mean. No one wants to be slandered. Nonetheless, when it happens, we can pray that the person gains peace and overcomes the prejudices, misconceptions, and mental instability that must be at work. My teacher, Dilgo Khyentse Rinpoche, said, "To reply with kindness and compassion to negativity and harm is the swiftest way to progress in overcoming ego and fulfilling the Bodhisattva path."

SELF-EXAMINATION: Do we have the inner strength and fortitude to respond both intelligently and gently to the inevitable diversity of opinions that exist in our world?

15. Even if someone insults and criticizes us in front of others, describing our flaws to anyone who will listen, instead of feeling anger, consider that person like a spiritual friend and advisor. Listen quietly and show respect; we can always learn from honest criticism.

The Sons and Daughters of the Buddhas all follow this practice.

COMMENTARY: There is a distinction between this practice and the one immediately preceding it. Here, the person who is pointing out our flaws may be abusing us with harsh words, but nonetheless, the criticism has some validity. We are doubly advised against becoming defensive and angry because this person has taken on a role not unlike that of a true teacher who helps us see our shortcomings so we can work on ourselves. Dilgo Khyentse Rinpoche said, "If someone criticizes us, why should we be unhappy? Someone else may be praising us at the same time. How does either really affect us?"

SELF-EXAMINATION: Am I open to constructive criticism and learning from even hostile opinions?

16. **If someone we have nurtured and cared for as one would a cherished child becomes resentful, angry, and hurtful, we should become even kinder and more giving; we should be understanding.**

The Sons and Daughters of the Buddhas all follow this practice.

COMMENTARY: Many of us have had the experience of trying to treat someone with kindness and love only to have the person turn on us for reasons we don't fully understand. Unkindness from someone we love is so much more painful than abuse from a stranger. Even so, we are encouraged to maintain our affectionate and loving attitude as if toward someone who is ill or not in his/her right mind.

SELF-EXAMINATION: Can I continue to feel love and empathy even for those who I feel have betrayed me?

17. **If someone is contemptuous or treats you without respect—even if that person is not your intellectual or spiritual equal—repay them with honor as you would an admired teacher.**

The Sons and Daughters of the Buddhas all follow this practice.

COMMENTARY: We train ourselves to swallow our pride; as we do so we realize that every time someone treats us with contempt and lack of respect, we are being given a lesson in humility. This lesson is all the stronger when it is delivered by someone we don't want to think of as our equal or qualified to correct us. This helps us loosen attachment to ego. With this practice, we can begin to realize that we are all equally important; we all have our opinions and a right to express them.

SELF-EXAMINATION: Do I genuinely understand the valuable lessons to be found through humility?

18. No matter how dire your emotional, physical, or financial condition, stay true to your practice, your inner principles, and your intentions. Continue to walk the path of awakening for yourself and all beings.

The Sons and Daughters of the Buddhas all follow this practice.

COMMENTARY: In Buddhism we are taught to bring everything in our lives—good and bad—onto the spiritual path. Some of the most inspiring practitioners are those whose lives are filled with serious problems, illness, and personal loss; even so, they stay committed to the Bodhisattva Vow and the spiritual path. In this way, even stumbling blocks are stepping stones.

SELF-EXAMINATION: At the most difficult moments in my life, can I stay open-hearted and maintain my commitment to the path of enlightenment?

19. Success and fame can be detrimental to spiritual development. No matter how much wealth you accumulate or how much you are praised and admired, don't be swept away by worldly achievements or lose sight of what is real. Stay connected to who you are and what really matters.

The Sons and Daughters of the Buddhas all follow this practice.

COMMENTARY: When we are trying to have a spiritual practice, money and success sometimes present a genuine challenge. It's easy to forget that praise and gain are merely transitory and lack any real substance. We've all seen how easy it is for successful people to get swept away on ego trips and lose touch with fundamental values. This practice reminds us to stay grounded in what's real, true, and good.

SELF-EXAMINATION: It's difficult not to get swept up into an ego trip when everything is going well. Can I do it? Can I stay committed to an awakened heart and bring my happy days with me on the spiritual path?

20. Anger is an inner problem. When you feel anger, don't just strike out at others. Instead turn inward and call upon your resources of awareness, love, and compassion to heal yourself first.

The Sons and Daughters of the Buddhas all follow this practice.

COMMENTARY: It's been said many times: How can we heal others unless we can heal ourselves? The powerful emotion of anger can create havoc, causing us to hurt others as well as ourselves. Think about the situations that have made you respond or even lash out with anger. We heal our anger with forgiveness—forgiveness of ourselves as well as others.

SELF-EXAMINATION: Thich Nhat Hanh reminds his students that "anger makes us ugly . . . anger makes us suffer . . . anger makes us double up like a shrimp being roasted." Can I remember this insight the next time I feel anger arising?

21. The more we pursue our desires, the more our desires grow; it's like drinking saltwater. We find freedom by letting go of our tendencies to become obsessed and addicted to situations that will ultimately prove unsatisfying.

The Sons and Daughters of the Buddhas all follow this practice.

COMMENTARY: In life, we could all become more balanced and even. Recognize our desires for what they are: ways of keeping us stuck, attached, and addicted. Satisfaction arises from seeking wholeness and well-being rather than seeking excitement. All else is like a roller-coaster.

SELF-EXAMINATION: Am I sometimes like a moth who is attracted to a flame? Do I become consumed by the objects of my momentary desire?

22. Recognize that life is dreamlike and illusory, and that truth is beyond concepts, existence, or solid separate individuality. See what *is;* move away from a dualistic perception of reality.

The Sons and Daughters of the Buddhas all follow this practice.

COMMENTARY: This practice introduces the concept of absolute Bodhicitta, which recognizes that everything is infinitely vast, ungraspable, and unknowable. Shabkar, a renowned, enlightened Tibetan yogi of the nineteenth century, sang:

> *"I realized that the nature of this mind,*
> *The root of samsara and nirvana,*
> *Is an ineffable luminous void*
> *With nothing to cling to."*

SELF-EXAMINATION: Can I keep my perspective on my experience—can I watch and enjoy the sitcom or the movie of my life without being overwhelmed by the melodramatic moments? Can I see through myself and not take it all so seriously?

23. Don't be fooled by appearances, style, or form. The loveliest objects can be as insubstantial and fleeting as the

rainbows of summer. Let go of your impulsive, knee-jerk attractions to things that don't last.

The Sons and Daughters of the Buddhas all follow this practice.

COMMENTARY: Why are we so strongly attracted to beautiful people and beautiful objects? Why are we overly influenced by current styles? In this modern age, entire industries revolve around beautiful images from the shiniest new cars to the most exciting new fashion models. The teachings of the Buddha remind us to look deeper into ourselves, into each other, and into the face of life itself—not just living on the surface of things, and wading in the shallows of life.

SELF-EXAMINATION: In my life, am I able to differentiate between the commercials and the main story?

24. All of us face problems and suffering. Recognize the illusory nature of all things; regard even difficulties and tragedies as fleeting and dreamlike.

The Sons and Daughters of the Buddhas all follow this practice.

COMMENTARY: This meditation on illusion and dreams is meant to be particularly helpful for seekers who struggle with crisis, tragedy, and grief. It addresses the age-old question of why bad things happen to good people. Milarepa's beloved guru Marpa was a householder who suffered the tragic death of his teenage son. When his child died, Marpa cried, "Of course everything is an illusion, but the death of a child is like a nightmare." Then he cried some more.

When faced with our own tragedies, we need to remember that when it's time to grieve, we grieve; this is necessary. Our dreamlike emotions are just as valid within the dream as anything else. We keep in touch with the bigger picture by remembering that even tragedies are insubstantial and illusory.

SELF-EXAMINATION: Am I able to open my tender and

vulnerable heart and feel the suffering and vicissitudes of life even while recognizing its illusory nature?

25. If we truly want enlightenment, we must be prepared to give of ourselves and all that we own without any thought of personal merit or gain. Cultivate an abundant, generous heart.

The Sons and Daughters of the Buddhas all follow this practice.

COMMENTARY: This charitable practice refers to the first paramita, generosity. The Sanskrit word "paramita" is literally translated as "that which has reached the other shore." In other words, a paramita refers to a transcendental virtue. The most common translation for paramita is "perfection." Mahayana teachings tell us to cultivate six perfections or paramitas. The first perfection that a Bodhisattva cultivates is giving with an open heart—"open hands, open heart, open arms, and open mind." Giving in this sense refers to more than giving alms. It means giving boundless energy and unconditional love in whatever form is required.

SELF-EXAMINATION: Can I truly be there for others, responding generously to what they need—as opposed to just giving those things that are easy for me to share?

26. If we lack ethics, virtue, and morality in our own lives, how can we help others? Practice self-discipline and moderation, vowing to be moral and ethical in everything you do.

The Sons and Daughters of the Buddhas all follow this practice.

COMMENTARY: The second paramita that a Bodhisattva cultivates is virtue and morality, which is known as "sila." Thus budding Bodhisattvas strive to live always with ethics, honesty, straightforwardness, and virtue. This leads to character development,

self-mastery, and the spiritual refinement of an impeccable, fully actu-
alized human being.

SELF-EXAMINATION: Do I apply ethical principles to
my daily decisions whether they be large or small?

27. **Our worthwhile intentions are continually challenged by the negative and destructive situations we encounter. In the most trying circumstances, let go of anger
and resentment. Instead cultivate patience toward all.**

**The Sons and Daughters of the Buddhas all follow this
practice.**

COMMENTARY: The third paramita is "shanti"—the
perfection of patience, endurance, and forbearance. We can
learn to "go beyond" the expectations of this world and display
patience in the most intolerable situations. During his lifetime,
the Buddha's cousin tried to kill him. The Buddha said that this
cousin's behavior helped him develop even greater patience,
forbearance, and compassion. The Buddha referred often to this
cousin as one of his best teachers.

SELF-EXAMINATION: Do I understand the importance
of patience? Do I cultivate forbearance in myself in all situations?

28. **Many seek to reach enlightenment for themselves
alone; even they walk the path as though their hair is on fire
and only their effort will put out the flames of their spiritual
emergency. Think, therefore, of how much more energy is
required to strive for enlightenment for the benefit of all
who suffer. This goal requires total commitment, courage,
and diligent effort.**

**The Sons and Daughters of the Buddhas all follow this
practice.**

COMMENTARY: The Buddha's advice to his followers
was to meditate and strive for enlightenment as though their

hair was on fire. This practice refers to the fourth paramita, which is the perfection of perseverance and effort. All of us innately have within us boundless energy and inexhaustible resources. We have only to utilize these inner natural resources to fulfill our heart's desire.

SELF-EXAMINATION: Do I have a passion for truth and enlightenment or am I just going through the motions?

29. In order to penetrate the nature of reality and achieve real insight and deeper understanding, we need training and grounding in mental stability and focused attention. Mere spiritual highs are not sufficient to liberate and awaken our mind, or to achieve the result of "the heart's true release."

The Sons and Daughters of the Buddhas all follow this practice.

COMMENTARY: This practice corresponds to the fifth paramita, the perfection of meditation, of mindfulness, focus, and concentration. If, through contemplative practices, you develop mental stability and focused concentration, then you can use it to gain deeper insight into the nature of reality. This delivers us far beyond the merely temporary highs and lows of the path of spiritual experience. These experiences are like scenery along the great highway of awakening. Better to develop insight, wisdom, and stable awareness.

SELF-EXAMINATION: Do I make the practice of self-awareness through meditation and a mindful outlook a priority in my life?

30. The perfections of generosity, virtue, patience, effort, and meditative absorption alone will not bring us to enlightenment without the cultivation of wisdom.

The Sons and Daughters of the Buddhas all follow this practice.

COMMENTARY: Wisdom, or "prajna," is the sixth paramita. But when we talk about wisdom, we mean perfect or transcendental wisdom, not just knowledge. This is a wisdom so complete that it is liberated from concepts. It is taught that the highest form of wisdom is insight into the true nature of reality (which is emptiness), beyond the dualism or separatist framework of subject, object, and interaction. This is the realization of "sunyata"—infinite openness, emptiness, and oneness.

SELF-EXAMINATION: Am I accessing my inner wisdom and applying it through practical virtues? Am I understanding the emptiness of things and seeing how things work and fit together?

31. We need always continue to look inward and make consistent efforts to examine our faults in order to root out and let go of our own confusion and delusion. This requires a sincere and ongoing commitment to awakening from the sleep of illusion. Ideally we should embody the Dharma, not just pay it lip service.

The Sons and Daughters of the Buddhas all follow this practice.

COMMENTARY: It's very easy to get lax and lazy about self-examination, and even to fool ourselves. In all spiritual traditions, there are practitioners who only go so far before stalling on the side of the path, being satisfied to rest on a plateau. When he wrote this practice, Thogme Zangpo was telling us to "walk our talk," practice what we preach, and make it to the finish line. This is essential advice to the Dharma practitioner. Otherwise we may find ourselves becoming hypocrites who say one thing and do another.

SELF-EXAMINATION: Am I consistently practicing self-examination? Do I see myself realistically?

32. Don't speak ill of others, and don't criticize fellow seekers. The only faults we should mention are our own.

The Sons and the Daughters of the Buddhas all follow this practice.

COMMENTARY: This is simple and straightforward advice that discourages negative and judgmental criticism. Jesus' New Testament advice to his followers was, "Why do you see the speck in your neighbor's eye, but do not notice the log in your own eye?" The Buddha told his followers to refrain from gossiping and fault-finding. He told them to use words to help, not harm others. A Tibetan saying: "Don't look for the flea in others' hair and overlook the yak sitting on your own nose."

SELF-EXAMINATION: Am I resisting the temptation to judge and talk about others?

33. Sometimes our most intense emotions and arguments occur with family and good friends—those with whom we are most intimate. It can be difficult to study and reflect on the Dharma or meditate when all of our energy is engaged in domestic disputes. Avoid the strong attachments and emotions that these situations encourage.

The Sons and Daughters of the Buddhas all follow this practice.

COMMENTARY: When it was written several hundred years ago, this practical teaching specifically addressed the daily travails of household life. At that time, there was a different class and social structure. Tibetan society was divided into the royalty, the monastic community, and the lay householders who were often patrons. When a monk became embroiled in the domestic life of a patron, valuable time was spent. Dharma teachers were well aware then of how much energy gets absorbed in the melodramas of day-to-day life. The same thing, of course, is true today, but we also realize that we can't always walk away from family, friends, colleagues, homes, and responsibilities. Nonetheless, we should be able to employ mindfulness and spiritual intentions to become less attached and invested in the roller-coaster of daily life. Instead here and now in this century, we could utilize homes and workplaces too as opportunities for spiritual growth.

SELF-EXAMINATION: Am I doing all I can to find ways to integrate my spiritual philosophy into my relationships with my close circle of friends and family?

34. Unkind words can cause great harm. When we are angry and speak harshly to others, we lose our spiritual footing. We create pain, causing someone else's mind to become disturbed and upset. Give up abusing others with harsh language.

The Sons and Daughters of the Buddhas all follow this practice.

COMMENTARY: The Buddha was very sensitive to the amount of damage and abuse that can be caused through our speech. In this practice, we are reminded that someone who has the intention of helping another must remember to speak kindly and gently.

SELF-EXAMINATION: Are my communications—my words, the tone of my voice, and my body language—healing, harmonizing, and sensitive?

35. It's all too easy to fall into unconscious ways of acting and thinking. Mindfulness helps us more closely observe ourselves and thus keep our tendencies to form negative habits in check.

The Sons and Daughters of the Buddhas all follow this practice.

COMMENTARY: Pay attention; it pays off. This is probably the shortest yet most effective advice anyone can give on how to live an enlightened life. Otherwise, we find ourselves constantly trying to play catch-up, trying to undo mistakes and errors that we have made through a lack of mindfulness. For some mistakes there are no remedies. That's why it's wisest to stay awake and conscious of what you do, say, and think.

SELF-EXAMINATION: Today, am I living mindfully—consciously, and intentionally upholding my intention to live the spiritual life?

36. In summation: Whatever we do, whatever we think, wherever we go, whatever the circumstances, we need to look inward to examine our minds. The work of a Bodhisattva requires mindful, attentive awareness.

The Sons and the Daughters of the Buddhas all follow this practice.

COMMENTARY: Each time we renew our Bodhisattva vow, we are reminded that this path isn't always an easy stroll. The Bodhisattva's way of life calls for a full-time commitment to being more consciously loving and aware.

SELF-EXAMINATION: Am I remaining steadfast in my aspiration to a higher, more meaningful, and deeper life?

37. Dedicate our practice for the good of all. Share the benefits with everyone. Include all in your heart and prayers. Recognize the interconnectedness of all and make no distinction between beings; we are all equal in the spirit.

The Sons and Daughters of the Buddhas all follow this practice.

COMMENTARY: This final practice reaffirms the merits and good fortune to be found in practicing both relative and absolute Bodhicitta, without taking ourselves too seriously. This path is a joyous highway of awakening.

Within the Avatamsaka (Garland) Sutra, a Bodhisattva speaks several wonderful lines of poetry that get to the essence of Bodhicitta and the meaning of wisdom and nonduality.

> *"Be free from subject and object,*
> *Get away from dirtiness and cleanness,*
> *Sometimes entangled and sometimes not.*

*I forget all relative knowledge; my real
wish is to enjoy all things with all people."*

SELF-EXAMINATION: Am I including the welfare of all beings in my heart's prayers, my spiritual practice, and my life work?

This, I think, is Buddha's love.

About the Dzogchen Foundation

More information about Lama Surya Das and his schedule of lectures, workshops, retreats, tapes, CDs, local meditation group, and Dzogchen training can be found at:

www.surya.org

Those without Internet access, please write or call:

The Dzogchen Foundation
P.O. Box 400734
Cambridge, MA 02140
(617) 628–1702

To order a CD of companion chants called *Chants to Awaken the Buddhist Heart,* by Lama Surya Das and Steven Halpern, contact the Dzogchen Center at the above address or at www.dzogchen.org.

DZOGCHEN
FOUNDATION

INDEX

A
Absolute Bodhicitta, 37,
    234
Absolute truth, 191
Acceptance
    learning deeper, 200–207
    openness and, 79–80
    of others as they are,
        110–12
    of self, 72–75
    of suffering, 184–85
Agendas, hidden, 96
Airbrush reality, 25
Analytical meditation, 155
Anger. *See* Feelings
Animals. *See* Creatures
Appearances, 234–35
Assumptions, challenging,
    124–26
Atisha, 208
Attachments. *See also*
    Nonattachment;
    Samskaras
    persona, 68–70

romantic, 31
tonglen and, 211
Attitude Transformation
    Trainings, 208
Authentic listening, 99–100
Authentic presence, 61–80
    being true to self, 61–63
    dropping personas, 70–72
    groundedness, 63–65
    image issues, 65–68
    imitating, 75–76
    life as not easy but real, 25
    meaningful relationships
        and, 126–27
    persona attachments, 68–70
    as spiritual practice, 76–80
    self-acceptance, 72–75
Avalokitesvara, 102
Avatamsaka Sutra, 36–37,
    242–43
Aversions, 49–53, 90, 211
Awareness
    authenticity and, 80
    choiceless, 87

existential, 8, 10
mindfulness and, 58 (*see also*
    Mindfulness)
of self vs. of others, 215–16
spiritual intelligence, 10–12

B
Baba, Neem Karoli, 32–33
Balance, 188–90
Bardos, 25–26
Behavior, 90, 96
Berry, Thomas, 135
Big picture. *See* Spiritual
    intelligence
Blame, 52
Blofeld, John, 191–93
Bodh-Gaya, 27, 100–101, 102,
    153
Bodhicitta
    Dharma and, 122
    essence of, 242–43
    practices, 221–43
    relative and absolute, 37
    tonglen and, 208–17
Bodhisattvas
    courage and, 120
    practices of, 221–43
    as spiritual warriors, 34, 38
    vow of, 34–35, 242
Body awareness, 58
Boorstein, Sylvia, 81
Breath
    meditation and, 58–59, 98–99
    riding the moving, 213–14
Buber, Martin, 197
Buddha, 15–16, 24, 26, 30, 37,
    48–49, 207, 212
Buddha Fields, 37–38, 190–91
Buddha-nature, 1, 74, 91–92, 191
Buddhavatamsaka Sutra, 36–37
Buddhism
    Dzogchen, 191, 245
    Kadampa school, 208

Mahayana, 28, 34–38
    Tibetan medical diagnosis, 12
Buddhist heart
    practices (*see* Meditations;
        Practices)
    relationships and, 1–2 (*see also*
        Relationships)
    as spiritual center, 10–12
Buddhist Peace Park, 146
Buttons, samskara, 49–53, 90

C
Calmness, 188–90
Caring. *See* Love
Castaneda, Carlos, 73
Causation. *See* Karma
Center, spiritual, 10–12
Chain of Conditioned Arising,
    18–21
Challenges, 175–80, 185–88. *See
    also* Suffering
Chandi (dog), 92, 142–43, 156
Chants CD, 245
Chékawa, Geshe, 208–9
Chodron, Pema, 213
Choice, 41–42, 167–70
Choiceless awareness, 87
Clarity, 15–16, 47
Clinging, 97–98
Co-dependent relationships, 54
Common ground, 138
Community, 225–26
Connection reflex, 107–9. *See also*
    Meaningful relationships
Connections. *See* Relationships
Conscious speech, 129–30
Contemplation, 55–57
Control issues, 79, 96
Courage, 119–20
Crazy Wisdom, 167
Crazy wisdom, 157–74
    connecting to holy fool, 163–67
    elevator antics, 170–71

foolish choices, 167–70
holy folly, 162–63
laughter, humor, and, 157–62
mental constructs and, 171–73
spontaneity, 80
wise fool's meditation,
173–74
Creativity, 78
Creatures
learning from, 142–48
loving, 139–42
Criticism
as lesson, 230–31
openness and, 79–80
personas and, 71–72
relationships and, 112–13
Crowfoot, 224–25
Crystal, Billy, 65

D
Dak-nang, 190–96
Dalai Lama, 1, 4–5, 11, 35–36,
63–65, 107, 206, 215
Dana Paramita, 115, 236
Darshan, 144
Das, Bhagwan, 162
Das, Lama Surya, 9, 33, 35, 45–46,
66–67, 84, 92, 142–43, 156,
168–70, 200–201
Dass, Ram, 31, 105
Death, 24, 186–88, 224–25
Denial, 48
Dependency, 97–98
Desires, 233–34
Dharma, 22, 26, 122–23
Dharmakaya, 191
Difficulties. See Challenges
DNA, spiritual, 3, 10
Donne, John, 108
Drala principle, 145
Drom, Lama, 209
Dudjom Rinpoche, 182–83, 189,
193

Dzogchen, 191
Dzogchen Foundation, 245

E
Earth connections. See Nature
connections
Ego clinging, 71–72
Eight Worldly Winds or Eight
Traps, 52–53
Ekajati, 73–74
Elevator antics, 170–71
Eliot, George, 41
Emotions. See Feelings
Empathizing, 124
Emptiness. See Openness
Enemies, loving, 202–3, 229–30
Energy, giving, 117–18, 119–20
Enlightenment, 47, 67. See also
Path, spiritual
Events, awareness of, 58
Exchanging, 208–17
Exercises. See Meditations;
Practices
Existential awareness, 8, 10
Expectations of perfection, 92–95
Exploitation, 97

F
Fall meditation, 155
Fame, 52, 232–33
Family, 240–41
Feelings
awareness of, 58
meditation and, 87
noticing and embracing, 89
perspective and, 15
reactive, 223, 233
reflecting on, 90
samskaras and, 49–53, 90
First Thought, Best Thought, 166
Five Defects of a Vessel, 103–4
Flower Garland Sutra, 36–37,
242–43

Flower meditation, 152–53
Folly, holy, 162–70. *See also* Crazy wisdom
Forgiveness, 200–207
Foundations of Tibetan Mysticism, 86
Four Mind Changers, 22–26
Four-step mindfulness practice, 89–90
Friends, 240–41

G
Gain, 52
Ganges River cremations, 186–87
Garland, Judy, 23
Garland Sutra, 36–37, 242–43
Generosity
    with courage and energy, 119–20
    with gift of Dharma, 122–23
    with kindness, 118–19
    with knowledge, 121–22
    love and, 33–34
    with money and gifts, 116–17
    practicing, 236
    as receiver, 123
    relationships and, 114–23
    with time and energy, 117–18
    tonglen practice, 208–17
Giving. *See* Generosity; Tonglen
Golden Rule, 113–14
Goodall, Jane, 139
Goodness, 1
Gorman, Paul, 105
Gossip, 97
Govinda, Lama Anagarika, 86–89
Great Perfection teachings, 191
Groundedness, 63–65

H
Hamlet, 61–62
Hanh, Thich Nhat, 36, 59, 94, 199, 207, 233

Happiness
    furthering, 22–23
    others as source of, 215
    as spiritual path, 182–85
Harm, doing no, 226–27
Hearing. *See* Listening
Heart. *See* Buddhist heart
Heart as Wide as the World, A, 27
Heart Sutra, 102
Hidden agendas, 96
Hoffer, Eric, 119
Holy folly, 162–70. *See also* Crazy wisdom
Holy Grail, 162–63
Holy Now, 55, 60
Holy Spirit, 199
Home Depot, 148–49
Honesty. *See also* Truth
    love and, 31–32
    relationships and, 96–99
How Can I Help, 105
Human bond, 107. *See also* Relationships
Humility, 231–32
Humor. *See* Crazy wisdom

I
Ikebana, 152
Image issues, 65–68
Imitating authentic presence, 75–76
Impeccable Communication. *See* Right Speech
Impermanence, 24, 224–25
Inner practices, 7, 150–56. *See also* Meditations; Practices
Inner tyrant, 113
Inner warrior, 53–55, 73
Intelligence. *See* Spiritual intelligence
Intentional behavior, 90
Interbeing, 36–37

J
Jesus, 67–68, 210, 229
Joy. *See* Crazy wisdom
Joyce, James, 78
Judgments. *See* Criticism
Jung, Carl, 68
Just this meditation, 60

K
Kabir, 30, 103
Kadampa school, 208
Kado, 152
Kalu Rinpoche, 21–22, 35
Karma
  as carried always, 25–26
  as cause and effect, 18–21
  Earth's, 6, 135–39, 148–50
  improving, 148–50
  life experience and, 47
  meditating on, 155
  samskaras as, 50
Kennedy, John F., Jr., 63
Khenpo, Nyoshul, 143
Khyentse Rinpoche, Dilgo, 185,
    221, 225, 230
Kindness, 118–19, 230
Knowledge, sharing, 121–22
Kornfield, Jack, 180
Kuan Yin, Bodhisattva, 101
Kushner, Rabbi Harold, 203

L
Lama Foundation, 34
Lao Tzu, 173
LaRocca, James, 202
Laughter. *See* Crazy Wisdom
Lessons, 175–96
  balance and calmness, 188–90
  challenges as, 175–80, 185–88
  creatures and, 142–48
  criticism as, 230–31
  happiness/suffering as spiritual
    path, 182–85

karma and, 20
  of life experience, 43–47
  loving what we don't like (*see*
    Loving what we don't like)
  pain/suffering as truth, 180–82
  pure perception/sacred outlook
    practice/meditation, 190–96
Letting go. *See* Nonattachment
Life
  experience (*see* Life experience)
  lessons (*see* Lessons)
  living in past, 98
  preciousness of, 22–23, 222–23
  reality (*see* Truth)
  shortness of, 23–24
Life experience, 41–60
  challenges of, as choice, 41–42
  contemplating, 55–57
  Eight Worldly Winds or Eight
    Traps, 52–53
  inner spiritual warrior and,
    53–55
  lessons of, 43–47 (*see also*
    Lessons)
  Mindfulness of Breathing
    meditation, 57–59
  paying attention to, 47–49
  present moment meditation,
    60
  as spiritual path, 42–43
  understanding samskaras, 49–53
Like vs. love, 199–200. *See also*
    Love
Listening
  authentic, 99–100
  awareness of sounds, 58
  silence and, 103–4 (*see also*
    Silence)
  with third ear, 100–102
Living Buddha, Living Christ, 199
Lo-jong, 208
Loneliness, 4, 109
Loss, 52

Love, 27–39
  Bodhisattva Vow and, 34–39
  of creatures of Earth, 139–42
  as energy and being, 27–28
  like vs., 199–200 (see also
    Loving what we don't like)
  relationship and, 5–6 (see also
    Relationship)
  self-acceptance as, 72–75
  subtleties of, 28–34
Loving-kindness, 1, 28–34
Loving what we don't like, 8,
    197–217
  acceptance and forgiveness,
    200–207
  love vs. like, 199–200
  people we don't like, 197–99
  tonglen practice, 208–17

M
McCarty, Osceola, 207
Maharaji, 32–33
Mahayana Buddhism, 28, 34–38
Mahayana Mind Training, 208
Makransky, John, 113–14
Mani stones, 145
Manure Principle, 182
Marks, Adrian, 119–20
Marpa, 235
Marx, Groucho, 157
Masks. See Personas
Maun practice, 105
Meaningful relationships, 107–33
  acceptance and, 110–12
  being present, 126–27
  Bodhicitta practices, 225–26
  connection reflex and, 107–9
  conscious speech and conscious
    relationships, 129–30
  criticism and, 112–13
  day of Right Speech practice,
    130–33
  empathizing with others, 124

generosity and, 114–23 (see also
    Generosity)
  Golden Rule and, 113–14
  integrating, into quest, 109–10
  meditative tools for, 84–90 (see
    also Nonattachment)
  openness and, 124–26
  Right Speech and, 127–33
Medical diagnosis, Tibetan, 12
Meditations. See also Practices
  breathe, smile, let go, 98–99
  Fall analytical, 155
  Mindfulness of Breathing, 58
  on open nature of reality, 213
  perfection of, 238
  present moment, 60
  pure perception and sacred
    outlook, 193–96
  as relationship tools, 84–90
  seasonal, 150–56
  self-reflection, 55–57
  Spring flower, 152–53
  Summer water-gazing, 153–54
  traditional, 84–86
  Winter walking, 155–56
  wise fool's, 173–74
Meher Baba, 105
Mencius (Mengzi), 68
Mental constructs, 171–73
Milarepa, 101, 151, 160, 224
Mind, suffering and, 188–89
Mind and the Way, The, 94–95
Mindfulness
  authenticity and, 80
  four-step, 89–90
  as path to love, 199
  paying attention, 47–49, 57–60
  practicing, 241–42
  as relationship tool, 84–90
Money, sharing, 116–17
Morality, 236–37
Muir, John, 7
Murden, Toni, 175

N
Naturalness, 78
Nature connections, 5, 135–56
  Earth's karma, 135–39
  learning from creatures, 142–48
  loving creatures, 139–42
  outer practices to improve
    karma, 148–50
  seasonal meditations, 150–56
New Millennium Resolution, 219
Nirvana, 16, 67
Nisker, Wes, 167
Noble Eightfold Path, 109, 128
Noble Silence, 104–5, 148
Nonattachment, 81–105. *See also*
    Attachments
  authenticity and, 80, 90–92
  authentic listening, 99–102
  Bodhicitta practice and, 228–29
  breathe, smile, let go
    meditation, 98–99
  expectations of perfection and,
    92–95
  five defects of a vessel
    reflection, 103–4
  meditative relationship tools,
    84–90
  Noble Silence practice, 104–5
  relationships and, 81–84, 96–99
  silence and, 103–4
  suffering and, 184
  third ear listening, 100–102
  traditional meditation
    instruction, 84–86
Norbu Rinpoche, Thinley, 183
Norlha, Lama, 179
Nyingmapa practice, 182–83

O
Obstacles. *See* Challenges
Om Mani Pedmé Hung mantra,
    43
Opening the Wisdom Eye, 11

Openness
  authentic presence and, 79–80
  meditating on, 213
  relationships and, 124–26
  sunyata as, 16, 37, 239
  wisdom of, 115
Outer practices, 7, 148–50. *See also*
    Practices

P
Pain. *See* Suffering
Paramitas, 115, 236–39
Passages, 25–26
Past, living in, 98
Path, spiritual
  dropping personas on, 70–72
  happiness/suffering as, 182–85
  life experience as, 42–43
  Noble Eightfold, 109, 128
  relationships and, 109–10
  as warrior's path, 53–55, 73
Path with Heart, A, 180
Patience, 237
Patterns, 8–10, 19, 46–47
Paying attention. *See* Mindfulness
People. *See* Relationships
Perception, pure, 190–96
Percival, 162–63
Perfection, 92–95
Perfections, 115, 236–39
Perseverance, 237–38
Personas
  attachment to, 68–70
  dropping, 70–72
  self-acceptance and, 72–75
Perspective. *See* Spiritual
    intelligence
Pleasure, 52, 227
Pot, *See* Five Defects of a Vessel,
    103–4
Practices. *See also* Meditations
  accepting suffering as spiritual
    path, 184–85

Bodhicitta, 221–43
choosing to be authentic, 76–80
crazy wisdom, 170–71
day of Right Speech, 130–33
Five Defects of a Vessel, 103–4
Four Mind Changers, 21–26
four-step mindfulness, 89–90
improving karma, 148–50
inner vs. outer, 7
listing people to forgive, 204–7
Noble Silence, 104–5
perseverance in, 232
pure perception/sacred outlook, 190–96
tonglen, 208–17
Praise, 52
Prajna, 238–39
Prayer, new millennium, 219
Preciousness of life, 22–23
Presence, sacred, 144. *See also* Authentic presence
Present moment meditation, 60. *See also* Mindfulness
Pure perception, 190–96

Q
Quest. *See* Path, spiritual

R
Ramakrishna, 153–54
Rampa, Lobsang, 11
Rangdrol, Choying, 160
Rashomon movie, 49
Reality. *See* Truth
Receiving, 123. *See also* Tonglen
Reflex, connection, 107–9. *See also* Meaningful relationships
Relationships
authentic and honest, 96–99
to big perspective (*see* Spiritual intelligence)
Buddhist heart and, 1–2
co-dependent, 54

with family and friends, 240–41
to holy fool, 163–67 (*see also* Crazy wisdom)
image issues and, 66
to life experience and lessons (*see* Lessons; Life experience)
meaningful (*see* Meaningful relationships)
meditative tools for, 84–90
to nature (*see* Nature connections)
nonattachment and, 81–84 (*see also* Nonattachment)
to what we don't like (*see* Loving what we don't like)
Relative Bodhicitta, 37
Relative reality/truth, 16
Relativity, 94
Reps, Paul, 203
Riding the moving breath, 213–14
Right Speech, 128, 130–33. *See also* Speech
Romantic attachments, 31, 93

S
Sacred outlook, 190–96
Sacred presence, 144
Salzberg, Sharon, 27
Samsara, 24–25
Samskaras, 49–53, 90
Saraha, 160–61
Seasonal meditations, 150–56
Self
acceptance of, 72–75
authentic, 23, 61–63 (*see also* Authentic presence)
cherishing, 215, 228
examination, 31–32, 239
mastery, 20
personas (*see* Personas)
reflection exercise, 55–57
relationships and authentic, 90–92

Seven Points of Mind Training, 209
Shabkar, Lama, 183, 234
Shah, Idries, 159
Shame, 52
Shanti, 237
Shantideva, 38–39, 202, 211–12, 228
Sharing. *See* Generosity
Shichiri, 203
Shmelke, Rabbi, 197
Shortness of life, 23–24, 224–25
Sila, 236–37
Silence
    listening and, 103–4 (*see also* Listening)
    meditation and, 87
    Noble, 104–5, 148
Simplicity, 79, 223–24
Six perfections, 236–39
Six Principles of Enlightened Living, 115–16
Solitude, 223–24
Solzhenitsyn, Aleksandr, 178
Soul mates, 7, 93
Sounds, 58. *See also* Listening
Speech
    conscious, 129–30
    day of Right Speech, 130–33
    gossip and tale telling, 97
    kind, 230, 241
    relationships and, 127–33
    using, to help, 239–40
Spiritual intelligence, 3–26
    big perspective as, 9–10, 13–15
    components of, 12–21
    Four Mind Changers practice, 21–26
    lessons (*see* Lessons)
    practices (*see* Meditations; Practices)
    reality and, 15–18
    relationships and, 3–10 (*see also* Relationships)

spiritual center and, 10–12
spiritual path (*see* Path, spiritual)
spiritual warriors, 53–55, 73 (*see also* Bodhisattvas)
    understanding karma and, 18–21
Spontaneity, 80
Spring meditation, 152–53
Steindl-Rast, Brother David, 111
Stockdale, James, 178
Stress, 189–90
Success, 232–33
Suffering. *See also* Challenges
    mind and, 188–89
    pain and pleasure samskara, 52
    recognizing, of others, 227–28
    as spiritual path, 182–85
    truth of, 180–82, 235–36
Sumedho, Ajahn, 94–95
Summer meditation, 153–54
Sunyata, 16, 37, 239. *See also* Openness

T
Tales of the Hassidim, 197
Tale telling, 97
Tao Te Ching, 173
Teachers
    availability of, 21
    death as, 24, 186–88, 224–25
Tendencies. *See* Samskaras
Teresa, Mother, 4
Third ear listening, 100–102
Third Eye, The, 11
Third Zen Patriarch, 95
Thirty-seven Practices of Bodhisattvas, 221–43
This is it teaching, 42–43
Thoreau, Henry David, 79
Thoughts, awareness of, 58
Three Jewels, 226
Thurman, Robert, 12
Tibetan Book of the Dead, The, 42, 95
Tibetan medical diagnosis, 12

Time, 23–24, 117–18
Tonglen, 208–17
Trainings. *See* Lessons;
    Meditations; Practices
Transitions, 25–26
Troubles. *See* Challenges
Trungpa Rinpoche, Chogyam, 61,
    73, 161–62, 165–66, 181–82
"Trust in the Heart Sutra," 95
Truth
    absolute reality, 191
    authenticity and, 63–65, 90–92
    (*see* Authentic presence)
    distinguishing, 15–18
    dualistic perception of, 234
    life journey and, 24–25
    letting go and (*see*
        Nonattachment)
    openness and nature of, 213 (*see*
        also Openness)
    of pain and suffering, 180–82
    realism and, 48–49
    reconnecting to, 78–80
    self-acceptance and, 72–75
Tulkus, 124

U
Unkindness, 231–32, 241

V
Vajra, 182

Values, superficial, 97
Vessel, Five Defects of a, 103–4
Virtue, 236–37
Vow, Bodhisattva, 34–35, 242

W
Walking meditation, 155–56
Warriors, spiritual, 53–55, 73. *See
    also* Bodhisattvas
Water-gazing meditation,
    153–54
Waving, 38–39
Way of the Bodhisattva, The, 211
Web site, Dzogchen Foundation,
    245
Winter meditation, 155–56
Wisdom
    authenticity and, 80
    behavior and, 90
    crazy (*see* Crazy wisdom)
    of openness, 115
    perfection of, 238–39
    three kinds of, 103
Wisdom eye, 11
Wise fool's meditation, 173–74
Wizard of Oz, The, 23
Words. *See* Speech

Z
Zangpo, Thogmé, 221, 239
Zen Flesh, Zen Bones, 203

A CROWDED ARK

A

CROWDED

ARK

Jon R. Luoma

Houghton Mifflin Company

Boston *1987*

Library of Congress Cataloging-in-Publication Data

Luoma, Jon R.
  A crowded ark / Jon R. Luoma.
    p. cm.
  Bibliography: p.
  Includes index.
  ISBN 0-395-40879-2
  1. Zoos. I. Title.
QL76.L866 1987   87-17784
590'.74 4—dc19   CIP

Printed in the United States of America

P 10 9 8 7 6 5 4 3 2 1

For Pam

Acknowledgments

Dozens of zookeepers, curators, veterinarians, directors, and assorted others willingly and graciously offered me their time and insights during the many months that this book was in progress. I'd particularly like to thank William Conway and John Gwynne at the Bronx Zoo; George Rabb and Sandy Friedman at the Brookfield Zoo; Ed Maruska, Betsy Dresser, and Milan Busching at the Cincinnati Zoo; Bob Hoage, Jon Ballou, and Devra Kleiman at the National Zoo; Jeff Jouett and Marvin Jones at the San Diego Zoo; Clayton Freiheit and John Wortman at the Denver Zoo; and most especially, at the Minnesota Zoo, former directors Ed Kohn and Steve Iserman, current director Kathryn Roberts, Nancy Gibson, Nick Reindl, Austin McDevitt, Jim Pichner, Mike DonCarlos, Frank Wright, John Lewis, and Ron Tilson. Steve Graham of the Detroit Zoo not only provided information and hospitality, but loaned me a large carton of important, and in many cases rare, zoo books from his superb personal library.

This book truly would not have been possible without the early and continuing help of Tom Foose of the American Association of Zoological Parks and Aquariums, Nate Flesness of the International Species Inventory System, and Ulysses S. Seal of the U.S. Veterans Administration Hospital in Minneapolis.

I'd also like to thank Gary Soucie at *Audubon* magazine

for planting the seeds that grew into this book, John Fleischmann at *Ohio* for suggesting the title, William Strachan at Houghton Mifflin for insights, aid, and patience, and my wife, Pam Hendrick, for assuring that I did not take myself too seriously even while taking this work seriously.

Contents

I

THE ANIMAL FAIR

1

2

A CROWDED ARK

37

3

THE FROZEN FUTURE

73

4

GOING HOME AGAIN

124

5

BARNUM AND BIOLOGY

150

Selected Readings

197

Index

200

A CROWDED ARK

THE ANIMAL FAIR

DAKOTA COUNTY, MINNESOTA, lies just south of the Twin Cities of Minneapolis and St. Paul in the north central United States. About twelve thousand years ago, a retreating glacier left behind huge mounds of glacial sediment here, so that today the county terrain looks like the sea during a storm: great rolling waves of eroded glacial drift.

Once the hills were forests of oak and maple and box elder, willow and prickly ash, witch hazel, dogwood, and sumac, dotted with ponds and potholes, home to the Sioux. Grizzlies lived here, and timber wolves and flocks of the slate gray and rose-breasted bird called the passenger pigeon. In the nineteenth century, fur trappers, traders, lumberjacks, missionaries, sodbusters, and soldiers came up the Mississippi River to the growing settlements of St. Anthony, north of what is now the Dakota County line, and Pig's Eye, a village that took its name from a notorious local saloonkeeper. The villages grew into cities, and the Roman Catholic missionaries canonized Pig's Eye in the name of St. Paul; the Protestant fathers across the river secularized the name of their city to Minneapolis.

In time the Sioux were pushed west into the Great Plains; the grizzly, the wolf, and the passenger pigeon disappeared. Into the burgeoning cities north of the county came lumber barons, railroad barons, banking barons, grain barons, and later, Scotch-tape barons. Still, only two or three decades ago Dakota County was dominated by cornfields and woodlands.

Recently, the county has undergone what urban planners call growth. The woods have been cleared and the fields graded to make way for tracts of "town homes," "patio homes," and "executive homes"; billboards planted into the glacial mounds announce the names of coming developments — Ridgecliffe, Vienna Woods — and the price of the American dream — "From $1,500 Down. No Closing Costs!" The dominant flora in the developments are Kentucky bluegrass and fescue, guaranteed "weed-free" and shaved into green flat swards around the houses. Green and yellow tank trucks prowl the county's winding streets, seeking to wipe out any broad-leaf plants that manage to survive. A network of urban superhighways gropes down into Dakota County today, and more highways and tracts of housing and shopping malls are planned.

But in the Dakota County suburb of Apple Valley is a patch of woods — five hundred acres of second-growth oak forest, dotted with ponds and laid out along a moraine named Johnny Cake Ridge — barely out of sight of the tract houses.

In the afternoon light, Nick Reindl and I are standing on a blacktop path near the edge of that island of hilly woodland. Directly before us is a low, thigh-high, concrete wall, but its back is sheer, dropping down maybe fifteen feet. Beyond its base a small grassy, shrubby clearing, littered with granite boulders, surrounds a tiny pond. Beyond the pond is an abrupt hillside, deeply wooded, the sun shafting between the trees. A brook flows down the hill, then through the clearing and into the pond. But there's something askew about this scene, and it might take a second look to catch what it is. The pond and the little brook are lined with concrete, and the boulders look vaguely phony.

Reindl, with a round Germanic face and dark-rimmed glasses, has the look of a bookish midwestern farm boy. He's wearing khaki trousers and a matching shirt with epaulets, a safari get-up, and a set of keys is attached to a chrome canister on his belt, janitor style. Reindl steps up to the concrete wall, reaches to his belt, pulls forward the keys, and barely jingles them.

There's movement in the trees, a big, sudden splash of yellow, white, black. Up on the hillside in the thick undergrowth an animal lifts itself, deliberately, like a yawn. Here on Johnny Cake Ridge in suburban Apple Valley, Minnesota, is a tiger, a big one, and it is sashaying down the hillside through the trees. There's no sound but a chickadee's two-note whistle in the woods behind us as the three-hundred-pound cat slides into the clearing. Another tiger and still another come out of the woods, out of perfect, striped camouflage from the sun-dappled forest and into the clearing. Now there are three by the pond, their amber eyes bright. One calmly mounts a boulder and sits. All three study Reindl on the wall above. They are Siberian tigers; larger than their widely known Bengal kin, they are the biggest of the world's cats.

This spot in Dakota County lies almost exactly halfway between the North Pole and the equator, near the forty-fifth parallel. If you were to follow that latitude west, you'd come to a region near the Amur River on the Sino-Soviet border. Once thousands of these magnificent giant felines roamed the north Asian taiga, stalking, pouncing, and pulling down Siberian wapiti for a meal and, some observers say, rolling and sliding down snowy slopes of a moonlit night. Today, at the very most, only about three hundred of the planet's largest cats remain in the wild, only in scattered parcels of wild land. Population biologists say that even if the destruction of tiger habitat can be abated, the Siberian tiger population may be too small and too scattered for the species to survive.

Most tiger experts are not sanguine about the cat's future. The few remaining wild Siberians are under a host of pressures: habitat encroachment, poaching, isolation in "islands" of habitat too small to prevent inbreeding, and subsequent declines in fertility and increased infant mortality. Reindl is a curator responsible for one of the largest captive populations of this critically endangered species. Some believe the tiger's survival may depend on places like this wooded refuge in Dakota County, an exhibit on the grounds of the Minnesota Zoological Gardens.

2

No one knows when prehistoric humans first began to capture wild beasts. Wolves, and perhaps jackals, were domesticated early—litters of their young carried back to a human camp—perhaps to be eaten, but some allowed to live because their playful behavior amused a hunter. The pups proved exceedingly loyal to their captors, for they had been programmed genetically to fit the intensely social interactions within a pack. They would fiercely guard their master's property and his life. With their speed and power and most especially their superb sense of smell, they would assist mightily in the hunt. Soon the human captors found that they could breed into succeeding generations behavioral or physiological traits they found useful—size and speed for pulling down deer, a tranquil temperament for harmony around the family fire. In time the wolf or jackal became the domesticated dog. Archaeologists have found in Europe what they believe is fossilized dog dung in the remains of human encampments of the Paleolithic Gravettian culture believed to be at least thirty-five thousand years old and a complete skeleton of a dog fossilized in Mesolithic, or middle Stone Age time, in a human encampment about ten thousand years old.

In India, elephants were hauling cargo and perhaps human passengers by 2500 B.C., and there are carved figures of apparently domesticated roosters and rock hens from about that period. The domestication of hoofed stock was complete by around 1400 B.C., for murals from ancient Thebes show slaves herding two breeds of cattle, one short-horned, the other lyre-horned, both probably domesticated from an ancient wild bison, the aurochs.

Zoos, however, appeared only after the domestication of humanity. There is no evidence of desire by any hunter-gatherer culture or primitive, agriculturally based society to collect numbers of wild animals for display. But the moment civilizations, wealthy royalty, and cities appear in history, zoos also appear.

The first known zoo-type collections were assembled about 2500 B.C. in Egypt. Pictographic records in the archaeological digs at Saqqara show pet monkeys, antelope, mongooses, hyenas, oryx, ibex, addaxes, and gazelles. One set of pictographs portrays an antelope wearing a collar, and some images appear to show stockades. There are detailed hieroglyphic records of one ruler who kept an immense collection of wild creatures, including 1,308 oryx and 1,135 gazelles.

During the fifteenth century B.C., Thutmose III kept in his temple gardens at Karnak exotic plants, birds, and mammals from Syria. His stepmother, Hatshepsut, who had an extensive palace zoo, once sent a collecting expedition to the land of Punt, probably present-day Somalia, more than a thousand miles on the Red Sea from Karnak. The party returned with monkeys, leopards, exotic birds, and even a giraffe, all of which were consigned to the queen's palace zoo. Rameses II owned giraffes, lions, and ostriches.

Ashurbanipal, the last powerful king of Assyria, had a zoological garden, and Nebuchadnezzar, king of Babylonia in the sixth century B.C., was a collector of lions.

King Solomon was a royal animal collector: "For the king's ships went to Tar'shish with the servants of Hu'ram: every three years once came the ship of Tar'shish bringing gold and silver, ivory, and apes, and peacocks." Indeed, the wise Solomon was a great collector in general, and perhaps the greatest of ancient royal wheeler-dealers, trading silver shekels for chariots and horses, hoofstock, and exotic birds by the thousands with his father-in-law, the pharaoh, and his neighbor, King Hiram of Tyre.

According to Confucius, sometime around 2000 B.C. an Empress Tanki built a marble "house of deer." Later, during the Chou dynasty, Emperor Wen Wang established a fifteen-hundred-acre menagerie called the Garden of Intelligence, which included samples of such fauna as the giant panda from throughout the vast and ecologically diverse Chinese Empire.

The ancient Greeks, too, were animal collectors. By the seventh century B.C., pet monkeys and birds began to appear in the gardens of rulers and nobles. By the sixth century B.C., they were importing exotic cranes, purple gallinules, and African domestic cats. A century later, the Greeks were building aviaries for finches, nightingales, jackdaws, magpies, pheasant, quail, and flamingos. Peacocks became such an immense attraction that owners could charge admission to see them.

By the fourth century B.C., the time was ripe for Aristotle to begin the first systematic zoological survey. His encyclopedia, *The History of Animals*, described about three hundred known vertebrates, primarily from studies of animals in menageries, especially those of Aristotle's former pupil Alexander the Great.

Probably the largest and most spectacular of the ancient menageries was founded by another Greek, Ptolemy I, whom Alexander had installed as ruler of Egypt. The zoo at Alexandria was expanded and enhanced by Ptolemy II, who sent expeditions for animals into Ethiopia and was probably the first to bring man's closest animal relative, the chimpanzee, into captivity. It is unlikely that any survived longer than a few months, considering the difficulty of keeping apes healthy in unsanitary cages where they were pummeled by exposure to human diseases. Sometime around 285 B.C., Ptolemy II ordered a huge animal processional to celebrate the feast of Dionysus. The great parade of beasts included teams of ostriches in harness and thousands of other birds: parrots, peacocks, guinea fowl, pheasant, and "Ethiopian birds." One hundred fifty men in procession carried "trees to which were attached wild animals and birds of all sorts." There were ninety-six elephants drawing chariots; wild asses, goats, twenty-four hundred hounds, two hundred Arabian sheep, one hundred Ethiopian sheep, twenty Euboean sheep, oryx, oxen, lions, leopards, cheetahs, camels, a "white bear," huge snakes carried by teams of slaves, and—what must have been remarkable sights among remarkable sights—a giraffe and a rhinoceros.

The collections of the Romans ran to a peculiar sort of practicality. Lucullus had a huge walk-through aviary at his country house, but the birds were not there purely for aesthetic purposes. Once nicely fattened, they became dinner—eaten, by the way, at a table in the aviary. The Romans had a similar attitude toward—or appetite for—

the strange and brilliant peacock. Sacred in their native India, peacocks were immensely expensive to obtain — two thousand times the price of an ordinary fowl. Thus it was a double sign of status for the wealthiest Romans not only to have obtained a peacock, but to serve it, roasted and redressed in its own stunning plumage, to honored guests.

Around the third century B.C., Roman animal-keeping took its ugliest turn: bull elephants captured in battle were turned against each other in the Roman arenas. Gladiators began fighting bulls — a sport that endures today in Spain and Mexico; large cats, a lion and a cheetah, were thrown together in an arena to fight to the death. Around 60 B.C., the generals began to toss army deserters into the arenas with animals that tore them to shreds amid cheers and applause.

By about 170 B.C., the Roman Senate attempted to legislate the blood-sport events out of existence, primarily by outlawing the importation of large, dangerous African animals. The new law was ostensibly to prevent escaping animals from terrorizing the countryside, but the aristocratic senators were probably more interested in preventing their plebian political opponents from buying votes through the sponsorship of such popular events. In any case, the law was overturned soon after it was passed. The games not only continued, but worsened. The bloodthirsty public began to pressure the provincial governors to acquire exotic beasts, particularly the fierce and powerful, for the games.

Around 55 B.C., Pompey sponsored a series of spectacles where animals, or humans, were simply slaughtered for public amusement. In one gruesome grand finale, gladiators massacred twenty-one elephants that Pompey had acquired from Egypt only after swearing that the great pachyderms would not be injured. The gladiators killed the elephants slowly, spearing them with javelins, the beasts flailing their great tusks, falling to their knees, trumpeting and wailing fiercely. Even many of the brutality-inured spectators were so appalled that they "rose and cursed Pompey for his cruelty." The statesman Cicero wrote afterward that he felt enormous pain for the elephants' death, indeed that he felt that the elephant "is somehow allied with humankind."

Caesar Augustus built a great menagerie between 29 and 14 B.C., but its primary purpose seemed once again to be the provision of stock for public blood-sport events. About thirty-five hundred of his beasts, most of them presumably large mammals, were killed in the arena during the twenty-six such spectacles he presented. One winter he received a gift of tigers from India, and though they were possibly the first ones ever seen anywhere in the Western world, they were dispatched into the arena to show their ferocity—and to die.

It only got worse. Caligula held one event during which four hundred bears and four hundred African animals were slaughtered; Nero had an arena floor sealed and flooded so that gladiators, floating in boats, could spear seals to death. Historian W. E. H. Lecky wrote in 1869,

The simple combat became at last insipid, and every variety of atrocity was devised to stimulate the flagging interest. At one time a bear and a bull, chained together, rolled in fierce combat across the sand; at another, criminals dressed in the skins of wild beasts were thrown to bulls, which were maddened by red-hot irons, or by darts tipped with burning pitch . . . In a single day, at the dedication of the Colosseum by Titus, five thousand animals perished. Under Trajan, the games continued for one hundred and twenty-three successive days. Lions, tigers, elephants, rhinoceroses, hippopotami, giraffes, bulls, stags, even crocodiles and serpents were employed to give novelty to the spectacle. Nor was any form of human suffering wanting . . . Ten thousand men fought during the games of Trajan. Nero illumined his gardens during the night by Christians burning in their pitchy shirts. Under Domitian, an army of feeble dwarfs was compelled to fight . . . So intense was the craving for blood that a prince was less unpopular if he neglected the distribution of corn than if he neglected the games.

By the end of the sixth century, arenas for blood sport were all over Europe, including twenty-five in France and a large one, with a huge supporting menagerie, at Constantinople.

There is little written detail concerning animal stocks and their care in the Roman menageries, and there was certainly little reason for anyone to keep such records, considering that the facilities themselves were little more than temporary holding areas until the next public slaughter. What does remain are the stories of the games themselves, which were of much more interest to commentators and observers of the time than the physiologies of the animals involved. There are even fewer records of animal capture and transport, but one thing is certain: for every beast that arrived in western Europe to meet its fate in the arena, many, many others must have died in capture.

A picture found at an ancient Roman villa in Algeria shows an animal hunt in which cheetahs, lions, and leopards were driven into a stockade of netting and thornbushes. The Romans also caught large cats in traps, sometimes using a small, yelping dog as bait. Hoofed animals were so plentiful along the banks of the Nile in the Sudan that captors simply herded panicked creatures, with inevitable broken legs and necks, into corrals.

The wholesale brutality appears to have abated with the fall of the Roman Empire, but animal collections were maintained during the Middle Ages, usually by powerful royalty. (However, the monks at St. Gallen in Switzerland built a "modern" zoo, with paddocks for hoofstock and work areas for the keepers.) In the eighth century, Charlemagne had three menageries with lions, bears, camels, monkeys, an elephant, and exotic birds. In the twelfth century, King Henry I of England had a small menagerie in Oxfordshire with lions, leopards, lynx, and camels. Holy Roman Emperor Frederick II, in the thirteenth century, collected elephants, camels, leopards, cheetahs, and monkeys, and sometimes exotic creatures would accompany him on his journeys.

As the Renaissance started, western civilization began exploring the world, and the travelers found zoos along the routes. Marco Polo discovered a great zoo at the palace of Kublai Khan, with elephants, hippos, big cats, bears, deer, asses, boars, horses, camels, monkeys, civet cats, fish, and so many falcons that the monarch retained one hundred falconers.

In 1519, Hernando Cortés reached Montezuma's zoo in Mexico, which included huge aviaries ablaze with colorful quetzals and cardinals, chachalacas, and quail. There were ten ponds of waterfowl, and birds of prey, too—falcons, eagles, and condors. There were iguanas, giant turtles, rattlesnakes, monkeys, bears, armadillos, sloths, and great hand-wrought bronze cages holding jaguars and pumas which, according to expedition diarist Bernal Díaz del Castillo, were "fed the flesh of dogs and human beings." (For that matter, Montezuma had human beings—dwarfs, bearded women, and others with physical deformities—placed in cages, where visitors threw food at them.) Nurses provided veterinary care, and three hundred keepers worked solely in the huge aviaries.

The explorers brought back the strange and wonderful animals as items of curiosity and, probably, proof of their exotic journeys. With the influx of animals, the sixteenth century saw the birth of large urban zoos in Europe and North Africa. They appeared in Cairo, Karlsburg, Constantinople, Chantilly, Saint-Germain, Siena, Ebersdorf,

Dresden, Prague, Naugebau, Elsinore, at the Louvre, the Tuileries, and Fontainebleau. The menagerie at Chantilly exhibited such curiosities as a giant anteater and a sloth. At Versailles, Louis XIII's sculptors and painters created what amounted to excellent records of the monarch's animal collection, which included such species as American tapirs, lemurs, birds of paradise, contingas, toucans, and condors. Charles IX of France had a substantial menagerie at his palace at the Louvre, including an arena for bullfights, and at least one king, Elector Augustus II in Dresden, revived the Roman practice of brutal animal spectacles in arenas.

The oldest existing zoo, Schönbrunn, was built in the late eighteenth century by Holy Roman Emperor Francis I as a present for his wife, Maria Theresa, queen of Hungary and Bohemia and archduchess of Austria. Situated at the very center of the grounds was a pavilion where the queen could dine surrounded by camels, elephants, and zebras.

Through the entire history of zookeeping, remarkably little had changed: menageries were the province of royalty; animals were caged for royal amusement and as symbols of status and power. But changes were to come.

Carl Hagenbeck of Hamburg was the most famous European animal dealer of the nineteenth and early twentieth centuries. His father, a fishmonger, opened a small menagerie in the mid 1800s and established himself as an animal trader. Carl began running the little zoo himself, in 1859, at age fifteen, and soon had become a great success as a collector of and dealer in wildlife, selling seals, elephants, giraffes, zebras, lions, and hundreds of other animals to zoos, circuses, and sideshows worldwide, including that of P. T. Barnum.

As a trader, Hagenbeck was responsible for hundreds, even thousands of animal deaths. He once noted that young elephants and rhinos "cannot as a rule be secured without first killing the old ones." Hoofed stock were collected by men on horseback who simply chased herds until the weakest animals fell back, exhausted. But capturing a young elephant required commissioning a group of African horsemen to kill its mother by slashing her hamstring muscles with swords and, once the bellowing pachyderm was rendered helpless, severing her leg arteries until she bled to death. Apes and monkeys faced a similar fate, for shooting protective mothers as a means of obtaining young primates persisted into the 1970s, and almost certainly continues among poachers and unethical traders. Former wild animal trafficker Jean-Yves Domalain described such "collecting" of a baby gibbon in his book *The Animal Connection*.

> Down below, the hunter rams the double charge of gunpowder down the barrel with a thin iron rod, then the lead shot. The spark flashes from two flints, and the gun goes off in a cloud of white smoke . . . Overhead there is an uproar. The female gibbon, mortally wounded, clings to life. She still has enough strength to make two giant leaps, her baby still clinging to the long hair of her left thigh. At the third leap she misses the branch she was aiming for, and in a final desperate effort manages to grasp a lower one; but her strength is ebbing away and she is unable to pull herself up. Slowly her fingers begin to loosen their grip. Death is there, staining her pale fur. The youngster flattens himself in terror against her bloodstained flank. Then comes the giddy plunge of a hundred feet or more, broken by a terrible rebound off a tree trunk.

No trucks or helicopters existed to haul the beasts off the African plains or out of the jungle. According to Hagenbeck's account, such large animals as elephants or giraffes would be hobbled and driven like crippled cattle in a huge, dusty parade. Some of the smaller beasts, baboons and young cats, might be placed in a cage strapped to the back of a camel, while a juvenile hippopotamus might be contained in a cage suspended by poles from the backs of two camels and followed by a half dozen water bearers who dealt with the hippo's unquenchable thirst.

The exotics were not the only animals in the odd parade, for an entire herd of domestic creatures was also necessary: "Hundreds of head of sheep and goats are driven along with the procession; the nanny goats providing a constant supply of milk for the young animals, and the remainder being used as food for the carnivores," wrote Hagenbeck. No records tell how many captured animals died on these forced marches or on the subsequent voyages from North Africa to Europe, but given the state of knowledge of animal care and that many of the captured beasts were young separated from their mothers, mortality must have been extraordinary.

But in the 1900s, the same Carl Hagenbeck, using the profits of his animal trade, his existing menagerie, and his circus, began construction of a dream: the Carl Hagenbeck Tierpark at Stellingen, a wholly new vision of what a zoo should be. He wrote,

> Now at last I am in a position to carry out my long-nursed project of founding a zoological park of a totally different kind from anything that had been before attempted. I desired, above all things, to give the animals the maximum of liberty. I wished to exhibit them not as captives, confined to narrow spaces, and looked at between bars, but as free to wander from place to place within as large limits as possible, and with no bars to obstruct the view and serve as a reminder of captivity . . . A certain point must be fixed in the garden from which might be seen every kind of animal moving about in apparent freedom and in an environment which bore a close resemblance to its own nature haunts.

Indeed, when the zoo opened in 1907, the giraffes and zebras were in grassy meadows, the wild sheep and ibex on a large artificial rock mountain. At the zoo's exemplary

African Plains exhibit, visitors were surprised to see no fences, no cages, no bars; instead they saw a naturalistic exhibit with gazelles and African flamingos, storks, cranes, zebras, and antelopes, and, most startling, basking peacefully in the sun directly behind and within a few feet of those animals were the natural enemies of some of them: an entire pride of lions. The paying guests could not see, between the forward area where the prey were located and the rear area where the predators reposed, the deep, large moat. The zoo in Hamburg was a remarkable engineering achievement. The entire site had been shaped, dug out, bermed, and dotted with artificial pools and ponds in a time before the era of great earth-moving machines.

It was a great leap of imagination—Hagenbeck had removed the cages and bars, the hardest edges of captivity. During the exhibit day, at least, the animals had more room. The park was a garden, replete with trees, flowers, and green grass. Most important, rather than pacing in dirty, dark animal prisons, these creatures were set in simulated wild habitats. Suddenly, they were no longer just animals on exhibit, but animals in some relationship to their own environmental framework. It was no longer just lions and gazelles, but a vision of Africa, of creatures of the savanna inextricably linked to the land and to one another. For the first time, a zoo designer was able to hint strongly at an ecological relationship. Hagenbeck's concept provided the framework for the zoo of the twentieth century, and perhaps beyond.

3

Out for a walk on a cool, gray day in the spring of 1972, I happened to wander with a group of friends into Potter

Park, along the Red Cedar River in Lansing, Michigan. The park itself was pleasant, if a bit muddy, the grass just greening up after the snows.

The park was deserted—picnic season was still weeks away—and we strayed through it and into the Potter Park Zoo, a small menagerie. The memory has dimmed, but I still recall a dark, dank brick building filled with cramped, steel-barred cages and a powerful stench of animal waste. In one cage, a mangy-looking lion paced an impossibly small, endlessly repetitive to-and-fro route. In another cell, a chimpanzee screamed and clawed through the bars of his cage toward a chubby boy in a crew cut, out of reach behind an iron railing, who was shouting and laughing at the ape in a raspy voice. From time to time, the boy hurled a peanut, usually so hard that it bounced off the chimp or the bars and out of reach. The boy's parents stood by, laughing, too.

Just twenty-one years old then, I could have counted on one hand the number of times I'd seen animals in captivity, for zoos are urban phenomena, and I had grown up in the northwoods country of Michigan's Upper Peninsula and the northernmost reaches of Maine. As a small boy, I had made one visit to the Detroit Zoo and two or three visits to a tiny collection of caged raccoons and penned-in deer in a park in a northern Michigan town. Once, too, I had had the dubiously educational experience of sliding several bottles of what surely was colored sugar water in well-used cherry soda bottles down a wooden ramp into the cage of a black bear. The enormously fat bear lived in a low, cramped cage outside a roadside saloon in upper Michigan, earning its keep by grasping the bottles in both paws and chugging the sugar water which, of course, the proprietor sold to tourists at a hefty profit.

With the addition of Potter Park to that sum of experience, I vowed, as my friends and I left the menagerie, never to set foot in a zoo again. Zoos, after all, were animal prisons. Even *if* the lion and chimpanzee could have lived in cleaner, larger cages, they were still jailed. As one who was interested in the future of wild places and wildlife, I could see no justification for such places, where animals ripped from natural environments are put on display for human gawkers, their social and psychological needs ignored. The place for chimps and lions was in the wild. To heap horror upon horrors, zoos probably were helping to deplete wildlife from wild places to keep their cells stocked.

But I went back to Potter Park more than a decade later, just to check. Unfortunately, little had been done to change my first impression. There were some nominal improvements — a free-flight aviary outdoors and a not-unpleasant grassy paddock for hoofed animals — but there also was Tombi, a small juvenile elephant the zoo had recently acquired. To view her, one entered a building and looked down through steel bars into a concrete-lined pit. She was hobbled by one fat iron-link chain that ran from a shackle on her right hind leg to the rear wall and another from a shackle on her left foreleg to the front wall, her movement so severely restricted that swaying side to side was the best she could manage.

A grandfather opened the glass door and ushered in a little girl. They stood silently for a moment.

"Why do they put a chain on him?" the girl finally asked, almost whispering.

"He can't move around," said the grandfather, as if he hadn't really heard the question.

"Do they *have* to put a chain on him?" she asked. The grandfather didn't respond. As they walked out the door, he said, "Poor little guy."

The zoo did offer an explanation in the form of a sign on the back wall. "The size and strength of elephants makes them potentially dangerous to handle in captivity. Keeper contact is necessary for their proper care. Maintaining control at night by leg chaining enforces the discipline of the keeper and enables him to work more safely around the elephant."

Beside it, crudely hand-lettered on yellow cardboard, was another sign that compared a few physical attributes of African and Indian elephants: weight, shape of back, size of ears. It seemed to be the only educational information offered anywhere at the menagerie.

Nearby, the brick Mammal Building was even darker than I'd remembered, and the stench was worse. A fan rattled somewhere above. A lion slept on a shelf in its tiny cage; two tigers paced on the wet concrete floors of other cages. In still another cage, a group of spider monkeys huddled together; a tortoise lay like a rock on the concrete floor of a cage down at the end of the building. Across the way, where the angry chimp once had been, was a solitary mandrill.

Mandrills—gregarious baboons from rocky and forested regions of South Cameroon, Gabon, and the Congo—live in the wild in hierarchical troops of up to two hundred animals. They can be crowd pleasers for zoos, both because all primates tend to thrill their distant cousin Homo sapiens and because male mandrills wear the astonishing bright colors of a tropical bird: purple or brilliant blue rump, purple and cherry red muzzle, and yellow or green beard. However, the mandrill at Potter Park was not, to my mind, a crowd pleaser. A beast genetically programmed and behaviorally driven to thrive in communities, he sat alone on a shelf mounted halfway up the back wall of his cage, staring steadily through the bars. He was motionless, as if stuffed or catatonic.

In visiting this dreadful place, I'd broken my old promise to myself, but I had recently been spending a great deal of time at zoos, for good reasons. Not the least was that in the years between my first and second visits to the menagerie in Lansing, I'd talked with serious conservationists who worked in zoos and insisted that not only was degradation of zoo animals unnecessary and wholly avoidable, but that zoos could play a critical role in the preservation of a natural world that is under enormous pressure. I'd also come to understand the distinction between a zoological garden and a rank menagerie—and that the Lansing example was a relic. In design, operation, and philosophy, it had far more in common with the menageries of the Romans and medieval kings than with even a zoo like Carl Hagenbeck's, which had been "modern" nearly a century earlier.

It took time, but Hagenbeck's ideas about how animals should be displayed eventually spread. For those who haven't noticed, there is a new sort of zoo, one where visitors see animals in swamps, deserts, grasslands, or rain forests, not in cages.

Just a few hundred miles to the east of Lansing, in the suburbs of Toronto, another male mandrill on exhibit is a member of a troop of mandrills displayed in a large, sunny, indoor pavilion. There is not a bar in sight, and the exhibit is asplash with living African plant life. Like their kind in the wild, the mandrills here spend their days in a gregarious group, grooming each other, mothers tending to their young, the young riding on their mothers' backs around the exhibit, playing with each other, or teasing the old male.

Nearby, a family group of lowland gorillas populates another nature-duplicating exhibit. Down a path are West African dwarf crocodiles, huge cannibalistic numbskull frogs, meerkats popping out of burrow holes—all in a green, humid set piece done up to immerse a visitor in an African rain forest with an explosion of palm trees, screw pines, sausage trees, tamarind trees, kapok trees, fig trees, banana trees, papyrus, and flowering vines. Outdoors, large mammals—elephant, musk ox, white rhinoceros, chee- tah, lions, tigers—have room to move in spacious sur- roundings. There is little sense of prison. Sometimes the visitors are separated from the visited by panels of glass, sometimes only by low walls or a moat. These natural barriers are drawn from an extensive base of knowledge about what sort of boundary a given animal will not cross: a tiger will swim happily across a wide moat, but won't attempt to cross a deep, wide gully—provided it is deep and wide enough. A white-handed gibbon, which won't have anything to do with getting wet, can safely be en- closed on an island with a ribbon of moat.

At the Brookfield Zoo in Chicago, primates live in a cavernous building, Tropic World, where from walkways visitors look out over deep and wide expanses of re-created Asian, South American, and African rain forest in three separate exhibits. Here, you might be standing on a wooden bridge over a deep canyon with gorillas by a waterfall on one side and colebus monkeys in the trees on another. From far away comes the sound of thunder, and as it approaches, booming, the colebus monkeys suddenly become active, most moving for cover. Suddenly an artificial rain showers on all sides, neatly missing the walkways. An older build- ing houses a more modest mammal exhibit, a darkened glass-walled room where dozens of bats soar and spin away from the walls in free flight.

At the San Diego Wild Animal Park, visitors enter a spectacular jungly garden and pass thatched-roof African huts in Nairobi Village on their way to an aerial electric monorail that coasts above a valley of grassland in the California chaparral. Rhinos, zebras, camels, and giraffes roam freely in a huge amphitheater encircled by the monorail track. The train passes within feet of a cliffside where the goats, ibex, and Himalayan tahr do a nimble quickstep.

In Minnesota the deeply wooded Siberian tiger setting is one of the most spacious large-cat exhibits in any zoo — too large and too wooded to see the animals, complain some visitors — a component of Nick Reindl's Northern Trail, a zoogeographic outdoor display featuring birds and mammals from the coldest Holarctic latitudes — Bactrian camels from Mongolia, musk oxen from the Canadian taiga, wapiti, bison, pronghorn, moose, woodland caribou, and wolf in forested parcels or on a broad expanse of rolling grassy hillside — trumpeter swans, Canada geese, white pelicans in ponds and potholes.

Nearby is the zoo's Tropics Trail, a living rain forest on multiple levels enclosed in a vast 1.5-acre building that claims to offer a sample three-thousand-mile walk through another zoogeographic region, the humid forests of Southeast Asia. It is a five-story ramped cascade of plants, pools, cliffsides, and waterfalls where hundreds of tropical birds are in free flight. Dolphins swim in one pond. On an island in another, a family group of gibbons, surrounded by paddling Oriental ducks and dozens of pink flamingos, swings in the trees. Not far away, the Minnesota Trail features local birds, fish, and mammals — most spectacularly, a functioning beaver pond, complete with a lodge and dam, dissected with a giant picture window so that visitors can view the exhibit from above and below the water's surface.

Good exhibitry need not be a multimillion-dollar proposition. Only about forty miles from Potter Park, in Battle Creek, is another small-city Michigan zoo. There are no elephants or tigers in Binder Park; the site is at least as much nature center as zoo. A secluded nature trail winds through the grounds, featuring nothing more exotic than southern Michigan woodland, bog, and swamp. It high-lights a low-maintenance, high-activity prairie dog town, ponds filled with waterfowl, and a fine, thickly wooded Canadian lynx exhibit. Visitors stroll into a three-sided, mock trapper's cabin along the zoo entrance walkway, viewing the long-eared cats through a picture window that looks out on the wood. Elsewhere, decklike boardwalks curve through dense woods. As the forest floor descends into a low valley, the boardwalks are suddenly up at the margin of the tree canopy. And below — in distinctly sep-arate exhibits — dwell timber wolves and deer.

The Cincinnati Zoo and the Smithsonian Institution suc-cessfully exhibit insects, surely some of the smallest and cheapest to feed of animals. The Cincinnati exhibit is par-ticularly superb, replete with leaf- and twig-imitating in-sects, giant Madagascar hissing cockroaches, bee and ant colonies, and a lush, moist, free-flight garden solely for butterflies. Admittedly, Cincinnati's Insect World is exten-sive — and expensive: it cost more than $1 million to de-sign and build. But keeping a pair of tigers costs, at minimum, about $5,000 per year. For that, virtually any small zoo that houses big carnivores could mount a fine insect exhibit featuring more than a few especially beautiful or frightening or peculiar representatives of the largest class of animals.

None of this is to suggest that small zoos should not keep big carnivores or that they must display Madagascar hissing cockroaches. Rather, within the limits of their re-sources, zoos can be more than the foul menagerie I found in Michigan's capital city as recently as the mid 1980s. And even Potter Park is at last undergoing something of a trans-formation. Thanks to pressure from the American Asso-ciation of Zoological Parks and Aquariums, which threatened not to accredit inadequate zoos and to remove them from its membership rolls, the zoo has shut down the squalid

Mammal Building and plans to remodel its exhibits in order to move at last into the twentieth century.

Does an Asian lion or a bottle-nosed dolphin care whether it is a captive? As serious scientists, most animal managers would scoff at any suggestion that animals necessarily suffer merely because they are contained. There is no evidence that even the most intelligent animals have any perception of captivity, far less a negative one. A compelling case could be made that, if one considers the best interests of animals as individuals, they are *better off* in zoos than in the wild. Animals in the wild are subject to a Homeric catalogue of parasites and diseases. In good zoos, they receive, from extensively trained staff veterinarians, far better medical care than many of the earth's humans ever will enjoy. They are free from sudden, painful death by predation. They live longer lives, their toenails clipped, cataracts removed, lacerations stitched, boils lanced, bumblefoot salved, and hunger sated with carefully balanced, sometimes vitamin-enriched foods. Animals in inhumane, overcrowded, filthy exhibits forced to live outside natural social groupings or denied the opportunity to practice natural behaviors may indeed suffer. But Heine Hediger, the renowned director of the Zurich Zoo, once opined, "If all the needs of an animal are adequately met, the zoo offers its inhabitants a manmade, miniature territory with all the properties of a natural one. The animal will then consider the territory its own: it marks and defends the area and does not feel imprisoned."

All of which may well be accurate. Zoo animals do indeed live far, far longer than their counterparts in the wild, where mortality among the newborn each year is often extraordinarily great. And zoo animals do define and defend territories in much the same way that animals in the wild do. And although neither Hediger nor anyone else has ever had the opportunity to query a macaque or musk ox on the matter, observation would probably lead most reasonable persons to agree that many animals appear quite content, provided an environment is designed to meet their behavioral needs: Toronto's mandrills living in an extended family troop in their African rain forest, Minnesota's gibbons living in a nuclear family high in the trees on their island.

In the end, the aversion to animals in captivity may be a purely human one. My own disgust with an old prison-style menagerie comes in large part from that love of wild places and wild creatures and subsequently from a sense of dismay that magnificent creatures are so demeaned—presented for the purpose of being gawked at in a tiny, barred cell.

But to some who care about wildlife, even the most elegant Hagenbeckian naturalistic exhibit is still a container for creatures not meant to be contained. Despite whatever verdant elegance a designer may have given a box, it is still a box with wild animals living in it rather than where they should be. Yet that, most compellingly, is the rub. In many cases "where they should be" isn't there anymore. Put simply: (1) *habitat*, an ecologist's word, is the area where a plant or animal lives; (2) habitat is limiting—the number of brook trout in a mountain pond cannot increase beyond the pond's physical and biological limitations; (3) habitat is vanishing at a staggering rate. Grasslands, freshwater and saltwater wetlands, and most of all, the moist forests of Africa, Asia, and South America are being torched, chainsawed, bulldozed, filled, and drained out of existence. Consequently, the species that live in those habitats are losing their homes, and they are vanishing, too.

My son, Benjamin, who was two years old when he accompanied me on my second visit to Potter Park, will finish high school in the year 2001. If the prevailing view of some of the world's leading biologists is correct, one fifth of the species that existed on earth on the day of his birth will have been extirpated by then.

4

A few dozen feet from the Cincinnati Zoo's vanguard Insect World exhibit is a blacktopped, flower-bordered path that leads to a small, pagoda-like building with a red tiled roof and ornately carved wooden doors.

I once stationed myself inside that building for several minutes on a busy summer afternoon at the zoo. Not far away, crowds were lined up at the newly refurbished cat exhibit, more crowds pushed through Insect World, more people shoulder to shoulder at the wide, panoramic lowland gorilla exhibit. Few found their way into the little pagoda. Those who did enter, like the twentyish couple in matching khaki shorts and sneakers who were holding hands, invariably strolled rapidly around the interior, glanced at the contents of the glass-sided display cases, and left.

She: "I don't think there's anything here. Just those stuffed birds."

He (under his breath as they strolled out): "Everything's dead. I don't know why they have dead animals in a zoo."

They were correct about the animals in the exhibit; the pagoda *is* a shrine to dead, or more accurately, extinct things.

Some ornithologists believe that the North American birds called passenger pigeons were the most numerous birds on earth. John James Audubon once estimated that a single flock he observed passing over southern Ohio contained about two billion birds. "The air was literally filled with pigeons," he wrote: "They darkened the sun as in an eclipse." Ornithologist A. W. Schorger estimated that passenger pigeons composed one third of *all* land birds in the diverse, still rich, still spectacular avifauna of the North American continent in the middle of the last century.

In less than a single human lifetime, this amazingly abundant species vanished, its forest habitat disrupted, its members gunned out of the skies by the millions. The last one seen in the wild was "the Sargents' pigeon" shot by a curious Ohio farm boy in 1900. Passenger pigeons survived for a time in a few zoos, but in 1914 the last passenger pigeon on earth, a bird called Martha, died in a cage in the Cincinnati Zoo. A similar fate awaited the only North American member of the parrot family. In 1918 the last Carolina parakeet, a bird named Incas, also died at the Cincinnati Zoo. Martha's remains, stuffed and staring out of glass eyes, reside in a glass cage at the Smithsonian in Washington. However, the Sargents' pigeon, also stuffed, lies in the red pagoda. So does Incas, on its back, beak open. R.I.P.

These animals' extinction through human intervention rdly unique. The last dodoes — flightless, pigeonlike, turkey-sized birds — were last seen on their island home, Mauritius in the Indian Ocean, in 1681. In 1844, a couple of Icelandic fishermen clubbed to death the last two great auks, also flightless, on an island in the North Atlantic.

By the late 1800s, European colonists in South Africa had done to the blesbok what Americans had to the bison—reduced populations that once numbered in the millions to a virtual handful; and by 1881 they'd driven the quagga, a brown zebra, into extinction. Like Martha the passenger pigeon, the last quagga died in a zoo.

In a time when civilization was synonymous with subduing the earth, there was little alarm about extinction. Yet forces already in motion would come to help humans understand the consequences of the butchery they unwittingly had begun to practice on their own life-support system.

Young Charles Darwin was a month away from his twenty-third birthday when he set out, two days before Christmas 1831, with the crew of a survey ship, the *Beagle*, which was bound for South America on a mission to map the continent's coast. Darwin, who joined the crew as an unpaid naturalist, was to collect plant and animal samples and observe and record the geology of the coastal regions the ship would visit. The trip was often difficult for Darwin. He was cramped into a tiny cabin with ship captain Robert Fitzroy. Darwin often was homesick and, worse, seasick. "Nothing, not even Geology itself, can make up for the misery and vexation of spirit," he wrote home in one letter. But he later recalled that while the ship was in Good Success Bay at Tierra del Fuego, he decided "that I could not employ my life better than in adding a little to the natural science."

And add "a little to the natural science" he did. Darwin filled a thousand pages of notebooks with tightly scrawled notes about geology, collected thousands of animals and animal skins and plants, kept a diary that was to grow to eight hundred pages, collected another four hundred pages of notes on botany and zoology and filled twenty-four more notebooks with immediate impressions. He climbed mountains, pushed his way through coastal jungle, slogged along beaches. In the Galápagos he dissected iguanas, threw terrified sea lizards into the sea to observe their responses — though frightened, they instinctively swam back to the beach where Darwin stood. He measured the speed of turtles (360 yards an hour), kept samples of mosses, ferns, lichens, herbs, and weeds and carefully noted the forms of lava flows and black beach sand.

While still visiting the islands, he wrote, "In both time and space, we seem to be brought somewhere near to that great fact—that mystery of mysteries—the first appearance of new beings on this earth."

Contrary to popular myth, Darwin did not begin formulating his solution to that mystery of mysteries during the voyage. In fact, his notations on the structural differences in the famous Galápagos finches were often haphazard, and he investigated barely at all the islands' vice governor's comment that the tortoises varied significantly from island to island. Captain Fitzroy did bring aboard a few living tortoises, but the crew made stew of their meat and tossed the carcasses overboard long before landfall in England. But back in England, Darwin began to puzzle about how species might evolve from a common ancestor. The catalyst for his theory came when he read the *Essay on the Principles of Population*, by the Reverend Thomas Malthus, published in 1789, which argued that populations always reproduced at rates greater than their food supply's ability to feed them.

The result, Darwin realized, was that many individuals would die before reproducing. And he received this inspiration: the patterns of death would not be random; those individuals best adapted to acquire food and reproduce would survive and pass their traits to offspring. Where new sources of food existed, organisms would, over many generations, tend to be wedged into what ecologists intellectually descended from Darwin would come to call niches. It would explain how, in the recently colonized Galápagos, one finch had evolved with a stout beak to exploit seeds as a source of food and another with a long, woodpecker's beak to exploit wood-boring insects. (Actually, because the latter lacked the long tongue of a woodpecker, it had evolved a remarkable behavior: using a twig to probe the holes it dug in wood.) "It at once struck me that under these circumstances favourable variation would tend to be preserved and unfavourable ones destroyed," Darwin wrote in his *Autobiography*.

In the *Third Transmutation Notebook* he wrote, "The final cause of all this wedging must be to sort out proper structure and adapt it to changes . . . One may say there is a force like a hundred thousand wedges trying to force every kind of adapted structure into the gaps on the economy of nature, or rather forming gaps by thrusting out weaker ones."

According to Darwin, speciation, the process by which one species splits its way into two or more, is slow—measured in tens of thousands of years—so slow that in the century and more since Darwin finally published *The Origin of the Species* no biologist has documented a single case of speciation having occurred. (Evolutionary change on a less sweeping scale has been documented, however. Consider the adaptation of insect populations to agricultural pesticides.)

But the process of extinction is also implicit in the theory of evolution. Over time—immense amounts of it, in human terms—any species can be supplanted by another that evolves more useful adaptations. In fact, from 90 to 98 percent of all species that have ever lived on earth have become extinct. (Estimates of the total number of species that have existed in the earth's history range from 100 to 250 million. Estimates of extant species range from 5 to 10 million, although only some million and a half have been formally classified.) It's fair to say, then, that almost any species exists a few tens of millions of years, at best, then becomes extinct. As the death of an individual in a population makes room for others, extinction of species makes way for other life forms to prosper: the end of the age of reptiles opened the door to the beginning of the age of mammals—and the eventual descent of man.

So, as a friend once challenged, "There have always been extinctions; why worry about them now?"

Or as Sam Witchell, a public relations consultant, wrote in a May 3, 1974, *New York Times* op-ed article, "Give Me the Old-Time Darwin," "The Darwin people tell us that species come and go, that this is nature's way of experimenting with life. The successful experiments survive for a time; the failures disappear to no one's detriment."

Why be concerned? Witchell asked.

Because extinctions are occurring at a rate unprecedented in the planet's history.

Because the rate of species extinction is far outstripping the rate of new species formation.

Because the result is a drastic loss of biological diversity on the planet, the consequences of which are unknown, with entire evolutionary lines vanishing completely rather than evolving into new forms.

Because many species that some people happen to care about deeply are among those most at risk.

During the age of reptiles, the dinosaur species went extinct at a rate of perhaps one every thousand years—that "sudden" extinction occurred over hundreds of millions of years. From the birth of Christ until around the time the Pilgrims had established themselves in the New World, about twenty species may have gone extinct. Now, according to ecologist Norman Meyers's projections, a half dozen plant or animal species became extinct yesterday; an equivalent number will have vanished by the time you wake tomorrow. And Meyers states that this species-per-day rate is middling compared with what's to come—one species per *hour* by the 1990s.

According to Meyers, the processes of evolution "are being altered more drastically than since the sudden disappearance of the dinosaurs . . . and possibly more than since the emergence of life's diversity three and one half billion years ago. And it is all happening within the twinkling of an evolutionary eye."

The wild environments of the earth are being destroyed as systematically as demolished buildings. When the trees of a jungle fall, down come with them the birds and mammals of the tree canopy, the creatures that lived in the understory, and the plants and animals that depended on the canopy of interdigitated leaves to keep the forest floor in cool shadow. Drainage accelerates, soils wash away, ponds and streams become polluted with silt. Even the regional climate may change if the initial damage is widespread.

The dense evergreen forests of the tropics represent only about 20 percent of the land area of the world, yet they hold enormous ecological wealth, including approximately 80 percent of the planet's total biomass of terrestrial vegetation and an estimated two fifths to one half of all of earth's species. Some scientists have estimated that as many as forty thousand species may occupy a single hectare (about 2.5 acres) of Amazon rain forest. Worldwide every *minute*, day and night, the earth is losing fifty acres of tropical forest. Two thirds of tropical Asia's tree cover is now gone; another two thirds of the forest cover is gone from South America.

The Amazon region may be the richest biological region on earth, in terms of both sheer numbers of species (as many as one million) and total biomass in its lush tropical jungle. But by the 1980s, chunks of Amazon jungle equivalent to the area of the state of Indiana were being leveled every year, much of it to create new pasture for grazing livestock, especially beef.

In too many cases, the destruction makes little sense. In much of Amazonia, the newly created pastures on leached jungle soils produce grass for only six to eight years, eventually to be overrun by scrub growth. Similarly, in tropical Asia the effect of wholesale logging of tropical hardwoods is often more like the mining of irreplaceable and nonrenewable resources, because in the absence of tree root systems, the heavy, constant tropical rains often wash away the nutrients that the forests require to regenerate.

There are some 2.7 billion head of domestic hoofed stock on earth, and the number increases every year. Goats, sheep, and cows need grazing lands, and the only place to obtain more is through conversion of wild places. But that conversion too often means that the "girders" that support the entire environment will be cut away. Overgrazing of semiarid grasslands in Africa helped extend the Sahara into previously productive lands in Ethiopia and the Sudan, for intensively grazed livestock set loose a climatic chain reaction: with the grassy cover removed, water begins to evaporate more rapidly, the land becomes drier, fewer plants grow, overgrazing becomes more severe as the many livestock rip up the few remaining green plants, water begins to evaporate more rapidly, and on and on. Elsewhere— almost everywhere— marshes and swamps, "junk" property to farmers and land developers, the richest freshwater ecosystems on earth to biologists, are being drained and filled at a staggering pace.

The reason for all the lost habitat: one species, Homo sapiens, is enjoying immense reproductive success to the immense detriment of many others. For most of their history, humans have had a minimal effect on the earth as a whole. Until a few thousand years ago, there were, at most, a few million. Virtually all were simple hunter-gatherers, their Malthusian expansion capped, like those of other organisms, by nature's own limits to population growth, starvation and disease.

In geologically recent time, humans have converted to an almost entirely agriculture-based life. Forests are cleared and tilled, grasslands are grazed by domesticated stock, and wetlands are drained to help provide croplands for an exploding population. The need for land is pressing. In 1650 there may have been 500 million people on the planet. By 1987 there were 5 billion, half of them under twenty-five years old who have yet to (and will soon) reproduce. Even if the world reaches zero population growth by 2000, the planet will then hold more than 8 billion of us.

There stubbornly remains a vast public misunderstanding of the fundamental mechanics of extinction. Yes, the dodo and the auk were easily hunted down and clubbed (the dodo, after all, was named *doudo*, "simpleton," by the Portuguese). The quagga and passenger pigeon were overhunted. Today, poaching of black rhinoceros for the sale of their horns is pushing them to the brink of extinction. About four thousand were left in 1986, down from sixty-five thousand as recently as 1970. Owing almost solely to poaching, the rhino population in Kenya alone dropped from twenty thousand in 1970 to fifteen hundred in 1980, to at best four hundred in 1986. A small New World monkey, the cotton-top tamarin, is in danger because of its massive capture for research laboratories.

But species are endangered far more often because habitat is limited and vanishing, and the results of lost habitat for animal species are precisely what Darwin's theory suggests. Through natural selection, species have become highly adapted to their habitat, like keys that fit precisely in ecological keyholes. Without the keyholes, the keys cannot function.

Such is the story of the tiger. In about 1950, there were an estimated 100,000 tigers in eight subspecies. By 1982, one of those subspecies, the Bali tiger, had vanished, and the total world population was in the vicinity of five thousand animals. In 1987 two more subspecies — the Caspian and the Javan—have disappeared; the South China tiger is down to a few individuals and appears doomed in the wild (Chinese zoos have a few breeding South China tigers). Only a few hundred Sumatran tigers survive, along with around two thousand Southeast Asian tigers. The Siberian tiger is down to perhaps three hundred individuals. Only the Bengal tiger has been stabilized at as many as four thousand cats (although censusing methods have been questioned and there may be fewer), entirely because the governments of India and Nepal have launched an all-out effort, called Project Tiger in India, to preserve and, in some cases, restore wild forest habitat.

In any case, as the forests and grasslands of India came under cultivation, other species were lost—notably the Indian version of the cheetah.

Completely ignoring the largest phylum of animals, the insects and other arthropods, the list of creatures known to be at risk from habitat loss could go on for pages, ranging from Hawaiian, Mediterranean, and Caribbean monk seals to the Asian elephant, from the Amazon manatee to the Malayan tapir, from the wild Bactrian camel to the pig-footed bandicoot, from the desert slender salamander to the Orinoco crocodile to the surviving tortoises of the Galápagos, to New Zealand's large flightless parrot, the kakapo, to the monkey-eating eagle of the Philippine jungle.

There have been heated academic disputes about just how many species face extinction, partly because no one knows how many species there are on earth in the first place, but the argument, ultimately, is nearly irrelevant. The point is that an unprecedented biological disaster appears to be in progress. Zoos alone can do little to stem the furious tide of extinction. But it is in their own self-interest to become lifeboats for at least a corner of vanishing nature. If not, there will be no mandrills or gorillas or gibbons or elephants, rhinos, tigers, lions, leopards, or condors left to see in nature *or* in captivity.

A philosophical transformation, far more significant than Hagenbeckian design changes, has come about with astonishing speed in the zoo world. As recently as the mid 1960s, suggestions were made that zoos become agents for wildlife conservation, but that was far from a reality. The stamp-collection-style zoo was still the norm—the "best zoo in the world" was one with the most animals and the most species. Specimens were guarded jealously, and although there were deals and sales and trades of animals, breeding loans to perpetuate a captive population were far less common than "collecting" expeditions to Africa or Asia. At a conference of the American Association of Zoological Parks and Aquariums in Cincinnati in 1964, Robert Bean, then the director of Chicago's Brookfield Zoo, told a reporter, "It's all talk so far. People aren't doing enough fast enough. The idea of a bank with animals from different zoos to be borrowed when they're needed, sure, it's a nice idea, but it's going to take fifty or sixty years before it catches on."

But it didn't take that half century.

Later on that summer day when Nick Reindl stood on the wall summoning tigers in Dakota County, I walked around the wooded hillside to another exhibit—a rolling grassland where a herd of stubby, dun-colored, brush-maned Przewalski's horses, a couple of foals wobbling around their mothers, grazed. These Mongolian wild horses, which are genetically distinct from all the domestic equines, are biological relics. Extinct in the wild, they survive only because zoos have succeeded in breeding them. If zoos had been able to provide such a service to the passenger pigeon, what once may have been the world's most abundant bird would not have vanished forever. If zoos can extend that service to other wild animals — as they claim they can — we may, after all, not be the last generation of humans to cohabit the planet with Sumatran, white, and black rhinoceroses, Bali mynahs, gorillas, orangutans, black lemurs, Siberian tigers, cheetahs, naped cranes, or even Aruba Island rattlesnakes and Puerto Rican crested toads.

TWO

A CROWDED ARK

TOM FOOSE, conservation coordinator for the American Association of Zoological Parks and Aquariums (AAZPA), likes to produce a drawing rendered by his wife, Ellen, a graphic artist.

At the center of the picture is an ark. Siberian tigers and Przewalski's horses stand on its decks, peeping out of portholes and over the gunwales. A giant panda is up to its neck in the water, but at least near the hull of the ark and hanging on precariously by a life rope. Sumatran rhinos, a scimitar-horned oryx, a wisent, a California condor, a monkey-eating (or Philippine) eagle, a Chinese alligator, and a king cobra are adrift on rafts. The eagle, wearing a bandage across its breast, looks particularly battered. On the roof of the boat are the words ZOO ARK, and above the ark, nestled in a puff of cloud, is a dodo with a halo over its head.

"Even if it's becoming a trite metaphor, this is really how we envision ourselves," Foose says, propping the cardboard image on one knee. "As a sanctuary."

Even without the cartoon at hand, Foose slips into that metaphor often and easily. "It's a question of not enough space on the ark to do everything we'd like to do," he says to point up the physical and economic limitations of zoos.

Foose, who holds a Ph.D. in animal physiology from the University of Chicago, works out of a cavernous, cluttered basement storeroom-cum-office in the Biological Services Building at the Minnesota Zoo, but as an employee of the AAZPA.

Even though interzoo cooperation began to improve remarkably in the 1970s, coordination to identify species most in need of attention was critically lacking. For example, in 1979, 801 bird species were bred in zoos, but only 37 of those came from the ranks of the 433 species of endangered, rare, or vulnerable members.

That lack of coordination was why the AAZPA hired Foose away from his position as curator at the Oklahoma City Zoo to work full time on its captive wildlife preservation program, now called the Species Survival Plan. His position was created by the association at about the same time the Minnesota Zoological Gardens opened, and the zoo offered to provide space for Foose. Bespectacled, a bit pudgy, with a Chaplinesque mustache, and an academic air, Foose found his way to the zoo world in the 1970s after spending months in India following rhinos for research on his dissertation, which concerned the relative evolutionary merits of multiple stomachs versus single stomachs in hoofed animals.

Since he became involved with captive breeding, his research has changed course. Dr. Ulysses S. Seal, a world leader in the captive breeding movement, calls Foose "the prime mover in applying demography to captive populations." Nate Flesness, whose own basement office is just around the corner from Foose's, once said that Foose was the "political action committee—or maybe it's the revolutionary council" for the North American zoo world.

There's more behind Flesness's hip-shot analysis than might seem apparent. Foose, armed with a mandate from

the AAZPA, has been rattling cages across the continent
—the cages of zoo directors and zoo boards of directors
and zoo employees—and even the zoo public. His mission
is to plan the future and oversee the lives of zoo species
that have been formally awarded a space aboard the ark
under the Species Survival Plan (SSP).

The program was born in 1978 when the AAZPA resolved to make conservation the primary goal of member
zoos. Zoos would, according to the resolution, work vigorously to educate the public about the catastrophe in progress in the wild and follow a recommendation from the
great British naturalist Sir Peter Scott to become "a Noah's
ark operation" for endangered species. Today, the zoo-as-
ark may be at least tentatively seaworthy. But unfortunately, the solution is far more logistically complex than
marching endangered animals into the gates of zoos two
by two. In short, small captive populations face enormous
pressures.

To understand the problems that the zoos and Foose
confront—and they are multitudinous—it might be well
to begin at the beginning.

In the mid-nineteenth century, there lived an Austrian farm
boy whose simple goal in life was to become a teacher.
He was accepted into the Augustinian Order of Saint
Thomas, a brotherhood of teachers, but after only a year,
he was dismissed from the university because, as his ex-
aminer put it, he "lacks insight and the requisite clarity of
knowledge."

Since the young, barely educated monk was hardly prepared for a teaching position, his order farmed him out to
its monastary in Brno, presumably to live out his days
quietly. Had he become a teacher, the young monk might
not have had the time—or the inclination—to conduct

his experiments and keep his meticulous record books or even to think much about the new science of biology. Indeed, the order forbade monks to teach the dangerous and suspect subject to schoolboys.

For about eight years, beginning in the mid 1850s, the monk, Gregor Mendel, became a breeder and crossbreeder of garden peas. When he began, the existing view of heredity was based on common sense and the law of averages: cross a tall plant with a short one and, common sense suggested, the result would be an average of the two, a plant of medium height.

Yet Mendel discovered something startlingly different. When he hybridized short peas with tall, all the offspring were tall plants. When he crossed peas with wrinkled seeds with peas with round seeds, the offspring always had round seeds. When he bred plants with red flowers and plants with white, the offsprings' flowers were always red. Plants with inflated pods and plants with constricted pods always had inflated-pod offspring, just as plants with axial flowers and plants with terminal flowers always had axial-flower offspring.

He might have stopped there and come up with a theory: any breeding operation involving tall plants resulted in tall offspring, and so forth. His experiments seemed to bear that out. But Mendel pushed the experiment another, critical step. He bred the new tall plants — the offspring of the short and the tall — with one another. Same with the new round-seeded plants and red-flowered plants and the others.

This time the results were equally remarkable, equally startling. In almost exactly three out of every four cases, the tall plants bore tall offspring. But about one out of every four such matings produced a *short* offspring. And the same phenomenon occurred with the wrinkled versus the round seeds, the white versus the red flowers, and all the rest.

The characteristics that had dominated in 100 percent of the instances the first time around now dominated in only 75 percent. In the other cases, these grandchildren of the original plants assumed the vanished characteristics of their other grandparent.

Mendel pushed on. When he bred these short plants with one another, all the offspring were short. With some of the tall plants from the same generation, all offspring were tall. With others, almost precisely half were short, half tall. Breeding tall plants with short from this third generation yielded either 100 percent tall or 75 percent short.

The Austrian monk kept meticulous logs of the results; the same patterns repeated themselves consistently. When he crossbred plants, round seeds, red flowers, axial flowers, inflated pods, green pods, and yellow seeds always determined the characteristics of the offspring in the first generation. Then the characteristics began to diverge in a regular, consistent pattern — one-fourth, one-half, three-fourths.

In that day, almost nothing was known about the workings of a living cell. But almost intuitively, Mendel defined the mechanisms that determined heredity. He theorized that any single characteristic — tallness, texture, flower color — is determined by a pair of "particles," one from each parent. Should each parent pass down, say, a long-stemmed particle, the offspring will be long-stemmed; should each pass down a short-stemmed particle, the offspring would be short-stemmed. But what of examples in which each parent passed down a different characteristic, one long, one short?

The result, Mendel guessed, was that one particle would

always dominate the other according to a predictable pattern. Tall-stemmed particles would always dominate shorts. Reds (in pea flowers, anyway) would always dominate whites. But the shortness and whiteness characteristics would not vanish; instead they would resurface later in highly predictable patterns suggesting that such a particle could be passed down in what is called a recessive, masked form. (Remarkable though the discovery was, Mendel had no credibility in the scientific community, and although he managed to publish his findings in 1866 in an obscure periodical, the *Journal of the Brno Natural History Society*, no one paid any attention. It wasn't until 1900 that his journal article was suddenly "rediscovered" simultaneously by a number of scientists, at a time when the details of cell division were becoming clear. The article remains the only extant piece of work by Mendel, who was later, despite earlier concerns about his "clarity of knowledge," to become abbot of his monastary. After Mendel died in 1884, the new abbot burned all his papers.) The nut of the genetic framework that Mendel described: we are all, human and monkey, African violet and fruit fly, utterly unique individuals, because so many combinations of the particles define our physical makeup.

Mendel's "particles," which offspring inherit from their parents, now called alleles, are lengths of deoxyribonucleic acid, DNA. Two alleles, one from each parent, compose a gene. Mendel's selections for his initial short and tall pea plants were homozygous for height, meaning that both the alleles that determined height were coded for tallness. When he crossed the tall and short plants and wound up with tall ones, those results were heterozygous, that is, their two alleles were a dominant one for tallness and a masked recessive one for shortness. Though parents and offspring were the same in physical appearance, their hidden genetic makeup was quite different. A geneticist would refer to the appearance factor as the phenotype and the hidden, genetic factor as the genotype. Thus, the two pea generations were of the same phenotype, but separate genotypes.

Of course, beyond environmental influences—one pea plant, well watered and dosed with phosphorus and nitrogen, always grows taller and fuller than a nutritionally deprived specimen—there are other complications. Mendel somehow managed to pick clear-cut characteristics, "pure" forms of inheritance. There is also "intermediate" inheritance in which one allele does not completely dominate the other—cross red and white homozygous snapdragons and they yield pink snapdragons, for example. Moreover, a single characteristic can be determined by more than one gene—a guinea pig's hair color is determined both by a gene that controls pigment production and by another that controls deposition of the pigment in the hair. Even more complex, a single, primary gene controls the pigment in human eyes—blue or brown. Yet irises can be gray (really a variety of blue) or black (really a variety of brown) because other, secondary genes control the amount of pigment in the eye, others the tone of the pigment, and others the way the pigment is distributed. Still other complications include so-called sex-linked genes, which are responsible for sex-specific abnormalities like hemophilia.

Offspring can only exhibit traits for which their parents carry the genetic code. However, changes called mutations *can* occur in DNA molecules, and hence in alleles, and be passed down to offspring. Some mutation is necessary, for mutations produce genetic variation, and genetic variation is the engine that drives evolution. Such mutations are subject to the furious pressure of natural selection, and if the organism with the mutational change survives, it passes the new diversity down to offspring. Thus, in time, organisms tend to have genetic makeups different from their ancestors'. However, living organisms are the product of millions of years of adaptive evolution, and truly beneficial mutations are exceedingly rare. Most are either so minor as to be meaningless (a slight shift in hair color) or harmful. Harmful ones work against an organism's general fitness.

A fatal mutation can occur in either a dominant or a recessive allele, but the results are strikingly different. A fatal allele in dominant form usually selects itself out of existence for carriers usually will die before reproducing.

But *recessive* alleles for lameness or blindness or infertility are another matter. Because they are usually masked by dominant, beneficial traits, they can survive passively in a population for hundreds of generations. What if, say, a single individual antelope develops a mutated recessive gene for lameness? If its mates have no matching recessives (unlikely, given the immense odds against any particular mutation occurring at all, much less twice), the offspring will be, phenotypically, healthy and swift. However, one out of four, on average, will carry a little genetic time bomb.

If successfully passed down, the time bomb is there, to be moved further along through dozens and hundreds of generations, steadily spreading through the population. Eventually two parents, each carrying the recessive lameness allele, could produce offspring that would be homozygous for lameness. Such matings are inevitable in any population.

If I produced only two children, and they and all their descendants produced only two each, I could have one thousand descendants in only ten generations. If everyone produced three, the number would be closer to sixty thousand. If four, over a million. These figures are based on the assumption that this rate of compounding fecundity would continue with no reproductive failures, no death before reproduction of one's quota, and no diminution of its mathematical power by any descendant breeding with another. Somewhere along the line, it becomes almost inevitable that at least two very very distant, umpteen-times-removed cousins will find each other. Should they both carry the same deleterious and recessive allele from a single mutation in a common ancestor, they could produce offspring with that negative trait.

Almost all individuals carry some deleterious genes, usually in recessive states. Dr. Victor McKusick, a geneticist and professor of medicine at the Johns Hopkins School of Medicine, says that each human carries an average of three abnormal, recessive genes. Other estimates run to five or more such genes per individual. I may be carrying one gene for clubfoot, another for muscular dystrophy, and another for a form of genetic mental retardation. My wife may carry a gene for albinism, another for deafness, and a third for cleft palate. However, although the recessive alleles may move to our children, they will not manifest themselves unless they exist in both parents.

The rate of birth defects in individuals not obviously related is relatively low. But mating by closely related persons is another matter altogether, for the likelihood of two deleterious, recessive alleles existing in the same position along a chromosome rises astronomically if the two parents have recent, common ancestors. A parent-child mating creates an extraordinary risk of producing defective offspring: a fifty-fifty chance of activating a deleterious recessive trait. Even at the first-cousin level, the odds that two individuals carry the same deleterious gene are one in eight; with sibling matings they are one in four.

Medical research has firmly established that children of closely related parents are often beset with physical or mental genetic abnormalities. McKusick has helped provide medical care for and studied genetic abnormalities among the Amish, a tightly knit, small religious group with about eighty thousand members in Pennsylvania, Indiana, and Ohio. The Amish avoid first-cousin marriages, but second-cousin pairings are abundant. McKusick says that in a 1973 study, "we found many couples who were related as second cousins about two or three times over" — their parents and grandparents were second cousins as well.

That study established an inbreeding coefficient "as though every married couple was related as something halfway between first and second cousins. People leave the group [the Amish population], but no new genes come in. And that in itself increases the coefficient of inbreeding, which keeps going up with each generation."

Among the Amish, typical recessive inherited abnormalities include a rare form of anemia, phenylketonuria — an enzyme abnormality that can lead to retardation — and two forms of dwarfism.

That consanguinous mating can cause such problems is no new discovery. Taboos against incest pervade human societies. (It's easy to imagine how one could perceive a curse from the gods for those who intermarry, considering the near inevitability of abnormalities and sometimes startling physical deformities that crop up among the children of very close relatives.) Even before Mendel's work was rediscovered, scientists had proved that inbreeding among animals caused damage, although they didn't know why.

In 1868, Darwin said of livestock breeding, "That any evil directly follows from the closest inbreeding has been denied by many persons, but rarely by any practical breeder." A study with rats begun in 1887 showed that within thirty generations of parent-offspring and sibling matings, the average litter size decreased from 7.5 to 3.2 offspring and mortality by four weeks of age increased from 3.9 percent to 45.5 percent.

However, as recently as 1977, there was virtually no hard evidence that inbreeding had any serious negative effect among zoo animals, and close parent-offspring inbreeding was rampant in the small, postage-stamp collections of most zoos.

There were some early warnings. The often intense inbreeding at zoos "is likely to result in low fertility, low survival of young, the outcropping of abnormalities," wrote geneticist R. Bogart in a 1966 issue of *Parks and Recreation* magazine.

Yet at most zoos, record keeping was so poor that any reasonable analysis of inbreeding for many animals was impossible, although studbooks for a few species did exist. Not until the late 1970s did the warnings began to quicken. By then, such biologists as Ulysses S. Seal and the World Wildlife Fund's Thomas Lovejoy had begun to warn that the effects of inbreeding depression were likely in zoo animals. Then, in a 1977 paper presented to the Second World Conference on Breeding Endangered Species in Captivity, Nate Flesness showed that by plugging inbreeding and reproduction numbers into a computer, he was able to document that highly inbred Przewalski's horses were less reproductively successful than less inbred animals. At the same conference, a Dutch couple, Jan and Inga Bouman, who had painstakingly assembled an analysis of the Przewalski population using some three thousand note cards, demonstrated the same problem in, as Flesness puts it, "simultaneous and 100 percent overlap."

As the Boumans' presentation bluntly stated, "No new blood has been introduced from the wild since 1947, and we believe that certain trends revealed in the course of our investigations give cause for alarm." According to Fles-

ness, his presentation and the Boumans' did indeed cause
some alarm in the zoo world, not so much because of the
possible genetic threat to horses as of the political threat
of outsiders' meddling in the zoo business. Flesness was a
graduate student of Seal's at the University of Minnesota.
Jan Bouman was a furniture maker and Inga Bouman a
child psychologist. Flesness is now the director of the International Species Inventory System (ISIS), which keeps
track of tens of thousands of zoo animals. (It has been
referred to as "computer dating for animals," a description
that makes Flesness wince.)

"We generated some heat," says Flesness. "We ruffled
some feathers in various directions. It didn't come through
channels. And none of us worked in a zoo. Our advice
hadn't been solicited by the zoo world, but we offered it
anyway. And there were some people who had already
decided that the idea of genetic management was bad—
that it meant that outsiders would come in and tell you
what to do with your animals. For them, we became an
example of all the problems that were probably going to
come their way if they started thinking about genetic management." But Flesness adds that the feathers began to
unruffle almost immediately as data that was increasingly
difficult to ignore appeared.

A breakthrough came when two National Zoo researchers, Katherine Ralls and Jonathan Ballou, began to analyze
the unusually good records that the Smithsonian-operated
institution had kept. They examined breeding records for
forty-four species of mammals representing seven orders,
twenty-one families, and thirty-six genera. To some degree, Ralls and Ballou had to approach the problem prepared for a few rough edges. Zoos successful at breeding,
and that included National, sell or trade animals, making
lifelong tracking a difficult, sometimes impossible task.
That problem is less evident today because of Flesness and

his work with ISIS. The two scientists compared the survival rates of animals that had related parents with those from nonrelated parents.

They later wrote, "The results were dramatic."

Among ring-tailed lemurs, for example, more than 30 percent of the inbred offspring died within six months of birth, compared with fewer than 20 percent of the non-inbred offspring. Among black spider monkeys, 58.3 percent of inbred offspring died compared to 18.2 percent of noninbred. And nowhere was the evidence more powerful than among scimitar-horned oryx: 100 percent of inbred offspring died, while only 5.4 percent of the noninbred died in their first half year of life.

In all, inbred offspring died at a higher rate in forty-one of the forty-four species. To look deeper into the possibility that the numbers may have been skewed by other statistical variables, Ralls and Ballou did a follow-up study on all twelve hoofed animals involved in the original one and showed that the higher mortality rate was not because of birth order or season, changes in animal management or the creatures' living environment, or any discernible difference between offspring of wild-caught versus captive-born mothers.

Ralls and Ballou then plugged their data about the National Zoo's wildebeest herd into a mathematical model, essentially posing three different "what if" scenarios.

One: What if the zoo continued the breeding program it had practiced between 1960 and 1970?

Two: What if the zoo used its existing population but instituted a complex breeding scheme to avoid inbreeding as much as possible?

Three: What if a new, unrelated male were brought in as a breeding stud each year to eliminate inbreeding?

The ultimate question Ralls and Ballou were attempting to answer is: what was the probability of the wildebeest population's surviving at all under each scheme? From the results of that model they produced a graph that shows dramatically what inbreeding might mean to a zoo population.

Under the first, "do nothing" scheme, the graph looks like the most precipitous of ski slopes. For about twenty years, according to the projection, the odds that the zoo's wildebeest population would survive are close to 100 percent, but then, suddenly, there is an astonishing decline. Forty years out, there is only a fifty-fifty chance. By just over fifty years, the probability is near zero. In other words, if the zoo continued its practices, it was highly likely that within fifty years it would have no wildebeests at all.

The second scheme — avoiding-inbreeding — fared a bit better, with the population maintaining between 100 percent and 90 percent probability of survival for fifty years. But then, suddenly, the probabilities of survival again begin plunging — to about 80 percent at sixty-five years, about 50 percent at seventy-five years, 40 percent only five years later, and at just over ninety years, once again close to zero.

The no-inbreeding scheme provided close to 100 percent probability that the population will survive an entire century.

The National Zoo studies were some of the first. More recently, geneticist Bob Lacy in the new Conservation Biology Department at Chicago's Brookfield Zoo has found evidence suggesting that inbreeding effects vary so much from one species to the next that any generalization is questionable. "Simple little rules and formulas don't apply," he says. "But until we find a way to predict which species are more or less affected, it would be a mistake to inbreed any species if we can avoid it."

The bottom line is that careful management to avoid inbreeding can increase the probability of survival for many zoo animals. But the only way to ensure long-term survival is to introduce new, unrelated animals regularly and relentlessly. Not to do so could repeat the experience of laboratory mouse breeders, who attempt to create special laboratory strains by inbreeding. Sometimes it works. Most of the time, however, the line goes extinct. For breeding plans to succeed over many generations, zoos would have to begin exchanging animals regularly.

Inbreeding does not necessarily destroy a population. Some highly inbred, tiny populations *have* survived. Early this century, the European bison, or wisent, almost jumped into the void of extinction. Yet thanks to vigorous zoo-based breeding programs in Europe, the population managed to pass through a genetic bottleneck with a population of only seventeen animals. In the years directly after the bottleneck, zoos were able to breed the bisons rapidly enough that those with seriously abnormal traits could die, leaving enough healthy animals to maintain the population.

Something similar must once have happened to cheetahs in the wild, although how far back in history no one really knows. Scientists Stephen O'Brien, David Wildt, David Goldman, and Carl R. Merril have analyzed cells of fifty-five South African cheetahs from two geographically isolated populations. The researchers found that the animals were near clones—genetically the same at every one of forty-seven allele locations, a level "dramatically lower than levels of variation reported in other cats and mammals in general." The evidence, they wrote in *Science*, suggested "a severe population bottleneck followed by inbreeding."

The St. Louis Zoological Garden intentionally pushed a population of Speke's gazelles through such a bottleneck in the 1970s and early 1980s. A single male was a common ancestor of all the animals. The zoo used a complex breeding scheme involving increasing the population size rapidly, and not breeding animals that showed deleterious traits, eventually creating a breeding nucleus that, although highly inbred, had had deleterious alleles winnowed out.

But the cheetah, the wisent, and the captive Speke's gazelle have not escaped forever the residue of the bottleneck. Although the cheetah as a species did manage to move through the population constriction and survive, the long-term implications for the threatened cat may not be rosy.

The reason? Although the population has survived the threat of deleterious alleles, in the process it has lost its genetic diversity. If zoo breeders don't pay attention to genetic management, Foose says, a gene pool can turn into a gene "puddle" as alleles vanish, or "drift," from the pool. And limited genetic diversity can make a species less fit to endure environmental change.

In a large population—over ten thousand individuals —significant genetic drift is minimal, simply because the odds are overwhelming that any remotely prevalent gene will carry on through one or another bloodline. But as the population shrinks, or effectively shrinks by becoming isolated into subpopulations, genetic drift becomes not only possible, but almost inevitable. And since genetic diversity is what makes a species adaptable, constriction of the pool to a puddle can create a less adaptable population.

There is an analogy between the lack of genetic diversity in a population and the lack of species diversity in the trees, or what's left of them, on the street outside my house. Early in the century, the city of Minneapolis, like many others, planted elms for their grace and beauty and shade. The city did not plant oaks or maples or lindens. In the 1970s, when Dutch elm disease reached the region, it mowed

like a scythe through the city, wiping out a huge propor-
tion of the monoculture of trees. Had there been a diversity
of species, we would still have a reasonably full comple-
ment of shade trees on the street.

In effect, the cheetahs, genetically speaking, are all elms.
With little variation in the species, it could be far more
susceptible to changes in its environment than it would
otherwise be.

"By whatever mechanism," the cheetah researchers reported in *Science*, "a successful and specialized species has
been produced with little genetic plasticity, one which could
be the least adaptive in a time of perturbation of the ecological niche."

For zoos, the implications are obvious. Part of the intent
of the Species Survival Plan is simply to keep populations
alive. Avoiding the harmful effects of inbreeding will help
do that, but another key requirement is to maintain as
much genetic diversity as possible, in the hope that when
and if the day comes for reintroduction into the wild, a
relatively intact species can be returned.

2

These days, Tom Foose is a student of demographics.
He looks at tigers or okapis in much the same way that
political pollsters look at voters. Foose doesn't simply
want to know how many tigers he's got, any more than
the pollster simply wants to know how many voting-
age Americans there are. The pollster wants to know how
many women between thirty-five and forty-five years of
age with a high school education favor a candidate and
how many Catholic senior citizens do, in order to fling that
data into a computer along with data about how many
women between thirty-five and forty-five are likely to

vote and how many Catholic senior citizens will vote on a rainy day.

Foose wants to know how many tigers, from which bloodlines, of which sex, and of what age have to breed with one another, and when, to produce a sound population. The story of the tiger in captivity illustrates the reason for Foose's concern with demographics: tigers almost became a victim of their own reproductive success.

Clayton Freiheit, director of the Denver Zoo, says, "Twenty years ago, the zoo with a breeding pair of tigers would write its own ticket. Relatively few zoos reared tigers successfully, and there was a high demand for cubs." But beginning in the 1960s, zoos began to learn more about how to assure that tiger cubs survived. Soon nearly every zoo with a male and female of breeding age was a tiger factory.

Consider what happened with Siberian tigers. In 1970, there were only sixty-six of them in U.S. zoos. But there were dozens of successful births in the next four years, and by January 1975, there were more than three times as many tigers—215—in U.S. zoos. If that trend had continued, by 1985 there would have been more than twenty-three hundred Siberian tigers in U.S. zoos.

In the wild, nature would have dealt, in its harsh way, with the problem of "surplus" individuals. The least fit cubs—not necessarily weak, but relatively weaker than their kin—and the oldest adults would perish, and the population would stabilize at or near its ecosystem's carrying capacity.

In a zoo, regular feeding and veterinary care and shelter from the weather preclude this natural culling—only the profoundly unfit, those with fatal deformities or disease, are at any great risk. By the late 1970s and early 1980s, zoos began to face a tiger surplus, and the situation had totally reversed—zoos were beginning to have trouble not

only selling tigers, but *giving* them away. To compound
the problem, the shift in philosophy among zoos and their
animal managers had led to increasingly stringent dispo-
sition policies. For ethical reasons, many would not sell or
give an animal, for example, to a circus to be trucked
around the country and perhaps trained with a whip. They
could have built more cages—but when to stop? It costs
thousands of dollars a year—about $2,500, according to
one estimate—to feed and care for a single tiger. A population growing at a rate of, say, 14 percent per year will
be twice as large in only five years, four times as large in
ten, and eight times as large in only fifteen.

Clayton Freiheit faced this problem in 1980, when a
Bengal tiger at the Denver Zoo gave birth to a litter of
four cubs, one female and three males. For the full summer,
the zoo enjoyed the benefits: a big, dangerous cat like a
tiger with a litter of playful cubs always attracts crowds.
When the summer season was over, Freiheit decided to
keep one of the males and trade the female for another
young female to give the zoo a future, unrelated breeding
pair. Two males remained; Freiheit advertised them for
sale in an AAZPA bulletin.

"There were no takers and we steadily dropped the price
to 'gratis to approved zoo,' " says Freiheit. In short, the
zoo's tiger breeding program was a victim of the laws of
supply and demand. Everyone was breeding tigers; other
zoos were attempting to unload surplus tigers, too. Moreover, Bengals had been supplanted in popularity as exhibit
animals by the paler, larger Siberians, which had the double
allure of an intensely endangered status in the wild and a
physical position as the biggest cat on earth. Freiheit eventually found a taker for one tiger for the cost of shipping.

"The remaining male is still with us," he said. "A beautiful three-year-old cat that nobody wants."

For the Denver Zoo, as for others, the oversupply of

tigers led to the only obvious solution. Many zoos simply ceased to breed them, often putting their females on "the Pill"—a contraceptive implant the size of a .45 caliber bullet surgically fitted under the skin. For other animals, population control has been more permanent. Denver, for example, has given vasectomies to hamadryas baboons, coyotes, grizzly bears, and African lions and castrated various hoofed males.

For zoos, birth control can be a blessing. The best institutions nuture their animals so successfully that many captive species reproduce easily. Surpluses are inevitable and returning surplus animals to the wild is, in most cases, infeasible, not least because wild habitat is constricting. But uncoordinated birth control can be a terribly mixed blessing. In fact, for Siberian tigers birth control nearly led to the destruction of the captive population in North America.

When this issue comes up, Foose starts pulling out his charts and graphs, the most telling of which are those showing the age and sex structure of the Siberian tiger captive population.

An idealized graph representing a tiger population in nature might look like a blocky Christmas tree.

The bottom bar on the graph shows all the tiger cubs under one year of age. The bar above it represents the one-year-old tigers and so on up to the oldest. Males are represented at the left of the vertical line, females at the right. This natural age and sex distribution contains a roughly equivalent number of males and females in each age group, shown by bars of equal length on either side of the line. Just as important, the greatest number of tigers is found among the new cubs; there are slightly fewer one-year-olds, fewer two-year-olds, and so forth.

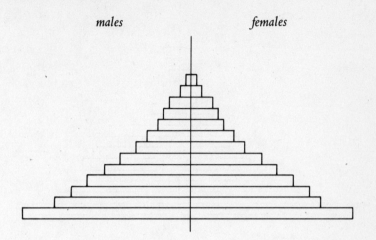

males   *females*

Foose insists that a graph of the captive population should resemble the Christmas tree structure of a wild one. Indeed, his graph for Siberian tigers in North American zoos for the year 1973 at least roughly resembled this sort of natural distribution, for in those days zoos were breeding their animals willy-nilly.

But in the 1970s, as zoos began to reach their carrying capacities for Siberian tigers, they stopped or severely restricted breeding. These limitations caused the distribution by age to become severely distorted. By 1978, of the hundreds of adult tigers in zoos, only a handful were young of the year or one-year-olds. In 1977, only seven male Siberian tigers had been born, and if the trend continued, there was every possibility that, some year soon, there would be no new tigers born in an entire year.

By then, the chart depicting the demographics looked more like the python that had swallowed a pig.

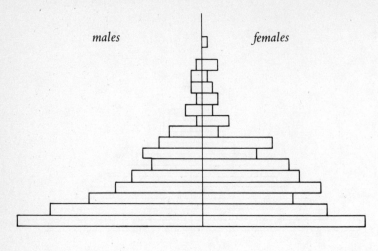

males   *females*

1973

There was a big bulge at the ages of four, five, six, seven, and eight—the prime breeding years. But beneath that bulge, few youngsters were ready to move into the breeding age group as the population aged. Certainly someday, as the tigers in the bulge aged, there would be a renewed demand for Siberian tiger cubs. Certainly, since an implant prevents conception only temporarily, there would *seem* to be every reason why a breeding program could begin anew.

But not quite so. For by that time, many tigers would be past breeding age, and the few remaining animals capable of reproducing would not represent the genetic diversity in the entire population. Suddenly, but too late, the zoo world would realize that its huge cohort of elderly tigers was about to die off, much of its genetic uniqueness lost forever for lack of breeding. Even worse, the remaining tiny breeding population would be more vulnerable to extinction simply through random bad luck. If, for example, only

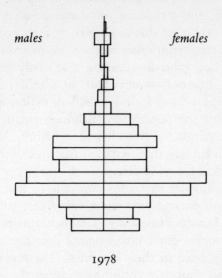

males   *females*

1978

five breeding-age females survive, odds are relatively high that disease or an accident or a natural disaster could wipe them all out before any produced a fertile daughter.

It was the old inbreeding demon, this time haunting zoos in a hidden way. A population of, say, 250 animals can, if mixed and matched properly, retain its genetic diversity and avoid most inbreeding for hundreds of years. But *only* assuming that it is a reasonably normal population in demographic terms — structured like a tree, not a satiated snake.

"If this trend had continued," Foose says, "within another ten years we would have produced a population of geriatric [and therefore infertile] tigers, and we would have been in very real danger of destroying the North American Siberian tiger population."

Foose later wrote that this demographic mangling "has probably been an appreciable cause of effective extinction in individual zoos and of instability in captive populations as a whole, and would be more conspicuous if zoos had not frequently been able to rejuvenate their populations by stock obtained from other institutions or from the wild."

But, demographically speaking, that's only the beginning.

Imagine that only twenty pairs of Siberian tigers are left in the world — forty individuals, half males, half females. Assume that the population, although small, fits reasonably closely into the tree-shaped structure. At least there are enough animals that, with management, inbreeding can be controlled for generations.

Imagine further that zoos continue to maintain a population with enough new cubs every year to support the structure, but do it unevenly. That is, six pairs breed every year, producing eight litters before they age. Another six breed only once in their lifetimes. The remainder don't breed at all. Enough young to support the program are being born, but any unique genes among those that don't breed at all will be lost. Unique genes among those that breed only once will be diluted in the group or, if they don't show up in the few offspring, may vanish. Once again, the effective size of the population shrivels.

In fact, by 1980, the four hundred Siberian tigers in North American zoos were descended from only seventeen ancestors brought to the continent over previous decades. According to Foose's charts and graphs, the distribution of descendants of these founders varied wildly. A single founder was the ancestor of fully 16 percent of the Siberian tigers in North America, while fewer than one percent were descendants of one of the other founders.

The situation worldwide was similar. A grand total of sixty-eight Siberian tigers have come out of the wild and into captivity. By 1984, twenty-nine of them were still captive — three in East Germany, the other twenty-six in the Soviet Union. Of approximately one thousand Siberian tigers in captivity, about 97 percent were captive-born and all descendants of, at most, the original sixty-eight. But only *six* ancestors had provided almost 70 percent of the founder genes to the captive population. Another six had provided about 19 percent.

The Przewalski's horse population genetics are twisted and similarly skewed. No wild horses remain to replenish the population's gene pool. The entire living sample of these horses began with fifty-three wild-caught animals in the early years of this century — again, not perfect, but enough to assure considerable initial diversity and room for plenty of mixing and matching to avoid inbreeding and much loss of diversity. But the whole population of around five hundred is descended from only seventeen founders, and only a dozen horses have contributed almost all the genes. (To make matters worse, a domestic mare got into the line early on.) Until recently, standard breeding practice for the little wild horses was to use a single male for every nine females.

Ulysses Seal says, "The animals that were not bred made no genetic contribution to the next generation. They were totally wasted in the maintenance program. They might as well not have been maintained."

Thus, says Tom Foose, the best way to move a captive population toward genetic stability is to promote demographic stability. A breeding program should first equalize the representation of the "founders" genes in the population. Once the original genetic mix is equalized, all animals in a breeding program should breed. There should be an equal number of males and females, and the age distribution should resemble a natural one. And the size of a captive population should never fluctuate much from year to year.

But there is another critical point. Ideally, keeping the gene pool large, diverse, and well mixed would be easiest with a large population. It would allow some sloppiness and less rigor in planning a breeding scheme. Unfortunately, zoos do not have that luxury.

At this writing, there is about enough space for one thousand large cats of the tiger-lion class in North American zoos. Of course, zoos could use their limited resources to build at least a bit more large-cat space. But what of the other animals that need those resources to come aboard the ark? Should the zoos also build more pachyderm space, more space for pandas and bears and endangered antelope? "We need to devote the *least* amount of space we can to Siberian tigers," says Foose, in order to leave space for Bengal tigers, Sumatran tigers, Asian lions, African lions, and jaguars.

The solution was a compromise, a decision based on computer analysis that inbreeding could be controlled and loss of genetic diversity minimized by maintaining 250 tigers in the breeding program. That number of animals would be managed intensively — so much so that an encyclopedic volume provided to each participating zoo mandates a type of musical chairs of tigers.

The Species Survival Plan is painstakingly specific. The entry for Toronto, for example, first notes that the zoo's Siberian tiger capacity was "6 maximum," then provides a census of tigers on the site by International Species Inventory System identification number and sex: "69 F [female], 360 F, 463 M, 876 F."

Under Breeding Instructions: "Do not breed 463 or 69 F for the SSP" (both tigers were highly inbred and their genes already widely preserved in the population); "360 has behavioral problems and is not recommended for breeding. Breed 876 F with 185 M from Minnesota in 1984."

Under another category titled Moves: "185 M from Minnesota to introduce three new bloodlines. Surplus 69

F and 463 F in 1983–84, 360 F in 1984, 876 in 1986–87, 185 M in 1992."

The word *surplus* was used as a verb. The Toronto Zoo was to move the named tigers into the surplus category in the given years. But the zoos were back to the old problem. For the genetic and demographic program to work—indeed, to save the tiger—the participating zoos were inevitably going to produce some animals that were surplus to the program, for mortality rates are so low in zoos that tigers can live long past their reproductive years and cubs much more often survive their first year of life. Further, there was no way to guarantee how large any individual litter would be. The average of just over two cubs per litter could range up to five.

The actual mechanics of the breeding program were that each male and female would be parent to two litters during its lifetime. Ten to fourteen litters a year would be produced from the entire population. Since litter size cannot be controlled, some of the one-year-olds might have to become surplus every year. All animals fifteen years old and older would become surplus. Throughout the zoo world, there would be an estimated twenty surplus tigers each year.

Already by the 1980s many zoos held surplus Siberian tigers—animals whose genetic lines were so overrepresented or whose ancestry was so uncertain that they could offer little to a planned breeding program. Given the limitations of space and resources on the ark and that most competent zoo directors refuse to sell their animals to roadside menageries, circuses, or other commercial sideshows, the only reasonable answer for most animals managers was "culling"—euthanasia.

That approach is hardly new. Wildlife managers conduct controlled kills of bison in the Yellowstone ecosystem and elephants in Tanzanian refuges to keep herds in check, not least to prevent the herbivores from overrunning nearby farms and ranches. Nor is it new in the pet arena. In the United States, humane societies and local pounds presently are killing about 15 million dogs and cats every year. And zoos themselves have always culled some species with impunity. Reptiles and amphibians, for example, have staggering reproductive potential, and no one has ever registered an objection to polywog euthanasia.

But elephants, monkeys, and tigers are quite another matter. After years of focusing its public's attention on individual animals, after claiming that its primary concern is saving endangered species, could a zoo actually get away with killing, no matter how humanely, a perfectly healthy, high-profile animal such as a Siberian tiger? Could the zoo-going and animal-loving public accept that individuals should die so that, according to the esoteric demographic calculations of a group of Ph.D.'s, the entire species might live?

The jury is still out on that matter. Only one zoo director in North America, Steve Graham of the Detroit Zoo, has established a clear precedent with his public and the local news media. In 1982, Graham walked into a firestorm when he proposed killing four Siberian tigers. His decision was not based on the Species Survival Plan. Rather, three of the tigers were old and ailing, one so crippled that it had to lean against the wall of its cage to stand up. The other had severe behavior problems. But the irony of killing endangered species was played to the hilt in the local news media. Graham, who has variously been described as outspoken, heroic, and a raving fool elsewhere in the zoo world, stood his ground, insisting that euthanasia was the only moral choice. A Detroit citizen and a group of animal rights organizations sued the zoo and Graham, but the court ruled for the zoo, and the three infirm tigers were killed. The precedent set, in 1985 the zoo culled four more Siberian tigers, these healthy, but surplus, then two lions in 1986. There were news stories in those cases as well, and public protests, but they did not approach the intensity of the 1983 outcry, and Graham continued to stand his ground.

Other attempts were far less conclusive. In 1983, the Toronto Zoo backed down from its plan to euthanize a healthy, albeit surplus, Siberian tiger to make room for another coming from Minnesota under the Species Survival Plan. In 1984, Minnesota itself faced a surplus problem. After repeatedly advertising a tiger, called simply Number 1918, first for sale and then gratis, in the AAZPA trading lists, curator Nick Reindl recommended, and the zoo's animal management committee agreed, to cull the female cat. Steve Iserman, then the director, concurred, but he decided to proceed without notifying the local media. The decision backfired when a local alternative weekly tabloid got wind of the plan and scooped the conventional press. In the two days after publication, television anchormen were intoning gravely that an endangered species had been "sentenced to death row" by the Minnesota Zoo. One of the daily newspapers reported that the zoo planned to save Tiger Number 1918's ovaries for reproductive research use. A local citizen telephoned, threatening to cut out a zoo employee's ovaries if the tiger were killed. Thousands of letter poured in. So many phone calls flooded the switchboard that the Apple Valley telephone system reached electronic gridlock, and nearby suburbanites could call neither into nor out of their homes. The governor called. At least one faded Hollywood star called. Dozens of callers offered to take the carnivore off the zoo's hands. And two days after his own firestorm began, Iserman announced at a news conference that the euthanasia had been called off. The tiger was eventually sent as a gift to the Shanghai Zoo, but the question of what to do with surplus high-profile animals remains, for the time being at least, unanswered. News spreads quickly in the zoo world, and since the Minnesota and Toronto experiences no other zoo save Detroit has proposed to cull such a popular animal.. The reluctance to cull has not yet been a disaster for the zoo ark. Aside from the Siberian tiger plan, most of the others are still in development, and the time hasn't yet come to trim the deck space down to the bare minimum for each species. Whether zoos can some day do that remains in some doubt. But the consequences of *not* being able to face the culling issue squarely may be worse.

William Conway, New York Zoological Society general director, said, in a speech to the 1983 AAZPA conference in Vancouver, "Only a substantial new contribution to Siberian tiger carrying capacity or a breakthrough in technology might sufficiently insure this program to reduce the need for the removal of surplus." He added, "The morally relevant SSP assumption is that preserving a viable population of a species justifies killing some individuals of that species; that permitting extinction of unique and irreplaceable life, when that can be avoided at the cost of some individuals, is not acceptable."

But Conway suggested that the entire question of euthanasia had to be "troubling" to the zoo profession, that "the very idea . . . is in conflict with what zoos treasure most, animal appreciation. We are not dog breeders, livestock farmers, or game managers inured to the necessity of 'cullings' and 'harvests,' " he said, and later wondered if any zoo professional could take the life of a healthy young gorilla.

The Species Survival Plan was to move forward, but a growing number of zoo professionals was convinced that saving the tiger and other endangered creatures was going to require persuading their coworkers, the public, and perhaps themselves that euthanasia was unavoidable. Conway later said, "The ultimate cruelty is extinction. The reason zoos are forced to these intense management techniques is to prevent this ultimate cruelty."

3

Cumulatively, there would seem to be many animals already in zoos. Among mammals alone, some fifty thousand individual animals represent eight hundred to a thousand species. Yet this sample is a poor representation of the diversity of the animal world. Insects and other arthropods (ticks, mites, spiders, and crustaceans) account for about 1.2 million of the known animal species. The Smithsonian's insect exhibit and Cincinnati's Insect World notwithstanding, zoos seem disinclined to get into the business of entomological exhibition on any large scale, and I've heard no talk of endangered species salvation programs for bugs among mainstream zoos.

Disregarding the fish, there are approximately twenty to twenty-five thousand vertebrate species — reptiles, amphibians, and birds — on earth, of which only about four thousand are mammals. Bats comprise about 20 percent of mammal species, but only about one percent of the species in zoos. On the other hand, the mammals at the top of the tropics food chains — big carnivores (primarily big cats) and primates (monkeys and apes) — together constitute about 42 percent of the species exhibited in zoos.

Zoos in North America average about fifty-five acres, with a total area of only about twenty thousand acres. All the zoos in the *world* — good ones, bad ones, those with excellent breeding programs, and those that are utter atrocities — could fit within the borough of Brooklyn. The

combined annual budget for operation of all the zoos in
North America with active breeding programs is about
$250 million. To put that in some perspective, it is less
than one tenth of the amount the United States government
spends annually on grants to help cities build new sewage-
treatment plants. And even at zoos with the most determined and aggressive breeding programs, only a fraction
of capital funds is devoted to facilities for breeding animals,
or exhibiting them. More goes to walkways, gardens, restaurants, and restrooms for human visitors, office space
for staff, heating facilities, plumbing, and wiring. Likewise, only a fraction of the zoo labor budget goes for
breeding efforts, for there are grounds to be maintained,
cages to be cleaned, education programs to operate, and
as a major fraction of the budget at any successful zoo,
vigorous marketing and public relations campaigns to get
enough visitors through the gates every year.

According to Ulysses Seal, if the zoo world indulged in
its past practices of loose, largely uncoordinated breeding,
it could hope to sustain perhaps one hundred endangered
vertebrate populations. With the application of aggressive
genetic and demographic breeding management schemes,
that number might rise to five hundred animal species.
The Bronx's Conway has done an extensive survey and
reports that, at the absolute outside, the zoo world could
theoretically support nine hundred endangered species in
adequate numbers to assure long-term survival.

Of course, it depends on which five or nine hundred
species one is talking about. There's a strategic difference
between sustaining an endangered population of tiny seed-
eating birds and one of carnivorous tigers. But given those
limitations, choices are going to have to be made. Most
crucial: Which species to preserve? Which to let fall?

Foose says, "Unfortunately, there isn't room enough on
the ark to do everything we'd like to do. There simply

isn't enough space to propagate in captivity all the species that are probably going to require sanctuary in zoos if they're going to survive. So we have to select."

To date, the zoo-based survival program has selected these species:

Puerto Rican crested toad
Chinese alligator
Aruba island rattlesnake
White-naped crane
Humboldt's penguin
Red panda
Black lemur
Lion-tailed macaque
Orangutan
Asian small-clawed otter
Snow leopard
Chacoan peccary
Black rhino
White rhino
Grevy's zebra
Okapi
Arabian oryx
Asian elephant
Red wolf

Orinoco crocodile
Radiated tortoise
Madagascan ground boa
Bali mynah
Andean condor
Ruffed lemur
Golden lion tamarin
Gorilla
Siberian tiger
Asian lion
Cheetah
Indian rhino
Sumatran rhino
Przewalski's horse
Barasingha
Gaur
Scimitar-horned oryx
Maned wolf

A glance at the list leaves no doubt that zoos lean overwhelmingly toward large animals in general and mammals in particular. More than two thirds of the thirty-seven animals singled out so far by the AAZPA for its species-specific survival programs are mammals, and all are vertebrates.

Nate Flesness feels that there's some sense in such an approach. "That's what zoos do best. It's all *very* species biased toward large mammals and birds. But to some degree my argument is, 'Yes, zoos should preserve what they like. It's like an art museum preserving art for future generations.' But the art museum doesn't preserve all art—not even a representative sample of art—but the art that the curators and the museum's supporters happen to like. Luckily, it turns out that, in many cases, these are the species that are the most endangered anyway."

Tom Foose agrees. In these earliest stages of human-induced mass extinction, the big, exotic, and sensational mammals turn out to be those that often are among the most endangered. The megavertebrates, as Foose calls them, often suffer directly and early from the effects of an expanding human population, because it either restricts the wide range they need—tigers and grizzlies, for instance—or destroys the massive supply of food they need to survive—as with elephants—or poaches them for trophy or profit—rhinos and gorillas.

Indeed, zoos can't serve every animal, says Foose. They tend, if only for their own economic survival, to focus on creatures that the public finds most fascinating—animals with whatever charisma it takes to propel those visitors through the turnstyles. And that, says Foose, is where zoos can and will concentrate—on the big and attractive animals. He's fond of using a term that cropped up at a meeting of zoo biologists to describe those target animals: "charismatic megavertebrates."

There is another, more pragmatic, reason for such a focus on mammals. Zoos appear to be most successful with breeding certain categories of species. The Brookfield Zoo's Sandy Friedman says, "Our success in breeding reflects the phylogenic nature of animals. We're most successful with mammals and least with insects—with birds, fishes, and herps [amphibians and reptiles] somewhere in between."

A vital question for the Species Survival Plan remains how to decide which animals, even from the more limited range of charismatic megavertebrates, to target when the need is so great. Some of the criteria are almost mundane. There must first be a breeding nucleus so that the program can advance at all — since there is no breeding nucleus of giant pandas in the United States, there is no species survival program for them — as well as enough zoo people with biological knowledge of the animal to support the effort. And, of course, the creature must be in some sort of peril.

According to Foose, as more and more animals come under the threat of extinction, those limited criteria will leave more animals in need of space on the ark than the program can handle. At that point, the SSP may have to select only those species with the highest predicted probability of captive survival, or those that are one-of-a-kind animals at the genus or family level — and perhaps those which, one day, stand some chance of reintroduction to nature or can at least help support a constricted and genetically threatened wild population through some form of technological genetic exchange, such as artificial insemination and embryo transplantation. In the end, the species savers in zoos may have to do what battlefield doctors did on the fields of France during the First World War: perform a kind of triage. They divided casualties into three groups: those with minor injuries who could wait for treatment, those with serious injuries who needed immediate treatment, and those who were beyond all hope.

At this writing, most of the plans are only in early development stages, for a full-blown effort means, among other things, detailed computer analysis of the existing populations and development of the same sort of complex scheme for genetic and demographic management — the musical-chairs program — that was developed for the Siberian tiger.

But is this level of cooperation and sophistication something that zoos are prepared to cope with? Or does the entire program promise to be complex, each move so dependent on others that the structure resembles a house of cards? What happens when one zoo can't afford to move a rhinoceros? What happens when an animal dies prematurely? What happens when a zoo director bows to pressure from his or her mayor or board to keep a popular animal at the zoo rather than move it out as part of a breeding program? What happens when political and public pressure prevents several zoos, almost simultaneously, from culling their "surplus"? Some curious and unexpected problems have cropped up already. Stephen O'Brien, the geneticist who participated in the genetic analysis of the wild cheetah population, discovered in 1986 that virtually the entire captive population of Asian lions in North America had genes from the related subspecies African lion. As one member of the Asian lion SSP committe wondered, "Does this mean we cull them all and start fresh with tigers from India, or do we just go for a generic lion?"

Ulysses Seal admits that "seeing the level of detail required, a lot of zoo people are getting a little apprehensive. In fact, a lot of people are just getting frightened out of their wits."

And National Zoo researcher Jon Ballou says, "The SSP is in kind of a honeymoon period. You have to wonder what's going to happen when all the zoo directors who've signed up begin to find out what level of commitment this is really going to mean."

THREE

THE FROZEN FUTURE

EVERY THURSDAY MORNING for a half decade and more, Marialice and Ulysses S. Seal have driven the few miles from their suburban Bloomington house to Gate B of the Minnesota Zoo, an access off limits to the public. They wait at the high, steel-mesh gate while it motors slowly open for them, and Ulysses — "Uly," as nearly everyone knows him — steers their van along narrow blacktop roads to the doors of Large Animal Holding, a building in a little valley below. They unpack their gear — Marialice her clipboard and records, Uly his syringes.

Large Animal Holding was originally intended to provide temporary living quarters for camels, wild horses, bears, and tigers in quarantine on first coming to the zoo or while they were being treated for illnesses or convalescing. For Uly Seal's purposes, it also has come to be a more permanent home for four Siberian tigers, a male and three females.

The place can hardly compete with the zoo's state-of-the-art exhibitry. It is purely functional — like a kennel. Rows of steel-barred cages line either side of a service corridor. Hatch doors controlled by winch from the corridor open into exercise runs outside. Similar doors between cages can be opened to allow animals to interact with one another or to be shifted from cage to cage. But there is no reproduction of nature here, no simulated rockwork, no bubbling creek, no green plantings. Those types of things, the biologists tell you, are purely for human visitors — to heighten the illusion, to pull visitors into the natural world of an exhibited beast. The beast itself, they say, couldn't care whether it's enclosed by bars or by a cleverly disguised moat or whether its floor is of plain concrete or painstakingly molded fake rockwork. Tigers do prefer to have a large platform bed well above the cool concrete, a need provided for here. But this is no exhibit; it is a place for research into the substantial mysteries of big-cat reproduction.

As the Seals walk the long corridor between the cages, the four tigers rise, move forward, and nuzzle at the bars. Uly Seal murmurs softly to the cats. The Seals move through another set of steel doors at the back of the building and into a small room, the "kitchen." The kitchen isn't much to admire, either: a small, bedroom-sized cubicle with a spaghetti tangle of ducting and pipework suspended from its ceiling, fat rubber water hoses coiled in a heap on the floor in one corner, an air-drying compressor thrumming and clunking away in another corner. It is a kitchen only in that meals for the animal occupants of the building are prepared here.

The Seals are never alone in the kitchen on these Thursday mornings. On one cold March day, Ron Tilson, then the zoo's research director and later its director of animal programs, has set up on a table and is removing items from a plastic tackle box labeled EXCALIBUR FISHIN' BOX. The items are a can of compressed butane, tranquilizer darts, and bottles of anesthetic drugs. Ann Beyers, a master's candidate in reproductive biology, has set up a steel centrifuge on another table. The centrifuge, squat and blue-green, looks like a flying saucer from a 1950s B movie. Terry Kreiger, a part-time zoo vet and a doctoral candidate in reproductive biology, is there, too, huddled over the table with Tilson, rapidly filling dart syringes with drugs.

Uly Seal shrugs off his parka and steps over to a small, head-high, barred window on one wall of the kitchen. The opening, about the size of a portable television screen, is covered with a smeared and scratched Plexiglas pane. Seal slides open the window and clicks his tongue. Suddenly an enormous feline head appears on the other side of the bars; it is an adult tiger, its whiskers only a foot from Uly Seal's own.

"Hi there, girl," Seal says quietly. Six feet up, the tiger's face nuzzles against the bars, her huge front paws side by side on the sill.

Ulysses S. Seal, improbable moniker and all, is one of the towering figures of the wildlife research world. Six-tyish, lanky, big-framed, six-feet-plus, he has a great salt-and-pepper woolly beard that billows to his chest. In a brown cardigan, Levi's corduroys, and hiking boots, Seal, father and grandfather, looks as though he could outpace men half his age on a mountain trail. Born in West Virginia and raised in Alabama, he speaks in a voice rich with tones not often heard in Minnesota. ("Ah cain't *hep* you with that right now, Marialice.")

Dr. L. David Mech, the world's leading authority on the Eastern timber wolf, once told a reporter that he likes to involve Seal as a collaborator on projects not only for his skills as a physiologist and endocrinologist, but also for the company of an "all-around genius."

International Species Inventory System director Nate Flesness has said that if Seal only had the sort of personality that compelled him to devote his considerable mental and physical energies to a single facet of a single field, "He'd be Nobel Prize material." Whether or not Flesness is over-stating the case, Seal is fairly idolized—maybe even, as a large-cat specialist, lionized—by the senior biological staff at the zoo.

But Seal does *not* focus on a single facet of anything. He has directed a national biochemistry lab for prostate cancer research for the Veterans Administration's research branch, is former chairman of the VA's nationwide research advisory committee, serves as a research proposal reviewer for both the National Institutes of Health and the National Science Foundation, and is simultaneously an adjunct professor in three departments at the University of Minnesota (Biology program, Department of Biochemistry, and Department of Entomology, Fisheries, and Wildlife). For starters.

As a sort of freelance wildlife scientist, Seal is regarded as an expert in developing drug regimes for immobilizing wild animals. When the New Delhi government sought help in developing a program for immobilizing its Bengal tigers, Seal was dispatched to India, along with his colleague and friend timber wolf expert Mech. He has been called in to consult in developing anesthesia for deer in Wisconsin, pronghorn antelope in Idaho, wolves in Minnesota, seals in Antarctica, and wild horses and burros in the American West—and at the same time to study endocrinology, reproduction, behavior, and nutrition in various of those creatures. In 1978, at just the time that Seal had become convinced of the need for the introduction of new genetic stock into the North American Siberian tiger gene pool, he was sent to Moscow to chair a joint U.S.-USSR animal immobilization project. There, he wangled an introduction to the director of the Moscow Zoo and officials of the Ministry of Agriculture and, before he'd left, had arranged for transfer of three valuable Russian tigers to zoos in the United States.

Seal sat on the committee overseeing the fate of the nearly vanished California condor and has been directly involved, as a captive-breeding adviser, in the program to save the rarest mammal in America, the black-footed ferret, of which there are, at this writing, just over a dozen in existence. He sits on the U.S. government's wild horse and burro management committee, supervises, with Mech, a timber wolf research colony near Minneapolis, a first-of-its-kind biochemical/behavioral study that has now become a model for others, and seems to appear at most major mammal management symposia, not uncommonly as a featured speaker.

Those in the kitchen at Large Animal Holding that day knew Uly Seal as one of the world's reigning experts on tigers and on the tiger's needs for long-term survival in captivity.

As recently as the early 1970s, tiger cubs born in captivity had extraordinarily high mortality rates. St. Paul's Como Zoo personnel called in a biochemist to help them understand why the cubs were dying, and he provided a key bit of research. The cubs' immune systems were failing because the zoo was attempting to hand-rear them on formula milk; the cubs were dying of pneumonia because they weren't gaining their mother's passive immunity from antibodies in her colostrum and milk.

The biochemist was Uly Seal. And it was his work with the Como tigers that started his long involvement with zoos and captive breeding. When a new type of zoological garden was proposed for Minnesota, Seal was appointed to the board and was its chairman through its final phases of construction and first few months of operation. Later he became chairman of the Captive Breeding Specialist Group of the Species Survival Commission of the International Union for the Conservation of Nature and Natural Resources — blessedly, more commonly known as the IUCN — based in Geneva, Switzerland. When the zoo world needed an all-inclusive data bank on the demographics and genetics of its multitude of animal populations, Seal invented ISIS and for five years was its director, designer, and computer programmer. When the captive breeding world needed an initial species survival plan as a model for others, it was Seal who realized that the painstaking, detailed Siberian tiger studbook kept over many years by East German Seigfried Seifert provided one of the best data bases for such a document, Seal who modified a business bookkeeping computer program to design the complex breeding and trading scheme, and Seal who developed the prototype plan, itself an encyclopedic work designed to stabilize Siberian tiger genetics by orchestrating the cross-continental game of zoological musical chairs.

When the tiger surplus problem began developing, and zoo vets begin wishing for cat contraceptives, someone invented a hormone implant that can be inserted under a female's skin, blocking estrus and ovulation for months at a time. The device, now used for many mammals at zoos around the world, cannot be purchased commercially. If you're a zoo director who wants several of them, you call or write the inventor: Uly Seal, endocrinologist. And on a quiet Sunday, the Seal family will build them for you at their kitchen table and provide them to you free of charge.

His furious pace might suggest that Uly Seal is overworked, humorless, and compulsive. He has been accused by other zoo researchers of some sloppiness born of fingers in too many pies—of data too hastily assembled without all the statistical I's dotted and T's crossed, although follow-up work nevertheless continued to verify his conclusions. At times, he speaks rudely and sharply to someone who's assisting him, particularly Marialice. But no one has ever accused Uly Seal of humorlessness.

To the contrary, he often has the aspect of a man having a better time than anyone around him, a man on the verge of sharing with everyone a joke on himself. He has an an occasional proclivity toward bad puns, and an often-employed, distinct chuckle: "Heh, heh, heh, heh."

I managed to get Seal to sit down for a single formal interview, on a Sunday afternoon at his home. We sat in his living room, a noisy dishwasher gushing and humming in the adjacent kitchen, I on the sofa with Marialice, two of his daughters at the dining area table, and Seal in an office chair beside a big steel desk with a large personal computer atop it. He was in the process of analyzing population data when I arrived, and I asked him why he does all this.

"An inexhaustible curiosity about everything," said Marialice.

"I just enjoy solving problems," Seal said, shaking his head. "And there's an inexhaustible supply of problems to solve."

Later Seal, who also holds an undergraduate degree in philosophy, added, "Here's my utilitarian-ethical explanation. I can find no way to justify not making a maximum effort to help maintain the earth's genetic diversity. If I don't make a maximum effort, I impoverish my children and my grandchildren. I can find no way to justify impoverishment of the future in terms of nonrenewable resources like species."

Then he paused and grinned. "But, really, it's all just a lot of fun and games."

In Large Animal Holding, while the others are getting their supplies ready, Seal is at the window clucking and talking to tiger number 368. Its head is surprisingly wide, virtually filling up the little window and rotating side to side to nuzzle the back of Seal's hand. "Yeah," says Seal, hero of the antianthropomorphizers, to the tiger. "Yeah. Hey, girl, your toenails need clipping, don't they? Not getting worn down enough in there, are they? We'll have to take care of that, won't we? Yeah, girl. Yeah. Heh, heh, heh."

Tiger number 368 finally lowers itself from the window and pads away. "Just a magnificent animal," Seal says. "Just a beautiful, magnificent animal."

On that February day, no one should have known better than Seal that surplus tigers were a potential problem. Seal's own Species Survival Plan for tigers makes it absolutely clear that, at some point, more possibly very early in their life cycles, some tigers will be considered surplus, with no value as breeders in a zoo world where cage space is so limited that perhaps only active or potential breeders should be housed. The four tigers in Large Animal Holding are already surplus to the program, so breeding them would seem to make even *less* sense—any cubs they produce would just be more chaff.

Yet on this cold Minnesota Thursday, in this minimally heated building, Uly Seal expects, or at least hopes, after years of painstaking preparation, to effect the first successful artificial insemination of a tiger. If it works, he will indeed have created some surplus cubs—a whole litter of them, he hopes. And Seal has his reasons for doing that, after all.

2

Terry Kreiger steps out into the corridor with a plastic blowpipe about the diameter of a dime and maybe five feet long. The anesthetic dart, packed inside the pipe, is a simple device—a hollow needle out front, a slip valve, then a small, two-compartment canister: anesthetic in the front compartment, compressed air or gas in the back one. At the end are a couple of plastic or fabric "feathers" to assure the thing flies right. The vet will raise the long pipe in both hands to his mouth, aim at a tiger's flank, pause for just a second while he steadies the pipe, then suddenly fill his cheeks. You cannot see the dart in flight. There's a quick, soft release of air — poof — and suddenly the Day-Glo orange hypo appears against the tiger's fur, the drugs already into the animal's muscle. The drug in the hypo was under pressure from the gas — butane, in this case. As the short needle penetrates the tiger's flank, the animal's hide pushes back the sliding valve at the needle's base, and the gas pressure forces the drugs out.

The vet must be careful. The idea is to get the needle into muscle, not a major blood vessel. The dose is too high for direct injection into veins and, if taken intravenously, could kill the animal. But it is almost impossible to hit a major vessel on a tiger's rump, Kreiger says, and an experienced dart blower seldom misses.

"The accuracy you can get is amazing," Frank Wright, the zoo's principal vet, once said as he blew a couple of quick darts across his operating theater into a corrugated box target. "If you practice a few times, all the mystery and intrigue of it would be lost. But when you've got a healthy animal, there's always the danger of its spinning around, maybe moving its eye into your range at just the wrong time. If it happens in that instant when you've already made the neuromuscular commitment to shoot, you can't stop. There's nothing you can do about it. But if you can keep from getting the jitters, it's pretty easy."

Pretty easy, comparatively speaking. Generations who've grown up watching "Wild Kingdom" on television might assume that darting an animal with a tranquilizer is as easy as giving aspirin to a child.

But even in human medicine, physicians, anesthesiologists, and insurance companies consider anesthesia to be one of surgery's greatest risks, probably the greatest risk. And before human surgery, doctors know a patient's weight and when he last consumed food or liquids. The anesthesiologist, a medical doctor with specialized training and reams of case-study literature at his disposal, administers the drugs slowly through vein or respirator, monitoring the patient's progress, ready to intervene with drugs or oxygen should problems occur. Human drug doses have been highly refined through millions of tests, all on the same species. Anesthesiologists without the requisite skills and knowledge are never certified; those who make serious errors are likely never to work in the field again. Most important, the human druggers can afford to *underdose*: there's little chance that a patient will suddenly leap from the surgical table and rip apart his doctors.

An animal, on the other hand, is drugged quickly, intramuscularly, often with a relatively massive dose for a margin of safety. Too often it is drugged by wildlife field staff who have little anesthesiology training and only scant knowledge of the best dosage for the species — frequently with no species-specific knowledge at all, merely guesswork based on weight and perhaps the responses of similar species. The human patient does not charge out of the hospital and into the bush to hide before sinking into a too-deep stupor. There is no danger that an opportunist predator will devour the drugged and crippled patient before his doctors can get to him. (Hyenas will even attack drug-crippled lions.)

All too often, animals are given the wrong dosage, if only because no one knows what the dose for that species should be. San Diego Zoo staffers once went to Africa intending to collect wild giant elands, assuming that a commonly used drug called M99 would knock them out effectively. Only five milligrams of M99 would normally bring down a four-ton rhinoceros, but the erstwhile hunters couldn't knock out any of the five-hundred-pound elands with a dose four times that amount and returned home empty-handed. In the 1960s, one polar bear capture expedition used a dose extrapolated from experience with grizzlies. The team quickly managed to kill five of six darted bears with what turned out to be a gross overdose. (The sixth got away, but it was shot the following day by a hunter.) Further, each individual has its own response to anesthesia, and that can be influenced by other variables. Once, vets at the National Zoo discovered that to knock out a two-hundred-pound young polar bear they needed a dosage six times higher than the one they had used to put down a nine-hundred-pound adult bear. A dose that knocks out a two-hundred-fifty-pound zoo lion accustomed to humans may have little effect on an adrenaline-supercharged two-hundred-fifty-pound wild lion being chased across a grassland by a roaring Land Rover.

Even if the dose is correct, darting animals is always risky. In 1985, the Minnesota legislature responded to angry farmers near the hamlet of Grygla, where the state's sole remnant elk herd was reputed to be eating up whole swaths of the local sunflower crop. The state's wildlife officials recommended a limited hunting season to keep down the size of the herd but, caught in a political squeeze between the farmers and demands from some animal lovers that the elk not be harmed, the legislature instead ordered the state's wildlife agency, the reluctant Department of Natural Resources, to tranquilize and translocate the animals to nearby Indian reservation lands. Promptly, the DNR's shooters darted a magnificent bull elk that, terrified by the chase, proceeded to charge into a marsh before the drugs took effect. By the time the DNR found the animal, the drugs indeed had worked: the bull had collapsed in a few feet of water and unconscious, with its nose submerged, had drowned before the wildlife team could reach it. (The herd never was relocated. A judge finally ordered the DNR to cease and desist in response to a lawsuit from animal rights organizations and the Sierra Club, to the publicly expressed joy of the DNR itself.)

It used to be worse. The "capture gun" was first introduced at a wildlife symposium in 1957; it was proclaimed a marvelous technological advance and promptly became a major devastator of wildlife. Using the gun seemed a simple alternative to conventional means of capture. During the first decade of its use, untrained anesthetic shooters killed a great deal of wildlife, with mortalities for some capture teams running to 100 percent.

Used properly, the capture gun can be a great boon, especially in zoos. Before development of the dart, zoo animals needing treatment had to be restricted in "squeeze cages" with one or two movable walls to compress the space enough that the occupant — by then often stressed to the point of terror — could be poked with a hypodermic on a stick.

But even in the controlled environment of a zoo, where all reasonable caution is used, accidents are inevitable. A tranquilized animal might stumble and injure its leg. For whatever reason, its heart may fail under anesthesia, or it may go too deeply under and simply stop breathing. Or a dart shot into a hip that is almost entirely muscle mass may nevertheless happen to penetrate a blood vessel, converting what should be an intramuscular dose into a deadly intravenous overdose. In 1986 the Minnesota Zoo had its first-ever anesthesia death: ironically, of all the species at the zoo, it was a Siberian tiger, a young male being tranquilized for shipment to Seoul to serve as one of two Minnesota zoo tiger mascots for the 1988 Olympic games. A necropsy showed that the male had become unconscious with its neck over a small ridge in a hatchway between two cages and quietly strangled while the veterinary staff was working furiously on its Seoul-bound companion, which itself had overreacted to the drugs and was having difficulty breathing.

There are other problems. Animal drugs are packaged for more conventional veterinary uses. Wright says, "You take out the little written insert in the package and it gives you the dosage for a forty-five-pound dog or a kitten, but it doesn't say a thing about Siberian tigers or lesser pandas." Indeed, I once watched Wright blow-dart an ailing red panda five times before the animal was dopey enough to be handled for a physical exam. (That wasn't all lack of knowledge: the vet had started out with a low dose for a margin of safety, fully prepared to dart the animal twice.)

Until Seal began working with tigers, no one knew much about the amount of these anesthetics to use with them, especially with those about to be ejaculated. Seal discovered that one reason researchers had trouble obtaining viable sperm from anesthetized cats was that the commonly used veterinary drugs, phenothiazine, promazine, and acepromazine, indeed knocked an animal down but, in males being artificially ejaculated, caused a retrograde ejaculation into the animal's bladder. Now he uses a combination of other drugs—ketamine, Rompun, and Valium—which together act as anesthetic, analgesic, and mild amnesiac. The drugs do not knock the tigers out completely, but instead plunge them into a deep, open-eyed, and—for a first-time visitor—disconcerting trance.

Early in the research program, Wright was skeptical about the effects the weekly knockdowns would have on the cats. "I was worried that after a week or two we'd have a bunch of physical and emotional basket cases on our hands," he says. But it isn't so. When the Seals or Wright or Tilson or any of the research regulars enter the building, the cats invariably rise to greet them, nuzzling against the bars. Only when Seal or a vet steps into the room with the blowpipe in hand do the cats show signs of distress, slinking toward the back of the cage, letting out an abrupt roar as the needle penetrates.

"Some of these cats have been down two hundred times — once every week for four years," says Tilson. "When I come in here tomorrow, I won't see any change. They'll greet me. They'll roll over and purr." There is a food intake chart for the tigers on the wall of the kitchen, one of the simplest indicators of health. The chart shows little change in eating habits over the course of months. Further, when one of the research tigers died of a common viral disease in 1984, the zoo did an extensive necropsy and pathological assay to find out what physical changes the drugs were causing. "No change in muscle, in liver, in kidneys — absolutely nothing," Tilson reported.

According to Seal, the blowpipe itself is an important addition to the technology of anesthesia. Unlike the air pistol in use at some zoos, this gadget is virtually silent, so at least the animals have no apprehension that they're going to hear a loud noise, which could further boost adrenaline levels, interfering with the anesthesia. Still, Wright has on hand in a cabinet in the vet complex a carbon dioxide pistol, a brace of CO_2 rifles, and a rifle that uses an explosive charge. Sometimes an animal is too distant to reach with a blow dart, and the speed of the carbon dioxide air guns is too slow for some others. I once stood with Wright in the Tropics Building, across a moat from the white-handed gibbons. We were far beyond the gibbons' island, looking at a lame flamingo below. But Archie, the male gibbon, who could see us through the foliage that intervened, had sailed, arm over arm, through the island's artificial branches to the point nearest us across the moat. He regarded the vet steadily, warily.

"I'll show you why we need an explosive gun sometimes," said Wright. "Watch this." He looked up to Archie and quickly put two fists to his mouth, as if they were holding a blowpipe. In virtually the same instant, Archie spun backward, grasped one tree limb, then another, and nearly flew, swinging and brachiating through the trees to a hiding spot behind a tree trunk at the far end of the island.

Seal didn't set out to conduct research on animal anesthesia, but his findings have constituted an incidental breakthrough in veterinary medicine. Rompun is a drug of choice for many anesthesias for animals, for it is considered to be safer, with fewer side effects, than a number of others. But it still can present problems. There is a natural inclination to err on the side of safety for the attending humans, so doses for much wild animal tranquilization tend to be higher than necessary. Good precedent exists for that much caution: veterinarians and researchers have been attacked by animals they thought had gone under. On one occasion, Dr. Charles Sedgwick, a Los Angeles Zoo vet, examining a Bengal tiger's swollen jaw, had the cat's head in hand when he realized that the tiger's eyes were those of a still-conscious, and very frightened, animal. The drug dose caught up with the tiger, but not before he'd clawed the vet. As a grizzly bear researcher once told me, "I'd rather be safe." But being safe means giving an extra margin of drug, which may not be so safe for the anesthetized animal.

There were eight deaths of tigers under anesthesia in 1984 and 1985 alone. "I'm quite certain they were from overdoses of Rompun," Seal says. The standard dose is about one hundred milligrams, but Seal uses only about one-half that, carefully parceling out more shots of much milder dosages over a longer period of time. Seal has found, too, that the minimum required dose varies between individuals. Some of the difference might have to do with how high-strung an individual animal is. That is why everyone must wait in the kitchen while the big cats are being knocked out — to keep the animals' stress levels, and subsequently their adrenaline levels, down. One result of Seal's low-dose approach, however, is that human adrenaline levels can increase. A tiger drifting in open, liquid-eyed dreamland for twenty minutes can suddenly stir and, with vets and researchers huddled around him, rise from the floor of his cage, still too hazy to attack, but only moments away from a clearer head. Tigers with clear heads don't take kindly to a group of humans invading their territories, to say nothing of how a fully conscious tiger would react to the processes that two of the cats in Large Animal Holding are about to undergo.

3

Large cats have been artificially inseminated only twice, ultimately with poor results. In one case, the London Zoo artificially inseminated a puma; the cub died soon after birth. In another, a tiger insemination at Cincinnati apparently worked, but the embryo never developed to term.

Almost all artificial insemination in zoos has been done with hoofed animals biologically closest to cows and sheep, with which it has been practiced for more than thirty years. But there have been some successes in the zoo world, notably with giant pandas. The London Zoo's Chia-Chia is the father via artificial insemination of Chu-Lin at the Madrid Zoo. National Zoo also attempted to employ Chia-Chia as a remote father for its female panda, Ling-Ling, in 1984 after officials there became concerned that her mate, Hsing-Hsing, had failed to impregnate her during an estrus. (They had mated, but Hsing-Hsing's technique seemed questionable to zoo officials.) Ling-Ling bore a cub. Although it died of respiratory failure, analysis later showed that the artificial insemination had been unnecessary: it was Hsing-Hsing's offspring after all.

The Basel Zoo has successfully impregnated a captive female African elephant with semen electroejaculated from a wild bull elephant, and in 1984, a baby gorilla conceived through artificial insemination was born at the Melbourne Zoo. (Although the newborn was rejected by its mother and had to be hand-reared, Melbourne did its best to educate her: a member of the Nursing Mothers Association, analogous to the La Leche League in the United States, had given the pregnant ape daily live demonstrations of human breast-feeding, to no avail.) Artificial insemination could be a boon to any captive breeding program.

Moving an animal from zoo to zoo is expensive for the zoo and stressful, sometimes even dangerous, for the beast. The shipped animal often experiences additional stress on relocation, finding itself in unfamiliar territory with keepers who are strangers. Every time a listed endangered species is shipped, the zoo must obtain permits from the U.S. Fish and Wildlife Service. An international transfer involves the approval of two governments and even more paperwork.

Imagine, then, the advantage of shipping a few milligrams of sperm cells rather than a four-hundred-pound male Siberian tiger — no long-term anesthesia, no shipping and relocation stress, no permit problems, no need to quarantine the animal at the receiver zoo. And there's another benefit.

In small wild or captive populations — and in the case of the Siberian tiger, both are relatively small — there's always the risk of random accident — stochasticity — causing the loss of rare alleles. Suppose such an allele, available in only one bloodline, is lost when a virus to which that strain is especially susceptible sweeps through the population. But if sperm had been collected and banked in a nitrogen freezer, the genetic balance could still be preserved, virtually in perpetuity.

In the case of the Siberian tiger, if sperm from all the male founders of the captive population had been saved and artificial insemination were possible, the genetic health of that population could have been stabilized sooner and better. In a "frozen zoo" genetic diversity could be preserved with far less concern for the demographics of the living population: with assurance that all original genes were preserved, no tiger would have to be declared surplus. It might even mean that the size of the captive population could be reduced, freeing exhibit space and resources for a broader range of species.

But there is another reason for perfecting artificial insemination—the future. When Ulysses S. Seal designed his genetic-demographic SSP model for captive tigers, he envisioned a breeding program that would yield a stable, genetically fit population for a thousand years. In the very long term, he says, artificial insemination might someday help to save the tiger in the wild.

As habitat vanishes, the only hope for many animals will be wilderness reserves. But population biology theory now suggests that with migration cut off, animals in such habitat "islands" may be subject to the same pressures as zoo populations: inbreeding, loss of diversity, demographic glitch, extinction. For species to survive, reserves will need to be restocked with new blood. Zoos may be able to provide that stock, but there's a rub: introducing some captive animals to the wild will be difficult. While a wild tiger cub learns how to hunt and defend a territory, zoo cats learn to salivate over the crinkling of a horsemeat wrapper. Some zoo tigers may be able to learn to survive, but training would be expensive, time consuming, and probably only occasionally successful.

But what if the "tiger" could instead be introduced to the wild in the form of a sperm cell removed, with a few million others, from a captive male and transferred to the wilderness to mature in the womb of a wild mother? The resulting cub or cubs would be raised in the wild by their mother, learning the ways of the stalk and the kill, learning to seek out and defend their own territories as they matured to adulthood. Conversely, what if new genetic stock could be brought into captivity to strengthen the gene pool by merely darting a male in a Siberian reserve, extracting its sperm, and airmailing it transcontinentally?

Is it science fiction? Probably not, although some prominent researchers, including National Zoo research director Devra Kleiman, have expressed skepticism that such reproductive technology can yield results among enough species to be meaningful anytime soon.

Ron Tilson says, "I really perceive it all as at a very medieval stage. We don't yet have much knowledge of even the basics, like endocrine [hormonal] systems, because the endocrine system is so massively complicated. So there's a lot of trial and error, a little like we're saying, 'Let's bleed 'im a gallon and see if 'e recovers from the plague.' But even though our state of knowledge is still medieval, we're rapidly moving into an enlightened age. We've accepted the importance of small steps. Everyone wants to take big jumps. But we've got to methodically try to approach the problem one step at a time and establish a base so that not only will we have a capacity to make it work, but a capacity to repeat it."

As part of the project's movement into the enlightened age Tilson has begun to invite scientists and specialists from outside the zoo world to get involved in the Minnesota Zoo's—and Uly Seal's—artificial insemination project. It is an invitation in the purest sense: there is no money to pay anyone to help, so anyone who lends a hand does it for the love of knowledge or wildlife or for the pure novelty of it. Novelty may yet be the saving grace. Tilson, outwardly not a timid man, said he was apprehensive about approaching busy scientists to ask for help gratis.

"But you get a positive reaction when you walk in and say, 'Hey, would you like a few mils of tiger semen?' People have been eager to help. They say, 'I can't wait until I tell my friends what I did today.' "

Among the volunteers is Edmund Graham of the University of Minnesota Veterinary School, considered by his colleagues to be the father of modern cryobiology. Beginning in the 1950s Graham pioneered techniques now widely used to freeze livestock semen and later embryos. Hugh Hensleigh of the university's medical school runs an experimental program for in vitro fertilization—test-tube babies—for human couples. Ann Beyers, in the kitchen with her centrifuge, who is one of Hensleigh's graduate students, will ferry pellets of tiger sperm back to a university lab for fertility tests and freezing.

Martha Garcia and Mel Fahning are highly respected veterinary researchers and entrepreneurial proprietors of a western Wisconsin gamete-freezing firm. Early in the research effort, Seal learned how to obtain semen, but so far, despite repeated artificial insemination attempts, he has not gotten a single cell to find its way through a female tiger's womb to an ovum. That's why Garcia and Fahning have been invited into the project. They've performed hundreds of inseminations in domestic hoofed stock, a technique so perfected that, with cows, it works more than 90 percent of the time.

The previous year, Tilson and Seal had thought an insemination had worked. "Last year," says Tilson, "we monitored the endocrine levels. When a female went into estrus, we ovulated her [induced ovulation with hormones]. We got high estrogen levels and thought we had a pregnancy. Fifty days later—crash—false pregnancy. Not to be discouraged, we started all over again this year. But this time, with help from Fahning and Garcia, we're going to try to transport sperm all the way up into the uterus itself."

Fahning and Garcia come into Large Animal Holding dressed for the office: he, balding and mustachioed, in white shirt, vest, tie, and cowboy boots; she, a petite, pretty woman in stubby high heels. They step into blue jumpsuits with their company logotype, CRYOVATECH, on the chest. Fahning opens a rubber surgical glove and holds it for Garcia, who drops her rings and watch into it. He tucks away the glove on a chair. She rolls up her sleeves and pulls elbow-length surgical gloves onto her hands and arms. Not incidentally, she has very small hands.

Kreiger has finished his work with the blowpipe. The team files from the kitchen into the service corridor between the cages. There are four anesthetized tigers in the holding area. The animals are soundly under anesthesia, yet their eyes are wide open—wet, amber disks the size of silver dollars.

Despite their reputation, tigers in the wild are generally not a danger to humans, usually avoiding people where possible. But like grizzly bears, they have little innate fear of anything. A tiny percentage of tigers become man-eaters, and these can be remarkably aggressive—raiding villages, crashing into huts. In the lagoons and backwaters of the Sundarbans in India, man-eaters have been known to leap out of dense shoreline vegetation and into the boats of fishermen for a Homo sapiens dinner.

But zoo animals do regard their enclosures as their own territory, and they can protect it ferociously. With no option to flee, many will attack if a human merely crosses the

artificial barrier. In 1985, a young keeper who violated all
the rules of procedure and crossed a fence into an occupied
tiger enclosure at the Bronx Zoo was mauled and killed.

Seal nonchalantly slides open the cage door. The male
tiger inside is flat on the floor, clearly drugged, but for me
there is still the knowledge of how quickly and efficiently
one of these immensely powerful cats could relieve one of
an arm or snap a neck. My consternation passes in a moment, however, if only because everyone else is blasé.
Oddly, it is less disconcerting to bend low, step directly
into the cage, and sidle up to the immobile, nearly quarter-
ton male. In nearby cages Uly Seal is already drawing
blood from the legs of the females for endocrine assays.

Marialice Seal is at her usual station in the center of the
room, feet on a plastic tub to keep them off the cold floor,
clipboard on lap, cages of drugged, prone tigers on either
side of her. The service corridor is cold, somewhere in the
mid-thirty-degree range, for it is near zero outdoors.

One drawback to Uly Seal's anesthesia technique is that
it must be repeated every twenty minutes. Marialice serves
as a station master, calling out dosages and times, tracking
the duration of each injection, keeping an eye on the tigers
to assure that they're breathing normally and that they're
still incapacitated. There is always the danger that the drug
will begin to wear off too soon because Seal and the vet
may be preoccupied and thus a few minutes late with the
needle.

The research team tends to recruit help where it is available. On this day, as I am standing near the supine tiger's
huge head in the cramped cage with three or four other
people, all of whom have other assignments, Tilson assigns
me a job. "If he starts to lift up his head, put both your
hands on it and push it down. If he still tries to lift it, put
your knee right there."

"Right there" is the tiger's neck, which is the diameter

of a reasonably mature red pine. "And then just push his head down," Tilson says. "I'm not kidding. It's important."

I am grateful that the tiger does not attempt to stand during the next half hour.

Breeders have developed a number of ways to obtain sperm. Some bulls have been trained to mount an artificial cow; some stags have deposited semen in an artificial vagina attached to the rear of a live teaser doe in heat. At the San Diego Zoo, a male cheetah has learned to allow himself to be masturbated by a researcher, as have killer whales at Sea World. But by far the most commonly used technique is electroejaculation.

This method is effected with the aid of a white, tapered plastic cylinder-shaped probe that looks like a large version of what might euphemistically be called a marital aid. The zoo's electroejaculation kit includes probes in varying sizes, intended for various animals. The probe for the tiger, the size of a large cucumber, has gleaming stainless steel electrode bands running along its surface. Kneeling, Tilson lubricates the probe, pushes it into the male's rectum, and wrinkles his face as a fecal odor suffuses the air.

From the service corridor, Uly Seal bends low and enters the cage. Straightening, he peers down at the prone tiger, lifts his head to regard the rest of us and says, "Well, glad to see everyone here for the seminal event. Heh, heh, heh, heh."

Seal kneels to the control panel on the small, portable electroejaculator, a box the size of a toaster oven. The control panel has a couple of knobs and gauges and a long, insulated wire running to the probe. Seal begins turning a dial steadily and rapidly. With each turn of the dial, the needle on a voltmeter jitters upward and back down. Tiny zings of electricity, measured in milliamps, are sent to the electrodes along the probe. Tilson has buried his hands in abdominal fur, aiming the tiger's penis into a small beaker.

"Twenty-five volts, forty milliamps," intones Seal.

"No erection, no fluid," says Tilson.

"Okay," says Seal. "Up to thirty." Then he turns the dial up and down twenty times more. "Thirty volts, ninety milliamps."

"Plus-minus erection and no fluid," says Tilson.

Seal goes to thirty-five volts at two hundred milliamps and, as before, twenty repetitions. From the male comes a deep, low moan.

The repetitions over, Tilson pulls the beaker away from the animal's abdomen and holds it up to the light. It contains just a bit of clear liquid. "I have a positive erection, and I have . . . oh . . . about one mil of semen," he says.

Seal fiddles with the dials again, raising the power to forty volts and four hundred milliamps. As he begins the repetitions, the tiger becomes vocal, letting out an astonished, low roar: "Mrrrowwwwww." The cat's hind legs extend in a long, leisurely, feline stretch and, as the repetitions continue, suddenly begin pedaling at the air.

Tilson pulls the beaker away, cupping it in his hand to keep it warm. "Great. I have four more mils for a total of five," he says. For now, the procedure is over.

Back in the kitchen, Tilson peers through a microscope at a semen sample smeared on a warm slide and invites me to have a look through the second eyepiece. To an untrained eye, it is a remarkable enough sight: thousands of tadpolelike sperm cells, swimming furiously.

Tilson isn't pleased; the sperm density seems low. But within half an hour there's a second electroejaculation, which yields what everyone is hoping for, a sample literally packed with cells. "Wall-to-wall sperm," says Tilson. Through the microscope, it is an awesome sight — millions of swimming, wildly active cells, densely packed. It is a superb and healthy sample.

A technician examining a semen sample looks primarily

at three things: the sperm concentration within the seminal fluid; how many are moving, as opposed to dead, and moving properly, swimming ahead rather than in senseless circles; and their morphology, or physical appearance.

The count of sperm per milliliter is accomplished simply, if tediously, by tallying the number of cells within sectors of a grid in a device called a hemacytometer counting chamber, then performing some simple math to factor upward to a milliliter. The percentage of motility estimate is similarly done by an experienced guesser. A reasonably high amount — up to 20 percent in even a healthy sample — will somehow be deformed and incapable of doing the job. The varieties of abnormalities are almost endless: megalosperm (with giant heads); microsperm (with tiny heads); pyriform sperm (with heads like inverted pyramids); sperm with generally misshapen heads; bicephalic sperm with two heads; sperm with their midpiece (the short section between head and tail) attached akilter on the head rather than symmetrically; sperm with double or coiled or bent midpieces; sperm with tightly coiled or double tails or endless varieties of bent tails; sperm with free-floating unattached heads.

Because sperm characteristics vary widely among species, there's little hope of extrapolating experience with one to the next, even among closely related species. Gorillas, for example, have extremely low sperm counts, so low that it seems a miracle, extrapolating from human experience, that gorillas can reproduce at all. John Wortman, the Denver Zoo's chief curator, says, "The sperm count in a normal gorilla is so low that if it came from a human, he'd be considered infertile." Varieties of semen among animals are just as wide. A horse, for example, normally provides about a pint of ejaculate. The upper limit for a single ejaculation from a Siberian tiger, however, is only a few teaspoons.

Part of the sample Beyers is centrifuging will be used fresh to inseminate a female tiger today in Large Animal Holding; another portion will be ferried to the University of Minnesota to be frozen; a third amount is for Beyers's own research. She will expose the sperm to hamster ova as part of her master's thesis research. Hensleigh, her adviser, has found that if one removes the cumulous mass and zona pellucida, barriers of tissue that surround and protect ova, one can subject living human sperm cells to the treated eggs and reliably measure the potency of the cells. Sperm that are adequately robust enter the egg and cause an acrosomal reaction — quite literally, the instant of conception, when one sperm "takes" and seems to blow up in the egg, excluding all others. Beyers is attempting to discover whether the same test will work for tigers. (A friend who had the fertility test, which is still controversial for humans, discovered that the clerks at Blue Cross were more than a little perplexed when a bill for fertilizing hamster eggs arrived.)

Even if the sample that is to be stored for the future is healthy and normal and handled properly, freezing is by no means an assured success. "We lose a lot of motility in the process of freezing and thawing," says student Sue Adams, who was working with cryobiology pioneer Ed Graham on the tiger project. "From 70 percent right down to 100 percent." The ideal freezing and thawing rate, she says, varies from species to species and must be worked out for each one.

The centrifuging process concentrates the cells and allows Beyers to remove the seminal fluid. Surprisingly, the natural fluid is far from the best medium for sperm survival, especially if the cells are to be frozen. At least that's true for humans and some other animals. "Of course," Beyers says as the centrifuge runs, "we're all very limited in what we know about tigers."

"In general," says Ed Graham, "seminal plasma is the worst possible medium for storing sperm — it's a medium that is there for natural breeding, not for putting in a test tube and storing for a hundred years." Graham has developed a "sperm extender" that better protects the membranes around an individual sperm cell, typically chemicals called TES and TRIS, some egg yolk to protect the membrane, "and a little bit of sugar for energy." Beyers isn't so elaborate. She suspends some of the cells in "BWW medium," a saline solution. But she wonders aloud whether the team's plan of bypassing the vagina will work. Obviously, injecting cells directly into the uterus should make it much easier for them to reach ova. But, in humans, chemicals in the vagina "capacitate" sperm cells, stripping away certain proteins that, if not removed, can sometimes prevent fertilization.

In the cage of female tiger number 732, Martha Garcia has been trying, with only gradual success, to work a catheter through the sleeping cat's cervix. The catheter is a thin, very long, strawlike, rigid tube. In a cow, it would pass easily into the uterus, but the tiger's cervix is not only less dilated, but the route is convoluted. Garcia has inserted her plastic-gloved left arm halfway to the elbow in the cat's rectum. With her left hand, she can feel the cervix. "It feels like a rubber eraser," says Fahning. She is palpating it, trying to manipulate it into a better position in order to coax in the catheter. John Lewis, the zoo's biological services director, has dropped by and is standing in the cage, holding a work light for Garcia. Garcia has just become, Fahning remarks, "the world's first tiger palpation specialist." Lewis asks if I won't please hold the tiger's tail.

Beyers brings the concentrated sperm samples to Fahning in the female's cage. Garcia has managed to work the catheter about three fourths of the way through the cat's cervix, but can get no farther. Fahning forces the concentrated sperm sample into the long, clear catheter with a syringe. Uncertain that it has all reached the catheter's terminus, he removes the syringe, bends over near the tiger's rump, and blows steadily on the catheter.

"We got a few hundred million in there, anyway," says Tilson finally.

Whether the attempt at artificial insemination will work is anyone's guess. In one week, the team will perform a laparotomy on the female tiger, inserting tubes into her uterus to flush out any fluid and cell matter. If there are any embryos, they will be of about one hundred cells by then, floating in that fluid, large enough to be just visible to the naked eye. If there are any embryos, the team may have begun to find the key to making artificial insemination as routine in cats of the lion/tiger class as it is in cows.

4

On a warm August day in 1983, Betsy Dresser boarded a flight in Los Angeles, bound for Cincinnati. She and Earl Pope had slipped through airport security without drawing any attention, although carefully taped under Dresser's left arm was a suspicious-looking stainless steel vial.

Dresser probably wouldn't fit the skyjacker profile. As a youngster, she must have been a sterling example of the all-American kid, with a mop of curly blond hair, an easy grin, and boundless energy.

"While other little girls were thinking about dolls," she says, "I was thinking about animals."

As a teenager, Dresser became a fixture at the Cincinnati Zoo—first as a "junior zoologist," later as a volunteer tour guide—constantly bothering director Ed Maruska to teach her more about animals. Maruska says that in recent years Dresser has taught *him* a thing or two about animals.

Between 1971 and 1979, at the University of Cincinnati and later Ohio State University, undergraduate, then master's and Ph.D. candidate Dresser played the game, by and large, by the rules. She was interested in wildlife biology, particularly wildlife reproductive biology. Ohio State is one of the largest land-grant universities in the nation, part of an academic industry with strong ties to agribusiness and an institution that devotes millions of dollars and thousands of person-hours yearly to a tiny corner of the animal world where only horses, pigs, cows, sheep, and chickens reside. There were no gorillas, no bongo, no tigers. So Dresser did her graduate research on what was available.

"My advisers in college told me right away to forget about exotics," she says. "They advised me that there were no jobs available for serious researchers working in reproductive biology with exotics, that I should go into the industry where the jobs were."

Dresser's master's thesis was on the effects of a fat-free diet on pregnancy and placental development in the run-of-the-mill laboratory mouse. As a doctoral candidate, "I did the first test-tube sheep," Dresser says, laughing. "But that wasn't where my heart was."

Dresser's advisers were at least partly right: there were virtually no jobs available for researchers working on the reproductive physiology of exotic wildlife. So she invented one. She accepted a faculty research position in the Department of Obstetrics and Gynecology at the University of Cincinnati and promptly began pestering Maruska at the zoo once again. This time, she wanted him to set up a research program into the technologies of artificially aided wildlife reproduction. Maruska admits that he resisted the idea. At the time, the measure of a new zoo's success was its breeding record, especially its ability to breed the most reproductively intractable of species.

"Betsy had to talk me into it," Maruska says. "I thought that doing these things was an admission of failure, an admission that we weren't providing the proper environment for breeding. I was obviously wrong. Betsy opened my eyes to the point that I see it now as the *only* solution for many species."

Dresser still holds an associate professorship at the University of Cincinnati, but she is preoccupied with the joint venture that grew out of her arm-twisting with Maruska, the Cincinnati Wildlife Research Federation. Her federation, born in 1981, is a consortium of the zoo, the university, and the animal collection at nearby King's Island Wild Animal Safari, a for-profit adjunct of a huge amusement park.

In her role as director of the federation, Dresser has become a zookeeper, although different from the kind who feed and clean up after animals. Her animal collections take the form of microscopic bits of life. That day on the airplane, she was actively zookeeping, lending body heat to a collection of endangered species in the container under her arm.

As she buckled the seat belt, Dresser turned to her colleague Pope and asked, "What do you suppose people on this plane would think if they knew there was a herd of bongo on board?"

A bongo is a rare, shy, big-eared, forest-dwelling African antelope. Dresser's and Pope's day had begun early, around 6:00 A.M., with veterinary staff at the Los Angeles Zoo anesthetizing a bongo female that had been "superovulated" with hormones and then allowed to mate with a male. If the hormone injection had worked, it would mean that several eggs were present when the mating occurred and that, optimally, several of those would have become multicelled blastocyst embryos. The domestic cattle-breeding industry routinely uses surgery to remove embryos at this point, but Dresser is adamant that with exotics surgery should be avoided when possible. Rather than slicing into the female bongo, the vets in Los Angeles used a Foley catheter, a rubber device that, once inserted through the cervix into the uterus, leaves three separate tubes exposed. The first is a conduit for air that, pumped in, inflates a balloonlike midsection of the device to form a firm barrier against the cervix. The second is a conduit for pouring a buffered phosphate flushing solution into the uterus, the third a conduit for drawing the solution back out after it has washed through the womb.

After flushing the uterus of the bongo, Dresser wound up with about two quarts of solution in a glass dish. She set the dish aside for about half an hour to allow any solid matter to settle to the bottom, then siphoned away most of the fluid from the top. Sorting carefully through the bits of tissue that remained, she found five tiny, very alive specks — bongo embryos, each only about the size of the period at the end of this sentence.

The flight from Los Angeles would arrive in Cincinnati at 7:30 that evening, but the biggest part of Dresser's and Pope's day was still ahead of them. Getting embryos out is ultimately meaningless unless they can be put back in.

Fewer than a thousand wild bongo still live in parts of Africa that once harbored tens of thousands, and the creature is listed as endangered by the IUCN. Fewer than one hundred live in captivity in North America, nearly one third of those at a single institution, the Los Angeles Zoo. The bongo clearly is in need of a larger, more stable population, both in captivity and in the wild. Dresser's plan was to try to prove that technologies that work for farm animals can be made every bit as applicable for African antelope. She intended to transplant the bongo's embryos into the wombs of surrogate mothers in Cincinnati.

Dresser's rationale from a conservation standpoint was much the same as Seal's for artificial insemination. Embryo transfer could mean easy exchanges of animals across international borders. It could allow more precise management of the gene pool. It could mean that new bongo could be introduced in the wild in embryonic form, a genetic-demographic double whammy that would introduce the genes of both a new mother *and* father.

But there was even more potential here. From her work in the world of agriculture, Dresser knew that science fiction types of procedures had become routine: superbulls mated with supercows that had produced hundreds of embryonic offspring in a single year; embryos frozen for months, years, maybe decades, then thawed and allowed to recommence development in the wombs of surrogate mothers. What if surrogate mothering were possible for endangered species? What if several embryos of every endangered mammal species could be stored in a tank of nitrogen for posterity? One could keep a frozen zoo or, as one scientist calls it, a library of life. What if it were possible to intervene in the process of extinction to the point that extinction was reversible: if the bongo should become extinct in the wild, a few withdrawals could be made from the library of life, placed into the wombs of a surviving antelope species, and, voilà, reorigination of a species. Through the wonders of cryobiology, common house cats could reoriginate rare spotted sand cats. Holstein milk cows could reoriginate gaurs. If the tiger disappeared, the tiger as species could become Lazarus in the womb of a lion.

Such a scenario is not farfetched and perhaps not too far in the future. On her way from Los Angeles, Betsy Dresser was only a matter of months—the average gestation period for bongo—from proving just how possible it was.

After forming her federation, Dresser began testing reproductive technologies on eland, a low-risk approach because they, another, larger African antelope species, are abundant both in zoos and in the wild. Success came early. In 1982, Dresser succeeded in hormonally superovulating a female eland, Toledo, who subsequently was bred with a male; about a week later, Dresser flushed the uterus and collected thirty-one embryos. Fifteen of them went into the wombs of domestic cows. ("I didn't think it would work. But I wanted to see what would happen," Dresser says.) Although pregnancies began in two of the cows, neither lasted more than one hundred days. But of three of Toledo's embryos that were transferred to other *eland*, one took. On June 14, 1983, a healthy calf conceived of Toledo was born of a surrogate mother named Millie. The calf quickly was dubbed E.T., — for "embryo transplant," although the sci-fi overtones were not coincidental.

By the time E.T. was born, another first was already in progress. In April 1983, Dresser pulled from a tank of liquid nitrogen at the zoo another of Toledo's embryos, which had been frozen for nearly six months. Once thawed, that embryo went into the uterus of another surrogate, Molly, and the following December 2, Molly delivered a full-term, seventy-seven-pound female calf. Although it died of complications from a breech birth, it was fully developed and completely normal, and there was no indication that its breech position was anything more than the normal vagaries of delivery. By 1984, another frozen embryo developed to term and entered the world whole and healthy.

Meanwhile, the effort was moving ahead leapfrog-style. By the time E.T. was born, Dresser had already negotiated with the Los Angeles Zoo for its cooperation in the transcontinental transfer. Of the five bongo embryos she and

Pope brought back, one went into a bongo mother. She inserted four more into the wombs of eland, hoping to prove that the much more common eland species, classified by taxonomists as of another genus, could be a bongo surrogate.

There was some precedent in the zoo world for Dresser's hunch that the interspecies transfer could work. As a result of a 1981 embryo transfer, a Holstein cow named Flossie gave birth to a gaur calf at the Bronx Zoo. In 1984, a horse gave birth to a Grant's zebra foal at the St. Louis Zoo.

If the entire procedure worked, there would be some firsts. The bongo-to-bongo transfer would be the first transfer of embryos between females of the same endangered species. The bongo-to-eland transfer would be only the second between an endangered species and a nonendangered one. (The gaur to the Holstein was the first. The Grant's zebra transferred in St. Louis is not endangered.) It would also be the first interspecies transfer among antelope. But for Betsy Dresser, there was more at stake. Although Ed Maruska and King's Island's Bob Reese had agreed to cooperate fully as partners in her federation, they did not provide much funding. Dresser says she had been spending 75 percent of her own time fund-raising, rather than doing research. Without question, an embryo transplant success would provide a burst of razzle-dazzle to the program and attract more donations. To no small extent, the future of the Cincinnati Wildlife Research Federation was at stake.

By now, inserting catheters into African antelope and coaxing tiny embryos into the womb was becoming routine for Dresser. By midnight, she and Pope were done.

A few weeks later, Dresser palpated the four would-be surrogates to check for pregnancy. The first two eland surrogates had none of the uterine swelling that signify pregnancy. Dresser checked the third. By the time she withdrew her hand, she was visibly shaking. She had felt a fetus. The bongo also appeared to be pregnant.

By late spring, both the bongo surrogate and the eland surrogate were fat with calf. Through the month of May the pregnant females were isolated in the veterinary center and under constant surveillance via remote video. On the night of May 31, Dresser stayed at the zoo late and drove home reluctantly.

"I went to bed that night with all my clothes on. I had a sense it was very close, that this was it for one of them," Dresser said. Back at the zoo's vet center, a volunteer was standing night watch, monitoring the televised picture of the pregnant antelope in their isolation cages. Just before 2:30 A.M., the eland went into labor. According to the protocol set up for the event, the volunteer dialed only the night watchman, then went back to observe the screen; the watchman telephoned veterinarian Lynn Kramer; Kramer called Dresser and said four words: "She's on her way." Dresser knew she might have only a matter of minutes if she wanted to be at the zoo in time to observe the birth.

So in the depths of that night, Betsy Dresser, solid citizen, sometime teacher at a local Bible college, became a scofflaw, racing through the streets of Cincinnati in her Honda Accord to the gates of the zoo. She ran from her car just in time to see the tiny bongo calf's head appear, and, with Kramer, the volunteer, and the night watchman, to cheer as the calf slipped out of the birth canal. The birth took only about fourteen minutes.

"It was such an easy birth," said Dresser. (Bongo calves, at about forty-five pounds, are only about half the size of eland.) "Next time maybe we'll give her twins."

Six days later the bongo surrogate gave birth to the biological twin of the eland's new baby. This calf, like the first, was born intact and healthy, but there was a small irony. Particularly in captivity, mammal mothers sometimes reject their offspring, and the bongo did just that. But curiously, the eland surrogate appeared not to know that this strange-looking calf was not hers and calmly began to nurse the bongo baby.

5

When I first heard about Betsy Dresser's frozen zoo, I suppose I imagined a largish, high-technology laboratory replete with gadgets, glassware, and white-coated assistants. But at the Cincinnati Zoo's Goetz Animal Health Center, Dresser led me though a pair of cluttered offices, down a short length of hallway, and into the door of her laboratory. We did not step in very far, because we could not: in a few steps we would have traversed the lab. Dresser's entire cryogenics facility is housed in a former darkroom, a fairly cramped one at that.

"I call it my giant cupboard," Dresser said, grinning.

Small worktables were pushed against two walls. Atop one of the tables sat Dresser's programmable liquid nitrogen freezer, about the size of a small microwave oven and labeled L'AIR LIQUIDE MINICOOL. Two blue canisters, also with the Air Liquide logotype, were stowed beside one table. Dresser pulled the small cap from one canister. A thin white cloud puffed out: nitrogen at minus 383 degrees, vaporizing instantly as it met room temperature air.

History's first embryo transfer occurred long ago, in 1890, when Walter Heape at Cambridge University successfully extracted the embryo of a pregnant rabbit and surgically implanted it in the womb of another rabbit. Today, both sperm and embryo transfer and freezing is a multimillion-dollar business with domestic livestock.

Commercial breeding operations have been storing and transferring semen for nearly three decades and embryos since the 1970s. The modern domestic cattle industry, in particular, has embraced reproductive technology, for it means that a single prize bull or cow—say, a cow that produces abnormally large amounts of milk or a bull that produces particularly prime beef—can become parent to literally thousands or tens of thousands of offspring. Best of all, scions of parents that are genetic blue bloods—from a cattleman's perspective, at least—can come to term in the wombs of low-grade, plebian mothers.

It is big business. Rio Vista Genetics, a Texas firm, is the world's largest embryo transfer operation, in 1980 delivering some five thousand little clumps of life at a cost to cattle producers of up to $2,500 per transfer. One prize supercow was thus biological mother to eighty-six calves in a single nine-month period.

Freezing an embryo is a complex process. Living cells contain more water than anything else, and a cell frozen too quickly would rupture, like a burst bottle of frozen beer. Therefore, a technician adds glycerol to extract most of the water from the cells, dehydrating them to prevent the formation of ice crystals during freezing. The first cooling stage is an extremely gradual process called equilibration. Over a period of one-half to twelve hours, cells are brought down to household refrigerator temperature, about 40 degrees: cool, but far from as cold as they have to be. Then, in a matter of minutes, the computerized liquid nitrogen freezer exposes the cells to nitrogen vapor, steadily drawing away heat energy until the cells drop from refrigerator to deep-freeze temperatures, then deeper and deeper until they are at about minus 150 degrees. Remarkably, the cell still isn't in a frozen-solid state—that will come in a single instant. Dresser or an assistant will plunge a forceps into the tank of nitrogen and touch the supercooled steel to the cells — a process called seeding. Instantly, the cell molecules within the embryo will snap into solid, crystalline formation. Then the embryo is put into the tank for storage.

Dresser pulled from the misting tank an embryo, a domestic cat. She is just beginning experiments that she hopes will someday allow house cats to carry the fetuses of rare, small, exotic counterparts like the jungle cat and sand cat. It's impossible to see the frozen cell mass because it's been drawn into a long thin cylinder, not unlike a soda straw, capped with a polyvinyl plug.

This tank was really a spare, used only for storing the few domestic cat embryos. The other tank, complete with an alarm system to warn of any leak or change in temperature, was the real frozen zoo, and the sum total of it. In it were only a few dozen bongo and eland embryos, but Dresser hoped it would someday hold gametes of rare creatures ranging from jungle cats to lowland gorillas. Dresser has a special interest in gorillas and hopes her work will lead to the application of reproductive technologies to the apes. But she adds, "Despite whatever rumors you may have heard, I am emphatically not interested in transferring gorilla embryos into humans."

There is one interesting twist. Animals have long been used as laboratory models for developing medical techniques for use in humans. "In this case," says Dresser, "so much more is known about human reproduction than gorilla reproduction that we'll end up reversing the process — humans will end up serving as a model for future work with apes. So far, it doesn't look as if we're an ideal model. It seems to be easier to do in vitro fertilization with humans than with some of the nonhuman primates."

Dresser warns that as valuable as they may have been, her successes might create a false impression. "There's no reason to believe that it will be this easy very often. I may have been just lucky with these animals. Maybe the techniques we used will only bring about a successful bongo-to-eland transfer one out of one hundred times, and I happened to hit that time."

Even if the same techniques prove to be ideal for bongo and eland, they might not work as well for other antelope species—to say nothing of gorillas.

Ulysses Seal once noted that, with all the reproductive technology that had been developed for farm animals, adapting them for use with tigers or rhinos would be a relative breeze. He says, "We assumed, on the basis of past experience with domestic animals, that in due course we'd have success." After half a decade and thousands of hours of research, he's learned a great deal about the subtle and intricate chemical and behavioral controls of reproduction in tigers, but, as I write this, has failed to prove that artificial insemination is even possible in the large cats. Researchers at the National Zoo have also been trying, with no more success, to inseminate Siberian tigers and have attempted to inseminate clouded leopards many times without success.

Says Dresser, "There are hundreds and hundreds of animals we just don't know what to do with. We don't know the endocrine levels. We don't know how to collect semen. We don't know estrous cycles. We don't know how to handle the sperm or the embryos once we get them. We have to get those fundamentals down first. We have to know what a reproductive tract in a rhino or an eland is supposed to feel like. Or can we even get in there to feel the reproductive tracts? We have to determine what kinds and sizes of catheters to use, what other equipment and tubing we might need. We have to find out if we can use hormones and get results. And with each new species, we have to start back at square one."

6

I once heard a scientist scoff at the notion of anyone "stealing the secret" of the atomic bomb, as if the secret were a page or two of classified information that, once microfilmed and spirited away, would result in a usable weapon. "It isn't a 'secret,' " the scientist said. "To build a hydrogen bomb means inventing an entire industry."

Reproductive technology is, similarly, no single secret. Any success will depend on much trial and error, collecting massive amounts of biochemical and behavioral data, and developing a breeding protocol involving rigorous timing, rigid adherence to proven standards, and still some blind luck. "We do have some common knowledge to build on," says Betsy Dresser, "but we still basically start at the beginning with each new species."

The first step is detailed understanding of the biochemistry of reproductive cycles. Males of species are usually excellent biochemical monitoring devices — a male chimp or antelope always knows when a female of its kind is receptive. But the signs are almost always less obvious to a human observer. Researchers generally know so little about the reproductive cycles of the animals they're dealing with that they have little or no way to predict when the female will be receptive to breeding.

The peaks and valleys of the reproductive cycles for cows, horses, and dogs are well known. But characterizing the normal range of reproductive cycling for any species means monitoring several individuals for months. (And it is a range. Each individual is unique, with all its attendant quirks.)

Ovulation must occur in the following sequence: something must direct an egg-containing follicle to appear on the surface of the ovary, something must encourage the follicle to ripen, then burst, releasing the egg. Something else must induce the lining of the uterus to prepare for reception of a fertilized egg.

That something is the endocrine system, a network of glands that produce hormones which, in turn, coordinate the activities of the relevant cells and organs. When it comes to reproduction, the organ of primary importance is the pituitary, a tiny gland located in the head.

Think of it as a biological stage play. Like a stage manager, the pituitary cues the actions that lead to pregnancy: curtain up, actors enter, lights up. As in a play, built-in feedback mechanisms are present in the endocrine system. A line spoken by an actor may cue the stage manager to ring a doorbell persistently. In response, the actor may open a door on stage, which cues the stage manager to shut off the bell.

Only by tracing the flux and flow of the important hormones that stage-manage reproduction can researchers like Dresser and Seal hope to piece together the reproductive mystery play for a given species.

The female reproductive process begins when the pituitary releases follicle-stimulating hormone (FSH). A smidgen of FSH travels from the pituitary and into the bloodstream, eventually reaching the ovaries. The arrival of FSH is a signal to the follicles on the surface of the ovaries to begin developing. The curtain is up.

Over a period of days, the follicle ripens and the egg inside approaches the time of release. Meanwhile, the concentration of FSH in the bloodstream has increased to a feedback level that cues the pituitary to release another hormone, luteinizing hormone (LH). Once again, the hormone trickles into the bloodstream and flows to the ripening follicle.

The follicle itself is a type of endocrine organ: it can produce the hormone estrogen, and the reception of LH signals the follicle to do just that. The estrogen produced by the follicle flows through the bloodstream back to the pituitary. There it signals the pituitary to produce more LH, which flows back to the ovary to signal the follicle to produce more estrogen, which flows to the pituitary to signal for the production of more LH, which will stimulate the follicle to produce more estrogen, and on and on until, finally, an estrogen peak pulls a switch in the pituitary that will cease the production of that very first hormone, FSH, and send out a great surge of LH. At this point, the follicle should have developed to such a ripe state that it is bulging from the surface of the ovary, a reddish, swollen lump clearly visible to a surgeon who has punctured the abdominal wall and is peering through a laparoscope. As the surge of LH peaks, the follicle ruptures, releasing the egg into the uterine horn to begin a journey to the womb.

The increasing estrogen has simultaneously sent a signal to the uterus to begin thickening its lining in anticipation of the arrival of an embryo. The recent LH surge continues its work, signaling the ruptured follicle to transform into a structure called corpus luteum, literally, "yellow body," a yellowish clump of cells laced with capillaries. The corpus luteum continues to act as a tiny endocrine organ, secreting small amounts of estrogen and copious amounts of the sex hormone progesterone. The progesterone sends signals to the pituitary to cease secretion of the FSH — an important bit of feedback, since continued presence of FSH in the bloodstream would begin the ovulation process anew.

There's more. At the same time that its presence in the blood signals the pituitary to halt the ovulation process, progesterone is inducing the development of the endometrium, the uterine lining that envelops and protects any fertilized egg that happens to come along. If an egg isn't fertilized, if a tiny embryo does not implant itself in the womb, the endometrium responds by secreting prostaglandin which causes the corpus luteum to atrophy.

And the curtain is down. When the corpus luteum atrophies, there is no more estrogen production. The absence of estrogen in the bloodstream is a feedback signal to the pituitary to secrete, slowly at first, FSH, and a new follicle will begin to form. The curtain has risen once again.

To look at one of Uly Seal's charts, which simultaneously tracks the rise, plateau, and fall of several hormones, and to trace the entire elaborate web of stimulation and, through hormonal feedback, inhibition, is to marvel at nature as a reproductive Rube Goldberg device. Except that this impossibly elaborate and interdependent chemical gadget really works.

There are numerous complications. Some mammals have an extra player in the biochemical reproductive fugue, the nervous system. In humans, ovulation is spontaneous, occurring about halfway through the cycle. But tigers are induced ovulators: ovulation occurs only in response to the stimulation of copulation. In other words, humans ovulate and, if they happen to copulate at the right moment during ovulation, they can produce offspring. Female tigers, on the other hand, go into estrus, copulate with males, and only *after* the nerve stimulation from copulation is the biochemical trigger that induces ovulation pulled.

A birth control pill can exert authority over the mechanics of birth by manipulating the endocrine system. Similarly, a scientist who fully understands a species' hormonal cycles, or at least an individual's, may be able to intervene in the process to promote birth. For Dresser's embryo transfers to be successful, intervention is mandatory. The donor female and the surrogate-mother-to-be must be at about the same stage in their cycles. Obviously, the donor must have produced ova to be fertilized. But

the receiving female's hormonal cycle must have prepared the uterus chemically and physically for reception of
an embryo. It appears, in fact, that the receiving female's
cycle should be just slightly behind the donor's, because
the transfer procedure seems to stall the embryo's development slightly. The odds of that happening naturally are
slim. Researchers like Dresser have learned from the cow
breeders to use hormones to manipulate two females into
properly synchronized cycles so that the play can begin.

Pinning down the cycles is critical. Unfortunately, a
researcher can make few assumptions about them, even
based on extensive knowledge of the cycles of other animals. The most time-tested apparent truths do not necessarily translate from species to species. Progesterone levels
are generally considered to be an excellent test for pregnancy because the hormone is present in both blood and
urine soon after conception in many, many species. But
Keith Hodges, a researcher at the London Zoo, discovered
why giant panda pregnancies so often come as a surprise
— progesterone levels don't rise substantially until after the
third trimester of pregnancy.

Even testing for hormone levels is complex and difficult.
Until recently, taking blood was the only way to measure
them, and that involves the use of anesthesia. But William
Lasley of the San Diego Zoo has developed a urine test
that allows scientists to track some hormone levels in some
species with great precision. Early on, Lasley perfected the
procedure for at least one primate. As he was developing
the test, he began to collect routine urine samples from
women at the zoo's research center and found he could
predict with great accuracy, within a few hours every month,
the time their menstrual periods would commence. It works
with some other animals, too, but it is not a perfect solution. Obtaining a sample means that a keeper must pa-

tiently observe an animal until it urinates, quickly move the animal to another area, and collect a urine sample from the enclosure floor with a syringe before the liquid dries or flows away. With one animal at least, San Diego has simplified the procedure. Dr. Barbara Durrant has trained a scimitar-horned oryx named Rachel to urinate into a beaker on command. It is questionable whether most tigers would be as cooperative or whether any clear-headed keeper would be willing to give them the opportunity.

As for the future, zoo biologists may soon be able to make another major embryo breakthrough with the ability to transplant across wide taxonomic gulfs. A key problem in transferring embryos across more than one genus level is that the methods of placental formation vary among different animal groups. While the evolutionary link between closely related species may mean that placental properties are similar, creatures more biologically separated will reject foreign placental cells: their immune systems literally identify a transplanted embryo as a potentially harmful foreign organism and attack it.

The placenta and embryo are both part of the tiny clump of cells washed out in the uterine-flushing process. And scientists can identify the outer layer of cells—the trophoblast—that will form the placenta. Scientists at Cambridge University have proved it possible to slice open, with microsurgical precision, the trophoblasts of both goats and sheep, remove the inner embryonic cells like a hard-boiled egg from its shell, then transfer the sheep embryo to the goat trophoblast. It suggests that someday, perhaps reasonably soon, zoo biologists may be able to use cows as surrogates for endangered antelope or dogs as surrogates for endangered cats or even elephants as surrogates for endangered rhinos.

7

One week after Uly Seal and the artificial insemination team at the Minnesota Zoo had made their attempt, they all gathered, with assorted hangers-on and observers, in the large surgery in the Biological Services Building, just up the hill from Large Animal Holding. They brought tiger number 372 up slowly in a zoo van on a road that winds up the hill. The van backed up to the long, concrete loading dock, and the back doors swung open. Tiger number 372 was on a stretcher on the floor of the van. Quickly, Uly Seal, Ron Tilson, and a zoo volunteer were at the handles, and the huge anesthetized cat was toted across the loading dock and through the steel double doors of the surgery.

There were about a dozen people in the room, including veterinarian Frank Wright, Uly and Marialice Seal, zoo photographer Tom Cajacob, veterinary anesthesiologist Alicia Fagella, assorted students, tiger keeper Ross Taylor, and Nick Reindl. After a while, the Cryovatech team, Fahning and Garcia, drifted in. There was little conversation. The tiger was on her back on a stainless steel examining table, legs splayed. Tilson, with electric clippers, was shaving a spot the size of a saucer on the tiger's tail near its base. Fagella inserted a long tube into the big cat's mouth and down into its trachea, inflated a balloon cuff deep in the throat to assure that the cat got only the air that was intended for it, and started an anesthesia machine that would pour nearly pure oxygen, with just a trace of halothane, directly into the cat's lungs.

A heart monitor began softly thumping a signal with each beat, simultaneously blinking an orange light. Wright, in blue jeans, hiking boots, and a green surgical cap, shaved the cat's wide abdomen bald, steering clippers around the cat's nipples. Wads of pale yellow fur piled up on the floor around the examining table. Soon a veterinary assistant was slathering the cat's naked belly with yellow-green surgical soap. The lights were bright, and the odor of antiseptic powerful.

Wright tried, and failed, to poke an intravenous fluids catheter into the spot Tilson had shaved at the base of the animal's tail. He tried and failed again. He tried a new spot on the abdomen and failed again. And he tried again at the tail, cursing, then finally succeeding.

Seal said, to no one in particular, "It's always difficult to find a vein in a tiger. They're thin-walled. Move around a lot."

Wright had said hardly a word. But with the catheter in and the anesthesia machine working, he said, "Let's go."

Four men picked up the stretcher and portaged the cat through the glass-windowed doors into a smaller operating room. An entourage accompanied the stretcher — two people rolling in the anesthesia machine, one on the umbilically linked IV rig. Wright, Fahning, and Garcia, meanwhile, were lathering up with surgical soap at a sink in the main room, pulling on sterile gowns, gloves, masks, and caps.

The cat was in a deep, drug-induced sleep. Gas is safer than injected drugs for major surgery because of its responsiveness. If the tiger should need to be put deeper under, the gas mix can be coaxed upward; should the cat go so deep that it begins to have breathing difficulty, the surgery team can manually ventilate its lungs by squeezing the drooping reservoir bag, which was filling, then deflating with each breath.

A vet assistant tied one front paw back to an upright on the operating table with a thin strip of gauze to keep the paw from flopping back across the tiger's chest. In a blaze of white light from the big dome lights overhead, tiger number 372 lay sprawled out, looking vaguely human, belly shaved and yellow green with antiseptic, the wide exhale and inhale tubes joining at a valve at her mouth. The heart monitor was still thunking steadily, the reservoir bag filling and deflating.

"I think everyone agrees that if we don't see any CL there's no real reason to go on," said Seal, referring to the hoped-for presence of corpora lutea, which would give some indication that the cat had ovulated. "But I think it makes sense to go ahead anyway, to practice flushing."

Fahning, all but his eyes covered in cap and mask, holding his sterile gloves up, nodded. The Seals left to hurry back to Large Animal Holding to take their weekly blood samples from the other research tigers, promising to be back as the surgery progressed. Cajacob, a head taller than anyone else, worked his way into a corner and focused his Nikon on the cat's abdomen. Wright and his helpers were in a huddle around the table. Wright selected from a plastic tray a steel scalpel and instantly began to cut. But for the thunking heart monitor, silence prevailed. The operation Wright was about to perform is a relatively routine one, a ventral midline celiotomy, an incision from pubis to near the umbilicus, to gain access to the lower abdominal cavity.

Wright says later that the first time he performed surgery on a live animal as a student at the Michigan State University veterinary school, he drew the scalpel carefully across the skin and nothing happened—no blood, no incision, nothing. But on this day, countless thousands of incisions later, Wright worked quickly, the process of entering an animal's innards as customary as peeling an orange.

"There's an instant feel," he says, "a certain tug or lack of tug against the scalpel."

In two quick passes Wright cut through the cat's skin and the layers of fat below. He clamped four small bleeding blood vessels on the skin with hemostats and flipped the instruments to the side to help hold open the skin. Below lay a mass of abdominal muscle, which, to be cut through, would require extensive suturing of the muscle and its sheath at the end of surgery. Instead, Wright located the linea alba, a thin membrane that joins the right and left halves of the abdominal muscle mass. With a scalpel, he poked a small hole in the linea alba, then inserted a finger through it.

"Peritoneum . . . right . . . there," he said. The peritoneum, a paper-thin membrane just below the muscles, lines the abdominal cavity, enveloping the viscera. By inserting his finger into the hole, Wright could pull the peritoneum away from the intestines below and in one operation with scissors slice a long slit through both the linea alba and the peritoneum.

Below the new opening lay a weblike structure of blood vessels and fat called the omentum. ("Looks just like Irish lace," Wright says.) He pulled the omentum out of the way and, with an assistant holding the entire incision open with retractors, pushed aside white and pink loops of large bowel, small bowel, and the bladder until he could see the body of the uterus, then up the uterine horn to the ovary.

"There's the uterus," he said. "There are the ovaries. Look at that."

Fahning, standing across the table from Wright said, matter-of-factly, "No ovulations. No ovulations we can see." Wright checked the other ovary. "No ovulations," said Fahning, sticking a gloved finger into the cavity and probing gently. "These follicles are just forming now. We were too early."

There was no visible reaction from Tilson. Visible reactions are hard to come by, in any case, with surgical masks over the face. But certainly he was disappointed. There would be other opportunities to try for an insemination, but less than a month hence, experts from around the world were to gather at a tiger symposium in Minneapolis, sponored in part by the zoo. Tilson would dearly have loved to report to the gathered scientists that the zoo had achieved an insemination.

Moreover, it was Tilson who had developed what he called behavioral correlates of estrus in tigers. In other words, he thought he'd developed a sure-fire way to predict the stages of estrus in tigers. Through months of observations, he had categorized what he thought were clear signals — sequences of purring, rubbing the head against the cage, rolling on the floor, and moving into a cat-in-heat crouch, which zoologists sternly term a "full lordosis posture." Tilson had correlated the behavioral observations with Seal's biochemical assays, and judging by the tests, the protocol he developed should have been a good predicator. The technique had promise; a zookeeper could collect data daily; a female tiger's reproductive cycle could be tracked with no need for knockdowns to take blood samples, with no cost for the sample analysis. But in this case, the behavioral test hadn't worked.

Following Seal's suggestion, Garcia and Fahning decided to proceed with the uterine flush for practice only. This surgical flush, although more invasive than the techniques Betsy Dresser has been able to use with antelope, is a relatively simple procedure. It required no further cutting. Garcia only made a puncture in the top of the uterine horn, a second into the uterus itself, injected a buffered solution into the horn, and drew the solution out of the uterus with a syringe.

They had nearly finished the flush when Seal returned. "Look at this," said Fahning.

Seal peered over Wright's shoulder and into the shining globs of tissue beneath the abdominal incision. "She hasn't ovulated," he said. "Those follicles are just about ready, though. We were early. Well, I'll be stuffed."

Seal retreated to the corner, stood flat-footed in sneakers with hands behind back, palms against the cool concrete block wall. The rest of the team was still in the surgical huddle, peering down. The flush completed, Wright began to suture the peritoneum and linea alba. Seal said, to everyone's back, "Let me propose a scenario." There was no answer, just the continued thunking of the heart monitor and hands, arms, and shoulders moving in the huddle.

"We'll go ahead and practice flushing her now," Seal said. "We'll ovulate her in three weeks and try again." Fahning nodded.

But it wasn't to be. The tiger symposium was coming up. The leading experts from India, Malaysia, Indonesia, China, the USSR, East and West Germany, and the United States were to be there. Tilson, as the representative of the zoo, and Seal, as the representative of the IUCN, were the hosts. There would be no time for reinseminating the tiger. Besides, Wright would have concerns about beginning the procedure again so soon after surgery. After five years, another Siberian tiger reproductive season would pass without a successful insemination.

FOUR

GOING HOME AGAIN

ON MAY 3, 1984, a carload of scientists from the National Zoo and the U.S. World Wildlife Fund arrived at Brazil's Poco das Antas Biological Reserve, northeast of Rio de Janeiro. A welcoming committee included staff from the Rio de Janeiro Primate Center and the Brazilian Forestry Institute, the mayor and the secretary of education of the local village, Silva Jardim, members of a new local conservation group, and assorted reporters, photographers, and television cameramen from the Brazilian national press. The committee was not at the site to greet the North Americans so much as it was to see the animal guests they had brought with them, first by air, then in the car: fifteen tiny, brilliantly golden monkeys. They were not really guests, after all, but displaced natives.

For decades, a tiny New World monkey called the golden lion tamarin, the GLT to primatologists, had been one of the most popular of all small mammals among collectors and zoos around the world, particularly in the United States. The reasons for its popularity are obvious. Few creatures are so extraordinary to behold. GLTs are alert, and quick, sentient of eye, dexterous of hand, with a close, brilliant, golden-rufous coat and a lush spray of golden lion's mane about the neck. Among the tiniest of the monkeys, they weigh only about a pound and a half and, excluding the tail, are only about one foot high from head to toe. Canopy dwellers and great, mobile acrobats, whole family-based troops of ten or more GLTs once cruised through high treetops in the rain forest like little flashes of setting sun. The taxonomists have a wonderfully descriptive scientific name for the beast, *Leontopithecus rosalia.*

The North and South Americans at Poco das Antas worked their way through a swamp, batting away at insects, to the door of a huge, wire-mesh cage filled with felled trees and limbs. The North American team released the tamarins into the enclosure. Fourteen of the monkeys dashed in panic into their own, familiar nest boxes, brought to Brazil from Washington, D.C., for the occasion. One lone female remained out, inspected the new territory, found a banana, and peeled it for the benefit of the newspaper photographers and television cameras.

There was some atonement for past wrongs in all of this. Zoos had once participated in the primate's near destruction. Now, National Zoo, the World Wildlife Fund, and the Brazilian government hoped, in a matter of weeks, to acclimate the little monkeys enough that they would revert to a wild state. At best, some of the reintroducees would survive long enough to reproduce. At worst, the entire group would expire by year's end.

Whatever happened, the tamarin as a species didn't have much to lose. The GLT's exotic qualities had helped lead it nearly to extinction; between two and three hundred were exported to zoos and as pets between 1960 and 1965 alone, according to IUCN figures. Meanwhile, the usual pressures from Brazil's booming population and land development efforts were destroying the tamarin's habitat, a thousand-mile rain forest strip along the country's Atlantic coast.

That a place to reintroduce tamarins even existed by the 1980s was due to the heroics of a group of Brazilian conservationists, led by primatologist Adelmar Coimbra-Filho, who had been worrying publicly since 1962 that, between deforestation and collecting by zoos and traders, the species was going to vanish. In the late 1960s, he spearheaded an effort to pass a landmark Brazilian law preventing export of any endangered species. By 1977, he had convinced the Brazilian government to set aside the twelve-thousand-acre, swampy, mosquito-infested Poco das Antas reserve. Some of its rain forest was intact. Other of its lands had already been converted to farmland. Although the farmland was inferior because of poor drainage, at least one prominent Brazilian public official vigorously denounced the notion of taking land out of crop production, however marginal, for the mere purpose of protecting "some silly monkeys."

But by 1984, there was plenty of support for the fifteen monkeys from the National Zoo. Pictures of the female sitting on a nest box and peeling a banana would appear in every major newspaper and on both Brazilian television network news programs. Later in the year, Brazilian children would dress up as GLTs for carnivals.

Of all the hopes and dreams of the promoters of the new zoo as an environmental conservation resource, none is fonder than this — that zoos, once net depleters of wildlife from wild places, could become net producers of wildlife for wild places.

Is that a reasonable dream? *Can* an animal born and reared in a cage ever learn to adapt to the difficult life of a wild creature? If the deluge of habitat destruction can ever be abated, can the animals leave the ark for the slopes of Ararat?

Reintroduction promises to be one of the most difficult challenges the zoo biologists will face. There has been skepticism that it will be possible on any meaningful scale. V. J. A. Manton at London Zoo's Whipsnade facility once called reintroduction of zoo species a pious hope. But Manton may, after all, have been as wrong as North American zoo officials who, as recently as the 1970s, suggested that zoos were far too competitive and jealous ever to exchange animals in significant numbers for breeding purposes, which they are now doing weekly.

Habitat destruction is responsible for almost all wildlife endangerment. And appropriate habitat is, by definition, critical to the survival of species in the wild. The gibbon can survive only as a puzzle piece linked to an intact rain forest ecosystem. An African lion survives on the savanna not in isolation, but in its position at the peak of a biomass pyramid. It depends on the ability of plants to convert sunlight and nutrient chemicals from the atmosphere and soils into cell tissue and on the ability of a grazing prey animal like the Cape buffalo to convert that plant tissue into edible red meat.

K. S. Sankhala of India's Project Tiger once pointed out that "to ensure the survival of the tiger at the apex of [its] biomass, not only the animal itself, but the entire natural environment, must be preserved."

Yes, level the forest or overgraze the grassland and the gibbon or lion will inevitably vanish. But it does not necessarily follow that a devastated habitat can never recover.

The foundation of any ecosystem is its abiotic building blocks. The amount of rainfall helps determine whether a piece of countryside will be desert, prairie, or forest. The temperature, the amount of sunlight, the chemical and physical characteristics of soil and minerals, and the chemical composition of the rains determine what sort of ecological structure can be built. If those building blocks are seriously disrupted, there is little hope for a reconstituted ecosystem. In some tragic cases, that is precisely what has happened or is about to happen. The fragile soil base of a few clear-cut rain forests has virtually washed away in the absence of a root system; air pollution has fumigated most of the plant community in some intensively industrial areas, such as Ontario's ecologically devastated, moonlike Sudbury basin.

But where the foundations aren't demolished, some ecosystems *can* recover. A forest leveled for its logs or converted to farmland may someday regenerate into a new, mature forest, the ecosystem moving through stages of plant succession that might begin with grasses and mosses, progressing over time to become dense with shrubs, then a young forest of pioneer tree species, and eventually, a mixed forest that includes mature stands of "climax" tree species. Arid grassland that has degenerated into desert can at least be improved and, with intensive and proper management, reconstituted.

Domestic grazing animals, for instance, cows, can sometimes be used to help restore the quality of arid grasslands that have undergone desertification. According to theories promoted by African-born ecologist Alan Savory, such grazing animals as antelope in Africa and pronghorn "antelope" in the American West are keystones in arid grassland ecosystems. The native bunchgrasses that should be growing in the desolated ecosystems cannot go to seed without the benefit of hoofs to loosen the soil and distribute seeds. In parts of the West, overgrazed public lands where cows have been completely banned for years are still in extremely poor condition. According to Savory's ideas, ranchers or environmental managers can improve such areas by duplicating nature's process through intensive herding of domestic hoofed stock, returning what Savory calls brittle environments to biological diversity and productivity. Although the notion is still controversial in scientific quarters, Savory's so-called holistic techniques appear to have worked in some tests.

The point is not that there is reason to feel complacent about habitat destruction because zoos can save the day;

they cannot save much at all. They can be arks for only a few hundred out of the hundreds of thousands of species that are threatened with extinction. And, for individual animal species, there is no question that they reproduce, adapt, and prosper best in their native ecosystems. As Tom Foose once put it, "Zoos are a poor place to preserve endangered species. But for some species, they're the only place."

2

Many exotic animals have been successfully introduced to totally foreign habitats. Cockroaches, of course, have been introduced into new environments with terrific biological success. Part of one of the oldest animal groups on earth, some species of roaches have shown immense adaptability, thriving, despite all efforts at twentieth-century chemical warfare, in some of the world's finest kitchens thousands of miles from their native African and Asian homes. (In fact, zoos almost everywhere provide great cockroach habitat. On at least three occasions I've been sitting at meetings or interviewing a zoo official when the local exterminator strolled through the room with a sprayer, squirted some cockroach killer into the corners, and slipped away.)

Another well-publicized case of successful insect introduction is that of the African or "killer" bee. Imported for research—it is a prodigious honeymaker—to Brazil in 1956, it subsequently escaped. The species, which has since worked its way northward, a few hundred miles each year, is expected to reach the southern United States well before the end of the century, perhaps before 1990.

There are innumerable other stories of insect success,

notably insect *pest* success. The crop-devouring Japanese beetle annually devastates millions of acres of North American crops; the mosquito found its way to Hawaii as aquatic larvae that escaped when a ship cleared its freshwater tanks.

In 1869, the tree-defoliating gypsy moth was intentionally imported from Europe to Massachusetts as a potential source of silk. A few escaped and prospered in their new environment. The moth's caterpillar now defoliates millions of acres of trees yearly.

Insects can establish themselves in new environments with relative ease, for their reproductive potential is staggering — a single queen bee lays millions of fertile eggs in a three- or four-year lifetime. Insects' lives are short, sometimes only weeks or months. The combination provides a potential for rapid natural selection and rapid evolutionary adaption.

Many vertebrate species, which adapt more slowly, have also prospered in new and foreign environments. Consider the enormous success of the starling, imported from England to the United States in the nineteenth century by those who believed the bird could help control North American insect pests. Today, it is present in such large numbers that in some areas it has become a pest itself. The Chinese pheasant, brought to North America as a game bird, thrives where it can find a grassy nesting habitat.

Islands offer some of the best examples of the often unfortunate biological success of introduced vertebrates. The New Zealand archipelago broke away from the ancient continent Gondwanaland about eighty million years ago, before the rise of the mammals. Consequently, its only mammals are those that could fly there, the long-tailed bat and the short-tailed bat, or swim there, the fur seal. Birds evolved to fill many of the habitat niches occupied elsewhere by mammals. The weird flightless kiwi, for example, sniffs about like a rodent, searching the soil for invertebrates.

When Captain James Cook went to the islands in 1773, he donated the first European animals. Cook released into the New Zealand forest three pigs that would be, he wrote, "enough to stock the whole island in due time." Other colonists brought and released more pigs. Less than a century after Cook's first visit, the islands were overrun with pigs. After an 1862 visit to the colony, a Dr. Hochstetter wrote that a three-man team of professional hunters hand-killed some twenty-five thousand wild pigs in a period of only twenty months. Settlers brought in rabbits that thrived, as the pigs had. Then they introduced weasels, stoats—short-tailed weasels or ermine to Americans—and cats to try to control the garden-devastating rabbits. So the weasels, stoats, and wildcats prospered, eating not only the rabbits, but native birds like the kiwi that had evolved no defenses against mammal predators. A few dogs went wild, and the ships brought the usual Norway and ship rats. Homesick for the songs of the thrush and lark, the New Zealanders imported birds of their native Britain. For purposes of sport shooting they introduced red deer, mule deer, white-tailed deer, tahr, and chamois, particularly into the mountain country of the cooler-climate South Island. The imported birds do indeed sing in the gardens, as well as in field and forest; the ungulates are thriving, and opossums are everywhere—"Damned marsupials," as at least one New Zealander describes the tree-defoliating emigrants from Australia. The New Zealand government considers the pressure on native habitat from the hoofed animals and the damned marsupials so severe that teams of government cullers regularly gun them down from airplanes or the backs of flatbed trucks. (Predictably, the introduction of exotic competitors and the predatory mammals has devastated the native bird populations. Today, the residents of a nation with about the land area of the state of Wyoming include fully 11 percent of the world's listed endangered birds.)

The grasslands of Texas are home to at least a half dozen species of antelope, springbok and impala among them, which are often "preserved" for hunting. Countless thousands of feral dogs and cats survive and breed wild offspring in the forests and fields of America. A few may have been pets that wandered away from home. Many were dumped at roadsides by owners who no longer wanted to care for pets, but wanted to "give them a chance."

The point is not that such introductions are biologically sound, sensible, or in the case of the abandoned pets, most of whom starve to death, even humane. Rather, there may be lessons to be learned. The introductions have worked in ecosystems where such imported species did not specifically evolve, usually without a shred of planning or forethought on the part of the humans who effected their entry. Biological reasons for why one introduction works and another doesn't defy categorization. The springbok from an African grassland can survive on a Texas grassland largely because grass is grass and there is little effective predation on big ungulates in Texas anymore. The weasel can thrive in New Zealand because native birds evolved no specific defenses against predatory mammals.

There is far less information on conscious reintroductions of species into habitats they formerly occupied. "The literature is pretty slim," says Nate Flesness. "But reintroducing an animal into range where it used to exist would seem to have a better a priori chance of success."

When pressed for an example of reintroduction success, zoos point to two large ungulates, both bison: the American "buffalo" and the European wisent. In each case, herds had collapsed to critical levels and were nurtured in captivity. They survive only in a modified "wild," in heavily managed park and reserve settings.

The American bison reintroduction came in 1905, when the New York Zoological Society offered to the people of the United States a nucleus herd of fifteen animals to be relocated to a fenced sixty-two-hundred-acre stretch of grassland on the Wichita Forest Reserve in Oklahoma. The only additions to the herd were four bulls from another refuge in Nebraska. The protected herd went through a veritable population explosion. By the mid 1950s, the American bison was clearly out of danger. Nearly a thousand of them lived on the Oklahoma reserve, whose area had to be expanded to nearly sixty thousand acres.

The wisent, a forest-dwelling bison, once ranged over much of Europe, possibly as far as Siberia. But growing human populations and increasing conversion of forest to agriculture had the inevitable result. By the first decade of the nineteenth century, the Lithuanian race of the huge ungulate, which can grow to a ton and a height of more than six feet at the shoulder, had been reduced to a herd of three to five hundred animals in a single royal reserve in the Białowieza National Park of Poland. The only other subspecies, the smaller, darker Caucasian wisent, survived in smaller numbers in the mountains of the Caucasus.

Then came a century and more of wars, political upheavals, and more devastation of habitat. Not long into this century, the wisent was all but gone. By 1921 the herd at Białowieza had vanished; the last wild Caucasian wisent was killed in 1927. But seventeen European bison still survived in European zoos. The zoo breeders, without knowledge of the difficult demographic-genetic problems it could have faced, managed to propel this easy-to-breed species through the genetic bottleneck. By 1982, a viable wild herd of about twelve hundred individuals had been reestablished at Białowieza and a second, smaller Polish reserve, and approximately thirteen hundred survive in zoos in Europe and the United States. (There's an interesting irony in the wisent propagation story. For all the discussion of maximizing genetic diversity, there's proof that generalizations and averages don't always extend to the specific. One of those seventeen wisents was packed with deleterious alleles, far more than the averages would suggest. The other sixteen were closely related and apparently together carried fewer deleterious alleles than the single member did. The genetic problems that began to show up as the small but growing population inevitably interbred.)

Both species survive in heavily managed settings on islands of reserve, protected to such a degree that the distinction between captivity and life in the wild may be a bit muddy.

Another zoo reintroduction story, that of the Arabian oryx, is still playing itself out. Although initial signs may be promising, this safety net is by no means as secure as it is for the two bison. The last three wild Arabian oryx were found dead in the Rub'al-Khali desert in 1972. The species was the victim of the admiration of Bedouin, who prized the creamy white antelope, with its delicate, long, straight-up horns, as a symbol of speed and strength. According to some reports, the Bedouin believed that eating its meat would help cure bullet wounds. Oryx hunting, in any case, had a long tradition as a rite of passage among Bedouin men. Early in this century, it took the form of a walkabout with a camel, a jug of water, and a muzzle-loading rifle. The introduction of efficient semiautomatic and automatic rifles and all-terrain vehicles in Arabia led, through the 1950s, to wholesale slaughter. At one point, the rulers of the Qatari tribe equipped a motorized caravan and drove five hundred miles to the Rub'al-Khali for the sole purposes of gunning down most of one of the remnant populations of the beast and managed to kill twenty-eight of the vanishing antelope. Others were killed on desert safaris by Westerners employed by the oil companies that were moving into the region.

In the early 1960s, Britain's Fauna Preservation Society funded an expedition to the Rub'al-Khali to procure as many of the remaining Arabian oryx as possible. After an arduous hunt, its party returned with two males and a single female—the nucleus of a "world herd." The group was transferred to a safe and eminently Arabian type of habitat in the Phoenix, Arizona, Zoo. The herd was thereafter genetically refreshed by six new animals from captivity in London, Kuwait, and Saudi Arabia and by 1972 was able to expand into a second captive population at the San Diego Wild Animal Park. (A general philosophy of captive maintenance is that one population in one setting is inadequate. A single virus or natural disaster could wipe out the entire species.) Today, the world herd numbers some four hundred animals at San Diego and Phoenix, and reintroduction has at least begun. By 1987, about forty of the animals lived in the "wild" in Oman. They are guarded by the same Bedouin whose fathers and uncles shot most of the last of them, rifles and jeeps provided courtesty of the Fauna Preservation Society. The wild herd is reproducing, and at least eight more captive-bred oryx, again from the western United States, will be going home to the Arabian Peninsula every year.

The story of the golden lion tamarin goes a step further than that of the oryx. More than 98 percent of their habitat in Brazil has been leveled and plowed. By 1980, the IUCN Red Data Book noted that fewer than one hundred GLTs remained in the wild, with the addition, "Likely to be extinct by 1985–90." But while the oryx bred easily in captivity, the news on the GLT was as grim in the zoos as it was in the wild. In 1972, a survey showed that there were about seventy GLTs in North American zoos, but the situation was worse than it appeared. For years the tamarin population had been replenished with captives from the wild because there was little reproduction in captivity.

After export ceased in 1969, the captive population began a slow, steady slide. Efforts to breed the monkeys were only marginally successful, and the birth rate by no means kept up with the death rate. By 1975, only about 19 percent of the captive population came from wild-caught stock, compared with 62 percent in 1969. Over those six years, the total zoo population had declined by 13 percent, and the surviving wild-caught tamarins were aging. The sex distribution was skewed in the worst possible way, with more males than females. Females were, for unknown reasons, periodically killing each other, and there was every reason to believe that the decline could only accelerate. Even as the GLT faced extinction in the wild, the zoo world appeared unable to help. Some experts opined that it would be an even-money bet whether the monkeys would become extinct first in the wild or in zoos.

The National Zoo had long been a leader in turning zoos toward conservation, especially in zoological research. In the mid-1970s, research scientist Devra Kleiman, later the zoo's research director, decided to try to find out why the golden lion tamarin was such a reproductive failure in captivity and to attempt to correct the problem if possible.

Kleiman and her research team discovered not a *reason* that the GLTs were failing as breeders, but an entire syndrome. One set of problems was purely physiological. The scientists discovered that many of the animals were improperly nourished because a widespread assumption that tamarins in the wild are strictly vegetarians was wrong.

The National Zoo developed a new feeding regime, one now used, in some permutation, virtually everywhere in United States zoos that keep GLTs. Morning and afternoon, the tamarins receive a half can of commercial marmoset diet. In the afternoon feeding they also receive five raisins, a slice of banana, a segment of orange with peel attached, a small slice of apple, and for the protein charge the zoo researchers found missing, eight mealworms every Sunday, six crickets every Wednesday and Friday, and each Tuesday, two furless baby mice.

The zoo scientists also determined that about 6 percent of the animals were suffering from diaphragmatic hernia, a genetic defect that shortened their life spans. The zoo found it possible to detect the birth defects by barium X-ray and repair them surgically.

The zoo also began to control inbreeding. Groups of tamarins were separated to control the spread of infectious diseases; feces were screened for parasites. The research team decided that contact with other species of primates, including not only other monkeys, but also humans, had to be limited to prevent disease transmission. Tamarins, it turned out, are so highly susceptible to human measles and herpesvirus that exposure to a simple cold sore can be life threatening.

On the behavioral side, in one of its most important findings, Kleiman's team discovered that mothers so often ignored or abused or killed their babies because mothering was not an instinctive behavior for the monkeys, but rather one they had to learn as youngsters by observing other females in a family group. At the same time, as females mature they become competitively, aggressively territorial with one another. So the research team advised rigorously keeping females in intact family groups, removing them only after puberty to avoid confrontations. The monkeys were provided with nest boxes — places in which to rest and hide and defend as their own special territory.

Through the adjustments in diet, living quarters, and family groupings, the National Zoo was able to induce the golden lion tamarins to breed not only regularly, but with astonishing success. By 1980, then National Zoo director Ted Reed told me that the zoo was already seeking other zoos for long-term loans of the tamarins. That same year, at the urging of Coimbra-Filho, the Brazilian government allowed five animals to be shipped to Washington to alleviate concerns about a too-limited gene pool in a booming captive population. By 1984 the population in the zoo, at its off-site breeding facility near Front Royal, Virginia, and in about fifty other zoos that had signed GLT loan agreements with National, had grown to four hundred animals. Some females were producing triplets, and one gave birth to quadruplets; some females were producing two and even three litters in a single year. Soon National was having trouble finding quality zoo homes for its GLTs and, ironically, had begun to wonder what contraceptive methods would best control the booming population. Within a few years of predictions of the species' demise, enough animals were surplus to the captive breeding program that several could be risked in a reintroduction attempt.

Meanwhile, things had become much worse in Brazil. A 1980 survey showed that while there were still wild GLTs in the Poco das Antas Biological Reserve, cattle were grazing within its boundaries. There were large areas of only brush or second-growth forest. (The monkeys need more mature forests.) Further, the government was building a dam—a bizarre conflict of policy destined to flood 20 percent of a reserve that had supposedly been protected by government fiat.

By 1982 only about seventy-five GLTs were surviving in the wild in about ten family groups. In that year, Kleiman and the members of her team wrote, "Whereas the captive population is now secure, the species' future in the wild remains bleak."

Kleiman began discussing with the World Wildlife Fund

and Coimbra-Filho the possibility of returning tamarins to the wild. With no precedent, no one believed it would be easy. The zoo staff hadn't a clue about the most efficient way to reintroduce a captive monkey to the wild or if such an attempt had much chance of working. Nevertheless, Kleiman began to push the project forward, convinced after talking to the Brazilian conservationists that the project could have beneficial effects beyond reintroduction. The beautiful little monkey, so nearly lost forever, might serve as a flagship species to teach rural Brazilians about wildlife conservation and endangered animals and their needs. Its presence might encourage public and political support to restore and protect the reserve. It might help stabilize the current wild population and provide some more field data about the GLTs. At the very least, the team would learn something about release techniques. Even if every one of the monkeys failed to adapt or died, the researchers might at least learn what *not* to do.

In November 1983, the fifteen golden lion tamarins were moved to the Rio de Janeiro Primate Center to begin their acclimation to the land of their recent ancestors. At the National Zoo, primatologist Benjamin Beck had begun a training regimen that was continued at the primate center. In captivity the GLTs ate a diet of nicely chopped food presented in a dish; they did not have to capture any of the small animals they ate, for the insects and baby mice were dead. Now the monkeys began to learn how to search in scattered sites; their food was often hidden in crevices or tucked into rotten wood or rolled-up leaves. They had to learn how to eat their fruit whole; many didn't know how to peel a banana. The animals learned quickly, and on their own, to avoid insect prey that bit or stung. There seemed no need to teach the tamarins to avoid flying predators. Whenever a large bird's shadow fell into their cages, the monkeys scattered to their nest boxes, chattering alarms.

Considering that the primates had until then lived indoors, had never seen a predatory bird, and certainly had no reason to associate birds with anything particularly negative, the researchers wrote, "We suspect that this response may be genetically hard-wired."

Not so for other responses. The research team noted that the GLTs seemed to hold no fear of snakes—twice, monkeys tried to eat snakes. (After reintroduction, one was killed by snake venom.) The team presented a large toad to the tamarin group to observe their reaction to the poison-skinned amphibian. Within a few minutes two of the monkeys had taken a bite of the toad, and the researchers had to wrestle it away from a third.

"Both frothed, cried, and vomited while the others watched closely," the researchers noted soberly. Worse, one of the two went into convulsions "and barely recovered after four hours . . . Nonetheless, they seemed eager to get to the toad the next day."

Did all this mean that the tamarins had an innate fear of the predatory birds, but somehow in captivity had lost their fear of eating poisonous toads or approaching venomous snakes? There was no way to know. It was at least as likely that both captive and wild tamarins have no innate avoidance behavior for reptiles and amphibians and no particular capacity to learn to avoid them, at least not quickly. A wild tamarin might be as dumb around a toad as a captive one, eating it and dying if it was unlucky enough to find one. The researchers weren't destined to find out what repeated exposure to the snakes and toads could mean, noting that they were "methodologically handicapped because of wanting to avoid potentially fatal experiments."

To help the GLTs develop the monkey skills they would need for locomotion in the jungle trees, the researchers tried to entice them to climb and to hang. Once they had been translocated to Poco das Antas, the tamarins found themselves in a high, wire-mesh enclosure where felled trees in which they could climb about had been positioned. Many of the tamarins, especially the older ones, preferred clinging to and climbing about on the wire mesh, and it was uncertain whether they could function properly in the treetops.

At 9:40 A.M. on May 31, 1984, the researchers finally opened the hatch on the mesh enclosure in the reserve. Within two minutes, a young male tamarin had moved slowly into the rain forest of its ancestors. A few seconds later, his brother and sister tentatively followed him out. By 10:00 A.M. all the monkeys had moved out of the cages and into the trees, some climbing high on springy branches in the tree canopy.

There were difficulties. As the researchers later put it, some of the GLTs had trouble learning "to plot a cognitive route through the forest." In the treetops, the GLTs were as if in a maze. "Their movements were characterized by false starts, fruitless retracing of pathways to dead ends, and finally, descent to and travel across the ground. At best, travel through the trees by the reintroductees was hesitant. At worst, they got disoriented and lost. Some simply sat, appearing to give up, and had to be rescued." Unfortunately, two were killed shortly after release, one by a snake, the other by a feral dog.

If "success" is measured only by a high survival rate, the reintroduction could be seen as an outright disaster. By 1986, of the fifteen captive-born tamarins moved to Brazil and released in 1984, only three were still alive. But Kleiman and the others were delighted and considered the entire experiment a success.

That the three survived at all was clearly a success in biological terms. Some of the captive animals had assimilated surprisingly well, learning to interact with wild tamarins in a family setting. Eleven more GLTS were introduced in 1985, and by 1986 National Zoo officials reported that of the surviving reintroduced animals, two formerly captive males had joined with a wild female and were living in a family group that included two offspring sired by one of them. A second group consisted of a captive-born female and a wild male, plus the female's offspring, which had been sired by another captive-born male. A third group, consisting of a single female and a single male, both captive-born, had formed outside the formal boundaries of the reserve, but in private protected forest nearby. In all, two litters had been born in the reserve to formerly captive parents, and it appeared that more were on the way.

High mortality may be a price that has to be paid in any reintroduction program. But mortality rates should be considered in realistic contexts, not those based on the extraordinarily low rates of long-lived humans in the developed world. If the average life span for an animal is only four years, there would automatically be 25 percent annual mortality in any population even if all the individuals survived from birth to old age. But then there's the Malthusian rule: species always reproduce at rates greater than the capacity of their habitats to support them. The result is extra individuals, often many, especially in the youngest age class.

You may think you're seeing the same gray squirrels year after year on your city streets, or the same cardinal in your backyard, but mortality rates in either population could easily exceed 50 percent in a harsh winter. It is not unusual for mortality in a white-tailed deer population to reach 40 percent, even in a group not exposed to predation or hunting.

Patrick Redig, director of the Minnesota Raptor Rehabilitation and Research program, reports that roughly half of all peregrine falcons reintroduced to the wild in the state have perished before reproducing. But he points out that wild peregrines die at about the same rate.

However, considering that captive animals have not grown up with the wilderness equivalent of street smarts, it seems reasonable to assume that mortality in almost any reintroduced group will exceed natural rates. There was another complication for the GLTs at Poco das Antas: the monkeys were introduced into habitat with an existing population of wild tamarins. The rules of ecology suggest that if that habitat was already at or near saturation for tamarins, there was room for few more. In that context, the survival and reproduction of any at all may offer real hope for future reintroductions.

3

Zoo animals become accustomed to the shapes, sounds, odors, and movements of humans. Some of the consequences for reintroduction are obvious. Zoo animals come to associate the appearance of their human keepers with an impending meal. Zoo visitors are no threat to safety and might as well be invisible. Therefore, released wildlife could be far easier pickings for poachers, vandals, and general villains than they would normally be.

General villainy is a real problem. In the late 1960s, a cow moose appeared one day in a pasture just outside Caribou, a town in northern Maine. Moose are generally mighty shy of people, but this one stayed in the vicinity of the pasture, directly beside a public highway that ran to a nearby large air force base and carried a great deal of traffic. Before long, residents and tourists were approaching the impossibly tame creature, feeding it handfuls of browse, and taking its photograph close up. One day in 1968, a town resident simply decided to shoot the creature. In the summer of 1986, a beluga whale similarly became friendly with swimmers and sunbathers in Long Island Sound until it, too, was shot on a whim.

There is potential for a converse human-habituation problem: some animals that could be a threat to humans may be so overaccustomed to their presence that the normal flight or avoidance responses become inactive. Grizzly bears in the Yellowstone Park and Glacier Park areas are the last in the lower forty-eight states. Infrequently, but with huge splashes of publicity, a grizzly kills a human. Grizzlies have little instinctive fear of anything; they do, however, usually avoid humans. But proximity to people in the parks, in local dumps, and on surrounding ranches can cause some bears to associate the presence of humans with an opportunity for a full belly. Biologists who have studied the bears' behavior are convinced that the primary reasons for their attacks are that some bears become too used to garbage dumps or garbage cans or handouts.

Especially in the Yellowstone region, bear populations are small and under stress, but federal officials agree that once a bear appears to be so habituated that it poses a threat to people, it must be dealt with. Yellowstone's official approach to handling the apparently human-habituated bears is to capture them in a drum trap and relocate them deeper in the park's wilderness areas, once. If the problem-bears reappear and continue to show signs of habituation, such as raiding campgrounds for food, they are supposed to be helicoptered into remote northern Canadian wilderness or shipped to zoos. Yellowstone officials admit, however, that they often simply try taking the bear again into remote country in Yellowstone.

At this writing, about two hundred bears were left in the Yellowstone-region habitat "island," which includes surrounding Gallatin National Forest and nearby Grand Teton National Park. In 1983, according to some reports, only seven breeding-age females were left in the park itself. No matter how stressed the population, bears that have killed people are not given a second chance; they are captured and killed by injection.

Aside from these sorts of behavioral problems, other problems could be brought on by natural and artificial evolutionary selection pressures. Spotted leopards or white-handed gibbons that have bred well in captivity may be those genetically least stressed by the presence of humans. Therefore, selection may work against the preservation of "wildness" genes. Moreover, zookeepers have inevitably bred aggression or territoriality out of some captive species because they simply prefer to work with tamer, more docile animals.

There may be other natural selection pressures in captive settings. An ungulate in the wild may benefit from its ability to flee with total abandon from any perceived threat. A zoo animal doing the same would encounter a fence. As M. R. Brambell, once curator of mammals at the London Zoo, noted, "We cannot avoid some change. The antelope which in the wild runs first, fastest, and farthest is more likely to leave offspring than his more sluggish brethren, if only because he escapes being eaten. In captivity, he is more likely to end up . . . with a broken neck and so would be less likely to leave offspring than his more trusting brother."

Animals in better zoos are raised in optimum conditions that are eminently humane, but hardly reflective of natural selection pressures of the rugged, competitive life-and-death struggle in the wild. A captive rhino or chimp or giraffe receives optimum nutrition and is less exposed to the ravages of parasites and disease. Therefore, animals that may carry genetic susceptibility to certain parasites or diseases may survive in captivity when they would have perished in the wild.

A large offspring of a captive animal would be at no adaptive disadvantage in a zoo. Neither, necessarily, would a runt. However, in the wild, relatively large individuals need to find more food than their smaller kin in order to survive. That requirement could work against the general fitness of reintroductees in some species. With others, smallness may decrease an animal's ability to defend itself or to take prey efficiently.

For all the speculation, the actual evidence, one way or another, is slim. However, Janet Kear, avicultural coordinator at the Wildfowl Trust in Slimbridge, England, did suggest to participants at the Second International Conference of Breeding Endangered Species in Captivity in 1976 that her work with waterfowl shows that after they have spent some generations in captivity, "we are not left with the same species because of the limited variability in a population which was founded by only one or two pairs [of founders]."

Kear pointed to studies showing that a wildfowl female will not return to a nest site where she had lost eggs. Yet with some captive waterfowl species, including the Carolina wood duck and the Mandarin duck, when eggs are removed from nest boxes, the ducks continue to use the same box again and again. Kear suggested that it proves that "foolish" genes are being passed through generations of waterfowl in captivity. "If their progeny were released into the wild, presumably natural selection would have to start again, eliminating the many animals with 'foolish' genes and favouring those few individuals with 'wise' ones, always providing, of course, that there were any 'wise' genes left."

(Kear's conclusion about "foolish" genes is questionable. There is always the possibility that the female ducks simply behave differently in captivity than they would in the wild. To prove that the foolish behavior would be continued in a wild setting would require such evidence from experimentation or observation, which Kear did not offer.)

Other researchers have shown that brown rats taken into captivity alter their territorial instincts, sometimes in as little as six generations. Normally, males attack other strange males, driving the intruders out of their territory. But in heavily populated captive environments where plenty of food was available, males in the sixth and later generations began to coexist more peacefully in what might have been an adaptation to restricted living quarters. Some experiments also have shown changes in the digestive tracts of red grouse bred in captivity—shrinkage of the small intestine and the cecum, which researchers speculate is an adaptive change in response to a diet of mostly commercial, easily digestible food. The changes were striking. The ceca in birds after generations in captivity were only 25 percent the size of those found in wild birds, and the small intestine 72 percent the size.

Research with Bewick's swan, a high Arctic breeder, has raised another sort of behavioral problem. In nature, the male induces the female to lay her eggs by putting on a wing-display show. Without the show, the female doesn't lay. The male's displaying behavior is, in turn, brought on by a photoperiodic reaction—he begins to display in the breeding grounds in the high Arctic only as the days of late spring become exceedingly long. In European zoos, the swan is a poor breeder. In fact, only one line of males, descended from a single pair captured in 1950, has induced females to breed. Thus, all captive-bred Bewick's swans are related to that single line. By itself, that's a mildly interesting bit of zoological trivia, but there's hidden importance. Kear suggested that all of this is so because the original 1950 male carried a rare genetic code that induced him to display during a time of too *few* daylight hours. In other words, in the wild, he would have begun his mating display too soon and therefore have been a poor wild breeder. The more "normal" male swans were not triggered to display because none was far enough north to experience a near-midnight sun.

"Does it matter?" Kear asked rhetorically. For zoos, the answer seems obvious: as long as a gibbon looks like a gibbon and acts like a gibbon, it cannot matter much if its population has lost a few genes. But for reintroductees, loss of genes could be a disaster. In the case of the swans, if a captive population descended from this line of males were to be reintroduced, the males might be so genetically misprogrammed that they induce the females to lay eggs too early in the spring or too far south of the proper range for optimum breeding. In the case of the grouse with the truncated digestive systems, larger digestive systems may be necessary for digesting food in the wild. Even if appropriate genes are available somewhere in the gene pool, mortality—and expense—could become extraordinarily high while nature sorted out the deleterious genetic stock.

Despite those few reasonable-sounding theories and *those few* bits of evidence, ISIS's Nate Flesness notes that there simply isn't a lot of solid information about whether much selection has really occurred in captivity or how much genetic diversity may have been lost. Flesness himself has done some arcane computer studies based on arcane theories that provide some hints that some selection may have occurred. He says, "Selection has probably been understressed by zoo people and overstressed by their critics. The fact is, there isn't much data one way or another. And even if there is evidence of selection in captivity, the real question is, Would they change back? And the real answer is, We don't know."

But beyond the biological, there can be political obstacles. If the same social problems that caused the loss of habitat in the first place have not been resolved, reintroduction is meaningless. If peasant farmers in the area of a new reserve are still increasing their family size yearly, the reserve's resources will be in jeopardy. If the market for rhinoceros horn remains lucrative, the incentive for poachers remains powerful. In 1986, Zimbabwe was dispatching militia with automatic weapons to battle heavily armed poachers to protect its few remaining black rhinos. (It might be well to keep in mind that habitat and wildlife protection can have direct, short-term economic benefits: tourism based almost entirely on visits to wildlife reserves is the second largest industry in Kenya.)

And then there are problems that are more politically intractable. In the 1970s, plans were under way to reintroduce endangered Asian lions from India to Iran's forests, where the lions once thrived. The program was supported by the shah of Iran, who was deposed by the Ayatollah Khomenei and the Islamic revolution, followed shortly by a seemingly endless and bloody war of attrition with Iraq. Needless to say, even if the translocation of lions met the needs of the Islamic revolution, it would not be a priority item for the Iranian government.

FIVE

BARNUM AND BIOLOGY

FROM THE DAY it opened, the Minnesota Zoo's Siberian tiger exhibit was excellent — for tigers. At the front of the exhibit was a small open clearing; there was running water in the warm months, plenty of snow in the winter, and best, almost all of it was a fine, deeply shaded forest.

All of which often made it less than great for most visitors. During the peak weeks of midsummer, when both zoo attendance and hot humid days were at their height, the exhibit provided precisely the sort of environment a huge, thick-coated, largely nocturnal cat needed so it could do what it does best under those conditions: melt into the cool shadows and sleep.

Some visitors may have been satisfied just to know that two or three or more tigers were lurking *somewhere* back there in the trees, to marvel that the tiger's natural camouflage made the cat invisible. Some may have taken a certain pleasure in knowing that the exhibit was more a simulation of a visit to the wild, where one had to *look* for the tigers, and that the natural world was arranged for the benefit of its occupants, not the sightseers. Looking hard enough into the brush, especially with the help of binoculars, one might discern an ear twitching, then make out the cat's form. Or staring into a spot in the brush, one might suddenly realize that part of the scene was camouflaged tiger, the creature's form seeming to materialize out of the undergrowth.

But immediately there were complaints — phone calls and letters to the zoo, letters to the local newspaper. They all said the same thing: "You can't see the animals." A few months after the gates opened in 1978, the zoo staff, succumbing to the pressure, subdivided the exhibit by running two ten-foot chain link fences over the top of the wooded hill. It actually made some sense. As it had been set up, the two sides of the tiger exhibit were on opposite ends of the zoo's looping Northern Trail sequence, a good half hour apart by foot and several minutes by monorail. It was far enough that the tigers could be on the invisible side for any given visitor, then have moved back over the hill once that visitor reached the other side. Further, the zoo had made a commitment to keeping a large breeding group of Siberian tigers. Adult tigers are usually loners and can be fiercely territorial, so halving the exhibit meant that more cats were outdoors at any one time. The fence was so far back in the trees that it was largely invisible in the summer months, anyway. And the two exhibits thus created were still both huge tiger spaces, by zoo standards.

But the exhibit was still so large and so overgrown with brush that tigers remained out of sight too often. The complaints continued. Groundskeepers were regularly dispatched to the exhibit to hack out shrubs and clear back the vegetation. The complaints continued. Finally in 1985, the zoo spent around $150,000 on a raised boardwalk, covered at its terminus by a gazebo-type roof, which penetrated into the south-side half of the exhibit. On the north side, the fence line moved progressively downhill. Now one can usually see the tigers on the compressed north-side exhibit, for, thanks to a low electric fence, the tigers have been brought virtually out of the forest and into the front of the exhibit. (Asian lions have been moved into the other side.) The tigers have only two-thirds the space they once had, but whether or not that bothers them is debatable. It does mean that more visitors collect at the low wall looking over the moated exhibit, that they stay longer, and that the complaints have diminished. However, the tigers still sink back into the undergrowth on a hot midday, and the zoo remains the home of a great natural exhibit that works for tigers, but not so well for visitors.

Creating exhibits for a zoo used to be so easy. A cage can be relatively small or large, kept relatively clean or filthy. Animals were largely interchangeable in exhibits — the same cage could be used for a lion or a baboon or a baby elephant. But now that the zoo world has moved away from the traditional menagerie environment, it confronts thousands of unresolved questions about how best to present animals, and their stories, to the public. Zookeepers share a common base of knowledge about how to breed, nurse, and feed their animals, but there is far less unanimity about how a zoo animal should meet its public.

In its long history, zoo exhibitry has moved through four overlapping stages. The first was the bars-and-shackles menagerie stage, still evident in many zoos. By the nineteenth century, some zoos were attempting to do a bit more with the exhibit buildings, heightening the sense of theater by setting a mood believed compatible with an animal's origins, or its perceived origins. Curiously, all the mood-setting exhibits showed the creature not in relation to other fauna or flora, but to human cultures. At Cologne, for example, the elephant was housed in a building of distinctly Moorish design, complete with tiny, minaret towers. The ostrich house was a replication of a mosque. The zoo at Düsseldorf reproduced a ruined castle for its

Barbary sheep; Berlin built a "Hindu temple" for elephants. Nevertheless, the bars and shackles were still there, and little effort was made to suggest the animals' natural environment.

The naturalism, or lack of it, was hardly the major concern in the early days of even such scientifically oriented zoos as London's. Merely keeping animals alive on exhibit was enough of a struggle. Improved attention to animals' physical well-being constituted the second stage. Considering the state of knowledge about human health and the transmission of disease, it is no surprise that keeping animals healthy was often nearly impossible in the face of poor sanitation and sweeping ignorance of nutrition. Recall that Louis Pasteur put forth the germ theory of disease in the middle of the last century.

The zoo world's struggle to care for great apes in captivity demonstrates the early practical exhibit problems. The London Zoo first acquired a chimpanzee in 1835, but the animal died less than six months later. In 1845, the zoo acquired another chimp for the then staggering price of £300. That chimp, too, died before the end of the year. By the end of the century, chimps, the most common of the great apes, were being captured willy-nilly by traders and brought to zoos and amusement parks, even though virtually no zookeeper knew how to keep the primates alive for more than a few months.

The first truly successful maintenance of chimpanzees was accomplished at a private collection of Rosalia Abreu at the Quinta Palatino in Havana, where the apes were given sanitary surroundings, balanced diets, and attention that would have been the envy of most orphaned children of the day. By 1930 seven baby chimps had been born and raised at the Havana facility. (In 1931 the entire collection was transferred to Yale University under the care of Dr.

Robert Yerkes, considered the father of primatology, and became the nucleus of the breeding colony at what has become the Yerkes Institute.)

The existing records for gorilla survival outline a similar fate. One of the first known specimens survived only seven months at a menagerie in England. Another arrived in Europe, traveled to Hamburg and London, then perished in Berlin.

Not until well into this century did zookeepers come to understand that our own evolutionary cousins might be more susceptible to human diseases than any other animal. Nor, apparently, did it occur to anyone that fecal matter which was dispersed over a wide area and treated organically in the wild could cause disease if allowed to accumulate in cages.

Late in the 1950s, the larger zoos — London, the Bronx, Berlin — built ape houses that were air-conditioned, well ventilated, and assiduously cleaned. Keepers with influenza or other contagious diseases were kept away from the apes. And the captive primates were separated more strictly from humans either by glass walls or sheer physical distance. As a result, mortalities decreased and, in time, came the ultimate proof that these were far better living conditions: the first captive births. In December 1956 the first lowland gorilla was born in captivity at the Columbus Zoo in Ohio. In the next five years, two more were born at Basel and one at Washington's National Zoo.

The third exhibition stage — the Carl Hagenbeck revolution — suggested that animals could be shown in environments that at least hinted at the wilderness from whence they came. Modern copies of Hagenbeck's moated islands and mountains and grottoes can be found everywhere in the zoo world. In fact, the Hagenbeck family helped design African savanna exhibits and rockwork bear grottoes at the Cincinnati Zoo and similar ones at the Detroit Zoo in the 1920s. Much of the Milwaukee Zoo, built from the ground up in the late 1960s, is a series of superbly designed Hagenbeck knockoffs, including the African plains concept where cheetahs look over a herd of Thomson's gazelles, separated, of course, by the inevitable invisible moat.

A zoo devoted to barless display must know, or learn, how to contain an animal. Carl Hagenbeck tested his animals to see how far they could leap or what sort of barriers might contain them. Today, there is a well-developed literature on such factors as the leaping abilities of spotted leopards and the relative proclivity or aversion of one primate or another for water. An embankment graded downward is usually enough to contain a giraffe, for giraffes have a powerful adaptive aversion toward anything that might cause them to fall. But such approaches have failed occasionally, too, sometimes spectacularly and sadly. Both the Bronx and the Frankfurt zoos suffered early failures after World War II when they first brought gorillas out of the caged environment. Both zoos used deep moats as a logical barrier; both lost gorillas that slipped, fell, and drowned in the moats. (At the Bronx, a passing bird-keeper, George Scott, heroically leaped into the moat and pulled the huge ape ashore, but it was too late to revive the beast.)

Even though variations on Hagenbeck's naturalistic approach now dominate exhibit design, some zoos have opted to dispense with naturalism altogether, especially in primate exhibits, where the necessity for sanitary living conditions has sometimes overwhelmed other considerations. Despite its Hagenbeckian vistas elsewhere, the newish Milwaukee Zoo's Primate House is all ceramic-tiled boxes with one glass wall. Ditto at the Denver Zoo and others.

The fourth stage began when zookeepers started to recognize that beyond catering to their physical needs, an exhibit should be behaviorally satisfying to the animals as well. This stage advanced in recent decades with the growing knowledge that fulfilling the animals' powerful behavioral and social needs was part and parcel of humane, ethical zookeeping.

To be sure, the bloody Roman arenas featured "behavioral exhibits," after a fashion. A lion will naturally kill for food or to protect itself. If a convict or Christian or armed gladiator was in the path of those needs, it was all the same to the lion. For that matter, the first large flight cages for birds were behaviorally oriented exhibits. A case could be made that displays featuring bears conditioned to sit up and beg for scraps of food are behavioral exhibits, in that the mammals at least "do something" in response to a stimulus. In the middle ages and later, bear pits were popular attractions in Europe. The zoo at Bern featured a pit with a climbing pole that allowed the bear to ascend to spectator level, there to be fed buns as a treat.

Monkey islands were among the earliest exhibits allowing socially adapted animals to engage in something resembling normal social behavior. Except during the winter months, primates remained on the islands day and night, escaping into nest boxes during periods of foul weather. The Cologne Zoo built the first known baboon island around 1900. Another appeared at the Munich Zoo in 1928, and a burst of monkey islands appeared at zoos in the United States beginning in the 1930s. The islands were largely self-sufficient—a mound or minimountain of moat-ringed artificial rock. Keepers provided food and cleaning, but the primate residents otherwise ran their lives without human intervention and with the full dynamics of behavior. With the alpha male and alpha female dominating the hierarchical troop, the other members were positioned along a dominance-submission pecking order. The inevitable squabbles and, from time to time, briefly violent fights broke out as members attempted to move up. Early on came evidence that the primates could contentedly accept the islands as their "habitat." A female baboon at Cologne regularly waded the moat late at night, the threat of visitors long gone, to scrounge for food scraps in garbage cans on the grounds nearby, then waded back to her island, not once attempting to escape.

The social primates, difficult to breed in isolated, prison environments, tended to breed readily in the dynamic social groups. Early on, too, came evidence that serving the behavioral needs of the primates could also serve visitors' desire for amusement. The islands quickly became prime attractions at the zoos; many still are. At many older zoos, colonies directly descended from the first residents still occupy the islands. Such behaviorally oriented exhibits are not, however, without problems.

Troops and packs and herds in the wild are dynamic, with members moving in and out of the group according to the needs of the minisociety. Says Minnesota Zoo Tropics Trail curator Jim Pichner, "In the Japanese macaque exhibit, we see young males four or five years old trying to breed the females. They end up being attacked by the alpha male. In the wild that behavior might well occur, but in the wild they might be completely kicked out of the troop. They have places to hide in the exhibit, but there's not much you can do for a really dumb four- or five-year-old male with his hormones pumping and his proper social behavior not yet worked out."

In the late 1940s, Dr. Heine Hediger, director of the Zurich Zoo, undertook the first systematic analysis of the psychological needs of zoo animals. The results of his work, published in a series of books with such titles as *Studies of the Psychology and Behaviour of Animals in Zoos and Circuses*, molded much of the current thinking about behavior and exhibitry. Above all, Hediger emphasized that the suitability of a space was more important than the size of an exhibit and certainly more important to the animal than whether its surroundings looked natural to humans. An orangutan in a vast, realistic exhibit of rockwork, with no trees to climb and no other orangs to interact with, would quickly become bored and miserable. "In reality," Hediger wrote, "the quality of the space at the disposal of the animal is of the greatest importance for its welfare."

Suitability, however, is no constant. Beyond the obvious — an elephant has different needs from those of a baboon — animals have strikingly different ideas about what makes a quality environment. A wolf, like a dog or a man, will not befoul its own den. However, Hediger suggested, a zookeeper intent on keeping every exhibit assiduously clean would be making a big mistake for some animals. The slow loris, for example, considers its living space habitable only if it is sodden with its own urine. "Every time its cage is cleaned out this animal has to drink incredible quantities of water straight away and sprinkle the nice clean floor systematically just like a watering-cart. This shows that habitability must be treated subjectively."

The opportunity for the monkey-island, troop-based primates to interact in the social group would be suitable design. But to force such family-based creatures as the gibbon to live in a large group would be cruel — and probably fatal for many animals. "It is of fundamental importance for every species of animal in captivity to be kept in a natural family group or in larger social groups," Hediger wrote.

Beyond social groupings, zoo animals need territories they can establish and defend as their own, a concept Hediger adopted from the new and still developing science of behavioral biology led by such pioneers as Konrad Lorenz. If they could be placed in natural social groupings, and if indeed they could define a territory as defendably theirs, animals could easily adjust to life in captivity and live long, healthy, contented lives, insisted Hediger. The same viewpoint also served as a convenient rebuttal to those who complained that zoo animals were not free. Following Hediger's philosophical lead, David Hancocks, an architect and former director of Seattle's Woodland Park Zoo, once wrote, " 'Free as a bird' is a misleading expression." Animals in the wild are "prisoners in space and time. . . . [A wild animal's] enclosure is its habitat and its relationships with other animals."

Hediger wrote, "Contrary to the accepted notion, the space allotted to the animal in captivity, once it gets used to it, is not always a place from which it does its best to escape. Rather, it considers it as its own personal property, and will, if need be, defend it stubbornly." Hediger personally cared for a slow loris for several years, which, he says, "would never leave his cage of his own free will. The volume of the cage was only one cubic yard. The animal was quite tame; if it was ever taken out for a time, it immediately showed a marked desire to get back to its own territory again."

Still, few zoo animals can exercise the full range of natural foraging-migrating-stalking-hunting-fighting-fleeing behaviors. But does a caribou miss the opportunity to migrate or a wildebeest to flee from a cheetah? Does the cheetah feel miserable that it cannot exercise its destiny to run faster than any other animal on land? (In the case of the cheetah, apparently not. Busch Gardens once installed a long run for cheetahs to do just that. The cheetahs, thriving on a balanced diet, saw little need to bother.)

Hediger suggested that training animals could enhance their lives, creating substitute stimuli to instigate natural behaviors — stalking, jumping, running. Even then, it was a controversial idea among serious zoo biologists. But, in fact, animal shows once were standard fare at many zoos.

For years the London Zoo held regular afternoon tea parties for chimpanzees.

Today, many zoo directors and biologists abhor nothing more than such anthropomorphizing, circus-style programming, and probably none more vehemently than Steve Graham of the Detroit Zoo. The zoo's chimp show had long been a top attraction, but when Graham arrived in Detroit in the early 1980s, he had the chimp show amphitheater bulldozed to the ground. (He's building a new, multimillion-dollar state-of-the-art naturalistic chimp exhibit in its place, and the zoo will concentrate on chimps to the exclusion of all other apes. "We owe it to them. This zoo was built on the back of the chimpanzee," says Graham.)

The attitude of many of the new-zoo advocates toward animal training was perhaps best expressed by Ron Keller. "What kind of obliviousness, what degree of idiocy, of unthinking, unseeing callousness does it take to reduce such magnificent, noble creatures to clowns and jesters?" Only one problem—Keller was the director of a whale-rights organization, Project Jonah, and he was speaking of the only kinds of mammals that progressive zoos *always* train—cetaceans, the whales and dolphins. Zoos train them out of a specific conviction that the intelligent marine mammals profit psychologically from forming bonds with humans and, perhaps more important, that the intelligent marine mammals need regular, changing mental challenges. The training, incidentally, is affection- and reward-based.

"We're willing to compromise in these cases for the good of the whales and the dolphins," is the way Minnesota's Ron Tilson put it. But there's more. Minnesota's bottle-nosed dolphins and beluga whales perform their "behaviors" at intermittent feeding times throughout the day. The whale and dolphin feedings are the most popular attractions at the zoo and therefore economically important to it. On the other hand, the whales and dolphins are among the most expensive creatures to keep.

But if affectionate training can help provide a better environment for cetaceans, why wouldn't it help other intelligent mammals? And couldn't it be done in a way that showed natural behaviors and gave the beast a chance to exercise while offering an opportunity to teach the public about the animal and habitat preservation? Maybe. But to date, aside from supporting conservation-oriented bird shows featuring hawks and owls, few of the new-zoo biologists seem remotely prepared to consider anything that smacks so much of the old, rearguard circus days.

There have, however, been a few attempts to use electronic and mechanical technology for behavioral enrichment, most notably a series of experiments in the 1970s by Hal Markowitz. In one of his experiments at the Portland, Oregon, Zoo, Markowitz set up a fish-feeding device that catapulted fish into a polar bears' pool whenever one of the two bears growled into a voice-activated relay system. Theoretically, at least, the bears would then dive into the pool to catch the fish. The bears' access to food was not unlimited. Rather, the regulated electromechanical gadget allowed the animals to work for their daily normal ration if they so chose.

But the female bear, Ice-ter, quickly learned to approach the food delivery area and hold her mouth open whenever the male, Esco-mo, ordered food. Thus, she not only prevented her mate from obtaining any of the fish, but precluded the dramatic dive into the pool. The problem was solved by setting up a pair of catapults on the exhibit roof that flung one fish into the pool and another onto the dry part of the exhibit, so that each bear obtained a portion of food whenever one of them executed the growl order. Before long the male came to enjoy having the female order the food. She ordered by growling, devouring the fish that landed nearby, on "dry land." The male, meanwhile, having climbed to a high precipice in anticipation of the food order, dived into the pool. (Incidentally, the single criticism the zoo received was from a visitor who was dismayed that the evil researchers were forcing a polar bear to swim.)

At Portland, Markowitz also installed an elaborate system that enabled visitors to allow gibbons to feed themselves. The visitor would insert a coin in a vending box, and a light would automatically switch on in the gibbon exhibit. If a gibbon chose, it could then pull a lever that would release food from a container across the exhibit. In order to obtain the food, the gibbon would have to brachiate across the cage.

It was an interesting turn of events. Feeding the animals was a major attraction at many of the old menagerie zoos. Visitors brought bread, peanuts, popcorn, and bits of meat or fruit or purchased snacks from the zoo itself to give to the animals. Even without the occasional sadist's slipping a sharp object into a treat, the practice was unhealthy for the recipients. In most cases, it was impossible to monitor the caloric intake of the animals, much less hope to control the balance and quality of this volunteered diet or the spread of disease from humans to the animals. In general, creatures have been programmed over millions of years of evolution to gain body weight when food is available, storing its energy as fat. On the uncontrolled diets, of course, many animals became obese, malnourished, and ill.

Public feeding of animals has been all but abolished in the sensible sectors of the zoo world. Yet allowing people to interact somehow with their charges has a great appeal to some zoo directors. If the argument in favor of zoos is that they allow people to come to understand and love these creatures, what better pathway to interaction, reasoned Markowitz, than to allow people to help feed the animals portions of a controlled and balanced diet, at the same time allowing the animals to exhibit natural behaviors and perhaps indulge in some exercise?

Markowitz insisted that there was evidence that the gibbons liked the feeding system. After it had been in operation for some time, researchers shoved bits of the same food through the bars of the cage rather than activating the device. According to Markowitz, at least two of the animals seemed to be annoyed. Even though food had literally been thrust into their hands, they returned to the lever to see if they could get the device to work. It is, however, equally possible that the gibbons had become so habituated to the machine that they had difficulty obtaining and eating food without going through the motions, à la Pavlov's salivating dog.

In another experiment, at the Panaewa Rain Forest Zoo in Hilo, Hawaii, Markowitz attempted to add a behavioral enhancement system to a Sumatran tiger exhibit, which, for the visitor, was a pavilion overlooking a tropical swamp. Prominently positioned within it was a television screen explaining the differences between the exhibit and a real Sumatran environment and information about the state of the tigers and their behavior in the wild.

If the tigers chose to eat, they could activate the programmed feeding system by scratching an artificial tree trunk equipped with sensing devices — a fundamentally natural behavior, since tigers in the wild scratch trees to mark territory. Providing the tigers had not yet consumed their controlled daily ration, the video display then featured a message that the tiger wanted to hunt and asked the visitor to participate by helping to choose the order or type of activities. If no visitor was present in the pavilion, or if no visitor chose to participate, the computerized system itself initiated the "hunt." Depending on the visitor's or the computer's choice, either a metal "rabbit" or "squirrel" appeared in the exhibit, each part of a half-ton mechanical

structure designed to withstand the pounding of a pouncing tiger. The tiger pursued the mechanical prey, which
disappeared quickly into a hole after the tiger had caught
it. Depending on the structured sequence, the cat might
also have to pursue the other metal prey animal and then
leap to the top of a nearby six-foot berm, where a pressure-
activated plate signaled completion of that phase of the
exercise. The final stage featured the tiger charging directly toward the visitor's window, then quickly under the
pavilion for a morsel of meat from a refrigerated dispenser.

According to Markowitz, the tigers in the exhibit began
stalking immediately the first time they saw the mechanical
rabbit. They indeed activated the device, but not, he said,
constantly. Rather, they spent time splashing in the swamp
pool, batting at birds that had flown into the exhibit, playing
with one another, or attempting to capture a gibbon that
lived in the system of "trees" and "vines" above and out
of reach in the same tropical setting.

At the now defunct Marineland, of California, Markowitz designed a "short chase" for African lions. He admitted that lions had seldom been a focus of behavioral
enhancement "because their daytime behavior in zoos is
more comparable with that in the wild than is the behavior
of many animals upon which we have focused, namely,
lions sleep a lot. Although they sometimes show a great
perseverance in wearing down . . . animals, they are not
noted for great pursuit activities."

But Markowitz came up with a simple system to make
the lions more active, at least periodically. Their exhibit
on an island was viewed from a boat with a driver "guide."
A sonic gadget that made a warbling noise was placed in
a heavy artificial stump. When the boat drivers approached
the lion area, they used a remote-control radio to activate
the noise. If one or more lions felt like eating, the cats

approached the stump, which, of course, was near the water's edge to give the customers a good view. After the lions had come closer, the driver could, again by remote control, release food from a dispenser near the back of the exhibit, to which the lions raced, giving viewers the thrill of lions in motion, rather than in their usual repose.

Markowitz maintained that it was proper to design systems purely for the sake of exercising an animal. "Bicycles that go nowhere and rowing machines that go nowhere are regularly prescribed to improve the human condition." He added, "We are emphatically confronted with the proposition that other animals besides ourselves like to do things, see things change because of their efforts, to enjoy the pride of gathering their own food and drink, and to have some control over their lives."

Markowitz's ideas seem interesting, but it is rare to find such showmanship at any zoo. Minnesota's Jim Pichner, whose Tropics Trail contains the greatest diversity of exhibits in any of the biogeographical units at the institution, says, "Those kinds of things can be useful in some cases. But there is so much labor and capital cost involved in most of them, and so many mechanical problems, that it's almost impossible. We've tried a few things here. We had a hydraulic feeding system for otters that was supposed to release a fish so that people could see the predator-prey relationship when the otters slid into the pool and caught the fish. But in practice, we didn't get squat out of it. The otters learned after a few times that the sound of a motor or a click or two at the back of the exhibit meant that a fish was about to be released. They'd swim over to the device and—wham—they'd have that fish the minute it was out.

"Sometimes, the keepers put suckers [bottom-feeding fish] into the beaver pond for the loons [fish-eating birds]. And it's kind of interesting to watch, but it's not like a lake. The loons dive and go bam, bam, bam. And so much for the suckers. With a lot of those kinds of things, the animals figure out the timing of the device and sleep right in front of the feeding tube. You haven't solved any problems. If they were sleeping all the time before, they *still* sleep all the time. When they hear a relay click, they wake up just long enough to grab the food and then go right back to sleep. I think it's not exactly natural behavior or behavioral enhancement to have an animal sleeping in front of a pneumatic feeding tube.

"I think it's better to create diversity in exhibits to allow animals to do what those particular animals do best. I think we should create — or re-create — what there is about their habitat that makes animals comfortable. Rather than trying to use mechanical devices, you usually do better to design in as much exhibit furniture as you can to allow animals to behave naturally. The more complex and rich you make the exhibit, the more natural behavior you can get out of them."

An example, Pichner claims, is the zoo's clouded leopard exhibit. When they first arrived at the zoo, these leopards were housed in a bright, diurnal exhibit in the Tropics Building. The cats were, by and large, sleepy and inactive. In 1984, the zoo redesigned its tropical nocturnal sequence, a darkened tunnel lined with an array of exhibits for those animals that sleep by day and move about by night. Part of the redesign included a new, darkened space for the clouded leopards, replete with interlaced sculpted concrete tree limbs, sturdy enough for the cats to prowl about on. Now, much more often, the leopards are on the move, gliding from branch to branch, both horizontally and vertically. Even when resting, the cats prefer to climb into the limbs and drape themselves across them, eyes open, alert. Pichner says that if the zoo were going to design the exhibit all over again, he'd put in an even more extensive network of concrete branches.

Pichner believes that tigers, and lions, too, might be far more active if an exhibit could be focused on their behavior. "Tigers and lions are far more active at night," he says. "But they don't move vertically. They need more area. Yet who's going to build a nocturnal exhibit for tigers that's acceptable to them? Who's going to build a two-point-five-acre nocturnal exhibit for a tiger or lion?"

As another example of exhibitry that works, he points to the zoo's gibbon island. Unlike many primates, gibbons are strictly disinclined to large social groups. Rather, in the wild, a single family maintains and defends a limited territory in the treetops. The zoo's family of white-handed gibbons—a male, a female, and their single juvenile offspring—spend their days on a large rock island covered with a massive webwork of concrete trees with flexing, fiberglass limbs. Each joint between limb and concrete trunk is spring loaded. The mechanical arrangement allows superb opportunities for brachiation—the spectacular, long-armed, hand-over-hand cruise of these lesser apes through the trees. As far as anyone can surmise about the emotions of apes, the gibbons appear to be stable and content, grooming each other, with the juvenile learning swinging skills, somewhat clumsily at first and increasingly gracefully. Archie, the male, a particularly active swinger, is deservedly one of the major attractions at the zoo.

However, Archie and the tropical exhibit sequence, which was designed to be a mixed one, have a few problems. The gibbons would have their trees-and-island microhabitat to themselves, except that in the water around them dwell elegant Oriental waterfowl and stilting pink flamingos. From time to time, a duck roosts on the rockwork of the island and, from time to time, Archie swats the bird powerfully into the water, with little apparent detriment to the duck beyond several ruffled feathers. On a few occasions, however, a flamingo has come too close to Archie's territory, and Pichner thinks that on these occasions the ape may simply have been exercising his curiosity when he grabbed the bird's slender neck in his powerful hand. In any case, the gibbon has throttled a few extremely valuable flamingos to death.

Archie is also the zoo's most regular escapee, but the culmination of his efforts may reflect more about habitat and territory in zoo animals than anything else. The gibbons' territory is an island because gibbons hate and fear water. Pichner is convinced that, with his extraordinary leaping abilities, Archie could escape far more often than he does, but that his distaste for water discourages it. Further, it appears that the gibbon actually dislikes leaving his family's territory. His internal conflict involves his fierce territoriality and his programmed need to defend the family against real or perceived threats.

Pichner speculates that the gibbon's escape problems result, sometimes, from *too much* human pleasure at his behavior. He says, "He perceives showing teeth as aggression — as a threat." The gibbon brachiates to one side of the island, and there are people smiling, showing teeth. He goes to the other side, and there are more people showing teeth. The more excited he becomes, the more the onlookers display their teeth. Finally, Pichner hypothesizes, "As much as the gibbon hates water, all that instinct is working on him and finally he just loses his cool. If there's an opportunity — a branch grown too long on a tree across the moat — suddenly he's out in the Tropics. The problem is, once he gets out, he hates it. He's out of his territory, and that's even more frightening. He was just being defensive. It's his family and his island and he perceived a threat. He wanted to get out and give those people hell, but now he's off what is his and he's on what's someone else's. He knows from experience that there are going to be people running around with nets and tranquilizer guns."

Archie's intermittent escapes have become more manageable, Pichner comments, now that his behavioral needs are better understood. Rather than chasing the gibbon down with nets, the keepers simply string a strong rope from a handrail back to a tree on the gibbon island, and Archie usually seizes the opportunity to return, hand-over-hand, to his own, safe territory.

The zoo has struggled, much less successfully, to make its sloth bear exhibit more interesting for visitors and more behaviorally lively for the bear. The exhibit is attractive enough, set into small, vegetation-covered cliffs in the Tropics. The problem is that the bear usually does precisely what his name suggests: displays intense sloth. His favorite "activity" is sleeping at the back of the exhibit in the entrance to the short tunnel that leads to his behind-the-scenes kennel-home. In an attempt to stimulate the bear and make it more active, the zoo designed an artificial fallen log with a hole in it, into which went a bowling ball with several finger holes drilled into it. Keepers loaded the finger holes with honey, hoping that the bear would bat and slurp at the log, spinning the ball to get at the honey as it might from a hive. To visitors, the ball was virtually unnoticeable.

The idea worked, to a point. Pichner says that the bear quickly became so proficient at rolling the ball and slurping out the honey that he'd be back asleep in the tunnel in a matter of minutes. Then the staff tried smearing honey and placing a few choice mealworms into the cracks and crevices in the rockwork of the exhibit to make the sloth bear work for his treats. "The bear can glom up all the honey you can smear into the crevices and all the crickets and mealworms you can put out in ten or twenty minutes and be back sleeping in the tunnel," says Pichner. "Food is a successful way to keep an animal active only for a short period of time. We're going to have to find a better way."

Pichner notes that the Tropics Building exhibits were close to display state of the art when they were completed in 1978, but there still are difficulties and inadequate exhibits, often for lack of a base of knowledge about how to improve them. "That's the problem. You build on nothing. Often you build on what *didn't* work in the past. It doesn't say much about what *will* work. So you go through the literature. You try to find out as much as you can about the animal, and then you just try something."

2

Probably the most famous notion about zoo exhibitry came in the late 1960s from the Bronx Zoo's William Conway who, early in his tenure as director, challenged his colleagues to consider the feasibility of building a spectacularly successful exhibit around the most unlikely and mundane of creatures: the run-of-the-pond bullfrog. Conway's proposal was extravagant and fanciful. But his message was serious. A bullfrog is as meaningful, in a biological sense, as any zebra or lion.

Conway presented that idea to the members of the AAZPA as his dream in which an eloquent devil-figure in a red cape, known only as "M," raged at Conway, as director of the Bronx Zoo, for spending vast amounts of money on such exotic species as pygmy chimpanzees "when you don't have a proper exhibit of bullfrogs . . . Why, an

entire zoo could be devoted to the bullfrog; a major building is hardly adequate to present the excitement."

In the dream, "M" ranted further at zoo directors for
their inadequate exhibitry in general, for putting arboreal
orangutans in treeless exhibits that looked like bathrooms,
for "making a great deal of noise about barless moated
exhibits" that are so behaviorally inappropriate that they
might as well be bathrooms, for putting a "two-dollar
sign" on an exhibit featuring a $5,000 animal.

"M" led Conway's dreaming persona down into a tunnel and thence into the "World of Bullfrogs."

Inside, a windowed tunnel passed under the bullfrog's
pond. Beyond were walls of brilliant graphics explaining
evolution—using the bullfrog as an example, with "com-
parative graphics showing man's brief history." There was
a darkened exhibit entitled "A Spring Night at a Bullfrog
Pond," where carpeting completely muffled human steps,
but the air sang with the rustling of cattails and the
choruses of frogs, where artificial fireflies glowed and a
recorded barred owl hooted in the distance. Ecological
exhibits showed the frog in relation to the biosphere and
its ecosystem, including a pinball machine featuring a frog
ball that children could try to keep out of the clutches and
beaks and mouths of its natural predators.

"M" told Conway, "Of course, I could have used *any*
common animal . . . Its effectiveness . . . in terms of human understanding and appreciation and its suitability in
terms of animal well-being is the best justification for removing an animal from the wild. A poor display can destroy the wonder of the rarest, most marvelous creature."

In 1982 the AAZPA asked Conway to present an up-
dated view of the famous bullfrog talk. He reported that
he'd had "second thoughts" on the matter. His talk, he
said, "assumed that all species can be made of equal interest

to the zoogoer if only they are exhibited imaginatively enough, but they cannot."

Yet, to my mind, today's truly outstanding exhibits are those that, in one form or another, fit the World of Bullfrogs metaphor. Great exhibits, and great exhibit sequences, attempt to immerse visitors in nature, to tell a story that the visitors may not have heard before. At best, they enhance regard for a creature—or, better yet, a population, a community, an ecosystem, a biome—that visitors disregarded in the past, using vivid educational displays to help tell the wildlife and conservation story.

Granted, few of even the best exhibits come close to fulfilling their potential, but I've picked three examples of fine exhibitry for a closer look at how the bullfrog dream has at last been partially realized at Minnesota's Beaver Pond, Cincinnati's Insect World, and the Bronx's environmental-polemics graphics.

Minnesota's Beaver Pond rings true to some of the bullfrog ideal, for it manages to display reasonably natural living circumstances and a natural life cycle for these creatures. A beaver in a bland exhibit would undoubtedly be the most singularly dull scene one could imagine, and surely one of the most boring of animals. But designers of this exhibit succeeded in defining the beaver's behavioral needs and discovering a way to portray much of its behavioral range. The exhibit is a working beaver pond, about 45 by 60 feet, complete with a stick-and-mud lodge with an underwater plunge hole, filtered flowing water, and a dam with a center spillway, thus creating both an upper and lower pond. (Exhibit designers hoped that the beavers would regularly "repair" the spillway in the dam. But they don't, although the male occasionally halfheartedly picks up chunks of wood and slaps them against the dam.) At the back of the lower pond is a mud flat. It is too small to allow tree regeneration under the beavers' intense pressure, so keepers stock it daily, slipping thumb-thick aspens cut elsewhere on the zoo site into metal sleeves buried in the mud flats. At the flats, then, in clear view of the visitors, the beavers chop down the trees for food. Algal plankton grow in the pond, but the zoo's attempts to grow larger aquatic plants there have failed: the beavers eat them all. The beavers also thwarted early attempts to grow plants and small trees in overhanging planters in the "limestone" rockwork. Although the walls should have been steep enough to keep the animals from reaching the planters, the beavers came out at night to pile pond debris at the base of the wall— impromptu footstools to help them reach the plants. That problem was largely solved by installing rocky overhangs on the walls.

Visitors view the beavers through a series of windows on an inclined walkway that offers views of the pond both from and below the surface of the water. Inside the beaver's lodge, two low-light video cameras cablecast to a television set in the observation area, allowing visitors to watch the social behavior in the lodge, including mother beavers tending to and nursing their kits. (I did once hear someone object to such an "invasion of the beaver's privacy.")

Adult beavers' metabolisms slow down in the cold months, and they live almost entirely on body fat. But the youngsters need food. To provide it, beavers with young work furiously near the onset of winter to build up a cache of aspen twigs and saplings. They place the supply in a carefully engineered structure designed to hold saplings submerged, away from the frozen pond surface. Beavers in the wild usually embed the trees that serve as the cache's structural members in a muddy pond bottom. But at the zoo pond, with concrete rather than mud on the bottom, the beavers had to invent another approach to cache-building; they soon learned to intertwine the trees so that the interlocking weight of the entire hoard keeps it submerged.

"The animals took great care in choosing a location inside the cache for each tree, cutting them all to the proper length and trimming excess limbs for storage in the center of the cache," a team of authors from the zoo reported in the 1981 *International Zoo Yearbook*.

One could question keeping beavers in captivity at all, especially since Minnesota has no dearth of the animals, and even inner city residents could find the animals not much farther from their doors than the distance to the suburban zoo. But nowhere in nature can one obtain such an intimate look into the beaver's unique behavior. As zoo exhibits go, it is a fine one, yet it does not fulfill its potential. Sadly, the zoo, like most zoos, has entirely missed the opportunity to install signs and other educational graphics to tell people more about what they're seeing, the effects beavers can have on stream ecosystems, or even their cultural and historical importance to the state.

Cincinnati Zoo director Ed Maruska says that skepticism abounded when he suggested building a million-dollar-plus exhibit dedicated solely to insects. "When we decided to go ahead with Insect World, some of my colleagues from other zoos decided I had lost it totally. Here I wanted to spend over a million dollars for creepy-crawlies that bite and sting, that are totally alien and not very attractive to most people. One zoo director told me bluntly that better men than I had tried things like this and failed. But 90 percent of the terrestrial animal species are invertebrates. They pollinate our flowers and work our ground, and they are vital to every other form of life. They were being poorly represented in zoos. Their story just wasn't being told, so we decided that we had to tell it."

The headaches in planning, building, and filling the four-thousand-square-foot exhibit were severe. Where in Ohio does one find acceptable food for Brazilian insects? How does one control the inevitable problems of unwanted insect pests in the exhibit building — home-grown Cincinnati cockroaches, whiteflies, and pharaoh ants? Insect *pests* are a problem at virtually every zoo, but here, the usual response — spraying insecticides — would wipe out the entire collection of exotics in the exhibit. Further, how does one convince U.S. Department of Agriculture specialists, who have dedicated their careers to preventing new exotic insects from entering the country, to approve the intentional importation of a few hundreds of same?

Cincinnati got past the problems by hiring only graduate entomologists as curator and keepers in Insect World and talking the USDA itself into serving as consultant to help design a safe exhibit with no windows, screen-covered drains, and a sealed "clean" room for handling some of the more escape-prone species. The entomologists introduced tiny parastic wasps into the butterfly aviary to control whiteflies on the growing plants and used natural hormones to inhibit the growth of pharaoh ant larvae. They made some assumptions that insects from distant ecosystems might be able to eat the same food as relatives in the Cincinnati area, and most of the time it worked. The Hercules beetle, a huge Amazon scarab beetle, is taxonomically related to the local unicorn beetle. Insect World curator Milan Busching says, "We knew that unicorn beetles feed on ripe fruit, and we found that pieces of ripe banana would work well for the Hercules beetles."

The exhibit broke tradition with conventional zoo wisdom that visitors don't read signs and graphics. "Visitors," says Maruska, "don't read *crummy* signs and graphics."

Insect World is as much an entomological natural history museum as a zoo, with graphics straight out of the Conway bullfrog pond demonstrating everything from the various kinds of insect mouth parts to how insects camouflage themselves. Contrary to the views of pessimists convinced that people who go to zoos would find such detail dull, a survey showed that the average visitor spends half an hour moving through the exhibit sequence. Since one could stroll casually through it in five or ten minutes, Cincinnati's visitors must be stopping to read the signs and to study the exhibits in detail.

When I first stepped into the exhibit area, I was met with an entire wall of backlit small transparencies showing hundreds of specialized insect forms and by the sound of a schoolteacher's voice. "Hey, kids, look at this. 'All the insects on earth weigh twelve times as much as all the humans.' " The teacher's students, meanwhile, were weighing themselves on a large, old-fashioned scale that offered to tell them their weight in insects. Most weighed about 12 million insects; I weighed 34 million.

Inside, with echoes of Conway's bullfrog evolution room, is a section devoted to insect evolution, with text appropriate to a high school textbook. "Insects," a sign reads, "are thought to have evolved from a centipede-like ancestor which bore a pair of leg-like appendages on each of its many body segments. Entomologists (people who study insects) believe that in the course of time the first five segments became specialized as a head capsule, bearing the eyes, antennae, and mouth parts. The thorax was formed from the next three segments . . ." And so on.

There is information about an insect's immense reproductive potential: "A female aphid could theoretically give rise, over a four-month breeding period, to more than 500 quadrillion aphids if all her progeny should live." (However, the graphics do not explain what happens to all that reproductive potential.) Huge Oriental walking-sticks are displayed next to tiny springtails, the latter seen through a magnifying glass. There are living, spectacular examples of protective camouflage, including the large Javanese leaf insect, virtually a duplicate of the large, bright green leaves it lives on. There are insect predators, ranging from a tiny Callimico monkey to silver, black-spotted, flat-bodied archerfish, which acquire their food by shooting a precise stream of water onto the leaves of riparian plants. There are working termite nests and beehives. Near the exit, a vegetation-choked free-flight room is dedicated to butterflies—steaming, humid, and silent but for the trickle of an artificial waterfall.

Most important of all is a sign at the exit, which reads, "You have seen how some insects threaten human well-being by competing for valuable resources and by spreading disease. Despite these seriously injurious activities, insects have their beneficial aspects of vital importance not only to people but to the environment as a whole. Losses to insects are certainly exceeded by the good which the insects perform, and it is safe to say that we could scarcely live without them."

Maruska says that when the exhibit opened in 1978, the same zoo director who had previously accused him of harboring delusions walked slowly through the exhibit and left muttering, "You SOB, you did it."

The Cincinnati Zoo, perhaps more than any other, has made giant strides in recent years with educational graphics. Of Insect World, curator Busching says, "We try to do a combination of zoo and museum techniques—to not overdo the education so much that people shut it out, but still let them learn." Near Insect World, in Cincinnati's new cat exhibit, an electronic sign allows visitors to push buttons on a backlit outline of a wildcat skeleton to learn about the adaptive advantages of the cat's claws, whiskers, teeth, eyes, skeleton, feet, and tail. Close by, an electronic map of Cincinnati invites a visitor to punch in his or her neighborhood to see how many gazelles it would support if it were a tropical grassland and how many lions those gazelles would support — at one acre of grassland per hundred gazelles per one lion.

But so far, when it comes to conveying specifically the environmental conservation message, no zoo can compare with Conway's Bronx. Signs in the World of Birds include one with a row of ten ostriches, heads in sand, with a bulldozer moving toward them. Says the sign, "Africa's human population is doubling every 28 years. . . . In Uganda, 70 percent of remaining wild lands were converted to agriculture between 1929 and 1979. . . . Africa's wondrous variety of hoofed animals have been displaced by goats, sheep, and cattle. . . . The destruction of wild lands and wildlife in Africa is repeating the history of the development of North America, except that it is moving far more rapidly and despoiling a far more wondrous flora and fauna."

At the Siberian tiger exhibit, after establishing that there are only a few hundred Siberian tigers left in the wild: "There are more than 700 known paintings by Rembrandt. The last Rembrandt sold was purchased for more than 2 million dollars. How much do you think a Siberian tiger is worth?"

In the World of Darkness, the zoo's vanguard nocturnal exhibit, visitors are told that fruit-eating bats are important to ecosystems because they help distribute seeds, which pass from fruit into their digestive systems and out with the nutrient-rich fecal matter. As visitors leave the World of Darkness, they are reminded that this is "a world that represents only one part of the totality that is nature. The continuing increase in human populations combined with environmental destruction is rapidly destroying the world of nature. Therefore, the future of all wild land and wildlife depends upon education, human protection, and interest, and ultimately upon you."

In the Great Ape House, a small exhibit is labeled THE

MOST DANGEROUS ANIMAL IN THE WORLD. The front of the exhibit is a row of bars, behind which is a full-length mirror. "This animal," says the sign, "is increasing at the rate of 190,000 every 24 hours, and is the only creature that has ever killed off entire species of other animals. Now it has achieved the power to wipe out all life on earth."

And then there is a Bronx Zoo graphic that is one of the most stunningly effective bits of environmental consciousness-raising I've seen. But first, some background. In 1984, the Bronx opened its long-planned, long-anticipated $9.5 million Jungle World exhibit, a superb, verdant Asian tropics sequence, beautiful and theatrical, featuring a volcanic scrub forest, a mangrove swamp, a lowland rain forest, and a mountain rain forest housing animals ranging from leopards to gibbons to creeping water monitors.

The attention to detail is staggering. Where windows had to be used as barriers, they are made of nonglare glass, sloped downward and carefully lit to obliterate any trace of reflection. Dappled patterns of moonglow fall on the forest floor of the nocturnal areas — even on the floor of the adjacent visitors' walk. Cloud mist shrouds the rain forest, thanks to a hidden misting system. Looking closely enough, one can notice that the artificial trees, draped with real vines, have tiny, delicate lichens carved onto them. Bronx exhibit and graphics curator John Gwynne explained to me that some of the exhibit artists were so dedicated to their forgery tasks that they had to be told to cease carving lichens onto the *backs* of trees. Over the visitors' heads lies a wooden pergola, so that no one can be distracted by the building's roof, rafters, and skylights, and underfoot is a wooden bridge. Even the entry handrails are made of carved wood from Bali.

"While technology is cutting down forests at an incredible rate, we're trying to use technology to help teach people about why these forests should be saved. We want the people to feel they're in the tropics of Asia," says Gwynne. The exhibit does just that. It fairly plunges them into the environment, all the better to set them up for the simple message they'll find outside, just after exiting, on a wide, sloped sign on a pedestal labeled TROPICAL FOREST COUNTDOWN. The sign, which lies directly in the visitor's path, interrupting the flow of exiting traffic, is virtually impossible to avoid. "When Jungle World opened on June 21, 1985," it says, "the worldwide acreage of tropical forests was 2,215,384,320 ."

Directly below, a digital counter shows how much tropical forest acreage remains. It is not a static number. The rightmost numerals of the display blink steadily downward, as nearly an acre per second vanishes—fifty acres each minute, seventy-three thousand each day.

Just beyond that, a similar pedestal, with an upward-ticking LED, shows the growth of the world human population, at a rate of 216,000 new souls every day.

Following the emotional introduction to the tropical environments, the concise, cool, nonpolemical statement of facts and numbers conveys a far more powerful conservation message than all the preaching in the world. It suggests that zoos truly can find ways to use their unique, theatrical resources to tell the conservation story.

But do they? In general, they emphatically do not. Zoo biologists repeatedly told me that they see public education as the single most important role of the zoo. In fact, all the good zoos, and even some of the bad ones, offer seminars, lectures, and classes. But few provide effective environmental education to the great majority of their visitors, those who simply come to look at the exhibits and the animals.

Asked about the zoo world's general failure to practice what it preaches, Detroit Zoo director Steve Graham paused for a moment and said, "Well, yes, you're 100 percent right that we don't. I keep saying that the only reason I'm in this business is that zoos in the United State have more than 100 million visitors every year, and that offers an unprecedented opportunity to reach people with the conservation message. But the fact is, if you hear me say that and then visit my zoo to see how well I've acted on it, you'd walk away disappointed. We haven't found ways to devote enough resources to graphics. Some of that's because once we're done with maintaining exhibits and caring for the animals, there isn't much left over. I think more of it is that we know a lot more about taking care of animals than we do about how to tell our visitors about conservation."

The Bronx Zoo, however, seems to have learned some of the basics from the advertisers of toothpaste, automobiles, and Jockey shorts. Most people may not read an exhibit sign any more readily than they pay rapt attention to a television commercial, but there is real hope for reaching some visitors by creating a lively, perhaps offbeat, surprising message—better yet, a series of such messages—and following the three cardinal rules of advertising: repetition, repetition, repetition.

It seems as if the zoo world needs a new Carl Hagenbeck, one who can point the way toward wildlife and conservation education in the same way the original pioneered the path to improved animal exhibitry. Several zoo directors or curators have expressed dismay that the vast majority of visitors still don't seem to bother to read the signs. But the toothpaste advertiser knows that even reaching a small percentage of a market, in time, can be enormously profitable. And what toothpaste advertiser wouldn't be thrilled to have the opportunity to reach more than 100 million prospects each year?

3

Deciding *how* to exhibit animals is one thing; deciding *which* animals to exhibit is another. In the past, zoo directors as postage stamp collectors might have tried to obtain as many species as possible as a badge of status among their peers, concentrating on a few that happened to interest them personally. Any fiscally responsible zoo director has to be certain to have on site the kinds of species that will bring visitors through the gate. Since the zoos in the Western world had traditionally featured animals from colonial Africa, that once meant, at minimum, lions, zebras, elephants, and rhinos. As the National Zoo's public relations director Bob Hoage put it, "Look at what most people come to zoos for. It's pachyderms—the pachyderms and the big carnivores. As far as most people are concerned, if you lose the pachyderms, you don't have a zoo, even though they really don't represent much of the diversity of animal life." Ideally, a zoo director might hope to obtain a real showboat of an animal—a gorilla or two or, far more rarely, a giant panda.

But as zoos begin to see themselves as institutions dedicated to conservation, new questions about which animals to keep have begun to arise. Should zoos keep individual animals, no matter how attractive, if their breeding population is already large enough to maintain genetic diversity? Beyond that, should they maintain at all animals that are not endangered in the wild; given the limitations of resources for animals that *do* need help, should zoos keep bottle-nosed dolphins, giraffes, and wallabies, or for that matter, beavers and bullfrogs?

Denver Zoo director Clayton Freiheit thinks that zoos must "strike an equitable balance between rare and common species," warning that "the so-called common species today may be rare tomorrow if everyone stops breeding it." He also believes that zoos must maintain some popular species simply because pleasing the zoogoing public "is essential for our own survival."

Nowhere does the conflict between crowd pleasing and conservation rear its head more noticeably in the zoo world than with the so-called white phase of the Bengal tiger. White tigers are immensely popular with the public, and therefore have become immensely popular with circus trainers and some zoos. At the same time, the demand for white tigers has created a gold mine for the one zoo that breeds them most effectively, and the lucrative white tiger breeding program at Cincinnati has thrust director Ed Maruska into the center of a storm.

White tigers are not albinos with a total lack of pigment; they are not pure white at all. Their coats are usually a cream color with chocolate brown or gray stripes, their eyes a striking blue rather than the usual amber.

On May 27, 1951, in India, the maharaja of Rewa captured a white tiger, later named Mohan, and for nearly twenty years thereafter kept the remarkable blue-eyed cat in the palace courtyard at Govindgarh. The maharaja was eager to breed the tiger, but he was sorely disappointed when he bred Mohan with a yellow Bengal and produced litters of perfectly yellow offspring. But his cousin-in-law, the maharaja of Baroda, who knew more than a little of Mendelian genetics, said, "Rewa was upset. I told him the answer: incest, of course." Following Baroda's suggestion, Rewa bred Mohan to one of the yellow tiger daughters, producing a litter of three more yellow cats, but also one white one. With that success, Rewa became a breeder— and peddler—of white tigers. In 1960, Ted Reed, then National Zoo director, purchased one of Mohan's male offspring, a cat named Mohini, and introduced the white tiger to America. Mohini and his inbred offspring quickly became leading attractions at American zoos.

"It's difficult to say how much the zoo owes to that cat and his cubs," said Reed later. "They drew attention to the facility and made all our recent improvements so much easier."

But by the 1980s many in the zoo world had doubts about the white tiger and whether an ethical, conservation-oriented zoo should exhibit an animal simply because it represents a genetic quirk. Some have even offered the opinion that the white tiger is a freak. The Bronx's Conway compared it to "a two-headed calf." Detroit's Steve Graham puts white tigers in the same category as the hated "trash and flash" chimpanzee shows and, following Conway's lead, says, "I think it's true. I've always worried that some children's zoo will have a two-headed calf and some zoo director will be clamoring to put it on exhibit. There's absolutely no difference in my mind between a white tiger and a two-headed calf."

All of which makes Maruska bristle. He got his start in white tiger husbandry in the 1970s, when Cincinnati was temporarily housing a pair of the National Zoo's Bengals, both yellow but heterozygous for the white gene. In 1974 the pair bred and produced three white homozygous cubs and one yellow heterozygous cub. By 1986, fifty-two white tigers had been born at the Cincinnati Zoo, the National Zoo had completely ceased breeding them, and Cincinnati had become the major supplier of white tigers in North America.

"They are *not* freaks," Maruska, his eyes blazing, responded at the 1986 International Tiger Symposium. "I've never seen a two-headed calf in nature, have you? Mohan wasn't the first wild white tiger. There were seventeen shot by trophy hunters between 1907 and 1933, and many other reports of sightings. These animals were adults. Obviously, they were surviving in the wild. I don't know of a single case of a two-headed anything surviving in the wild."

Maruska acknowledges that the too-intense inbreeding of the white tiger lines has resulted in birth defects, but insists that the data for the tigers born at his institution show few such defects and that the animals are in generally good health. He has proposed for years that the white should be embraced by the Species Survival Plan and bred accordingly. Doing that would mean devoting a separate plan to the white tiger, for it could be maintained as a white variety only through some level of inbreeding. Yet to meet the SSP goal of improved genetic diversity would involve outcrossing more white tigers with yellow Bengals, devoting already scarce cage space and resources to the white tiger program. AAZPA conservation coordinator Tom Foose was always more than skeptical that the white tiger belonged in a conservation program. Then, in 1986, a detailed genetic analysis of white tiger cells resolved the issue. The North American whites weren't even pure Bengals. Apparently somewhere along the line a Siberian tiger had gotten mixed into the genetic stew, and its genes appeared to be in virtually the entire white tiger population. In the autumn of 1986, the AAZPA decided not to include the white cat in the SSP.

Maruska, however, intends to keep breeding and showing them. He'll breed them because of the demand: a healthy pair can easily fetch $125,000, as did a pair he sold to the Sigfried and Roy animal act in Las Vegas. He'll show them because they bring visitors through the gates.

"We fail in one area when we allow the public to become infatuated with an animal," says Maruska. "But that's what's already happened with the koala and the giant panda. I don't know of a single zoo director who wouldn't give his right arm for a giant panda. The white tiger is here to stay by popular demand."

Popular demand is one of the guiding principles at Cincinnati. Elsewhere, some staffers abhor even the notion of taking zoo animals off exhibit to parade them before television talk show cameras. At the Minnesota Zoo, the animal management team has firmly denied most requests to take animals off site for such a purpose. For that matter, there was once a confrontation at Minnesota between the animal management team curators and an operations director about whether the grass in the visitor areas should be mowed — long grass, though unsightly for the average visitor, provides far better habitat for native birds and rodents. Maruska, on the other hand, is happy to provide animals for television or advertisements, even dispatching a keeper and a tiger to every Cincinnati Bengals home football game. The grass is not only trimmed; the grounds at Cincinnati are bordered and carefully ordered, like an English garden.

"Zoos are here for conservation. And we do a pretty good job of it here," says Maruska. He's correct; few other zoos have built a shrine to endangered species, few can compare with Cincinnati for educational graphics, and only a handful support a reproductive biology program. "But we can't be financially irresponsible. Most of us in the zoo world depend on attendance. We have to come up with a few million dollars every year or we fail our community *and* our mission. If nobody comes through the gate, we won't have an opportunity to communicate the conservation message. I'd agree with P. T. Barnum. If we want to save wildlife, we have to tell people what's happening to wildlife habitat. But in order to tell them anything, first we have to get people under the tent. Without the visitor coming into the park for a family outing, Betsy Dresser's

research program wouldn't exist. Once we get people under the tent, if they walk through beautiful grounds and
find fine exhibits, then they might be in a mood to let us
tell them about conservation."

4

Early in this project, I visited a small group of environmentalists in St. Paul. Someone asked what subject I was
working on. I might as well have announced that I was
going to write a book about proctology. When I said I was
going to write a book about zoos, but not a denunciation
of same, there was a puzzled silence.

"I don't like zoos," one woman finally said quietly. As
we talked, it turned out that her experience with zoos had
been acquired in the 1950s and earlier and that she had
never visited the local zoological gardens. But the response
is similar to one I ran into repeatedly in the following
months and years. While I was writing the book, most
mainstream environmentalists—or conservationists, for
those who prefer the more traditional term—who learned
I was working on such a project—and worse, that I had
positive feelings about zoos—limited themselves to polite
silence. A few acknowledged, if somewhat grudgingly,
that for some species zoos might be the only hope, but
they didn't like them anyway. A few, ticked off, listed all
the bad things they had ever heard about zoos.

By no means based on a scientific survey, my impression
is that many environmental activists simply don't like zoos
on principle and deeply mistrust zoos' motives and their
real commitment to conservation. As Steve Graham once

put it, many conservationists hold zoos in about the same contempt that zoo people hold circuses.

Certainly, there are those whom the zoo world will never please, and zoo people doubtless would waste their collective breath trying to change them. Notably, Michael Fox, an official of the Humane Society of the United States (an organization that has, incidentally, gone on record in support of good zoos), commented, in a 1986 issue of *The Animals' Agenda*, an animal rights magazine, "With such high-tech innovations as operant training devices, behavioral monitoring, ova transplantation, and genetic engineering, the contemporary zoo is fast becoming emblematic of capitalist industrial technology."

Fox continued with the statement that zoos were providing animals to "lucrative game ranches in Texas" for trophy hunters to shoot; that he had divined that the animals were troubled because he had tried during a visit to the National Zoo to look into the animals' eyes and they did not look back; and that if zoo visitors were made aware of the suffering of the animals, "then this zoo, like all zoos, would be demolished and the animals liberated by a compassionate humanity." Where he would propose to liberate the hippos, lions, and pandas in a world of devastated habitat, Fox didn't say.

But more sensible voices have expressed concerns about zoos. Norman Meyers, a noted ecologist and author, once wrote quite correctly, in *The Sinking Ark*, that zoo scientists simply have too little knowledge to breed successfully many of the endangered animal species. He noted that the cheetah, penguin, and hummingbird—and he might have added the giant panda—have been difficult or outright impossible to breed. He remarked that zoos are not only far more expensive places to maintain wildlife than natural habitats, but that natural habitats preserve much more than a single species.

To preserve a species in natural surroundings means that man safeguards not only a single genetic system, viz., that of the species itself, but of several interlocking genetic systems that form part of the ecosystem of the species in question. In this way, man not only preserves a species known to science and recognized as threatened, but he also preserves many other species, some of which may not even have become known to science.

In a brief 1985 editorial in *BioScience*, zoologist Eric Pianka of the University of Texas wrote, "Like all biologists, I *love* zoos, but they aren't enough." In the process of explaining why they aren't enough, Pianka may have hit upon the key reason why so many ecologically oriented people are dubious about zoos altogether. He said that a zoo animal

> is totally out of context. Just as a word taken out of a paragraph loses much of its meaning and information content, an animal extracted from the wild no longer has a natural environment. Any given word is a subject, object, noun, verb, modifier, etc., with complex relationships to other words in the paragraph in which it resides; similarly, any wild organism is either a producer or a consumer and has its enemies, predators, potential competitors, and for many, its prey. Individuals also possess meaningful relationships to other members of their own populations, such as their own offspring, potential mates, neighbors on adjacent territories, kin, and so forth . . . For the population biologist, an animal in a zoo has been stripped of most of what is interesting about it; it is like an isolated word out of context.

There have been harsher criticisms. In one of the most ringing condemnations, *Not Man Apart,* a publication of the Friends of the Earth, printed in 1985 an article by David Phillips and Sandra Kaiser entitled "Are Zoos an Excuse for Habitat Destruction?" One of the three internal boldface heads of the article was "The Captive Breeding Boon-doggle." The authors wrote,

> The altruistic roles of zoos, the ones that are paraded in front of wealthy foundations and the public, are those of educator and nurturer of endangered species. But those roles are being increasingly challenged as it becomes apparent that the full measure of a specie includes the ecosystem that molds it. More and more people are coming to believe that animals have a right to exist in their own natural habitats, instead of being shown off for the amusement of humans.
>
> The overall effect of the zoos' attempts to be arks for endangered species may be to accelerate the loss of habitat. Zoos are giving a false impression that species can be saved, even if the wild is destroyed.

The authors also noted that zoos had reintroduced few endangered species to the wild.

Perhaps the zoo people quoted here have already answered most of these charges. No, tragically, zoos cannot save entire ecosystems or even significant pieces of ecosystems. No, unfortunately, zoos have reintroduced few endangered species, in part because the habitat problems that caused them to become endangered in the first place have not been resolved.

Yes, saving habitat is *the* critical issue. During my dozens, probably hundreds, of interviews and conversations with zoo biologists and administrators, that very theme recurred constantly. No professional biologist, and no reasonably astute amateur, would ever suggest otherwise. The best places to preserve species are intact wild ecosystems, with emphasis on *intact*.

But what happens when the wild habitat is lost? Is it reasonable for the ark to stay afloat? Is it reasonable for zoos to provide a buffer, a fallback, for those species — the Siberian and Sumatran tigers, the black rhino, the orangutan, and the others—that survive in the wild, but only tenuously? Some have argued that it isn't, that it is somehow nobler for a species to "die with dignity" in the wild than live through generations in captivity. But since no one can see fifty, one hundred, or two hundred years into the future does it not seem stunningly arrogant for a human being to suggest that an entire evolutionary line be allowed to terminate at the hand of humans when there is any reason, however slim, to hope that somehow, someday, that species might thrive again in the wild with the help of humankind?

Is there a danger that zoos can create a sense of complacency, the sense that "the zoos are saving the tamarin, so it must be okay to destroy the Atlantic coast forest"? Perhaps. It is no better an argument for shutting down zoo-based propagation programs than that a hospital should be shut down because it encourages people to avoid preventive medicine. But it is a danger the zoo world should take seriously, considering the propaganda skills of those who would commercially drain, fill, torch, inundate, stripmine, and otherwise desolate natural landscapes without regard for their biological importance. Yet the hard fact is that the planet already is losing plant and animal diversity—and habitat—at a staggering rate. Virtually none of it can be attributed to the deleterious effects of zoos, but rather to the human birth rate, hunger, poor land use, and bad politics.

Many sincere conservationists will probably continue to be vaguely uneasy, or outright suspicious, about zoos and their motives, not least because too many zoos continue to be animal jails or centers for carnival-like hucksterism at the expense of the animals.

For all the income generated by more benign attractions,

such as white tigers, the inevitable circus overtones may be contributing to a backlash that keeps the zoo world misaligned with many who could be its natural allies. In the end, zoos must confront the suspicion that all the talk of conservation is more than window-dressing to subdue criticism, that Barnum is far more important to zoos than biology.

Can zoos do all that? Conway, who often has led the struggle to turn the zoo world around, wryly refers to the diverse perspectives and agendas of zoos as "a United Nations problem."

Explains Nate Flesness, "It's important to keep in mind that zoos are not independent organizations. They are supported by county, city, state, and in one case, the national government. And, in fact, they have responsibilities to those governmental bodies rather than to any broader entity. So it requires considerable commitment for a zoo director to take this sort of thing on. Because he then has to report to his superior to say, 'I'm doing this for the good of the world's wildlife and the cooperative good of all zoos rather than for the good of visitors to this specific zoo and the local government that supports it.' "

The ark is sailing into uncharted waters. The zoo world's only hope as a conserver of wildlife is to continue and accelerate along the course. But can an ark succeed with the public as well as a menagerie or carnival? With enough dedication and imagination, maybe it can.

As the apparition "M" told William Conway in the bullfrog dream,

> Our urban populations have expanded so rapidly that whole generations are growing up without any natural contact with wild creatures; a new public opinion concerning wildlife and wild environment is arising unfettered by fact and unguided by experience. Except at the zoo, the opportunities to know or even become interested in living wild

creatures are largely vicarious ones for many city dwellers. Yet it is the Bronx bus driver and the corner pharmacist whose votes will determine the fate of the Adirondack wilderness, the Everglades, of Yellowstone Park. You must give your visitors a new intellectual reference point, meaningful and esthetically compelling; a view of another sensory and social world; a feeling of personal interest in diminishing wild creatures and collective responsibility for their future which is so closely linked to that of man. Zoos must be natural history and conservation centers of the future.

Beyond their educational dimension, and despite their inability to save everything, zoos can at least save something.

Says Conway, "To put it baldly, what zoos will end up doing is preserving those animals that mean a great deal to people for esthetic and emotional reasons. We're not even talking about preserving ecologically important species — if it's very rare it no longer has ecological value by definition. Zoos have no business suggesting they're going to preserve all of nature. I don't know of a single credible zoo director who would suggest it. The vast majority of the organisms on earth are far smaller than my little fingernail — virtually none will be present in a zoo's collection. Take it a step further: the biomass of termites of Africa is far greater than the biomass of elephants. Take it a step further: the biomass of plant life is many times that of all the animal life. No, zoos can't preserve plants and all those millions of creepy-crawlies. But at zoological gardens, if we can overcome our problems, we have the charge of preserving that very small portion of life that is at the tip of the iceberg — that which has inspired man, his attitudes, and his poetry. Of course it's not enough. *Of course* it's not preserving the diversity of life on earth. But at least we're making a stab at it."

SELECTED READINGS

INDEX

Selected Readings

American Association of Zoological Parks and Aquariums Species Survival Plan. Wheeling, W.Va.: American Association of Zoological Parks and Aquariums, n.d.

Campbell, Sheldon. *Lifeboats to Ararat*. New York: Times Books, 1978.

Cherfas, Jeremy. "Test Tube Babies in the Zoo." *New Scientist*, December 1984.

Conway, William. "How to Exhibit a Bullfrog." *Curator* 11, 4 (1968).

Durrell, Gerald. *The Stationary Ark*. New York: Simon and Schuster, 1976.

Ehrlich, Paul, and Ehrlich, Anne. *Extinction: The Causes and Consequences of the Disappearance of Species*. New York: Random House, 1981.

Fischer, James. *Zoos of the World*. London: Aldus, 1966.

Flesness, Nathan. *Status and Trends of Wild Animal Diversity*. Submission to the Congressional Office of Technology Assessment, 1985.

Fox, Michael W. "The Trouble with Zoos." *The Animals' Agenda* (Animal Rights Network magazine), June 1986.

Gold, Gerald. "A Jungle in the Bronx." *New York Times Magazine*, May 26, 1985.

Grosswith, Marvin. "The Guano Factor." *SciQuest*, October 1981.

Guppy, Nicholas. "Tropical Deforestation: A Global View." *Foreign Affairs,* Spring 1984.

Hahn, Emily. *Animal Gardens.* New York: Doubleday, 1967.

Hancocks, David. *Animals and Architecture.* London: Hugh Evelyn, 1971.

Hediger, H. *Man and Animal in the Zoo.* New York: Seymour Lawrence/Delacorte, 1969.

————. *Studies of the Psychology and Behaviour of Animals in Zoos and Circuses.* London: Butterworths Scientific Publications, 1955.

————. *Wild Animals in Captivity.* London: Butterworths Scientific Publications, 1955.

Kleiman, Devra; Beck, Benjamin B.; Dietz, James M.; Dietz, Lou Ann; Ballou, Jonathan D.; and Coimbra-Filho, Adelmar F. "Conservation Program for the Golden Lion Tamarin: Captive Research and Management, Ecological Studies, Education Strategies, and Reintroduction." In Benirschke, K., ed., *Primates: The Road to Self-Sustaining Populations.* New York: Springer-Verlag, 1985.

Lenard, Lane. "The Frozen Zoo." *Science Digest,* June 1981.

Livingston, Bernard. *Zoo, Animals, People, Places.* New York: Arbor House, 1974.

Markowitz, Hal. *Behavioral Enrichment in the Zoo.* New York: Van Nostrand Reinhold, 1982.

Meyers, Norman. *The Sinking Ark.* Elmsford, N.Y.: Pergamon Press, 1979.

Miller, Julie Ann. "The Mating Game." *Science News,* October 13, 1984.

Morris, Desmond. *Animal Days.* New York: William Morrow, 1979.

Perry, John. *The World's a Zoo.* New York: Dodd, Mead, 1969.

Phillips, David, and Kaiser, Sandra. "Are Zoos an Excuse for Habitat Destruction?" *Not Man Apart.* November–December 1985.

Pianka, Eric. "Viewpoint/A Wild Analogy. *BioScience,* December 1985.

Rabb, George. "The Unicorn Experiment." *Curator* 12, 4 (1969).

Ralls, Katherine, and Ballou, Jonathan D., eds. "Proceedings of the Workshop on Genetic Management of Captive Populations." *Zoo Biology* 5, 2 (1986).

Schoenwald-Cox, C.; Chambers, S.; MacBryde, B.; and Thomas, W., eds. *Genetics and Conservation: A Reference for Managing Wild Animal and Plant Populations.* Menlo Park, Calif.: Benjamin Cummings, 1983.

Seal, Ulysses S., and Foose, Thomas J. "Development of a Master Plan for Captive Propagation of Siberian Tigers in North American Zoos." *Zoo Biology* 2 (1983): 241–242.

Singer , Peter. *Animal Liberation.* New York: Avon, 1975.

Tilson, Ronald, and Seal, Ulysses S., eds. *Tigers of the World: The Biology, Biopolitics, Management, and Conservation of an Endangered Species.* Park Ridge, N.J.: Noyes, 1987.

Wright, Michael. "Zoo to the World." *New York Times Magazine,* July 19, 1981.

In addition to these books and articles, there is a wealth of material by various zoo scientists about zoos and their wildlife conservation efforts in the proceedings of the annual meetings of the American Association of Zoological Parks and Aquariums. Published late each autumn, they are available in zoo libraries.

The International Zoo Yearbook, published annually by the London Zoological Society, is available in zoo libraries and some public libraries.

Index

AAZPA (American Association of
Zoological Parks and Aquariums)
bullfrog talk to, 170, 171, 192
and Foose, Tom, 37, 38
and inadequate zoos, 22
and Species Survival Plan, 38, 39,
185 (*see also* Species Survival
Plan)
Abreu, Rosalia, 153
Adams, Sue, 98
Alexander the Great, 7
Alleles, 42, 43–44, 89–90
Amazon rain forest, 31–32. *See also*
Tropical forest
Amish, genetic abnormalities among,
46
Anesthesia (darting) for animals, 81–
88
Animal act, white tigers sold to, 185
Animal Connection, The (Domalain),
13
Animal habitats. *See* Habitats, animal
Animals
collecting of, 5–12, 13–14, 35
diversity of species among, 67
domestication of, 4–5
as endangered, 68–72, 182–83,
190–91 (*see also* Endangered
species)
evolutionary development of, 27–
31, 33, 176
"freedom" of, 159
genetic management of, 48, 50–
51, 52, 53, 61–64 (*see also*
Genetic management)

humans as threat to, 32–33, 178–
79
moving of, 89
public feeding of, 162
as reintroduced into wild, 126–
27, 132, 143–49 (*see also*
Reintroduction of animals to
wild)
as surplus, 54–55, 63–67, 80
survival in wild of zoo-raised,
90–91, 142–143
vanished species of, 24–27, 29–
31, 33–35
zoo life of, 17, 23–24, 157–59 (*see
also* Zoo(s); Zoo exhibitry)
Arabian oryx, 134–35
Archie (gibbon), 86–87, 167–69
Aristotle, zoological surveys by, 6–7
Ark, zoo as, 37, 39, 62, 69, 71, 129,
190
Artificial insemination of animals,
88–91, 111
electroejaculation in, 85, 89, 95–
96
Minnesota project in, 73, 80, 91–
100, 118–23
and surplus animals, 80
see also Reproductive technology
Ashurbanipal (king of Assyria), 6
Audubon, John James, 25
Augustus II (elector of Dresden), 12
Auks, extinction of, 26, 33

Bali tiger, 33
Ballou, Jonathan, 48–50, 72

Barnum, P. T., 12, 186
Basel Zoo, 89, 154
Battle Creek (Michigan), Binder Park zoo in, 21–22
Bean, Robert, 35
Bears, grizzly, attacks by, 144–45
Bears, polar
    and euthanasia, 83
    feed training for, 161–62
Bears, sloth, exhibit for, 169–70
Beaver Pond, Minnesota zoo, 172–74
Beck, Benjamin, 139
Bees, "killer," 129
Beetle, Japanese, 130
Behavioral exhibits in zoos, 156, 161–66, 169–70
Bengal tiger, 34, 55, 62, 76
    white phase of, 183–86
Berlin zoo, elephant exhibit at, 153
Bern zoo, 156
Bewick's swan, and captive breeding, 147–48
Beyers, Ann, 74, 92, 98, 99
Binder Park zoo, Battle Creek, 21–22
Biological diversity
    loss of, 30
    see also Genetic diversity
Birth control
    and reproductive intervention, 115
    for zoo animals, 56, 78
Bison. See "Buffalo," American; Wisent
Blesbok, extinction of, 26
Bogart, R., 47
Bongo, embryo transfer for, 102–8, 110–11
Bouman, Jan and Inga, 47–48
Brachiation, 167
Brambell, M. R., 145
Brazil, tamarins reintroduced into, 124–26, 135–43
Breeding
    animal anesthesia in, 81–88
    and artifical insemination, 88–100, 111, 118–23 (see also Artificial insemination of animals)
    and birth control, 56
    and demographic structure, 56–62

through embryo transfer, 102–8, 110–11
    endangered species' difficulty in, 188
    as genetic management, 48, 50–51, 52, 53, 61–64, 68–72 (see also Genetic management)
    inter-zoo exchange for, 35, 127
    as measure of zoo success, 101–2
    and reproductive technology, 112–17
    Uly Seal's involvement with, 77–79
    tigers as "success" story in, 54–56
    traits from, 4–5
    of white tigers, 183
    and zoo budgets, 68
Bronx Zoo, 155, 178–80
Brookfield Zoo, Chicago, 20, 51
Brutality toward animals
    by ancient Romans, 8–10
    by Hagenbeck's collectors, 12–14
    in zoo, 16–18
"Buffalo," American, reintroduction of, 132–33
Bull fighting, by Roman gladiators, 8
Bullfrog, and zoo exhibitry, 170–71
Busch Gardens, 159
Busching, Milan, 175, 177

Cajacob, Tom, 118, 120
Caesar Augustus, 9
Caligula (Roman emperor), 9
Captive maintenance
    two-site principle of, 135
    see also Wildlife conservation; Zoo(s)
"Capture gun," 84
Caspian tiger, 33–34
"Charismatic megaverterbrates," zoos' concentrating on, 70–71
Charlemagne, 10–11
Charles IX (king of France), 12
Cheetahs
    breeding difficulty with, 188
    in Frederick II's menagerie, 11
    genetic sameness of, 51–52, 53
    lost species of, 34
    and need to run, 159

Cheetahs (*cont.*)
  Romans' hunting of, 10
  on species-survival list, 69
Chicago, Brookfield Zoo in, 20
Chimpanzees
  and early zoos, 153–54
  London Zoo tea parties for, 160
  in Ptolemy's zoo, 7
Choice of animals for zoos, 69–71,
  182–83, 184, 192–93
Cicero, on elephants' death, 9
Cincinnati Wildlife Research
  Federation, 102, 106
Cincinnati Zoo
  Dresser, Betsy, at, 100, 108
  extinct/endangered-species shrine
    at, 25, 186
  and Hagenbeck family, 154
  Insect World at, 22, 67, 174–78
  and popular demand, 186–87
  and white tiger, 184
Cockroaches, introduction of, 129
Coimbra-Filho, Adelmar, 125–26,
  138–39
Cologne Zoo, 152, 156, 157
Como Zoo (St. Paul), 77
Columbus Zoo (Ohio), 154
Condor, California, and Uly Seal, 76
Confucius, 6
Conservation
  as AAZPA goal, 39
  and selection of species, 182–83
  zoos as educating for, 180–81,
    187, 191–92
  see also Endangered species;
    Wildlife conservation
Conservationists, and zoos, 187–91
Constantinople, 10, 11
Contraception. *See* Birth control
Conway, William, 66–67, 68, 170–
  72, 184, 192–93
Cook, Captain James, 131
Cortés, Hernando, 11
Culling
  of New Zealand mammals, 131
  of surplus animals, 55, 64–67

Dakota County, Minnesota, 1–3, 35
Darting (anesthesia), 81–88
Darwin, Charles, 27–29, 47
Death rates. *See* Mortality, animal

Demographics of zoo populations,
  53–56, 61–62
  and Przewalski's horses, 61
  and Siberian tigers, 56–61
Denver Zoo, 55–56, 155
Desertification, 128
Destruction of animal habitats, 24,
  31–34, 127–29
  Bronx Zoo exhibit on, 178
  and liberation of zoo animals, 24,
    56, 188, 190
  for megavertebrates, 70
  recovery from, 127–28
  for tamarin, 125, 135, 138
  zoos as excuse for, 189, 191
Detroit Zoo, 64–65, 66, 154–55
Diaz del Castillo, Bernal, 11
Dinosaur species, extinction of, 30
Displaying of zoo animals. *See* Zoo
  exhibitry
Diversity, biological, 30. *See also*
  Genetic diversity
DNA, 42, 43
Dodoes, 26, 33
Dolphins, show-training of, 160–61
Domalain, Jean-Yves, 13
Domestication of animals, 4–5
Domitian (Roman emperor), 10
Dresser, Betsy, 100–102
  embryo transplant by, 100, 102–
    8, 109–11, 115–16, 122, 186–87
  on reproductive technology, 112,
    113
Durrant, Barbara, 117
Düsseldorf zoo, 152–53

Ecological relationships
  and introduction of species, 132
  and Tierpark (Hamburg), 15
  and zoo exhibitry, 171, 172–74,
    177
  and zoos vs. natural habitats,
    189–90
Ecosystems, reconstitution of, 127–
  28
Education, as exhibitry function, 18,
  172, 174, 175–81, 192
Egypt, zoo-type collections in, 5–6,
  7
Elands
  anesthetizing attempts on, 82–83

embryo transplant in, 105, 106–8, 111

Electroejaculation, 85, 89, 95–96

Elephants
Hagenbeck's capturing of, 13
in Potter Park Zoo, 17
in Roman spectacles, 8–9
on species-survival list, 69

Embryo transfers, 102–8, 110–11
and commercial breeding, 108–9
freezing of embryo for, 109–10
and reproductive cycle, 115–16
taxonomic gulfs in, 117
see also Reproductive technology

Endangered species
vs. attractive species as zoo
exhibits, 182–83
Brazilian law protecting, 126
as difficult to breed, 188
and euthanasia, 64–65
and extinct species, 24–27, 29–31, 33–35
and habitat destruction, 24, 33, 70, 127 (see also Destruction of animal habitats)
New Zealand birds among, 131–32
shipping of, 89
shrine to, 25, 186
and SSP, 38–39, 71 (see also Species Survival Plan)
surrogate mothering for, 104, 106
tamarins as, 125
zoos for preservation of, 68–72, 129, 190–91, 192–93
see also Breeding; Genetic management; Reintroduction of animals to wild

Environment. See Habitats, animal

Environmentalists, and zoos, 187–91

Ethical considerations
in disposing of animals, 55, 64
in exhibiting genetic quirk, 184
and zoo exhibitry, 156

Euthanasia, for surplus zoo animals, 64–67

Evolutionary development, 27–31, 33
Insect World lesson on, 176
see also Natural selection

Exhibitry. See Zoo exhibitry

Extinction of species, 24–27, 29–31, 33–35
vs. euthanasia, 64, 66–67
see also Endangered species

Fagella, Alicia, 118

Fahning, Mel, 92–93, 99–100, 118, 119, 120, 121, 122, 123

Fauna Preservation Society, Britain, 135

Feeding of zoo animals, 162

Fitzroy, Robert, 27

Flesness, Nate, 38, 47, 48, 49, 70, 75, 132, 148, 192

Foose, Tom, 37–39
and genetic management, 52, 53–54, 60, 61–62
on selection of species, 69, 70, 71
and white tiger, 185
on zoo as ark, 37, 62, 69, 129

Forests, tropical. See Tropical forests

Fox, Michael, 188

Francis I (Holy Roman Emperor), 12

Frankfurt zoo, 155

Frederick II (Holy Roman Emperor), 11

Freiheit, Clayton, 54, 55–56, 182–83

Friedman, Sandy, 70–71

Garcia, Martha, 92–93, 99, 118, 119, 122

Genetic bottleneck, 51–52, 133

Genetic diversity, 52–53, 59, 79, 90, 134, 182, 185

Genetic management, 48, 50–51, 52, 53, 61–64
artificial insemination in, 89–91 (see also Artificial insemination of animals)
embryo transfer in, 104 (see also Embryo transfers)
and euthanasia, 64–67
selection of species for, 68–72
see also Species Survival Plan

Genetic plasticity, 53

Genetics
and deleterious genes, 44–46, 52
and inbreeding, 45–52
and introduction into wild, 145–49

Genetics (*cont.*)
　　Mendel's experiments on, 40–43
　　and mutations, 43–44
Genotype, 43
Gibbons
　　Archie, 86–87, 167–69
　　as family-based, 158, 167
　　"collecting" of, 13
　　feed-training of, 162, 163
　　island for (Minnesota Zoo), 21,
　　　24, 167–69
Golden lion tamarin (GLT), 124–26,
　　135–43
Goldman, David, 51
Gorillas
　　early survival difficulties of, 154
　　moats as barriers for, 155
　　poaching of, 70
　　as showboat, 182
Graham, Edmund, 92, 98, 99
Graham, Steve, 64–65, 160, 180–81,
　　184, 187–88
Greeks, ancient, as animal collectors,
　　6–7
Grizzly bears, attacks by, 144–45
Guagga, extinction of, 26–27, 33
Gwynne, John, 179–80
Gypsy moth, 130

Habitats, animal, 24
　　adaptation to, 33–34
　　animal as prisoner of, 159
　　as critical issue, 190
　　destruction of, 24, 31–34, 127–29
　　　(*see also* Destruction of animal
　　　habitats)
　　introduction of animals into,
　　　129–32
　　reintroduction into, 56, 132–43
　　zoos contrasted with, 188–89
Hagenbeck, Carl, 12–15, 19, 154–55,
　　181
Hamburg, Germany, Tierpark in,
　　14–15
Hancocks, David, 159
Hatshepsut (queen of Egypt), 5–6
Havana, Abreu chimp collection in,
　　153–54
Heape, Walter, 108
Hediger, Heine, 23, 157–59

Henry I (king of England), 11
Hensleigh, Hugh, 92, 98
Heredity. *See* Genetics
Hiram (king of Tyre), 6
History of Animals, The (Aristotle), 7
Hoage, Bob, 182
Hodges, Keith, 116
Hsing-Hsing (panda), 88–89
Humane Society of the United
　　States, 188

Inbreeding
　　and demographics of Przewalski's
　　　horses, 61
　　and demographics of Siberian
　　　tigers, 59–60
　　and genetic abnormalities, 45–50,
　　　52
　　and genetic management, 48, 50–
　　　51, 53, 61–64 (*see also* Genetic
　　　management)
　　and wisent propagation, 134
Incas (last Carolina parakeet), 26
India
　　animal domestication in, 5
　　Bengal tigers in, 34
　　and peacock, 8
　　Roman tigers from, 9
　　Seal, Uly, in, 76
　　species lost in, 34
Innate avoidance behavior, of
　　tamarins, 140
Insects
　　exhibiting of (Insect World), 22,
　　　67, 174–77
　　as introduced into new habitats,
　　　129–32
International Species Inventory
　　System (ISIS), 48, 49, 63, 75, 77–
　　78
Interspecies transfer, 104–8, 117. *See
　　also* Embryo transfers
Introduction of animals, 129–32. *See
　　also* Reintroduction of animals to
　　wild
Iran, lion-import plan by, 149
Iserman, Steve, 65–66
IUCN (International Union for the
　　Conservation of Nature and
　　Natural Resources), 77, 103, 123

Jardim, Silva, 124
Javan tiger, 33–34
Jungle World exhibit (Bronx Zoo), 179

Kaiser, Sandra, 189
Kear, Janet, 146
Keller, Ron, 160
Kenya
  rhino population in, 33
  wildlife tourism in, 149
"Killer" bees, 129
King's Island Wild Animal Safari, 102
Kiwi bird, 130–31
Kleiman, Devra, 91, 136–39
Kramer, Lynn, 107
Kreiger, Terry, 74, 80–81, 93
Kublai Khan, 11

Lacy, Bob, 51
Lansing, Michigan, Potter Park Zoo in, 15–19, 22–23
Lasley, William, 116
Lecky, W. E. H., 9–10
Leopard
  in Middle Ages menageries, 11
  nocturnal exhibitry for, 166–67
  Romans' hunting of, 10
Lewis, John, 99
Ling-Ling (panda), 88–89
Lions
  Asian/African mixture of, 72
  "chase" designed for, 164–65
  Iran's import plan for, 149
  in Middle Ages menageries, 11
  nocturnal exhibit for, 167
  Romans' hunting of, 10
  on species-survival list, 69
Livestock
  overgrazing of, 32
  in restoring of habitats, 128
London Zoo, 153, 160
Lorenz, Konrad, 158
Loris, slow, 158, 159
Los Angeles Zoo, 103
Louis XIII (king of France), 12
Lovejoy, Thomas, 47
Lucullus, aviary of, 7

"M" (exhibitry critic), 170–71, 192
McCusick, Victor, 45, 46
Malthus, Thomas, 28
Management of genetic stock. See Genetic management
Mandrills, 18, 19, 24
Manton, V. J. A., 126
Marco Polo, 11
Maria Theresa (archduchess of Austria), 12
Markowitz, Hal, 161–65
Martha (last passenger pigeon), 26
Maruska, Ed
  and Dresser, Betsy, 100–101, 101–2, 106, 186–87
  and exhibitry, 174, 175, 186–87
  and white tigers, 183, 184–86
Mech, L. David, 75, 76, 77
Megavertebrates, zoos' concentrating on, 70–71
Melbourne Zoo, 89
Menageries. See Zoo(s)
Mendel, Gregor, 39–43
Merril, Carl R., 51
Meyers, Norman, 30, 188
Middle Ages
  animal collections during, 10–11
  bear pits during, 156
Milwaukee Zoo, 155
Minnesota Zoological Gardens
  artificial insemination project at, 73, 80, 91–100, 118–23
  Beaver Pond at, 172–74
  euthanasia plan by, 65–66
  Mongolian wild horses in, 35
  and off-site animal appearances, 186
  and Uly Seal, 77
  Siberian tiger refuge in, 2–4, 21, 150–52
  and Species Survival Plan, 38
  tiger anesthesia death at, 84
  Trail displays in, 21, 165
Mongolian wild horses. See Przewalski's horses
Monkey islands, 156–57
Monkeys
  cotton-top tamarin, 33
  golden lion tamarin (GLT), 124–26, 135–43

Moose, in town–appearance of, 143–44

Morality. *See* Ethical considerations

Mortality, animal
in wild and zoos, 23, 90–91, 142–43
of zoo apes, 153–54

Moth, gypsy, 130

Munich Zoo, 156

National Zoo, Washington
Bengal tigers of, 184
breeding records of, 48–49
gorilla births in, 154
and tamarins, 124, 136–42

Natural selection, 27–31
adaptation through, 33
and introduction into wild, 145–49
mutations' role in, 43–44
vs. zoo protections, 54–55

Nebuchadnezzar (king of Babylonia), 6

Nero (Roman emperor), 9–10

New Zealand, introduced mammals in, 130–31

Nocturnal exhibits, 166–67, 178

Not Man Apart (Friends of the Earth), 189–90

Nursing behavior
gorilla coached in, 89
viewing of beavers', 173

O'Brien, Stephen, 51, 72

Oryx, Arabian, 134–35

Otters, feeding mechanism for, 165

Overgrazing, 32, 128

Pachyderms
as chief attraction, 182
see also Elephants; Rhinoceros

Panaewa Rain Forest Zoo (Hilo, Hawaii), 163

Panda, giant
in ancient Chinese zoo, 6
artificial insemination of, 88
breeding difficulty with, 188
breeding nucleus lacking for, 71
in Foose drawing, 37
progesterone-pregnancy relation in, 116

public infatuation with, 185–86
as showboat, 182

Panda, red, on species-survival list, 69

Passenger pigeon, 1, 25–26, 33, 35

Peacock, as Roman status symbol, 7–8

Phenotype, 43

Phillips, David, 189

Phoenix Zoo (Arizona), 135

Pianka, Eric, 189

Pichner, Jim, 157, 165–70

Pigeon, passenger, 1, 25–26, 33, 35

Poco das Antas Biological Reserve, Brazil
tamarins reintroduced into, 124–26, 135–43

Polar bears. *See* Bears, polar

Pompey, 8–9

Pope, Earl, 100, 102, 105–6

Portland Zoo (Oregon), behavioral training at, 161–62

Potter Park Zoo (Lansing, Michigan), 15–19, 22–23

Primates. *See* Chimpanzees; Gibbons; Gorillas; Mandrills; Monkeys

Project Jonah, 160

Project Tiger, 34

Przewalski's horses, 35, 37, 47, 61
on species-survival list, 69

Ptolemy I (king of Egypt), 7

Ptolemy II (king of Egypt), 7

Public
and animal euthanasia, 64–67
animal extinction misunderstood by, 33
conservationists among, 187–91
conservation message to, 180–81, 187, 191–92
and selection of zoo animals, 70, 183, 184
zoos as appealing to, 68, 185–87
see also Zoo exhibitry

Ralls, Katherine, 48–50

Rameses II (king of Egypt), 6

Rats, territorial instincts of in captivity, 147

Redig, Patrick, 142

Reed, Theodore, 138, 183–84

Reese, Bob, 106

Reindl, Nick, 2–4, 21, 35, 65, 118
Reintroduction of animals to wild,
    126–27, 132
    for Arabian oryx, 134–35
    birth control as alternative to, 56
    for "buffalo," 132–33
    in criticism of zoos, 188, 190
    politics of, 149
    problems in, 143–49
    and SSP selection, 71
    survival probabilities in, 90–91,
        142–43
    for tamarins, 124–26, 135–43
    for wisent, 132–34
Renaissance, zoos discovered during,
    11
Reproductive technology, 112–17
    in criticism of zoos, 188
    humans as model for, 110
    primitive state of, 111
    and SSP selection, 71
    see also Artificial insemination;
        Embryo transfers
Rhinoceros
    poaching of, 33, 70, 149
    in Ptolemy's procession, 7
    on species-survival list, 69
Rio Vista Genetics, 109
Romans, ancient
    as animal collectors, 7–10
    and gladiatorial games, 8–10, 156

Sahara, extending of, 32
St. Gallen, Switzerland, monks' zoo
    at, 10
St. Louis Zoological Garden, 52
St. Paul, Minnesota, Como Zoo in,
    77
San Diego Wild Animal Park, 20–21,
    116–17, 135
Sanitation
    and display considerations, 155
    and early zoos, 153–54, 155
    relative need for, 158
Sankhala, K. S., 127
Sargents' pigeon, 26
Savory, Alan, 128
Schönbrunn, 12
Schorger, A. W., 26
Scott, George (zoo attendant), 155
Scott, Sir Peter, 39

Seal, Marialice, 73, 78, 79, 94, 118,
    120
Seal, Ulysses S. ("Uly"), 75–79
    and animal anesthesia, 85–86,
        87–88
    in artifical insemination project,
        73, 74, 91–92, 95–96, 118, 120,
        122–23
    and breeding program, 68, 90
    on Foose, 38
    on inbreeding, 47
    on Przewalski's horses breeding,
        61
    and reproductive technology,
        111, 113, 115
    and species survival plan, 72, 78
Sedgwick, Charles, 87
Seifert, Seigfried, 78
Selection of animals for zoos, 69–71,
    182–83, 184, 192–93
Siberian tigers. See Tiger(s), Siberian
Sinking Ark, The (Meyers), 188
Sloth bear, exhibit for, 169–70
Slow loris, 158, 159
Smithsonian Institution, 22, 26, 67
Solomon (king of Israel), 6
South China tiger, 34
Southeast Asian tigers, 34
Species Survival-Plan (SSP), 38, 39,
    53, 62, 67, 69–72
    and Foose, Tom, 38, 39
    and Siberian tigers, 62–67, 80
    and white tiger, 185
Starling, introduction of, 130
Sudbury basin, Ontario, 128
Sumatran tigers, 34, 62, 163–64
Surplus animals, 54–55, 63–67, 80
Surrogate mothering. See Embryo
    transfers
Swan, Bewick's, and captive
    breeding, 147–48

Tamarin, golden lion (GLT), 124–
    26, 135–43
Taylor, Ross, 118
Territoriality
    and gibbon island, 168
    outbreeding of, 145
    of rats in captivity, 147
    in zoo, 23, 158–59
Thutmose III (king of Egypt), 5

Tierpark (Hagenbeck zoo), 14–15, 19

Tiger(s)
artificial insemination of, 80
attacks by, 93–94
international symposium on, 122, 123, 184
nocturnal exhibit for, 167
Rome receives from India, 9
as surplus, 80, 90
vanishing species of, 33–34
zoo breeding of, 54–61

Tigers, Bengal, 34, 55, 62, 76
white phase of, 183–86

Tiger(s), Siberian, 3–4, 34
anesthesia death of, 84
artificial insemination of, 73, 79–80, 85, 90, 91, 92–100, 111, 118–23
birth control/demographics for, 54–61
Bronx Zoo exhibit on, 178
as competing with other tigers, 56, 62
and euthanasia plan, 64–66
genetic management of (SSP), 62–63, 69, 72, 78
infant mortality among, 77
Minnesota Zoo exhibit of, 2–4, 21, 150–52
numbers of in captivity, 61
and Seal, Uly, in USSR, 76
studbook for, 78
as surplus, 63–67
and white tiger, 185

Tiger(s), Sumatran, 34, 62, 163–64

Tilson, Ron, 74–75, 86, 91–92, 95–96, 118, 121, 123, 160

Titus (Roman emperor), 9

Toronto Zoo, 19–20, 63, 65

Trajan (Roman emperor), 9

Tranquilizers (darting) for animals, 81–88

Transplant of embryo. See Embryo transfers

Triage, for animal species, 71

Tropical forests
Bronx Zoo exhibit on, 179–80
Brookfield Zoo exhibit on, 20
disappearance of, 31

Tropics Trail, Minnesota Zoo, 21, 165

USSR, Uly Seal's visit to, 76

Wen Wang (emperor of China), 6
Whales, show-training of, 160–61
White (Bengal) tiger, 183–86
Wilderness reserves, 90
Wildlife. See Animals
Wildlife conservation
through artificial insemination, 90–91
and Species Survival Plan, 39 (see also Species Survival Plan)
by zoos, 34–36, 68–72
see also Conservation; Genetic management

Wildt, David, 51

Wisent
genetic bottleneck of, 51, 133
reintroduction of, 132–34

Witchell, Sam, 30

Wortman, John, 97

Wright, Frank, 81, 86–87, 118–21, 123

Yerkes, Robert, and Yerkes Institute, 153–54

Zoo(s)
animal preservation through, 34–36, 69–72 (see also Conservation; Endangered species; Wildlife conservation)
as animal prisons, 17
and animals' welfare, 23–24
as ark, 37, 39, 62, 69, 71, 129, 190
as art museum, 70
attitude of ecologically-oriented toward, 187–91
cooperation among, 35, 38, 126–27
and euthanasia, 64–67
genetic management by, 48, 50–51, 52, 53, 61–64, 68–72 (see also Genetic management)
inbreeding at, 47–50
public feeding in, 162

selection of animals for, 69–71,
182–83, 184, 192–93
total size and budgets of, 68
Zoo exhibitry, 19, 152
animal shows in, 159–61, 191–92
and animals' needs, 18, 23, 73–
74, 156–59
Beaver Pond (Minnesota), 172–74
behavioral enhancement in, 156,
161–66, 169–70
at Binder Park zoo, 21–22
at Bronx Zoo, 178–80
at Brookfield Zoo (Chicago), 20
conservation message in, 180–81
educational graphics in (Bronx
Zoo), 180
educational graphics in (Cincinnati Zoo), 177–78
Hagenbeck's contribution to, 14–
15, 19, 154–55, 181
historical stages of, 152–56
Insect World (Cincinnati), 22,
174–77
at Minnesota Zoo, 21, 150–52
as natural for animals, 166–69
natural barriers in, 20, 155
negative example of (Potter
Park), 16–18
nocturnal, 166–67, 178
and popular demand, 186–87
at San Diego zoo, 20–21
at Toronto, 19–20
and "World of Bullfrogs," 170–72
Zoo history
in antiquity, 5–6
and Hagenbeck, 12–15, 19, 154–
55
and Middle Ages, 10–11
in modern Europe, 11–12
and Montezuma, 11
and Renaissance travelers, 11

Zoological survey, by Aristotle, 6–7
Zoos (various locations)
Basel, 89, 154
Battle Creek (Binder Park), 21–
22
Berlin, 153
Bern, 156
Bronx, 155, 178–80
Busch Gardens, 159
Chicago (Brookfield), 20
Cincinnati, 25, 174–78, 186–87
(see also Cincinnati Zoo)
Cologne, 152, 156, 157
Columbus (Ohio), 154
Denver, 55–56, 155
Detroit, 64–65, 66, 154–55
Düsseldorf, 152–53
Frankfurt, 155
London, 153, 160
Los Angeles, 103
Melbourne, 89
Milwaukee, 155
Minnesota, 2–4, 21, 150–52,
172–74 (see also Minnesota
Zoological Gardens)
Munich, 156
Panaewa Rain Forest Zoo (Hilo,
Hawaii), 163
Phoenix, 135
Portland (Oregon), 161
Potter Park, 15–19, 22–23
St. Louis Zoological Garden, 52
St. Paul (Como), 77
San Diego Wild Animal Park,
20–21, 116–17, 135
of Smithsonian Institution, 22,
26, 67
Toronto, 19–20, 63, 65
Washington, D.C. (National),
48–49, 124, 136–42, 154, 184